THE
KENNEDYS
AT WAR

Also by Edward J. Renehan, Jr.

The Lion's Pride

The Secret Six

John Burroughs

THE
KENNEDYS
AT WAR
1937–1945

Edward J. Renehan, Jr.

DOUBLEDAY

New York   London   Toronto   Sydney   Auckland

PUBLISHED BY DOUBLEDAY
a division of Random House, Inc.
1540 Broadway, New York, New York 10036

DOUBLEDAY and the portrayal of an anchor with a dolphin are
trademarks of Doubleday, a division of Random House, Inc.

All photographs appear with the kind permission of the John F. Kennedy Library.

Library of Congress Cataloging-in-Publication Data
Renehan, Edward, 1956–
The Kennedys at war, 1937–1945 / Edward J. Renehan, Jr.—1st ed.
        p.   cm.
Includes bibliographical references and index.
1. Kennedy family. 2. Kennedy, Joseph P. (Joseph Patrick), 1888–1969. 3. Kennedy,
Joseph P. (Joseph Patrick), 1915–1944. 4. Kennedy, John F. (John Fitzgerald), 1917–1963.
5. Kennedy, Kathleen, d. 1948. 6. Politicians—United States—Biography. 7. World War,
1939–1945—United States. 8. World War, 1939–1945—England—London. 9. London
(England)—Biography. I. Title.
E747 .R46 2002
973.9'092'2—dc21
2001047518

ISBN 0-385-50165-X

Copyright © 2002 by Edward J. Renehan, Jr.

All Rights Reserved

Printed in the United States of America

May 2002

First Edition

Book design by Lee Fukui

1   3   5   7   9   10   8   6   4   2

Dedicated to my daughter
Katherine Eleanor Renehan

Contents

THE
KENNEDYS
AT WAR

1

Kennedy Confidence

A SKED IN 1959 how he had come to be a war hero, Senator John F. Kennedy quipped ironically: "It was easy—they sank my boat." Several years later, referring to the tale of PT 109 as related in the film starring Cliff Robertson, President Kennedy told a friend that the popularly accepted account of his heroics in the Solomons was more screwed-up than Cuba. Still, those who studied Kennedy closely understood that his time in the service always remained an important part of him, regardless of how glibly he sometimes appraised it. "Everything," wrote *Los Angeles Times* journalist Robert T. Hartmann, "dates from that adventure." Hartmann perceptively added that Jack's several days of pure survival after the loss of PT 109 were "the only time Kennedy ever was wholly on his own, where the $1 million his father gave him wouldn't buy one cup of water." Likewise Hartmann noted that "Kennedy's superabundant charm is never more engaging than when he leaps back to wartime reminiscence with a receptive veteran of the Solomon campaign."

Of course, Jack Kennedy's war record provided a great practical political benefit. Every campaign he ever ran emphasized his status as a warrior and a hero. He displayed his Purple Heart and his Navy and Marine Corps medal in each of his several offices. He kept on his desk, preserved in plastic, the coconut shell on which he had scratched his dramatic—if redundant—rescue plea after the sinking of PT 109. A float in his inaugural parade featured a full-size replica of the vessel he'd made famous (or was it the other way around?). And male visitors to the Kennedy White House routinely received PT-boat tiepins as souvenirs.

But it would be a mistake to believe Kennedy looked back on his experience of the war cynically, or viewed it as little more than a useful PR tool. Quite the contrary. He considered World War II to have been the seminal, defining event in his life. "I firmly believe," he once wrote, "that as much as I was shaped by anything, so was I shaped by the hand of fate moving in World War II. Of course, the same can be said of almost any American or British or Australian man of my generation. The war made us. It was and is our single greatest moment. The memory of the war is a key to our characters. It serves as a breakwall between the indolence of our youths and earnestness of our manhoods. No school or parent could have shaped us the way that fight shaped us. No other experience could have brought forth in us the same fortitude and resilience. We were much shrewder and sadder when that long battle finally finished. The war made us get serious for the first time in our lives. We've been serious ever since, and we show no signs of stopping."

Elsewhere Jack commented that though the war might have made him, it had "savaged" his family. "It turned my father and my brothers and sisters and I upside down and sucked all the oxygen out of our smug and comfortable assumptions. We still, with the old battles long over, have great confidence: great Kennedy confidence, which is the main strength of our tribe. But we sons and daughters no longer have that easy, witless, untested and meaningless confidence on which we'd been weaned before the war. Our father had us pretty well trained to appear to ourselves and others as unbeatable and immortal—a little bit like Gods. Now that's over with. Now, after all that we experienced and lost in the war, we finally understand that there is nothing inevitable about us. And that's a healthy thing to know."

Writing in 1999, Richard D. Mahoney said World War II breached the Kennedy family—and, most important, its patriarch—"like a wrecking ball." This book tells the story of that breach, an act of destruction that enabled the redefinition of a family and the making of a man.

. . .

WHO WERE THE KENNEDYS before the breach? How did others see them? How did they see themselves? What testimony do we have about this vivacious and sometimes conflicted clan who seemed so full of real yet unexamined and unreflective promise in the years before the war?

They were, indeed, an unambiguously confident bunch—those young people who rushed so happily through the 1920s and early 1930s with no thought of any destiny other than one defined by wealth, comfort, and—of course—conquests. Eunice Kennedy Shriver—the fourth of the nine Kennedy children, born 1921—recalls the family motto as "*Finish First. . . .* I was twenty-four before I knew I didn't have to win something every day." The family filled its summer days at Hyannis with a succession of races: swimming, running, sailing. "And if we won," remembers Eunice, "[Daddy] got terribly enthusiastic. Daddy was always very competitive. The thing he always kept telling us was that coming in second was just no good."

A close family friend recalls Joseph P. Kennedy, Sr.—iconoclastic investor, entrepreneur, and sometime public servant—as someone who "didn't like anyone to be second best, and he expected you to prepare yourself better than the other fellow and then try harder than he did. Any other course of action in his mind suggested stupidity." As Jack—the second-eldest, born 1917—recollected during his presidency, "[My father] could be pretty caustic when we lost. He scared some of my contemporaries who visited the house." Joseph Kennedy's most astute biographer, Ronald Kessler, has likened him to a coach, and his children to a football team. "The aim," writes Kessler, "was to win at everything, no matter what."

The coach did not pride himself on his patience, nor was he known for his honesty. He once lashed out bitterly at Joe Jr.—the eldest child, born 1915—when the boy lost an important sailboat race. Then, by way of making up for his outburst, he purchased his namesake a new mainsail. Young Joe promptly started winning again. Later, Joe Jr. discovered that the new main ran nine inches too high, giving him an unfair advantage against other boats. The episode foreshadowed much of what was to come. Joe Sr. would always do whatever it took to improve his children's odds—lengthening their sails in many different ways throughout their lives. Only with the world war would he bump up against a contest he could not fix to the certain advantage of his offspring.

. . .

Joseph P. Kennedy, Sr., seems to have been at once awesome, terrifying, demanding, and benevolent: driving his children to compete and win with the same great ruthlessness he brought to bear in his pursuits of money, power, social prestige, and beautiful women. Every day in summer he would sit in his "bullpen" outside his second-story bedroom at Hyannis and bark loudly into his telephone as he negotiated a steady string of big-money deals in stocks, films, real estate, and the wholesaling of liquor. His loud voice carried over the beach and water, where his busy children could hear his incessant banter. They knew he was up there, watching them play their ceaseless contests, keeping his own score.

Football games sometimes concluded with fistfights between Joe's highly competitive sons. "It's touch," commented one guest, "but it's murder. If you don't want to play, don't come. If you do come, play, or you'll be fed in the kitchen and nobody will speak to you." Besides losing, the other unforgivable sin among the Kennedys was to refuse a challenge—any challenge. "I grew up in a very strict house," Jack would recall, "and one where . . . there were no free riders, and everyone was expected to do, give their very best to what they did. . . . There was a constant drive for self-improvement."

All the children rose to the occasion again and again: all except Rosemary. Joseph and Rose Kennedy's eldest daughter (born 1918, one year after Jack) remained on the periphery of the active and energetic family in her early teen years: a disconnected presence seemingly dumbstruck by the flurry of activity on which her brothers and sisters thrived. Nineteen years old in the summer of 1937, Rosemary—who had suffered brain damage during a botched delivery—barely possessed the mental capacity of a fourth-grader. Her brothers and sisters (eventually even the youngest, fourteen years Rosemary's junior) acted at various times as her protectors and caregivers. Eunice Kennedy Shriver recalls: "We all had the feeling [Rosemary] was just a little slow, so [we always made it a point to] jolly Rosemary along. . . . Then, also, the boys were very good with her. Like Jack would take her to a dance at the club, and would dance with her and kid with her and make sure a few of his close pals cut in, so she felt popular. He'd bring her home at midnight. Then he'd go back to the dance."

. . .

THOSE WHO KNEW the family best described the oldest boy, Joseph P. Kennedy, Jr., as the son most like the father. Handsome and athletic, Joe Jr. had a short temper and a penchant for fistfights. He often behaved like a bully, as even his adoring little brother Ted could attest. On one occasion Joe threw the boy into the ocean during an outburst after the two had lost a sailboat race. "On the way home from the pier," Teddy recalled, "he told me to be quiet about what had happened that afternoon."

Throughout his adolescence and young manhood, Joe regularly appeared content to gain superiority by knocking others down rather than elevating himself. He was careful, however, not to show this face to the tutors and instructors at his school—Choate (now Choate Rosemary Hall), in Wallingford, Connecticut. He was not at Choate long before he emerged as a star on campus: playing varsity football, editing the school newspaper, and generally performing well in the classroom (though this took great effort). He seemed the golden boy and—at a casual glance—popular. Nevertheless, a number of lowerclassmen—among them brother Jack—breathed a sigh of relief when he graduated.

He did not, like so many others in Choate's class of 1933, proceed directly to Harvard. Those in a position to know—even the Choate tutors who loved him—agreed the eighteen-year-old was just not ready. His father's alma mater would eat him alive. Better for him to spend a productive year sharpening his wits in the company of a tutor who could challenge and enlighten him. Then, if the gods took pity, he might just find himself in shape to face the rigors of an elite college. Heartily endorsing this plan, family friend Felix Frankfurter (of Harvard Law) suggested the one man he considered the greatest teacher on the planet: Harold Laski, socialist economist at the London School of Economics. British by birth and Jewish by upbringing, Laski embraced not only socialism but also atheism, and said he considered the Roman Catholic Church one of the "permanent enemies" of all that was "decent in the human spirit." Joseph Kennedy, Sr., told stunned friends that he was sending his son to the unlikely Laski in order that the boy might become versed in the ideology and methods of the have-nots, the left, *the enemy*.

Once ensconced in London for the academic year 1933–34, Joe Jr. struck Laski as an amiable but unbrilliant fellow: a student always anxious (though often unable) to please. "He was with me during a year when the three outstanding students in my department all happened to be at once Socialists and poor Jews from the East End of London," recalled Laski. "Nothing was more admirable than Joe's attitude toward them, a deep respect for their ability, an ardent promise that one day he would know enough to argue with them on equal terms. . . ." The day, as Laski implies, never came. Both in the classroom and during Laski's many famous Sunday teas—where he encouraged his generally precocious students to debate on a range of subjects—Joe repeatedly proved unable to hold his own. "I am just getting to the point," he wrote (optimistically) after several months in London, "where I can discuss matters intelligently and not be like a dumb ham."

In the midst of his year abroad, Joe Jr. went with Laski on an extended trip to the Soviet Union, where he saw little that he liked. Then, over Easter weekend of 1934, he journeyed with roommate Aubrey Whitelaw to visit Hitler's Germany. "I had been to Laski's many times to tea," he wrote his father, "and had heard him and many German socialists tell of the frequent brutalities in Germany." Nevertheless, Joe came to admire Hitler's program once he saw it up close, and he quickly adopted the Nazi version of recent history as his own.

> They had tried liberalism, and it had seriously failed. They had no leader, and as time went on Germany was sinking lower and lower. The German people were scattered, despondent, and were divorced from hope. Hitler came in. He saw the need of a common enemy, someone of whom to make the goat. Someone, by whose riddance the Germans would feel they had cast out the cause of their predicament. It was excellent psychology, and it was too bad that it had to be done to the Jews. The dislike of the Jews, however, was well-founded. They were at the heads of all big business, in law etc. It is all to their credit for them to get so far, but their methods had been quite unscrupulous. . . . The lawyers and prominent judges were Jews, and if you had a case against a Jew, you were nearly always sure to lose it. It's a sad state of affairs when things like that can take place. . . . As far as the brutality is concerned, it must have been necessary to use some, to secure the whole-hearted support of the people, which was necessary to put through this present program.

Joe took his favorable impression of the Third Reich with him when he entered Harvard five months later. He also, of course, brought along the memory of the poor Jews from the London slums who so frequently made him out a fool in Laski's living room. Several years later, during the autumn of 1944, Jack would question Laski's memory of the deep respect with which the normally truculent Joe had approached the Jewish students who were so clearly his academic superiors. "Is that really the way it was?" Jack asked Laski in a letter. "Or are you being generous?" Jack told the professor he thought it would have been "surprisingly out of character" for Joe to appear "at all gracious about not measuring up. He was, at heart, highly-competitive. And he usually had but one obvious wish for anyone who showed him up at anything: destruction." A friend from Joe's Harvard years recalls him mentioning that he did not mind Jews but, like his father, hated *Kikes*. One wonders, given his experiences among Laski's students and his positive reaction to Hitler's Germany, just how Joe Jr. defined the difference between the two.

. . .

REFLECTING ON THE MEMORY of her two oldest boys, the elderly Rose Kennedy would recall Joe Jr. as "older, bigger, stronger, . . . but Jack, frail though he was, could fight like fury when he had to." Rose remembered the two youngsters once racing round the block on their bicycles in opposite directions, each refusing to veer out of the other's path. Jack went to the hospital for twenty-eight stitches following the inevitable collision. Long after both Joe and Jack were dead, Bobby Kennedy—ten years younger than Joe and eight years younger than Jack—described how, as a boy, he would lie in his bed at night "and hear the sound of Joe banging Jack's head against the wall." When asked to reflect on Joe Jr. during an interview in the early 1960s, Jack commented: "He had a pugnacious personality. Later on it smoothed out but it was a problem in my boyhood."

Jack's health was also a problem during his boyhood—and after. As Robert Kennedy was to recall, "At least one half of the days that he spent on this earth were days of intense physical pain. . . . When we were growing up together we used to laugh about the great risk a mosquito took in biting Jack Kennedy—with some of his blood the mosquito was almost sure to die." Jack came very near to death from scarlet fever at age two. A slight defor-

mity of his back required the occasional use of crutches and a brace. He also
had asthma and was extremely thin. At six, his mother described his appearance as being "elfin." He received the last rites of the Roman Catholic
Church when he was fourteen during a potentially fatal attack of appendicitis, after which he became so thin that his grandfather—John "Honey Fitz"
Fitzgerald, onetime congressman and mayor of Boston—offered him a dollar for every pound he gained.

Jack's perennial complaints throughout his youth included a strange mix
of flulike symptoms—chills, hives, fevers, abdominal pain, and occasional
fainting—all of these stemming from sudden, unpredictable, and unex-
plained drops in his white blood cell count. Painful injections of liver extract
sometimes improved his condition. Whatever was wrong with him, it had
the interesting side effect of sometimes turning his skin to a jaundicelike yellow or, when he was lucky, the yellowish-brown of a healthy tan. (Jack's affliction would not be correctly diagnosed until 1947, when doctors at
Boston's Lahey Clinic finally identified their longtime patient as suffering
from Addison's disease: the steady decline of the adrenal glands and consequent degeneration of hormonal output, without which the body is not able
to adequately combat infections and other medical stresses.)

Jack's illness rose and then subsided unpredictably, with long hiatuses
of health in between the attacks. Still, he spent much time in infirmaries and
hospitals. Often confined to bed for weeks, he maximized his time by de-
vouring the complete works of Burke, Gibbon, Winston Churchill, and
other major writers on history and politics. When one of his father's friends
visited him at the Mayo Clinic in 1934 she found Jack "lying in bed, very
pale, which highlighted the freckles across his nose. He was so surrounded
by books I could hardly see him. I was very impressed, because at that point
this very young child [seventeen] was reading *The World Crisis* by Winston
Churchill." Interestingly, he also read Henry Pringle's life of Theodore
Roosevelt and, one might guess, took heart in the story of the sickly young
TR's rise to robust manhood.

It was perhaps not a coincidence that he subsequently went west, just
like TR, to work on a ranch and build his stamina, returning to play football
for Choate and later for Harvard's 1936 freshman squad. Like all the rest of
his family, Jack disdained self-pity, never complained, and always performed
to the maximum his strength and talent would allow. As the head coach at

Choate would recall, "Jack made up for what he lacked in athletic ability with his fight." Quick on offense and good at tackling, Jack nevertheless proved useless when it came to blocking or any other task where size mattered. "Guts is the word," said Jack's close friend and fellow Catholic, the Harvard gridiron hero Torbert Macdonald. "He had plenty of guts."

Jack's testosterone drove him not only into sports, but also into the arms of just about any woman who would have him after he lost his virginity to a white prostitute in a Harlem brothel at age eighteen. Although he would eventually master the art of seducing the girls he met in his social rounds, young Jack's sexual adventures during the first years of his amorous life most often involved prostitutes. He told friends he viewed whores as plentiful, economical, and convenient. He was busy, he said, and liked the idea of being able to go to a professional on his own schedule for some brisk and businesslike sex on demand.

His father's assistant Eddie Moore, who had ambitiously procured women for "the boss" for many years, took to supplying Jack as well sometime in late 1935 or early 1936. "Went down to the Cape with five guys from school [Harvard]," Jack wrote a friend in October of 1936. "EM got us some girls thru another guy—four of us had dates and one guy got fucked 3 times, another guy 3 times (the girl a virgin!) + myself twice—they were all on the football team + I think the coaches heard as they gave us all a hell of a bawling out." (Big brother Joe, meanwhile, disdained prostitutes and instead dated a succession of actresses, dancers, and older married women, all of whom he said he considered "safe." The self-supporting actresses and dancers tended not to be in the market for husbands; the same, of course, went for Joe's married dates.)

. . .

DURING HIS TIME at Choate, Jack ran counter to his brother Joe—two years ahead of him—and became a magnet for troublemakers. Untidy and disrespectful of authority, he made a distinctly negative impression on the faculty. He consistently earned mediocre grades, and his father worried that Jack might never reach his potential. He had above-average intelligence (scoring 119 on the Otis Intelligence Test), but simply did not seem interested in Latin, French, mathematics, or English. He earned his best grades in physics and history, the latter being his favorite subject. When he graduated, he ranked 65th in a class of 110. His closest friends at the school included K. LeMoyne ("Lem") Billings, the son of a Pittsburgh physician, and Ralph ("Rip") Horton, the son of a prosperous New York dairy owner. Billings recalled that Jack "had the best sense of humor of anybody I've ever known in my life. And I don't think I've ever known anybody who was as much fun."

Throughout his career at Choate, Jack demonstrated a healthy questioning of authority and a hearty disregard for the campus rules and regulations. When Jack's mother sent a crate of oranges from Palm Beach, Jack spent the better part of a day aiming them at the heads of friends who passed by his window. On another occasion, he collected all the pillows in his dormitory and packed them in the room of a classmate he did not care for. In his senior year, he and a group of twelve friends (among them Lem and Rip) formed a "Mucker's Club," the name fashioned after the headmaster's term for everything and everyone that was unwelcome at Choate. This secret society embarked on carefully planned search-and-destroy missions every morning, diligently striving toward the boys' long-term goal of violating each and every campus rule.

Jack's casual and, at times, rebellious approach to education continued after he moved on to college. Arriving at Harvard in the fall of 1936, Jack quickly dispelled any notion that his undergraduate career would be a serious one. In fact, he appears to have decided early on that he would leave it to Joe—a junior when Jack was a freshman—to be the serious, academically belligerent Kennedy on campus. Instead of focusing on his studies, Jack concentrated on the social scene, where his charm, good looks, and wealth brought him steadily increasing success with women. (Sensing yet another field of play on which he and his brother might compete, Joe sometimes sought to steal Jack's girls—but the ladies invariably came back to Jack. He had a charm Joe lacked. Joe's humor was biting, sarcastic, and routinely trained on others. Jack's, on the other hand, was self-deprecating and unassuming. He was, quite simply, more fun to be around.)

And despite his casual approach to studies, he did have a serious side. During a summer 1937 tour of Europe with Lem Billings following his freshman year at Harvard, Jack began to get a sense of the wider—and increasingly troubled—world. Visiting Munich, Jack and Lem quickly got their fill of the beer-guzzling brownshirts they encountered at the Hofbrau

House, site of Hitler's infamous beerhall putsch and a favorite watering hole for Nazi Party stalwarts. Lem remembered that he and Jack developed a terrible impression of Germans in general and the Nazis in particular—the latter always so anxious to demonstrate their superiority over Americans. "We just had awful experiences there," Billings recalled. The brownshirts "were just so haughty and so sure of themselves," still basking in the afterglow of their triumphal 1935 march into the demilitarized Rhineland, when neither France nor England had dared stand in their way.

.   .   .

IT CAN BE ARGUED that Lem Billings knew the young Jack Kennedy better than anyone. Thus we must pay attention to Billings's assertion in a 1970s interview that Jack's buoyant, charismatic, and stridently witty character sprang from a well of chronic unhappiness. We must also respect Billings's assertion that Jack's profound and abiding melancholia in turn flowed from his "very, very complex and stand-offish" relationship with his mother, Rose.

They were not close. "My mother never hugged me," the grown Jack told his friend William Walton with great emotion, "never, never!" (Jack's longtime associate Chuck Spalding once commented: "I think half of this activity with girls was making up for what he didn't have at home.") Delegating the care of her children to nannies and boarding schools, Rose frequently made herself even more remote by planning to be abroad at times when the school-age Kennedys returned home during recesses. Rose likewise left her husband—who'd already proved adept at cheating on his marriage—to go his own way in matters of the flesh after the birth of their last child, Teddy, in 1932. Sex, she said, was for procreation, not recreation. (Joe Kennedy, Sr., of course, felt otherwise.)

During his presidency, Jack would comment that Rose had not been around much during his childhood. "She was either at Paris fashion shows or on her knees in some church." Between 1929 and 1936, Rose made no fewer than seventeen extended international journeys. Writing in her 1972 autobiography, Rose amusedly—and clearly without realizing their import— quoted the words uttered by five-year-old Jack when he learned she would shortly depart on a six-week tour of the West Coast with her sister Agnes. "Gee," said the boy, "you're a great mother to go away and leave your children all alone!" During her long absences, Rose kept in touch by drafting a series of newsletterlike round-robin dispatches chronicling her travels—these designed for circulation to the whole family, thus saving her the trouble of having to write to each child individually.

On those few occasions when Rose did give any one of the children her undivided attention, it was usually to discuss the ancient pieties and devout rituals of the Roman Catholic faith. "We always had a rosary on our beds," remembers Pat, born one year before Bobby. "And of course, she'd hear our prayers, and our catechisms, which we learned every week." Jean—the second-youngest, born 1928—recalls being drilled relentlessly by her mother in the liturgy of the mass. All the children absorbed the lessons of the Church—especially Bobby. He served as an altar boy, energetically pursued the Latin of the Roman mass, and generally seemed the most receptive to his mother's religious zeal. Bobby truly looked forward to the time he spent with Rose talking about Jesus, the Holy Trinity, and the redemption of souls.

Like his father, Jack made a serious claim to devout Catholic piety while at the same time sinning with great gusto. He said prayers on his knees each night, attended confession at least once a week, received communion regularly, and slept with whores as frequently as possible. Despite the contradictions, Lem Billings thought that Jack's sinner's faith seemed quite sincere. Jack tempered his religiosity, however, with a lightly ironic (and thoughtful) detachment. He laughed out loud when, during their 1937 tour of Europe, Billings got sick with a fever after visiting the grotto in Lourdes where the Virgin had appeared to Saint Bernadette, a place renowned for miraculous healing. He also voiced open skepticism when presented with the relics of supposed miracles in Rome, among them Veronica's veil and the steps down which St. Peter's head was said to have rolled.

.   .   .

AS WE'VE ALREADY SEEN, Joseph P. Kennedy did not send his sons—at least not his oldest sons—to Catholic schools. "I figured," he recalled, "the boys could get all the religion they needed in church, and that it would be broadening for them to attend Protestant schools." What was more, they would eventually have to make their way in a world dominated by a Protestant elite. Joe believed that the sooner they learned to deal with (and perhaps master) the Protestant powers that be, the better. Rose, on the other hand, insisted that her girls attend parochial schools, where they could learn the skills most necessary for their future callings as Catholic wives and mothers.

With Rosemary receiving special instruction of her own, it fell to Kathleen—the second-eldest girl and fourth child, born 1920—to lead the way for her younger sisters in the rigid, often stifling world of Catholic convent education. Nicknamed "Kick" because of her vivacious good humor, Kathleen had just turned thirteen in 1933 when her mother—concerned that the girl demonstrated too much interest in the opposite sex—dispatched her to the school conducted by the Sisters of the Order of the Sacred Heart at Noroton, Connecticut. There—in a grim, forbidding mansion perched high above Long Island Sound—Kick and other pubescent Catholic girls studied under the strict discipline of nuns who believed self-denial and obedience to authority constituted the routes to all things holy.

Her face covered with a black veil, Kick attended mass every morning before breakfast. Afterward, she and her fellow students endured long periods of silence, which the nuns claimed would aid the girls' contemplation. Winter or summer, Kick and her cohorts bathed twice a week in cold water, the sisters citing this frigid rite as an invaluable tool for achieving physical and spiritual purity. Like other students, Kick was forbidden to be alone "two by two" with any other classmate—a rule meant to reduce the possibility of lesbianism. Later, at age fifteen, Kick spent a year abroad at the Convent of the Holy Child in Neuilly, outside Paris, where she and her colleagues practiced the same regimen—now being silent in French.

Visiting some older American boys during May Week at Cambridge in 1936, sixteen-year-old Kick fell instantly in step with the rhythm of the secular world—happily swapping her veil and her rosary for balls, regattas, and boys. When Kick returned to Noroton in the autumn of 1936, she was a different person: perhaps not a seductress, but certainly a flirt. She used several weekend leaves from school to sweep Jack's friend and sometime Harvard roommate Torb Macdonald off his feet. Then she shattered Torb—the poor scholarship student, the son of a gym teacher from the wrong side of the tracks—in the spring of 1937 when she dumped him quite suddenly for a far more desirable Catholic: Peter Grace, the Yale-educated heir to the Grace Lines shipping fortune. (Some of Kick's less generous contemporaries expressed amazement that either Macdonald or Grace would find Kick appealing, given her plain Irish looks, her big hips, and what she herself once called her "tree-stump" legs. Others noted that Kick's effervescent, chatty personality routinely won out over her figure, and made many men besides Torb and Peter look twice.)

.   .   .

L IKE ROSE, Joe Sr. spent great amounts of time out of the household. He nevertheless always made himself present in the lives of his children. In fact, he exchanged detailed, intensely personal letters with each of them on an almost daily basis. There was only one on whom he did not dote. In the final analysis, Joe Sr. would always—despite himself—exhibit a certain distaste if not for Rosemary, then for the fundamental inadequacy she personified. Through no fault of her own, Rosemary was a person her father stood incapable of understanding: a person defined by her limits rather than her capabilities. Try as he might, the father could never muster any genuine enthusiasm for the girl's pathetically small conquests: tying her shoes, dialing a phone, singing a nursery rhyme. Her fate, he must have realized, was written already. She would never be a winner.

2

The Ambassador

WHETHER OR NOT one cared for Joseph P. Kennedy, one had to admit he had a nose for opportunity. Those who disliked him—and they were legion—enjoyed characterizing him as a rather desperate social climber who grasped at wealth with a remarkable and single-minded tenaciousness. Those who opposed him in business usually wound up poorer for their trouble, and went away with grudging respect for the guile Kennedy was prone to display just when one least expected it. Those who thought to use Kennedy for their own ends soon found themselves used in turn, for Joe was never one to let a debt owed him, be it financial or political, go unpaid; and interest on things owed Joe had a way of compounding at quite a frantic rate.

President Franklin Roosevelt was well aware of this in the autumn of 1937, when he noticed the *New York Times*'s Arthur Krock and others of Kennedy's friends in the press mention him as a likely candidate to replace the ailing Robert Worth Bingham as ambassador to the Court of St. James's. The prominent Kentucky newspaper publisher had lately been a patient at Johns Hopkins University Hospital, where malaria, having already ended his career, now threatened to end his life.

While the gentleman of the press telegraphed Kennedy's desires indirectly, it was left to James Roosevelt, the president's eldest son and secretary, to bring FDR specific details on Kennedy's wants. Jimmy had, in recent years, received a large number of favors and gifts from Kennedy. The forty-nine-year-old financier had aided the younger Roosevelt—aged thirty—in building a lucrative Boston insurance business, had brought him and his wife along as guests on a European vacation, and was currently suggesting that in future he'd be pleased to help the easily flattered Jimmy make a run at the Massachusetts governorship.

Speaking years later about his role as messenger boy for the aspiring ambassador, Jimmy would recall his father laughing "so hard he almost toppled out of his wheelchair" when first presented with the prospect of sending Kennedy to London. During a dinner at his Hyde Park home, surrounded by WASPs like himself who had always had easy entrée to the society that had routinely been forbidden to the overambitious Kennedy, FDR said that to appoint a Boston Irishman as emissary to the king would be "a great joke, the greatest joke in all the world." FDR, a master at misdirection, did not tell his guests the joke might very well wind up being played. And he threw Treasury Secretary Henry Morgenthau, Jr., off the scent with the blunt assertion that Kennedy was "a very dangerous man."

Dangerous or not, there were, FDR told Jimmy, several simple facts to keep in mind. First of all, Joseph Kennedy had donated more than $360,000—the equivalent of over $3.8 million in today's dollars—to the Democratic campaigns of 1932 and 1936. He had also been instrumental in breaking a deadlock at the 1932 Democratic convention when he persuaded publisher William Randolph Hearst (who controlled no fewer than eighty-six delegates) to throw his support behind FDR, thus assuring Roosevelt the nomination. Now, FDR judged, had come the day of reckoning when he would be made to pay Kennedy back in spades.

FDR correctly guessed that Joe would not take no for an answer when it came to the ambassadorship, and that his desire for the London appointment was intense. Over the long years, Joe had been denied membership in the Harvard Clubs of Boston and New York, the University Club, the Knickerbocker Club, and numerous other bastions of old-money culture. In London, as ambassador, he would automatically be made a member of the Royal Thames Yacht Club, the Athenaeum, the Queen's Club, the Monday

Luncheon Club, the International Sportsmen Club, and many other elite establishments to which the best of American society often aspired in vein. It was just like Kennedy, the president told his son, to want to leapfrog those who would snub him and become a peer of their betters.

As FDR pondered Kennedy's appointment to London that autumn, he knew his old ally was unhappy. He also knew from experience that an unhappy Kennedy was a vengeful and vocal Kennedy, a Kennedy prone to talk too much to the press and say harmful things. FDR had, since 1932, dedicated great amounts of energy to containing the sometimes bitter, routinely passionate Irishman who was always so easily offended, and seemed so full of insecurities and brooding resentments. "The trouble with Kennedy," an exasperated FDR once explained to Henry Morgenthau, "is you always have to hold his hand." Joe, said Roosevelt, was far too thin-skinned and temperamental, and could become absolutely babyish when not doted upon. Roosevelt said he was getting tired of Kennedy's calling up and saying "he is hurt because I have not seen him."

Still, Kennedy had demonstrated abilities as a manager—abilities FDR first sought to exploit when he appointed him to head the new Securities and Exchange Commission in 1934. "Send a thief to catch a thief," Roosevelt told Morgenthau shortly before leaking news of Joe's appointment to the press. By the time Kennedy resigned one year later, even his harshest critics—among them *The New Republic's* John T. Flynn—had to admit the former Wall Street buccaneer had done a splendid job of taking the new SEC regulations and putting them to work. Flynn, who at first had staunchly opposed Kennedy's appointment, wound up bidding him adieu in *The New Republic* by saying, "I think it but fair to him to say that he disappointed the expectations of his critics. He was, I firmly believe, the most useful member of the Commission."

Subsequently, in the summer of 1936 (a presidential election year), Kennedy emerged with an audacious bid to court the ultimate in Rooseveltian favor. "I have no political ambitions for myself or for my children," Kennedy lied in the foreword to his book *I'm for Roosevelt*. "I put down these few thoughts about our President, conscious only of my concern as a father for the future of his family and my anxiety as a citizen that the facts about the President's philosophy be not lost in a fog of unworthy emotion." Kennedy published his little manifesto—ghostwritten by Arthur Krock—at his own expense. Subsequently Kennedy went on national radio (again at his own expense) to urge Americans to vote the Democratic ticket. For all these efforts, however, FDR rewarded Joe with only the smallest of morsels from the presidential table. Kennedy—who'd originally (and quite unrealistically) hoped to be handed Morgenthau's job as secretary of the treasury—instead received a lackluster appointment to chair the obscure Federal Maritime Commission, where he started in April 1937. It was from this bureaucratic wasteland that he now, only six months later, petitioned for release to exciting London.

. . .

IT DOES NOT DO to simply say these two Harvard men, Kennedy and Roosevelt, came from opposite sides of the tracks. They came, in fact, from opposing worlds and embraced opposing worldviews. Their philosophies, sensibilities, and agendas were always fundamentally at odds. Theirs was a complex, highly pragmatic, and entirely political relationship. Each often viewed the other cynically; each always did his best to use the other for his own purposes.

Only two generations removed from the Potato Famine, Kennedy inherited wit, stamina, and a respectable (though not vast) amount of wealth from his street-smart, entrepreneurial father. More important, however, he also inherited a driving ambition to maximize that wealth and assure his clan's advance in the world.

More than one contemporary speculated that Joe's one and only allegiance was not to country or to the general good, but to family. He had little civic feeling. He actively loathed what he once called "the dim and dull-eyed masses" for whom he produced sophomoric film entertainments and imported liquor. The general welfare of the non-Kennedy public was not, for him, a priority. (In an interview toward the end of his time as ambassador, Kennedy would look back on his New Deal service in the mid-1930s and loudly complain about First Lady Eleanor Roosevelt, whose main drawback was that "she bothered us more on our jobs in Washington to take care of the poor little nobodies who hadn't any influence than all the rest of the people down there altogether.") To Joe, the public was little more than a mass of outsiders to be conquered and manipulated to the best advantage of Kennedy interests. "I think," recalled one who knew him well, "the world outside his house was war for Mr. Kennedy."

Given his view of the public, it is no surprise that Kennedy did not approach public service altruistically. Having been repeatedly rejected by WASP society—a society he at first craved to be a part of and then, eventually, grew to detest—Joe came to view public service as a tool for gaining the respectability and acceptance that all his fortune could not buy no matter how many times he deftly doubled and tripled it. As the shrewd FDR must have surmised, Joe also saw public service as a stepping-stone to something far more profound and insidious than mere social acceptance. His most genuine ambition was one he would reveal bluntly only after his son had been elected to the presidency. When asked what had been his main aspiration in life, the confident and triumphant first father responded flatly: "I wanted power. I thought money would give me power and so I made money, only to discover that it was politics—not money—that really gave a man power."

Truth be told, Kennedy cared much more for power than he did for Roosevelt. He told friends he viewed FDR as clever, but also as an accident of privilege who did not know what it was to suffer. When word of these criticisms filtered back to Henry Morgenthau, the treasury secretary told a colleague that Kennedy had Roosevelt "figured out not at all." Morgenthau dryly pointed out that the crippled president could always, despite his privileged background, confidently say he knew a thing or two about suffering and struggle.

Still, unlike Kennedy, FDR had been raised from the cradle safe in the knowledge that he was one of the elite. FDR *arrived*, in every sense of the word, on the day he was born. His family name, the age of his money, and the facts of his pedigree on both sides of his family tree gave him an immediate place in the most rarefied precincts of the Eastern Seaboard. Like his father, FDR was an avid clubman. He was a member of the Century, Harvard, and University clubs, to name just a few of the establishments where Kennedy had been blackballed. Yet, despite his aristocratic roots, FDR was a democrat with a small *d*—one driven by a genuine concern for the welfare of the common man.

FDR's wealth, though modest compared to Kennedy's net worth of over $9 million, was enough to inoculate against the craven desire for more. By refusing to give his full attention to his few entrepreneurial ventures, the brilliant and inspired political tactician often proved a notoriously poor businessman who almost always lost money whenever he took a stab at private enterprise. Kennedy, on the other hand, had the veritable Midas touch in business. He was well known to be the shrewdest of generals when marshaling his forces on every and any financial front. He never missed a beat on Wall Street, saying and doing all the right things at just the right time, such as when he gleefully sold short into the plummeting stock market of late 1929, hastening the market's collapse and making millions in the process.

Previously he'd made substantial gains in the market by just the kind of activity he subsequently regulated as head of the SEC. Throughout the early 1920s, Joe had become expert in the subtle art of stock pooling: conspiring with other traders to bid up the price of a stock and then dumping that stock once the market had been fooled into buying at the higher price. He likewise enjoyed great successes not only in liquor distribution (legitimate and otherwise) and filmmaking, but also as a banker and real-estate speculator. Yet in politics he frequently misread popular sentiment and was prone to strategic blunders. He often made arbitrary and self-destructive public statements, and he had no knack for shaping the type of loyal alliances and practical compromises that were essential for long-term survival in public life. Thus FDR had good reason to wonder how Kennedy would fare as a diplomat.

· · ·

THAT AUTUMN FOUND the would-be ambassador's two eldest sons—Joseph P. Kennedy, Jr., twenty-three, and John Fitzgerald Kennedy, twenty-one—living in Harvard's Winthrop House. Here they energetically pursued their studies, sports, and women while at the same time balancing the biases and assumptions of the great seat of Protestant learning against the weight of their ancient Roman Catholic faith. As the Kennedys knew all too well, their unfashionable religious affiliation had its consequences not only at Harvard but everywhere throughout the society of the Northeast. Like "the old man" a quarter of a century before, Joe Jr. (now a senior) had been elected to the Hasty Pudding Institute in the autumn of his sophomore year only to see his career as a clubman come to an abrupt halt shortly thereafter. He was not chosen for any of Harvard's eight exclusive final clubs, and had to settle for lowly Pi Eta. "It was better than nothing," remembered one associate from those days, "but it created a bad feeling in him."

Jack—now a sophomore—hoped and planned to fare better. Of the two brothers, he was certainly the more likely candidate: amiable and without Joe's off-putting demeanor. (Joe Jr.'s Harvard tutor, Ken Galbraith, described Joe as "slender and handsome, with a heavy shock of hair and a serious, slightly humorless manner." Jack, on the other hand, was "gregarious, given to various amusements, much devoted to social life and affectionately and diversely to women.") Jack also tended to be the shrewder, more politically savvy of the two—something he demonstrated when he focused his ambitions on the Spee Club, the president of which, Ralph Pope, was known to deplore the anti-Catholic bias then dominating a host of Harvard institutions.

Looking around the campus for likely Catholic candidates, Pope had taken a pass on Joe Jr. two years before and now as well decided against Jack's friend and roommate Torbert Macdonald. Pope considered Joe to be pushy and a bit of a bully. As for Macdonald, Pope told friends the football star struck him as an intellectual lightweight. (Besides, Macdonald had yet another strike against him. He was poor.) Pope also thought both Joe and Torb were a little too likely to enforce, rather than destroy, Irish-Catholic stereotypes. Jack, however, gave off a completely different impression. By the time the rushing season ended at the start of December 1937, Jack had found himself a home. The Spee Club, recalled Jack's friend and fellow member Jimmy Rousmaniere many years later, gave Jack "a base and a social standing which his brother never had. Jack and Joe were good friends, but I think that Jack always felt happy that he was able to do some things that Joe couldn't do. And the Spee Club was the means of doing that."

Contemporaries recall Joe Jr.'s being visibly annoyed upon receiving word that his younger brother had made it into the Spee. Perhaps Joe's jealous and sour reaction was just a symptom of his personality. Or perhaps the timing of the news had something to do with Joe's response, for it came on the heels of one of the greatest disappointments in the young man's life: his failure to achieve his school's varsity letter, the large H.

Joe had played for the Harvard football team (first the freshman squad, and later the varsity) all of his four years on campus, but he had never advanced to the first string despite the fact that his position—end—demanded little in the way of technical skill. A friend, looking back, cited Joe's thinly veiled contempt for coach Dick Harlow as the reason why he'd spent so much time warming the bench. The same friend cited the same obvious animosity as the reason why Harlow, breaking with tradition, refused to give Joe and other second- and third-string seniors a chance to earn their letters during the last game of the '37 season. The date was November 20. The place: Soldiers Field, Harvard. The opponent: Yale. Harvard led by seven points as the final quarter neared its end.

"With six minutes to go," wrote Joe's biographer Hank Searls, "the Harvard bench writhed in anticipation: Harlow, in the lead, would surely start to substitute now. It was humanly impossible for the seniors to keep their seats. The coach sat impassively as the minutes flew. Some seniors stayed tight-faced; some, like Joe, fought tears; some could bear it no longer and begged. . . ."

Years later, Joe's Harvard contemporary John Edward Regan, Jr., would comment: "All those others who didn't get into that big game—the last game of the '37 season and the first Harvard win over Yale since 1933—had Joe to thank. Harlow—who knew Joe hated him and hated Joe right back—didn't want to give Joe the satisfaction, but at the same time Harlow couldn't make Joe the only one of the last-year men he left out. So an entire class of second- and third-stringers wound up leaving the school without those varsity letters: all thanks to Joe's unbridled, unconcealed, and unproductive animosity."

. . .

MANY MILES FROM HARVARD, FDR's inner circle appeared divided on the question of whether or not Joseph Kennedy, Sr., should be dispatched to Great Britain. Treasury Secretary Morgenthau—whose job Kennedy still coveted—did not like the idea and by now perhaps regretted having been the man who'd first brought Kennedy and Roosevelt together as political allies in 1930. Morgenthau reminded Roosevelt that Kennedy, though backing FDR for a second term, had nevertheless voiced frequent criticisms of FDR's economic policies, calling them too liberal and even socialistic. "England is a most important post," Morgenthau, by his own account, told FDR, "and there have been so many people over there talking against the New Deal. Don't you think you are taking considerable risks by sending Kennedy, who has talked so freely and so critically against your administration?" Roosevelt replied that he had made arrangements "to have Joe Kennedy watched hourly, and the first time he opens his mouth and criticizes me, I'll fire him." Besides, said Roosevelt, Kennedy was "too dangerous" to keep around in the States. If nothing else, the appointment would at least get Kennedy away from the domestic press corps.

Others in the administration—among them Tommy Corcoran (a Harvard-trained lawyer then working for FDR as a liaison to Capitol Hill) and Secretary of the Interior Harold Ickes—encouraged Kennedy's appointment in order to get him out of the way. Both expressed concern (to each other and to Morgenthau) about Kennedy's influence on Jimmy Roosevelt, who in turn had the presidential ear. As Corcoran complained to Ickes, Joe had to be gotten out of town in order to stop him from "pouring his conservative ideas in the sympathetic ears of Jimmy, who relays them to the president." Corcoran reminded Ickes of the words uttered long before by Lincoln's secretary of state, William H. Seward. "Some persons," Seward had said, "are sent abroad because they are needed, and some are sent because they're not wanted at home." Still, Kennedy's case was debated back and forth for quite some time behind the White House walls, with Morgenthau leading the arguments against Kennedy's appointment and the president eventually concurring—albeit briefly.

Arthur Krock happened to be at Joseph Kennedy's rented mansion outside Washington on December 2 when Jimmy Roosevelt showed up dangling a minor cabinet appointment, secretary of commerce, as bait to lure Joe away from wanting the London assignment. After Jimmy's departure, recalled Krock, "he [Kennedy] came back to me, clearly very indignant, very angry, and said, 'He tried to get me to take the Secretaryship of Commerce and I knew it was only an attempt to shut me off from London, but London is where I want to go and it is the only place I intend to go and I told Jimmy so, and that's that.' " FDR appears to have green-lighted Kennedy's London appointment within days of this rebuff. He nevertheless expressed his severe displeasure when Arthur Krock—apparently with Jimmy Roosevelt's approval, if not the president's—published advance word of Kennedy's new ambassadorial role in the *New York Times*, preempting the White House announcement.

Friends as well as foes pronounced themselves chagrined by the news. Journalist Boake Carter of the *New York Daily Mirror* and the *Boston Globe*—who, like Krock, was a frequent recipient of Kennedy largesse—went so far as to warn Kennedy that he should not take the job. The ambassadorship to Great Britain, wrote Carter, "needs skill brought by years of training. And that, Joe, you simply don't possess. Do not think me unkind in saying that. On the contrary, I'm trying to save you some heartaches. . . . Joe, in so complicated a job, there is no place for amateurs. . . . If you don't realize that soon enough, you're going to be hurt as you were never hurt in your life." Interestingly, even Kennedy's telegram to the president acknowledging his confirmation in mid-January would have a fatalistic ring to it. "Just got news of my confirmation . . ." Kennedy wired. "I want to say now that I don't know what kind of diplomat I shall be, probably rotten, but I promise to get done for you those things that you want done." FDR shared Kennedy's pessimism. Roosevelt's friend Cornelius Vanderbilt, Jr., would recall that in speaking in private of Kennedy as the future ambassador to Britain, "FDR did not hesitate to mention Catholic connections as a bar to political trust."

FDR told Morgenthau that "he was going to send [Kennedy] to England as Ambassador with the distinct understanding that the appointment was only good for six months and that, furthermore, by giving him this appointment, any obligation that he had to Kennedy was paid for." How true this was, and whether FDR was just trying to placate Morgenthau by telling the man what he wanted to hear, is perhaps indicated by the fact that Roosevelt subsequently told Postmaster General and Democratic National Committee chairman James Farley that he did not think Kennedy would stay in the job more than a year. Kennedy himself told Harvey Klemmer, a Maritime Commission aide whom he now recruited to accompany him to London as publicist and speechwriter, "Don't go buying a lot of luggage. We're only going to get the family in the *Social Register*. When that's done, we come back and go out to Hollywood to make some movies and some money."

Joe informed Tommy Corcoran that he wanted the London post chiefly to please his wife, Rose, forty-seven. Like her husband, Rose Kennedy viewed herself and her family as perennial outsiders marked as completely by their Catholic faith and Irish roots as they were, according to the dogma of the Church, by the stain of original sin. While the divinely ordained blemish could be washed away through mere baptism and contrition, the other birthmark had thus far proved much tougher to get rid of. Rose fervently hoped the mission to London would finally do the trick.

. . .

THE NEWLY APPOINTED ambassador scheduled his departure for February 23. Rose—sidelined by an attack of appendicitis—planned to follow him on March 9 with eighteen-year-old Kick and the four youngest children (Pat, Bobby, Jean, and Teddy). The *New York Times*'s society page published the timetable for the various voyages of the remaining Kennedys. The ambassador's eldest daughter, Rosemary—whom the *Times* identified as a student at Marymount Convent in Tarrytown—was to follow two months later accompanied by her sister Eunice, currently enrolled at the Convent of the Sacred Heart, Noroton. Then, finally, the ambassador's two eldest boys would journey to England as soon as they concluded their spring terms at Harvard.

Visiting FDR at Hyde Park the night before he embarked, Kennedy received an informal briefing from the president, who spent more than an hour describing the European situation as he saw it. FDR expressed concern at the recent break between Anthony Eden and Prime Minister Neville Chamberlain, Foreign Secretary Eden having resigned from Chamberlain's government two days earlier in protest over Chamberlain's apparent willingness to recognize Mussolini's annexation of Ethiopia. Like the firebrand Winston Churchill, Eden believed it would be better to fight the beast of Italian (and by extension German) militarism now, in the short term, rather than help it grow large with the spoils of appeasement. What, Eden had asked in an editorial published shortly after his resignation, would the fascists demand next, once they held a decisive geographical advantage in North Africa and Europe?

Eden, FDR insisted to Kennedy, was a good man. It was a pity to see him go. Still, FDR had heard good things about Eden's successor, the aged Lord Halifax (Edward Frederick Lindley Wood, third Viscount Halifax and later first Earl of Halifax). There were rumors that Halifax—a Yorkshire nobleman and grandson to Lord Grey of Reform Bill fame—did not share the yellow stripe FDR suspected ran down the back of Prime Minister Chamberlain. (Chamberlain's predecessor, Baldwin, had been much the same type of fellow, FDR complained, and was largely to blame for recent Italian and German provocations. After all, Hitler had been making noises for years about how he would reunite the millions of Germans separated at the end of World War I by the terms of the Treaty of Versailles. FDR believed the Führer had been sent a dangerous signal when, after ordering his forces into the Rhineland in 1935, he found neither France nor Baldwin's England disposed to stand in his way.) Complete dedication to the concept of peace was a dangerous predilection in those who would often have to speak and act from a stance of confident belligerence in order to avoid war. Britain, FDR knew full well, was rearming with a vengeance in the face of growing German and Italian territorial ambitions. Still, no amount of firepower would be enough for a ship of state commanded by officers without the spine to use it.

At the same time, FDR told his ambassador to caution Prime Minister Chamberlain that the United States—though supportive—would be hard pressed to come to Britain's aid militarily in the event of a face-off with Hitler. FDR reminded the sympathetic Kennedy that he was constrained not only by neutrality legislation, but also by the wishes of the vast majority of American voters, who stood stridently and squarely against the prospect of American involvement in another European war. As Michael Beschloss has pointed out, FDR by this time suspected that the dictator nations "must ultimately be faced down" and admitted to some in his inner circle "that the European picture looked dark and that American involvement in some form was a distinct possibility." But Kennedy—whom FDR regarded quite accurately as an isolationist of the first rank—received no such confidences.

Thus coached in FDR's concerns and priorities, Kennedy set sail on the 23rd aboard the *Manhattan* bound out of New York. Rain fell in torrents as Kennedy stood on the promenade deck, waving and blowing kisses down to his most cherished assets, his children, gathered far below on the drenched pier.

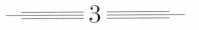

3

Rotten Row

"WELL," KENNEDY WROTE Jimmy Roosevelt early in the first week of March, "I am here after a very nice trip in the *Manhattan*. The ship rolled all the way across, but I have had much worse trips and on larger liners in the middle of the summer. The sailors and stewards couldn't have been nicer—no trouble and no Mickey Finns." A few days later, crossing his feet atop his ambassadorial desk and leaning back in his plush executive chair, Kennedy warned a friendly gathering of London journalists: "You can't expect me to develop into a statesman overnight."

While anxiously expressing his admiration for British society and culture in a steady stream of carefully crafted public remarks, Kennedy painted a very different picture in confidential letters home. His first impression was of a nation adrift and doomed. "I can tell you," he wrote Jimmy Roosevelt, "after forty-eight hours in this place, that England is faced with an economic problem that makes ours look like a tea party. The armament program is keeping the wolf from the door, but underneath is a condition that seems to me to be as dangerous as ours was during the year 1929. England has used up practically all of its aces. First of all, the debt is large; second, it's taxing about as much as it can; third, its cost of carrying the debt has been marked down;

it has already got the benefit of a tariff imposition and it is now spending all its money on armament and, boy, when this stops they're in for it, and I believe that this factor, considering our own situation in America, will be the determining factor in writing the fate of the world rather than the political side."

Kennedy's busy round of London calls began on March 2 when he visited Eden's successor, Halifax—a diplomat of the old school who, Kennedy remarked, "looks and acts like a Cardinal or Abraham Lincoln (without a beard)." Two days later, on the 4th, Prime Minister Neville Chamberlain received the new ambassador for an hour-long meeting during which Kennedy repeated the message he'd given Halifax: the Brits must not count on the United States to come to their aid in the event of hostilities with Germany. Kennedy told Chamberlain the American people were completely antiwar. Because Great Britain seemed to be the natural ally of the United States, the Americans must avoid creating the appearance of any entangling alliances. Grim, graceless, soft-spoken, and sincere, the aged Birmingham industrialist replied that he was indeed making his plans—for war or for peace, one hoped the latter—without counting on America. Kennedy noted in his diary that he had spoken to Chamberlain quite plainly and honestly, and that Chamberlain had seemed to take his candor in stride.

Kennedy quickly decided that he and Chamberlain were *simpatico*. He approved when Chamberlain condemned war as a resoundingly stupid and wasteful exercise from which all reasonable men should always recoil. Similarly, Joe agreed when Chamberlain stated emphatically, in terms the entrepreneurial Kennedy was prompt to sympathize with, that there were many smarter ways than military force for conducting the world's business. The ambassador wrote John Boettiger, a journalist in the employ of his friend William Randolph Hearst and also son-in-law to the president: "Chamberlain believes God has put him at the helm of the British ship of state explicitly for the purpose of steering her away from war. Secondly, he believes conciliation and appeasement are the only methods by which one can maintain peace with dictators like Hitler and Mussolini, two of the most belligerent and militaristic leaders the world has ever seen." Kennedy gave a similar report to Cordell Hull—the dignified former senator from Tennessee now serving as FDR's secretary of state—emphasizing Chamberlain's "realistic, practical mind" and assuring Hull that Chamberlain "has assumed the responsibility of trying to straighten out the Italian and German situa-tion. . . . He is convinced concrete concessions must be made to Germany and is prepared to make them to avert war."

After being duly impressed with the British prime minister, who had been in office since May, and equally impressed with Chamberlain's new man Halifax, Kennedy privately speculated that those at home, such as FDR, who so regretted the departure of the war-mongering Anthony Eden didn't know what they were talking about. Kennedy quite wrongly sized up Cham-berlain as a strong, decisive man in full charge of events. In letters, dis-patches, and diary notes, he repeatedly compared Chamberlain favorably with his shrillest political adversary, Conservative MP Winston Churchill, whom Kennedy had first met during a trip to England in 1935. At that time, the nearly teetotal and pacifist-leaning Kennedy had come away from a typ-ical Churchillian lunch disgusted by the liquor-sipping, cigar-champing mil-itarist. Churchill, Kennedy complained, had spoken of nothing except his dire forecasts of what would happen should the Western democracies fail to arm against the threat of European totalitarianism. Back home in the States, Kennedy had studiously failed to tell FDR of Churchill's suggestion that America and Great Britain join together in building a vast fleet of battleships to oppose the growing fascist menace.

Presenting his credentials to King George VI at Buckingham Palace on the 8th, Kennedy dressed formally in tails with slacks. He was self-conscious about being bowlegged, and for that reason had asked and received permis-sion to dispense with the knee breeches traditionally worn at court func-tions. (In a few weeks, describing the presentation of Mrs. Kennedy and several of the Kennedy children to the court, Winston Churchill's son Ran-dolph would comment dryly in the *Evening Standard* that "the only trousers at last night's court were those worn by the American Ambassador and some of the less important waiters.") Following the formalities, the king went out of his way to congratulate Kennedy on a hole-in-one scored several days ear-lier at the Stokes Poges golf course—a happy quirk of fate that optimistic British journalists trumpeted as a good omen.

Upon leaving the palace, Kennedy—in a major breach of etiquette—quoted his conversation with the king for interested reporters. These and other hiccups occurred much to the annoyance of the embassy's most senior professional diplomat, Herschel Johnson, a dignified South Carolinian who liked it best when the political appointees who showed up calling themselves ambassador kept to the script and stayed within the rules of conduct, saying what he told them to say when he told them to say it. Johnson and Kennedy were not to be friends.

. . .

ROSE KENNEDY DEPARTED for Great Britain with Kick, Pat, Bobby, Jean, and Teddy on March 9, sailing out of New York harbor. "It was an exciting and slightly hectic sailing," she recalled, "because so many friends of all ages were there to wish us *bon voyage* and a marvelous time in England, to say nothing of a great many members of the press. Among these was our old friend Mary Pickford, pretending to be a reporter because she was about to play the role of one in a movie and wanted to get a little practice in an authentic scene." A few days later, when their ship made its first port of call at Cobh, Ireland, Rose recalled the impoverished circumstances under which her forebears (and Joe's) had left that shore so many years before. "Now our family returned, momentarily, in circumstances that could hardly be more dramatically different. There were many thoughts in my mind that day."

Kick dominated the headlines early in the third week of March when Rose and the children made their triumphant landfall in Great Britain. While they were at sea, the *New York World-Telegram* had run a story incorrectly reporting Kick's secret engagement to Peter Grace. The newspaper went on to suggest that this connection lay behind lucrative federal subsidies Joseph Kennedy, Sr., had arranged for the Grace Lines during the former's time as head of the Maritime Commission. Neither the engagement nor the rumors of patronage were true. Nevertheless, on the day of the family's arrival in Britain, Kick found herself fending off reporters who in turn seemed to ignore her mother. When asked about young Mr. Grace, Kick insisted: "It's so silly. He's awfully nice. I like him a lot." Then, under more intense questioning, she changed her approach completely: "I do not know anything about him at all." Her father, in turn, repudiated the rumors of his daughter's engagement, declaring loudly: "She's only eighteen!" But none of these denials stopped the London *Daily Express* from running a two-column story headlined "Kathleen Kennedy, Aged 18, Is in Love."

In fact she was not in love. Far from it. Indeed, she was having huge second thoughts about Peter and had, before her departure from New York, told close friends that she looked forward to putting an ocean between herself and the shipping heir. It seems he was too pious for her. Like his devout father, Peter Grace practiced a most sincerely profound and consuming Catholicism. In this he was quite unlike the other Catholic men in Kick's life: her father and brothers. She had recently grown tired of not only Peter, but also Peter's close associate with whom the couple spent—so far as Kick was concerned—far too many evenings: James Keller, a Maryknoll priest with a penchant for cultivating the scions of wealthy Catholic families. Kick told her closest confidantes that she sometimes did not understand what to make of Peter, a young man with the world at his feet who preferred confessionals to cabanas and Jesuits to jazz. Why was Peter so serious all the time? Didn't he know how to have fun?

Arriving quite breathlessly in London that March of 1938, Kick seemed ready for a change. She was, at the very least, ready for some fun.

. . .

THE UPPER WINDOWS of Rose and Joe's new home, the official ambassador's residence at 14 Princes Gate, provided splendid views looking out over the Knightsbridge traffic to Hyde Park and the Kensington Gardens. Six stories high and boasting thirty-six rooms, the house lay just thirty minutes away by foot from the embassy at Grosvenor Square. French double doors on the second floor opened to a balcony with a good perspective down onto the bridle paths of Rotten Row, where Joe and several of his children would soon begin to ride in the mornings, taking on aristocratic British pretensions with great speed. As Joe was well aware, the mansion along with a lavish country house had been given to the United States of America several decades before by the family of J. P. Morgan—the same man whose son, J. P. Morgan II, had snubbed Joe on more than one occasion. Now Joe used the elder Morgan's bedroom and toilet, wrote letters at Morgan's desk, and garaged his black Chrysler (which he'd insisted the State Department ship for him) in Morgan's old horse stable.

Along with his car, Joe brought his own staff to shore up the already considerable collection of junior consular officials and attachés stationed at the embassy. In addition to Harvey Klemmer from the Maritime Commission, Joe imported several Hollywood cronies. For reasons that remain vague, Will Hays's Motion Picture Producers and Distribution Association of America supplemented the salary for one Arthur Houghton. A fellow Irishman and a former theatrical agent who had been friends with Kennedy for many years, Houghton's chief responsibility seems to have been to serve as gregarious company for the boss. "I hate like hell to take him away from you," Kennedy wrote one of Houghton's colleagues at the Motion Picture Association, "but, my God, London is cold, dreary and foggy during the winter." Kennedy needed Houghton, he said, "to make sure I have somebody over there I can have a laugh with."

Kennedy also brought several personal assistants whom he paid out of his own funds. These included Page Huidekoper, an attractive young friend of Jimmy Roosevelt's now destined to become a chum of Kick's; James Seymour, another one of Kennedy's Hollywood colleagues; and one Jack Kennedy, a rough-and-tumble bodyguard and *gofer* formerly employed by RKO. (This Kennedy would henceforth go by the nicknames "Ding-Dong Jack" and "London Jack" to differentiate him from the boss's second-eldest son.)

In addition to Houghton, Kennedy, Huidekoper, and Seymour, Ambassador Kennedy's perennial assistant Eddie Moore—a former secretary to Rose's father, Honey Fitz—would arrive shortly with his wife. Finally, Kennedy also hired Harold Hinton, a former reporter for the *New York Times*, to serve as his personal press liaison. "There is little doubt," the British chancery in Washington wired the Foreign Office, "Hinton has got his job through the influence of Arthur Krock. . . . It is given out that he is going to write the Ambassador's speeches and keep contact with the press. From what he himself hints it will appear that he will have other jobs to do in the Embassy. . . . If Mr. Hinton is representative of his paper's view, he will be welcomed, for the *New York Times* is as reasonable and as Anglophile as any paper in the United States."

The embassy in which Kennedy and his cronies were to work consisted of three recently renovated Georgian townhouses at the corner of Broad Street, facing Grosvenor Square's elegant central garden. Kennedy's personal office, on the second floor, was spacious, comfortable, and effeminate. "I have a beautiful blue silk room," he wrote Jimmy Roosevelt, "and all I need to make it perfect is a Mother Hubbard dress and a wreath to make me Queen of the May. If a fairy didn't design this room I never saw one in my life." A large portrait of Joseph H. Choate, American ambassador from 1899 to 1905, constituted the office's single masculine aspect. As Kennedy would recall, the old WASP "watched me daily as I began and closed my work. At times it seemed to me that I could hear him say, 'You are a cad, sir!' " It was from this blue room, laboring under Choate's disapproving glare, that Kennedy would run his ambassadorship, directing not only the small crew he'd brought with him from the States but also the standing staff of twenty-five consular officers plus no fewer than seventy-five clerks, secretaries, cooks, servants, and security guards.

. . .

JOE BARELY HAD a chance to get used to these new environs when the realities of Europe intruded on the glamour of his embassy, the elegance of his mansion, and the pretense of his high-sounding title. Hitler launched his Austrian Anschluss on the evening of March 11–12, and did so with full confidence that neither Britain nor France would move to block him. It took only about twenty-four hours for the Germans to proclaim the end of the Austrian Republic and the expansion of the Reich. Hitler himself visited Vienna on the 14th. Addressing Parliament on the crisis, Chamberlain emphasized that "the fundamental basis of British foreign policy is the maintenance and preservation of peace." Kennedy sent Krock word calling Chamberlain's speech a "masterpiece" and told his friend that "there will be no war if Chamberlain stays in power with strong public backing."

Writing of Austria to FDR, Kennedy stated the obvious when he said that "the U.S. would be very foolish to try to mix in." Foolish was right. If neither Britain nor France saw fit to try and stop the Führer, it was unlikely the United States, half a world away, would make the attempt. As Kennedy may or may not have realized, the only real question in Hitler's mind was whether or not his rival dictator, Mussolini, would challenge the Nazis' latest conquest in a country bordering northern Italy. Looking at the catalog of Kennedy's many cables, letters, and dispatches to Roosevelt and Hull at this particular hour, all of them rather frantically contrived to persuade the Washingtonians to steer clear of the highly unlikely possibility of U.S. involvement in the Austrian question, one is forced to wonder what homework, if any, Kennedy had done on the *Realpolitik* of the world he now endeavored to help manage.

Kennedy delivered what was traditionally the first address of every newly appointed American ambassador—a speech to the Pilgrims Society, the old and highly respected organization long dedicated to promoting goodwill and good relations between the United Kingdom and the United States—just six days after the start of the Anschluss. Sitting in an ornate ballroom at Claridge's Hotel, Joe's audience rewarded him with relieved applause when he dismissed as incorrect the notion that the United States would never fight any war short of one that threatened actual invasion of the American mainland. They were quiet, however, when he insisted that "the great majority of Americans oppose entangling alliances." And they were perceptibly grim when they heard the ambassador predict that the United States might likely remain neutral in the event of European hostilities. In any event, said Kennedy, the United States should only be counted upon to pursue whatever course was best for the United States. Little did the ambassador's glum listeners realize that his originally proposed remarks, sent to Washington for approval shortly before the Anschluss, had been even more provocative. Kennedy had intended to say the United States had "no plan to seek or offer assistance in the event that war—and I mean, of course, a war of major scope—should break out in the world."

It was Secretary Hull who, with approval from FDR, pulled the ambassador back from this rhetorical edge. Over time, Joe was to become increasingly restive under the wary Hull's close scrutiny, supervision, and censorship. Whenever possible, he would do end runs around the secretary, addressing letters and cables directly to FDR, to his son Jimmy, and to the likes of Jay Pierrepont Moffat, chief of the State Department's Division of European Affairs. Kennedy shortly wrote Bernard Baruch, as he would others including the president and Moffat, that "as much as I dislike saying it, Germany is really entitled to what she is asking for." Joe told Baruch the German peoples of Europe deserved reunification. What was more, he speculated that the real problems of Europe were not political or ethnic, but purely economic. "An unemployed man with a hungry family is the same fellow, whether the swastika or some other flag floats above his head." What Europe needed was booming stock markets and full employment, said the businessman turned diplomat. Then all would be well.

Such simplistic sentiments as these routinely addressed to Roosevelt and those around him would eventually prove Joe's undoing. More immediately, they perhaps helped inspire FDR to open lines of private communication with numerous members of the British opposition, among them the staunchly anti-Hitler Harold Laski. When FDR's ambassador got wind of the president's correspondence with the socialist economist, he expressed himself "on this score in vigorous language to James Roosevelt, suggesting that he call his father's attention to the unwisdom of such a procedure. As I look back, it was symbolic of much that was to come."

· · ·

As Hull began what was to be a long struggle to keep Ambassador Kennedy's rhetoric in check, doctors back in Boston at the same time struggled to keep Jack's illness in check. The young Kennedy's football career had come to an abrupt halt the previous autumn when, well short of making varsity, he suffered a ruptured spinal disk after being thrown to the ground during a scrimmage. Undaunted, Jack now set his sights on the Harvard varsity swim team, where he thought he had a good shot at achieving his large H. After all, he'd been a star backstroke artist the previous year on Harvard's undefeated freshman swim team. His dream was to qualify for the starting position in the mid-March competition against Yale—if only his troublesome body would not persist in betraying his tenacious spirit.

Jack spent the third week of February in the Harvard College infirmary with a severe intestinal infection. He was then briefly back in circulation on campus before being rushed to the New England Baptist Hospital the second week of March. During his time at the Harvard infirmary he arranged to sneak out for an hour's practice in the pool every evening. Subsequently, in the short period between his release from the infirmary and his admittance to New England Baptist, he stoically endeavored to make the team that would take on Yale. Physically exhausted by the grippe that plagued him, Jack nevertheless performed well (though not well enough) in the qualifying heat. Classmate Richard Tregaskis—who was later, like Jack, to make a name for himself in the Solomon Islands and would write the classic *Guadalcanal Diary*—beat him by three seconds. Jack's skill at swimming would, however, come in handy soon enough. The day was not far off when it would save his life.

4

A Wonderful Time

IRTUALLY ALL of the British and American press—save perhaps for Churchill's crotchety son Randolph—seemed at first willing to give the new ambassador and his family all the most benign and complimentary coverage possible. London newspapers regularly featured snapshots of Kennedy and his brood. British press photographers evidenced a special interest in photogenic little Teddy, while the prim editors of Britain's women's magazines queued up to have tea with Rose and ask her advice on the raising of large families. Henry Luce, one of the ambassador's many Republican friends, even sent a *Life* photographer to document Kennedy and his children at the ambassador's residence. One doubts whether FDR could have failed to miss the resulting article, which forecast Kennedy as a likely presidential candidate and compared the ambassador's family to that of Roosevelt's cousin Theodore: "[Kennedy's] bouncing offspring make the most politically ingratiating family since Theodore Roosevelt's. Whether or not Franklin Roosevelt thought of it beforehand, it has turned out that when he appointed Mr. Kennedy to be Ambassador to Great Britain he got eleven Ambassadors for the price of one. Amazed and delighted at the spectacle of an Ambassadorial family big enough to man a full-sized cricket team, England has taken them all, including extremely pretty and young-looking Mrs. Kennedy, to its heart."

As *Life* took pains to point out, no fewer than five former ambassadors to London had wound up as president of the United States: John Adams, James Monroe, John Quincy Adams, Martin Van Buren, and James Buchanan. The younger Adams had also served as a special assistant during his father's ambassadorship. (Perhaps noting John Quincy's career path, Kennedy decided Joe Jr. would stay in Europe for a time after his graduation from Harvard in June and be put to work in various as yet unspecified diplomatic functions.)

Throughout the winter and spring, Arthur Krock published numerous flattering accounts of the ambassador's diplomatic aptitude. According to Krock, Kennedy and his family had completely won over the British ruling class. Krock made sure to point out that the Irish kid from Boston was now welcome in even the most sedate and dignified British country houses. The subtext for Beacon Hill? Old Joe had finally arrived. Shortly, the Lowells and Cabots and Saltonstalls were to take it just as Kennedy intended—*personally*—when he announced that the U.S. embassy in London would no longer present mainland American debutantes to the British court. Such presentation would henceforth be restricted to daughters of American officials posted to London and daughters of American citizens who had lived in England for an extended period. "Even though his own pretty daughters would constitute 'official presentees,' " commented the New York *Daily News*, "Ambassador Kennedy had best be prepared for cries of 'foul' if one or more of 'em duck their plumed heads to King George VI and his Queen this Season!" (Joe would ignore this warning.)

Kick began getting good publicity well before her presentation at court. The press soon forgot about her supposed engagement to Peter Grace, who did not even rate a mention when Kick was profiled in the May issue of *Queen*, a magazine normally devoted to chronicling the social life of titled families. The editors singled Kick out as one of the "buds" of the coming Season. She was, said the magazine, "America's most important debutante." *Queen*'s reporter seemed enthralled: "I was impressed by her approximation to the best type of our own English girls of the same age. She had none of that rather sophisticated air and ultra self confidence which is sometimes associated with youthful Americans." Wearing a scarf, derby, and jodhpurs, the girl delightedly allowed herself to be snapped cantering down Rotten Row with her father. Urged on by publicist Hinton, the London *Times* even decided it was worth a photograph when Kick baked cookies and dropped them by London's Great Ormonde Street Hospital for Children.

Kick's parents appeared, on the face of things, to be just as popular as she. After a lifetime of snubs back in the States, it was refreshing and gratifying for them to enjoy the measure of social acceptance and prestige that came automatically with the title of ambassador. Looking at their calendar going forward, Joe and Rose eagerly anticipated what Joe described as "a fine ride." Invitations flowed in for virtually all the important events of the upcoming Season: the Royal Derby Ball and Derby race at Epsom Downs, the Royal Ascot Race and Gold Cup Day at Ascot Heath, the Henley Rowing Regatta, tennis at Wimbledon, and the Yachting Regatta at Cowes. "It was a wonderful time," Rose wrote years later, remembering that period of her life when Europe was in its death throes, ". . . so much excitement, so much anticipation, so much fun."

Rose immersed herself in the business of being the ambassador's wife, going at the job with a joyous certitude. For years, her husband had used his career as an excuse to be away from her. Now she was by his side, and he was to a large measure dependent on her skills as a hostess and household manager. Rose spent many hours preparing menus, planning parties, and supervising the embassy's twenty-five domestic servants. She cited her numerous responsibilities as good reason to send Jean and Pat away to the Convent of the Sacred Heart, Roehampton. She at the same time placed Bobby and Teddy, the only two children remaining at home, under the supervision of governess and registered nurse Louella Hennessy, whom Rose had brought over from New York.

Louella got the youngsters bathed, dressed, and fed every morning before delivering them to London's Sloane Street School for Boys. There, after being instructed by his father that he should avoid fighting at all costs lest he tarnish the image of the United States and her ambassador, Teddy hit a bully named Cecil in the nose—but only after receiving special permission to do so from Louella. Both Bobby and Teddy developed a great love for toy soldiers and deployed wave after wave of plaster men against each other's opposing forces in the upstairs hall of the ambassador's residence. Confronted with a steady round of social engagements that seemed to come automatically with being the son of the ambassador, twelve-year-old Bobby struggled, just as he had for a long time, to overcome his awkward shyness with people outside the family. He nevertheless went quite mute when introduced to Princess Elizabeth—someone his own age—at a garden party.

.   .   .

O N THE SAME DAY Bobby stumbled about for something to say to the heir, his father lunched with Winston Churchill and Churchill's son Randolph. This was in early April, on the heels of Chamberlain's recently negotiated Anglo-Italian agreement. Pouring down whiskey after whiskey but never seeming to get drunk, the Conservative MP expressed profound concern about the agreement by which Great Britain recognized Mussolini's annexation of Ethiopia in exchange for vague security assurances. Italy, Churchill insisted, was not to be trusted. Had she not withdrawn from the League of Nations the previous January? Had she not shown every sign thus far of at best tolerating and at worst abetting the ambitions of Germany? "Churchill was scornful of the gains that might accrue to England through the Anglo-Italian agreement," remembered Kennedy. In fact, Churchill denounced not only the agreement and those who made it, but also Italy's "secret partner" in the deal, Germany.

Churchill said he had recently "endured" a meeting with the German ambassador von Ribbentrop—soon to be recalled to Berlin and promoted to foreign minister. Churchill said he had become annoyed when von Ribbentrop demanded England give back the German colonies seized at the end of World War I. At the same time, von Ribbentrop said England should close her eyes to the ongoing process of *Lebensraum* and the situation of Germany's next most likely target for unification: Czechoslovakia. These things, von Ribbentrop insisted, did not concern Great Britain. Unlike Churchill, Kennedy was inclined to agree with von Ribbentrop on the topic of central Europe and with Chamberlain on the topic of relations with Mussolini. Ignoring Churchill's views, the naive Kennedy told Krock he considered the Anglo-Italian agreement to be "the high point in Mr. Chamberlain's foreign policy thus far. There is a general feeling here that Mussolini realizes now that he will be more comfortable with Great Britain as a friend than he would be in relying exclusively on Hitler."

Churchill would become quite unhappy with Kennedy shortly, when the ambassador began squiring Colonel Charles Lindbergh around official London. Recently returned from a visit to Germany, Lindbergh and his wife had come away mightily impressed by both the resolve and the military preparedness of the Reich. "There is no question of the power, unity, and purposefulness of Germany. It is terrific," Anne Morrow Lindbergh wrote in her diary. Colonel Lindbergh himself believed that "German air strength is greater than that of all other European countries combined. . . . [England and France] are far too weak in the air to protect themselves. . . . It seems to me essential to avoid a general European war in the near future. I believe that a war now might easily result in the loss of European civilization." In speeches to small groups of British decision makers, Lindbergh couched in somewhat more diplomatic parlance the stark verdict he enunciated more vehemently in his private diary: "England seems hopelessly behind in military strength in comparison to Germany. The assets in English character lie in confidence rather than ability; tenacity rather than strength; and determination rather than intelligence. . . . It is necessary to realize that England is a country composed of a great mass of slow, somewhat stupid and indifferent people, and a small group of geniuses."

Lindbergh's small group of British geniuses most often gathered at Cliveden (pronounced *Clivden*, with a short *i*), the Buckinghamshire country home of Waldorf Astor (second Viscount Astor, chairman of the Royal Institute of International Affairs) and his wife, Nancy Witcher Langhorne Astor. Dubbed by the British press "the Cliveden set," the appeasement-favoring (and, it was whispered, pro-fascist) politicians and journalists who routinely gathered at Cliveden provided a warm welcome for both Lindbergh and his fast friend the new American ambassador. After the war, when official Wilhelmstrasse papers documenting Nazi air strength became available, Lindbergh's estimates of German air superiority would be discredited and his unwitting role as a pawn in the German game of disinformation revealed. But in 1938, as A. L. Rowse told William Manchester many years later, Lindbergh was "treated as omniscient in air matters. . . . [London *Times* editor] Dawson quoted Lindbergh to me: he was made much of by the Cliveden set." (A member of the Cliveden set himself, Geoffrey Dawson worked for the Astors, who owned—among other newspapers—the London *Times*.)

The proprietress of Cliveden, Nancy Astor, had married Waldorf in

1906 not long after divorcing her first husband, Robert Gould Shaw II of Boston—an abusive alcoholic who inspired Nancy to despise liquor, and all those who drank it, for the rest of her life. American-born just like her husband, Nancy came originally from Virginia, where her father, a successful cotton planter ruined by the Civil War, had risen from the ashes of that defeat to make a small fortune during Reconstruction. Nancy's father-in-law, William Waldorf Astor, had emigrated to England in 1889 after an unsuccessful political career in the United States. He sent his American-born son to Eton and Oxford, and eventually encouraged the boy—by then thoroughly English—to become a naturalized British citizen in 1899 at the age of twenty. When Nancy and Waldorf married, their gifts from Waldorf's father included the famous Sanci diamond worn by Louis XIV at his coronation, several million dollars in cash, and the true jewel in the crown of Astor's British holdings: Cliveden. The guest wing of the house, maintained by a staff of thirty-four, accommodated forty visitors; the family wing, more modest, required only twenty indoor servants, while no fewer than forty-six gardeners maintained the grounds. The total bedroom count stood at forty-six.

The Astors also owned additional homes in London, Sandwich, and Plymouth, where, in 1909, Waldorf ran successfully for the House of Commons as a Conservative from the Sutton Division. The bipartisan Waldorf not only served in Parliament but did stints as parliamentary secretary for Prime Minister Lloyd George (a Liberal) and as chairman of the State Medical Research Committee. He was, however, forced from the House of Commons two years after inheriting his father's title in 1917, at which point the forty-year-old Lady Astor—who had no title in her own right and was thus qualified as a "commoner"—decided to run in the same district where her widely popular husband had served. She won election by a significant majority in the election of 1919 and would be returned to office many times, serving until 1945 despite some unorthodox religious views and some unsavory bigotries, none of which she made any attempt to conceal then or later.

"I'm glad you are smart enough not to take my anti-Catholicism, which so many others make so much of, personally," she wrote Kennedy not long after they first met. "The Catholic Church is a grand old battleship of a faith. I would hate to think what the world would be like without it. It does so much to define Europe, and rightly dominates the great countries and cultures of the mainland just as it does the culture of the working people in Ireland. The stand that I—a Christian Scientist married to an Episcopalian—take against the Church is simply that it has no role in the culture or politics of this great Protestant nation, this England so much shaped by the Reformation, so much defined by a unique history and world-view outside of that—and often contrary to that—propounded by Rome."

As Astor pointed out to Kennedy, she had many Roman Catholic friends—among them G. K. Chesterton, with whom she shared (if nothing else) a profound dislike for Jews. (Indeed, when Nancy made her first bid for Parliament and some criticized the idea of an American standing for office, Chesterton's newspaper the *New Witness* leaped to her defense, responding that since there were so many Jews in Parliament already, one more "foreigner" would not make any difference one way or another. In fact, said Chesterton, a Christian foreigner would be a welcome change.) For himself, Joseph P. Kennedy disliked Jews generally while at the same time maintaining close friendships with several individuals of Jewish descent, among them Arthur Krock. Indeed, Kennedy seems to have tolerated the occasional Jew in the same way Astor appears to have tolerated the occasional Catholic. Choosing to make nothing of Astor's anti-Catholic bigotry, Kennedy allowed her to beguile him. "I like her very much," he wrote. She was, he said, "a hard worker [with] a great heart." (Interestingly, Astor and her fellow Conservative Churchill detested each other. "If I were your wife I'd put poison in your coffee," she once hissed at Winston during an argument. "Madam," Churchill replied, "if I were your husband I'd drink it.")

Nancy Astor's anti-Semitism reinforced an urge toward appeasement that had its roots in her experience of World War I. She had known many young men who'd died in that carnage. "After two years . . . we did not look at the casualty lists anymore," she recalled. "There was nothing to look for. All our friends had gone." The government used Cliveden as a hospital during the Great War. A cemetery on the grounds contained the bodies of the many men who had died there. The war, Astor said, had turned her into something "very like a pacifist." Unlike Churchill, Astor had been delighted back in 1933 when the Oxford Union passed by a vote of 275 to 153 the resolution "That this House will in no circumstances fight for King and Country." She was likewise thrilled when the Cambridge Union voted shortly thereafter (213 to 138) for "uncompromising" pacifism.

Busy entertaining Kennedy, Lindbergh, and others of like mind that spring of 1938, Astor professed a profound disinterest in press accounts detailing the abuse of Jews in Austria. William L. Shirer reported: "Day after day large numbers of Jewish men and women could be seen scrubbing Schuschnigg signs off the sidewalk and cleaning the gutters. While they worked on their hands and knees with jeering storm troopers standing over them, crowds gathered to taunt them. Hundreds of Jews, men and women, were picked off the streets and put to work cleaning public latrines and the toilets of the barracks where the SA and the SS were quartered. Tens of thousands more were jailed. Their worldly possessions were confiscated or stolen." To Kennedy, Astor wrote that Hitler would have to do more than just "give a rough time" to "the killers of Christ" before she'd be in favor of launching "Armageddon to save them. The wheel of history swings round as the Lord would have it. Who are we to stand in the way of the future?" To this Kennedy replied that he expected the "Jew media" in the United States to become a problem in future, and that "Jewish pundits in New York and Los Angeles" were already making noises contrived to "set a match to the fuse of the world."

The grim events in Austria did nothing to stifle Cliveden's gaiety that Easter. "Spent Easter weekend at Lady Astor's," Kick wrote Lem Billings, "and it was really wonderful. . . . All the guests turned out to be very nice and the other four girls were really the best English girls I've met. The Duke and Duchess of Kent came for dinner one night. She is lovely but he is very disappointing. We all played musical chairs and charades. Very chummy and much gaiety. Dukes running around like mad freshmen."

All in all, the weekend provided a splendid foretaste of the London Season scheduled to commence, this year as any other, right after Easter with the First Spring Meeting at Newmarket and the opening of the summer exhibit at the Royal Academy. It would conclude, as always, with the Royal Garden Party at Buckingham Palace in late July. Throughout May, June, and July, Kick and other debutantes were to spend nearly every night at balls and dinner parties, and every weekend at country-house gatherings. The most lavish and ostentatious event of the Season was to be the Jewels of the Empire Ball, where some £1.5 million worth of jewels were traditionally worn by the assembled guests. After her Easter with "Aunt Nancy" Astor, Kick decided she was beginning to like the idea of England. She found herself not missing Palm Beach nearly so much as she thought she might. She was dazzled.

. . .

HER PARENTS, TOO, had been dazzled one week earlier when they spent Palm Sunday weekend (April 9–10) as guests of the king and queen at Windsor Castle. The place was, of course, more museum than home, decorated with Gainsboroughs and ornamented with many relics of Britain's great royal personalities. Other guests included Prime Minister Chamberlain and his wife, along with Lord and Lady Halifax. A Scots bagpiper walked about the rooms before dinner on Saturday, and a red-coated orchestra serenaded the royal couple and their guests throughout the meal's many courses. Sitting in front of the fire in their room later that evening, Joe said, "Rose, this is a helluva long way from East Boston." The couple took breakfast alone on Sunday morning and were then driven to a tiny Catholic church just off the grounds. "Palm Sunday," Joe recorded in his diary. "Read the long gospel in English. We had to stand."

At lunch following church, the ambassador found himself charmed by Princess Elizabeth, who, on hearing he had worked in the movie business, immediately volunteered how much she liked Disney's *Snow White* and especially the Seven Dwarfs. When Mrs. Chamberlain asked the heir what her favorite subject was in school, she said geography. She had just finished studying the Atlantic coast of the United States. Elizabeth also said she very much liked sports, especially swimming and horseback riding, and playing American baseball with Daddy and Mummy. Afterward, strolling with the king and queen through Windsor's grand grounds, Joe and Rose passed the tomb of the old Duchess of Kent (mother of Queen Victoria) and then went into a large garden, the gate of which the king himself unlocked, pulling out a big bunch of keys he carried around just "like a watchman." From the garden they went by cars to the large modern house the king used weekends when officially in residence at Buckingham Palace. Here tea was served and polite and pointless conversation indulged in until the ambassador broke away for a walk and talk with Chamberlain and Halifax.

Chamberlain told Kennedy that neither Austria nor Hitler's latest demands involving Czechoslovakia were worth fighting over. And he suggested that Konrad Henlein, the leader of the Sudeten German minority in

Czechoslovakia, had a point when he insisted on his people's right to reunification with the Fatherland. Looking beyond the question of Czechoslovakia, Chamberlain acknowledged Hitler's categorical statement in *Mein
Kampf* that Germany's future lay in southeastern Europe and the Ukraine.
He pointed out, however, that the Führer left it vague whether his inten-
tions were conquest by military means or by mere (and completely legitimate) economic penetration. "If he means economic penetration without
force," said Chamberlain as quoted in Kennedy's unpublished memoir of his
ambassadorship, "we cannot very well object. Besides, war wins nothing,
ends nothing. In a modern war there are no victors." The challenge, said
Chamberlain, was to keep the peace by pacifying the dictators while at the
same time making them realize no one's best interest would be served by a
general war and the accompanying "collapse of civilization."

It was in part to avoid such a collapse that Kennedy took it upon himself
to engage in a series of secret meetings with the new German ambassador
to the Court of St. James's, Herbert von Dirksen, shortly after von Dirksen's
arrival in London on May 4. As chronicled in von Dirksen's numerous cables to Berlin, Kennedy—acting without authority from the State Department—made frequent direct contacts with the German embassy. He advised
von Dirksen that President Roosevelt, the victim of Jewish influence in the
news media and government, was poorly advised on Germany and needed
educating as to the philosophy, ambitions, and ideals of the Reich. Kennedy
also made numerous inappropriate remarks concerning Chamberlain's genuine willingness to settle German's grievances without bloodshed. In so doing, Kennedy unwittingly strengthened Germany's hand in what amounted
to an enormous game of bluff poker. "Although Kennedy promised von
Dirksen that he would relate their conversations when he saw the president
in June," writes Michael Beschloss, "he was evidently acting on no authority
but his own." Citing Kennedy's friendship with Lindbergh (whom Hitler
would shortly honor with a medal) and his energetic work to stifle Winston
Churchill's call for a grand alliance against the dictatorships of Europe, von
Dirksen would eventually go on record as calling Ambassador Kennedy
"Germany's best friend" in London.

5

Worthy Successor

ROSEMARY AND EUNICE arrived in early May accompanied by Mr. and Mrs. Eddie Moore. Having been Joe Kennedy's right-hand man in the States, Moore—after whom Kennedy had named his youngest son—at first assumed he would serve the same function in England. This, however, was not to be. A tough and devoted business henchman and an expert purveyor of dirty tricks, Moore was not cut out for the role of diplomat. He was, however, skilled at handling all those most private matters his boss seemed unwilling to trust to others. For decades it was Moore who served as bagman for the bribes Joe paid to keep the wheels of his various business intrigues running smoothly. As has already been mentioned, Moore also acquired the whores Kennedy ran through in such high numbers. Now the ambassador handed Moore yet another touchy assignment. Kennedy purchased a modest home in South Ascot, installed the Moores, and ordered them to entertain Rosemary on weekends when she was furloughed from a nearby school for the mentally retarded. Joe did not want to see her in London save for a few special occasions when, closely supervised, she would accompany Rose and Kick to carefully chosen balls and social events.

The first of these was Rose's, Rosemary's, and Kick's introduction at court on May 12. While Rose and Rosemary wore elegant white gowns by Molyneux, a leading British society designer, Kick appeared at Buckingham Palace wrapped in a dazzling outfit she'd selected at Lelong during a weekend in Paris: this also a shade of white to go with the white plumes traditionally worn at such presentations. Rose, as a matron, wore a tiara borrowed from one of her new and fast British friends, Lady Bessborough. Rose recalled with childish glee: "I felt like Cinderella."

The mood and excitement were the same a few weeks later when the ambassador hosted a coming-out ball for Kick and Rosemary in the paneled French ballroom on the embassy's second floor. The evening began with a dinner party for eighty followed by a receiving line of three hundred, after which Ambrose's Swing Band—hired away from the Mayfair Hotel for the evening—struck up its tunes. Kick swung about the room dozens of times with the likes of Prince Frederick of Prussia and the Duke of Kent. Simple Rosemary danced every dance of the evening as well, but always with the same partner. Ding Dong Jack made it his business to occupy Rosemary and make sure the girl felt a full part of the party. All other eyes, meanwhile, focused on Kick. Newspapers gave big coverage to the event. Society columnists on both sides of the Atlantic dubbed Kick the most exciting debutante of 1938.

. . .

ACCORDING TO HIS close associate Arthur Krock, Joe Kennedy had never before been more sure of himself in all his cocky and confident life. He delighted in the sight of his daughters being accepted by the highest level of British society. He reveled in his easy intimacies with the businessman-turned-politician Chamberlain. And he believed every word of encouragement he received from his seemingly incisive Cliveden friends, all of whom thought him a most likely candidate for the White House.

"Will Kennedy Run for President?" asked *Liberty* magazine on May 21. The writer of the piece, Kennedy protégé and retainer Ernest K. Lindley, answered his own question in part when he suggested the country needed a man "who can make business and progressive reform pull together toward sound prosperity." Lindley went on to point out that "professional political handicappers will give heavy odds against him at this stage. But a few connoisseurs of Presidential material are willing to make long-shot bets that the next Democratic nominee for President will be Joseph Patrick Kennedy." Lindley adoringly chronicled the ambassador's many assets, which included "brains, personality, driving power and the habit of success" along with "an athlete's figure, a clean-cut head, sandy hair, clear straight-shooting eyes, a flashingly infectious smile and faultless taste in dress." Lindley's article failed to mention that a May public opinion poll had placed Kennedy fifth among potential Democratic candidates, assuming Roosevelt was not in the race (in which case he would have ranked sixth).

Other of Kennedy's friends in the press joined Lindley in predicting the ambassador would test presidential waters when he returned for a brief visit to the United States at the end of June. It was likewise rumored, wrote Krock and others, that Kennedy would pick up an honorary doctorate from Harvard on the same day Joe Jr. graduated—the degree itself no small step in the direction of the White House. "Did Joe Kennedy Sr. want to be President of the United States?" Krock asked rhetorically many years later. "Yes he did! Very definitely. He hoped to be nominated in 1940, without any question. . . . He was a very ambitious man. . . . He was shrewd. He thought his services had so impressed the country, and there was money behind it for a gigantic propaganda machine and it might work. All he wanted to do was beat Roosevelt in 1940."

Perhaps not beat, but definitely displace. "Mr. Roosevelt had made no announcement as to his attitude on a third term," Kennedy recalled of this period. "I knew that many of his closest advisors were urging him to break with tradition and run for the third time in 1940. There was little doubt he had the matter under consideration." At the same time, Kennedy realized Roosevelt did not like it when subordinates eyed his throne. "Mr. Roosevelt also had a quality—a failing, some have called it—of resenting the suggestion that he was to be succeeded and cooling perceptibly towards a man who might be considered, by his friends, a worthy successor. . . . I wanted no such false issue to arise between us."

Thus Roosevelt's would-be successor was coy and disingenuous with reporters when he disembarked from the *Queen Mary* at New York on June 20. Journalists noted the delight with which the ambassador waved off rumors that he would be the 1940 Democratic nominee for the White House. Kennedy grinned widely as he dismissed the New York *Daily News*'s recent

dubbing of him as the "Crown Prince of the Roosevelt regime." He announced emphatically that he had not returned to look into his presidential
prospects. He had simply come home to attend a momentous family event.
He said he hoped the assembled journalists would do a proud father a favor
and note Joe Jr.'s pending graduation, *cum laude*. Had they heard the boy was
chairman of the Class Day Committee? Neither his father nor the sitting
president of the United States had climbed that mountain. When once again
pressed on the matter of his presidential aspirations, Kennedy insisted: "I
enlisted under President Roosevelt in 1932 to do whatever he wanted me to
do. There are many problems at home and abroad and I am happy to be busy
at one abroad just now. If I had my eye on another job it would be a complete breach of faith with President Roosevelt."

On the morning of the 21st, after spending the night at the Waldorf-
Astoria, Kennedy traveled by train to Hyde Park to brief FDR on the situation in London. FDR listened attentively, uttered many complimentary
asides, and asked Joe to relay to Chamberlain the vaguest of presidential
commitments: should Chamberlain run into trouble maintaining the peace,
FDR would rush in to throw the "moral authority" of his office behind
Chamberlain's effort. Roosevelt was, by his own account, dumbfounded later
in the meeting when Kennedy asked him to refrain from criticizing fascism
in his speeches since, in the long run, the United States would inevitably
have to wind up with some form of fascism itself. "Joe Kennedy," Roosevelt
told Interior Secretary Harold Ickes shortly after the exchange, "if he were
in power, would give us a fascist form of government. He would organize a
small powerful committee under himself as chairman and this committee
would run the country without much reference to Congress."

Always one to keep his options open and his sources secret, Roosevelt
did not mention his very precise knowledge concerning Kennedy's now active though clandestine aspirations for the White House. Besides, the president had no legal authority for putting the FBI on the ambassador's private
mail as he had done, and he would have been hard pressed to explain his in-
timate familiarity with confidential correspondence exchanged between
Kennedy, Krock, Henry Luce, and others. Roosevelt was all smiles and well-
wishes as Kennedy departed Hyde Park, although what FDR smiled at was
probably not so much Joe as the idea of what was in store for him. Indeed,
FDR's torpedoes were already primed, aimed at the heart of Kennedy's am-

bition, and ready to be launched via the *Chicago Tribune* and *The Saturday Evening Post*.

Kennedy was somewhere around Springfield, Massachusetts—on the night train carrying him from Hyde Park to Boston—when he learned he would *not* be given the honorary degree he so desperately wanted and had been lobbying for. Harvard's honors would instead go to Walt Disney, writer and statesman John Buchan, Yale president Charles Seymour, and ten other worthies from the arts and industry. Nothing had changed since 1936, when the Yankees of the Harvard Corporation denied Kennedy a slot on the board of overseers and then leaked to the press his standing at the bottom of the long list of candidates. It was a measure of how naive and unrealistic Kennedy could sometimes be that he'd actually hoped, after his experience in 1936, to be made a recipient of the cherished crimson hood just two years later. In his unpublished memoirs, Kennedy attempted to depersonalize the rejection, framing it as just another example of anti-Catholic bigotry perpetrated by the old families of Beacon Hill. The argument, however, does not hold up. Archbishop William Cardinal O'Connell of Boston—who as a young priest officiated at the wedding of Joe and Rose Kennedy—had been granted an honorary degree just one year earlier.

To save face in Boston, Kennedy put out a release to the effect that he had been offered but declined the honorary degree because of a pressing family emergency. He said his need to stay at home in Hyannis, at his sickly second-eldest son's bedside, took precedence over Class Day. He'd traveled a great distance to see Joe Jr. graduate from Harvard, but now—to the son's bitter disappointment—he avoided the ceremony. He would be damned, he told those closest to him, if he would sit and watch Disney take *his* honors.

As for Jack, he spent Class Day (June 22) not in bed but at sea—captaining a boat for Harvard in the McMillan Cup Regatta conducted that year at Cape Cod's Wianno Yacht Club, not far from Hyannis. He'd been in New England Baptist Hospital the week previously, and several days of tests had revealed nothing new about his condition. ("I am once again confounding the best medical brains of the Northeast," he wrote a friend. "All agree I am a textbook case, but no-one knows quite what chapter.") He emerged rested on the 20th, and nearly immediately went to captaining one of the two Harvard boats in the McMillan series. Both Jack and his brother Joe had come in second for their respective divisions during the seventh series on the 21st, and Joe had come in third in the eighth and final series conducted for his division that same afternoon. Jack's second-place showing in the eighth series for his division on the 22nd assured Harvard's win over the nine other schools competing. But the victory came with a sharp edge. Ironically, the ambassador's lie to the press about why he'd "refused" Harvard honors caught up with him the moment Jack emerged as a star of the collegiate regatta.

.   .   .

DURING THE SAME hour Joe Jr. received his diploma with no family to bear witness and Jack expertly maneuvered his Wianno One-Design in the McMillan series off the Cape, presidential secretary Steve Early sat down with a reporter to speak of Roosevelt, Kennedy, and the election of 1940. The president, Early told Walter Trohan of the *Chicago Tribune*, was unhappy with his ambassador. Citing "positive evidence that Kennedy hoped to use the Court of St. James as a stepping stone to the White House," Early said FDR found Kennedy's self-promotion annoying and his ambition distasteful. Appearing on the 23rd, Trohan's *Chicago Tribune* story did not name Early as a source but nevertheless quoted him directly when explaining how "the chilling shadow of 1940" had fallen across the friendship previously shared by Roosevelt and Kennedy. Trohan further quoted a "high administration official" as saying: "Joe Kennedy never did anything without thinking of Joe Kennedy. And that's the worst thing I can say about a father of nine kids."

It took several days for word of the story to spread across the country. Kennedy himself—holed up at Hyannis until the 24th, when he traveled to Washington—only learned of it on June 25, the morning after a pleasant dinner with FDR. Kennedy later spoke of the "true Irish anger" that swept him when he read Trohan's piece. He immediately requested interviews with both Roosevelt and Hull, but was made to wait several days before finally being permitted access. ". . . I offered to resign," recalled Kennedy of his conference with Hull. "He sought to calm me down and I recall him telling me that I should not be so disturbed because, as he said, 'He [Roosevelt] does those things. He treats me twenty times as badly.' " The ambassador then had what he called "an angry interview" with Early followed by a brief and tense meeting with FDR, during which the president denied he had had anything to do with Trohan's reporting. This denial, Kennedy wrote later, "assuaged my feeling and I left again for London, but deep within me I knew that something had happened."

The second of Roosevelt's torpedoes hit a few days later, on the 28th, just as Kennedy and his sons made ready to board the French Line's *Normandie* for the voyage back to Europe. Reporters rushed Kennedy on the pier demanding his response to a critical article in the new *Saturday Evening Post*. The article claimed (accurately) that Kennedy, as owner of the Somerset Distilling Company, had used Jimmy Roosevelt to acquire preferential whiskey import permits and in turn had given Jimmy all the insurance business related to Kennedy properties in Boston. "Jimmy," said the piece, written by Alva Johnson, "has helped Kennedy to reach the two great positions he now holds—that of Ambassador to London and that of premier Scotch-whiskey salesman in America."

Kennedy angrily denied the facts as reported in the magazine. "I'll admit I am the American Ambassador," he said as he walked toward the ship, "but I'll deny I'm the premier Scotch salesman. I suffered by knowing Jimmy Roosevelt. If the rest of *The Saturday Evening Post* article is no truer than the part about my connection with James Roosevelt, it's all a lie." That said, Kennedy retreated up the gangplank as quickly as he could, putting the most distance possible between himself and the reporters he'd been so glad to see just a few weeks earlier. The wry smile and sardonic denials of his arrival now gave way to denials of a different type: bitter, framed in a scowl. Kennedy had been foolish and overreaching when he came home with hopes of being honored and courted as FDR's heir apparent. In the end he wound up humiliated by both his president and his school.

. . .

A S MIGHT HAVE been expected, the ambassador maintained a foul mood throughout the Atlantic crossing. He spent much time in his cabin, shunned casual well-wishers, skipped dinner at the captain's table, and seems to have wanted to make his sons share in his psychic isolation. Arthur Krock, traveling to Europe as Kennedy's guest, risked the ambassador's displeasure when he did his best to set both young men free. Krock recalled years later that there was a beautiful actress aboard with whom young Joe became smitten, "and that annoyed his father because he thought that the boy might be perhaps a little too impulsive and maybe this girl was making a play for a boy of his prominence, his wealth and so on—an attraction, I must add." Jack also "had a girl that I think his father didn't know too much about." When the ambassador imposed a curfew and insisted his sons retire to the Kennedy suite at a respectable hour, Krock sneaked the boys out a back door. "I don't know whether the old man found out about it or not," he said later. "At any rate the curfew was not maintained." It is interesting that the ambassador, given his own well-known penchant for actresses, so disliked the idea of Joe Jr. going in the same direction.

Whatever luck Joe Jr. enjoyed with women aboard ship, his fortunes declined perceptibly once he landed in England, where he slipped almost immediately into the role of ugly American. His sarcastic humor and lack of finesse were a problem. Many young British women seemed put off by what Lynne McTaggart has called Joe's "sexual aggressiveness and violent temper." It did not help that he was often heard parroting his father's isolationist views. Jack, on the other hand, fell quite easily into the round of the London Season. He was well liked by all the debutantes, adapted quickly to British manners, and won friends without effort.

"Joe looked much more mature than Jack," recalled Hugh Fraser, who encountered both brothers in London at this time. "I think Jack looked incredibly young for his age at 21. I think he was intellectual in a bright quick way, while Joe was much more serious and had a lumbering gravitas about him. He was the eldest boy in the family, and I think this weighed quite a lot with the Kennedys, who were sort of hierarchical." Fraser had the impression that Joe—painfully aware of Jack's smarts, boyish charm, and popularity—was at a loss as to how to compete. "While Jack was disarming in most social settings," commented Fraser, "Joe was simply disarmed." Still, Fraser did not see Joe as being in any particular competition with Jack, *per se*, but rather with "life itself." It seemed to Fraser that Joe was always struggling to "do the world one better, to have the last word, to be one-up on every and any person he encountered, be that person a brother or a stranger. And remember England was full of strangers."

When a reporter chanced upon Joe at London's popular 400 Club (also known as the Embassy Club, on Old Bond Street) during early July, he found the American seated amid an eclectic group—none of them Brits. Joe's cohorts for the evening included a Turkish pasha, a Greek shipping

magnate, an Argentine polo player, a Dutch baron, and the daughter of
American film star Will Rogers. Joe, the reporter wrote, was "a nice boy, easily recognizable as the son of his father. I asked him whether Kennedy *père*
had a chance of becoming President despite the fact that he is a Roman
Catholic." The reporter reminded Joe of the 1928 election, when Democrat
Al Smith—the popular but Catholic governor of New York—found himself
buried beneath a groundswell of mid-American WASP hatred. Joe wisely
offered no comment on the subject of the presidency. He instead described
his current job—which he would hold throughout the summer—as the ambassador's confidential aide and secretary. He also described, in this context,
his trip just a few days before with his father and Eddie Moore in a small private plane across the Irish Sea: the first time a sitting American ambassador
to Great Britain had ever visited the Emerald Isle.

Ambassador Kennedy did not have a reputation for engaging in any sen-
timental nostalgia for Ireland, nor had he ever actively supported the Irish
nationalist movement. In fact, he was known to privately mock as "Harps"
and "stupid Micks" those backward-looking Irish-Americans who tended to
romanticize the idea of Ireland and cling to Irish culture. And so, when he
himself turned up in the land of his fathers at the end of the first week of July
1938, it was not to rekindle fond ancestral memories but rather to salve a
wounded ego. What the Protestants of Boston would refuse, the Catholics
of Kennedy's homeland would gladly tender. Eire's Prime Minister Eamon
De Valera presided at the July 7 ceremony during which Joe received an
honorary degree from the National University of Ireland. As Joe Jr. told the
tale to the reporter at the 400 Club, the Irish PM and Ambassador Kennedy
hit it off instantly. They found they shared similar worldviews. In a few
years' time, when war came, Eire would identify itself as officially neutral.

·   ·   ·

WITHIN THE TRIO of Joe and Jack and Kick—aged twenty-three,
twenty-one, and eighteen respectively—it was vibrant Kick who continued to get most of the attention even after her photogenic brothers arrived in Great Britain. "The whole family is taking to London life with the
ease of the proverbial ducks to the pond," observed the Astor-owned London *Times*. "But it is Kathleen especially who is about everywhere, at all the
parties, alert, observant, a merry girl who when she talks to you makes you

feel as if you were seeing it all for the first time too." Kick attended a succession of London parties and balls, and on weekends she traversed the English countryside, traveling from one house party to another, eventually
winding up somewhere to sleep. She haunted such London nightspots as the
400 and the Café de Paris with her friends Deborah ("Debo") Mitford, Sally
Norton, and Dinah and Virginia Brand (both nieces of Lady Astor). She also
stepped out frequently with Sylvia ("Sissy") Lloyd-Thomas—the daughter
of Hugh Lloyd Thomas, onetime private secretary to the Prince of Wales
and one of the few Catholics in Kick's British set. Society columnists duti-
fully recorded Kick's growing list of escorts, most of them titled aristocrats,
all of them wealthy, and all of them Protestant.

Peter Grace found out about Kick's active social life the hard way. Kick
arranged to be away at the races in Sussex when Peter arrived at the ambassador's residence for a long-planned visit during the second week of July.
She did not return to town for another five days, by which time Peter was
wrapping up his scheduled one-week stay and preparing to depart for home
on one of his father's ships. Their meeting was brief and tense. Kick confessed to Peter that she was seeing other people, among them William
Douglas Home (destined to become a noted playwright) and Anthony St.
Clair Erskine, Earl of Rosslyn. Had Peter remained in London long enough
to pick up the next edition of *Queen*, he would have been rewarded with yet
another name to add to that list. *Queen* published a photo of Kick at the Sussex Races with William ("Billy") Hartington, the Marquess of Hartington,
whom she had met several months before through David Ormsby-Gore (a
cousin of Billy's, and the boyfriend—despite religious differences—of Kick's
chum Sissy Lloyd-Thomas).

Amid a sea of desirable aristocratic British bachelors, twenty-year-old
Billy—heir to the Duke of Devonshire, one of the wealthiest men in England—represented the quintessential prize catch. Billy's father, Edward
William Spencer Cavendish, the newly installed tenth Duke of Devonshire,
controlled some 180,000 acres of farmland throughout England, most of it
worked by tenant farmers. In addition to a London mansion and three estates in England, the duke owned a castle (Linsmore) in Ireland only a few
hours' drive from the Kennedys' squalid place of origin, and an abbey
(Bolten) in Scotland. As a result of the family's many aristocratic marriages
through the long years, Billy was positioned to come into not only the duke-

dom, but also two earldoms, two baronies, three Irish titles, and three Continental titles (one each in Portugal and Spain, along with a princedom in
the Netherlands).

Tall, bright, and cheerful, Billy had what Lynne McTaggart has aptly
described as "a lanky, coltish charm." Although a colt, he was also a thor-
oughbred. Rumpled, unself-conscious, and without airs, Billy's mild demeanor changed only on the cricket, rugby, and polo fields, where he traded
his easygoing generosity for a fiercely focused urge to win. Enrolled at Cambridge at the time he met Kick, Billy impressed his instructors as a bright
though unenthusiastic student. He much preferred the races to the classroom. He knew in his bones that his life was set, no matter what grades he
wound up getting. One small part of his attraction for Kick may have been
the fact that, unlike her older brothers, he did not sport around in search of
easy conquests with women. Billy instead approached dating with the high-
minded purity of one who was consciously in the market for a wife rather
than a short-term lover. His longtime friends, however, were surprised when
he began to see a lot of the somewhat plain, thoroughly American, and thoroughly Catholic Kick Kennedy.

Although fantastically wealthy at the time Kick first encountered them,
the Cavendishes would soon enough see their fortunes dwindle, just as had
those of so many other aristocratic British households throughout the first
half of the twentieth century. As a class, the British aristocracy had been in
decline since the death of Victoria, if not before. In recent memory they'd
been the victims of tax assaults by Lloyd George. They'd seen many of their
best young men fall in the Great War. And they'd fought against the slow
but inevitable breakup of their landed estates: all those old, unprofitable,
economic white elephants so out of sync with Britain's new industrial economy. In the midst of this tide of history, the Cavendishes held on as one of
the last truly powerful and prosperous clans of the old order.

Indeed, it appeared that social prominence—and fantastic wealth—simply came with the blood. Still, Billy's father was famous for wandering about
his properties (or, for that matter, London) in old and shabby suits, looking
quite like an impoverished clerk, albeit a clerk who projected the greatest air
of self-confidence. Like his father before him and his son after him, the duke
had been raised from infancy secure in the knowledge that he needn't prove
himself to any man. He knew who he was, and so did everyone else who mat-

tered. Fifty years old in 1938, the duke had served on the British delegation to the Versailles Peace Conference in 1919, where he'd done much to shape the treaty Hitler so despised. He had later spent fifteen years as member of Parliament from Derbyshire, and currently served as under secretary of state for dominion affairs. When Kick first met the duke he was still getting used to his title, which he'd ascended to only a few months before upon the death of his father, Victor Cavendish, the ninth Duke of Devonshire.

This randomly dressed aristocrat thought quite highly of Kick. "She is very sharp, very witty, and so sweet in every way," he wrote Lady Astor. "The Irish blood is evident, of course, and she is no great beauty, but her smile and her chatty enthusiasm are her salvation. I doubt, of course, she'd be any sort of a match for our Billy even if we managed to lure her out from under the papal shadow." The duke had recently spoken at length about the papal shadow in a self-published pamphlet meant to warn his countrymen of what he believed was a Romanist plot to "re-Catholicize" Great Britain through the marriage of RC girls to members of the British upper classes, especially the titled nobility. He would shortly go on record as being highly annoyed when Chamberlain and Halifax—at the secret behest of Ambassador Kennedy—sent a British warship to war-torn Spain with orders to rescue twenty-eight Spanish Sisters of the Sacred Heart after six of their number died in Nationalist air raids.

Later that summer, not long after the forlorn Peter Grace departed for New York, Kick visited several Cavendish homes, including Compton Place in Eastbourne, where she stayed during Goodwood Week, and Churchdale Hall, the family's ten-bedroom mansion at Ashford-in-the-Water, Derbyshire. When Kick called at Churchdale Hall, she found Billy's parents in the process of moving out. By Christmas, the new Duke and Duchess of Devonshire intended to be installed in the duke's official residence, Chatsworth House, five miles away.

As it happens, Kick had been introduced to Chatsworth, and had come to know it quite thoroughly, long before she ever laid eyes on the place. As an adolescent, Kick had fallen in love with Jane Austen's *Pride and Prejudice*. Sitting in her room at the convent in Noroton, she read and reread the great romance until she had practically memorized the book. The novel's Mr. Darcy lived in an imposing rural mansion called Pemberly. "It was a large, handsome, stone building, standing well on rising ground, and backed by a ridge of high woody hills," wrote Austen, "and in front, a stream of some natural importance."

As first seen by Kick in 1938, Chatsworth stood virtually unchanged from the place that more than 120 years before had enchanted Austen—who had adopted the house and grounds as her real-world model for Pemberly. It was, Kick told a friend, like something out of a fairy tale: a sumptuous pile of yellow stone surrounded by gardens, fronted by the River Derwent, and backed by a tree-covered hillside. Bess of Hardwick commissioned the original house in the late sixteenth century, but of Bess's construction only the Huntingtower on the hill above the house (built in the 1580s) remained for Kick to see. The first duke (Bess's great-grandson, who received the dukedom for assisting William of Orange during the Glorious Revolution of 1688) rebuilt Chatsworth in classical William-and-Mary style between 1686 and 1707. Lancelot "Capability" Brown landscaped the eleven-hundred-acre park surrounding the house during the mid-1700s. Brown widened the river and built a three-arched bridge approaching the house. The sixth duke (1790–1858) added a library, a north wing, and elaborate waterworks. Known as the "Bachelor Duke," this gentleman also built a complex system of interconnected artificial lakes, geysers, and fountains—all of them designed by his lover, the engineer Joseph Paxton.

Chatsworth stood closed and shuttered when Kick dropped in for a brief tour that summer. Sheets covered furniture, and the whole place seemed musty and ancient. Drapes needed to be drawn open before Kick could get a good sense of the house's grand foyer, called the Painted Hall, with its gilded iron balustrades and wall and ceiling murals by Laguerre depicting the life of Julius Caesar. Proceeding through the house, she pronounced herself awestruck by the sight of priceless tapestries, sculptures, and other art treasures. Room after room revealed oils, drawings, and engravings by Holbein, Da Vinci, Rembrandt, Gainsborough, Rubens, and Velásquez. Long hallways provided extra wall space for ancestral portraits executed by Sargent, Reynolds, and other masters.

Just like her parents, Kick had come a long way from East Boston.

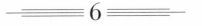

6

Peace with Honor

I T I S A N U N D E R S T A T E M E N T to say Jack had an affinity for Britain and British society. He was, in fact, essentially British in his manner, sensibilities, and values. When he came to London, this time as previously during several brief visits, he arrived with a strange sense of homecoming. His Choate friend Lem Billings had noted during their summer trip in 1937 that the Catholic Jack seemed strangely "un-at-home" and out of his element in the great Catholic countries of Europe—Italy, France, and Germany. Protestant England appeared more to his liking. He was, after all, the product of Protestant schools consciously conducted in the British tradition.

Billings and others who knew Jack well were not surprised, shortly, when he adopted David Cecil's *The Young Melbourne* as his favorite book. Jack found his predilections—both cultural and personal—closely mirrored in Cecil's portrait of the second Viscount Melbourne, William Lamb, political adviser to Queen Victoria. As Cecil would note (and Jack would underline), the aristocratic Melbourne had been a natural skeptic who wrestled with "the conventional prejudices of his rank and station." He'd likewise cherished the guise of a cynic who, though doubting the value of virtue, "never doubted the value of being a gentleman." Furthermore, though

Lamb made successful runs at many a serious political pursuit, he seemed to do so only because his political conquests (like his amorous conquests) amused him and provided an antidote to boredom.

Unlike Melbourne, Jack tended not to be a snob. The same went for his brother Joe. Although both had spent the bulk of their lives around affluent people and felt most comfortable in such company, neither appeared to take his privileged life for granted and neither chose friends based upon net worth. Each had close associates at Choate and Harvard who were scholarship students from modest backgrounds. Lem Billings, speaking of his trip to Europe with Jack, recalled: "I went over with very little money because my father [had recently died]. This is another side of Jack's character: he was perfectly happy to live at places for forty cents a night, and we ate frightful food . . . but he did it [because] that was the only way I could go with him."

In London, Jack and Joe made a point of befriending everyday embassy staff members, among them receptionist Terry McCulloch, a native of Scotland. "Joe was an awful good-looking young fellow," she told Joe Jr.'s biographer Hank Searls many years later. ". . . He and Jack used to kid me. We were about the same age. They called me 'Snow White' and they teased me and they'd pull my hair and chase me up and down the stairs. We had a lot of fun. Kathleen was less friendly. She didn't fraternize with the help, and criticized her brothers for doing so." Terry nursed an unreciprocated crush on Joe. He in turn focused his romantic ambitions on the ethereal and Catholic Virginia Gilliat (later Lady Sykes). He was also seen about town quite a bit with Stella and Anna Carcano (nicknamed Bebe and Chiquita, respectively), the beautiful Catholic daughters of the Argentine ambassador.

As had been the case with Melbourne a century earlier, Jack quickly tired of the "nice" girls he met at dress balls, posh nightspots, and embassy reception desks. While sometimes—though by no means always—fine for conversation, they were useless for other, more tactile pleasures. Thus Jack continued to rely on professionals, as well as the occasional inspired amateur, for sexual gratification. He made himself notorious in Kick's set for a week or more when he insisted on introducing them to a particularly vivacious but uncouth American. Apologizing to Hugh Fraser for the sometimes loud behavior of the ebullient "Honeychild Wilder"—a model recently dubbed Cotton Queen of Louisiana and flown to London to promote the Bayou cotton industry—Jack explained that the young lady was "quite necessary to keep around" for she was "remarkably talented at providing aid and comfort to Americans abroad, relieving their stress, and rendering them every service for the good of God and country."

Jack slowly developed skill at discovering other gifted amateurs, some American, some not. That summer when Joe and Rose Kennedy rented a mansion at Eden Roc near Cannes on the French Riviera, Jack rather delightedly bedded down another Eden Roc visitor, Marlene Dietrich: his first but by no means last movie star. Whether Jack's fling was before or after the ambassador's flirtation with Dietrich during the same holiday, we do not know. We do know, however, that Dietrich bragged for years about having had both father and son in rapid succession. Jack, in turn, bragged about Dietrich to one of his playmates that summer, Claiborne Pell, son of Herbert Pell, FDR's minister to Portugal. An heir to the Lorillard tobacco fortune, Pell would eventually be elected as a Democrat to the Senate from Rhode Island the same year Kennedy came into the presidency.

Pell—who had been Jack's classmate along with Billings and Henry Morgenthau III, son of the ambassador's nemesis in the Treasury Department, during a brief time Jack spent as a student at Princeton in 1935— dated Kick for several weeks at Eden Roc. Accompanied by Jack, the couple spent their days learning to water-ski and their nights in the lush nightspots of Antibes and Cannes. Joe Jr. occasionally tagged along with Jack, Kick, and Claiborne in the evenings, but by day he usually kept to the beach with the younger Kennedy offspring: sometimes good-naturedly, sometimes not. The challenger and tormentor was never far beneath the surface. Teddy would grow up to remember one occasion when Joe dared him to attempt higher and higher dives from Eden Roc until the ambassador stepped in to halt the exercise.

On nights when young Joe did not hit the clubs, he sat with his father on a terrace overlooking the Atlantic and talked of Europe's latest flashpoint, Czechoslovakia, where the rhetoric of Sudeten Germans and their supporters in the Fatherland became increasingly heated, belligerent, and ominous every day. Hitler had ordered the fortification of the Siegfried Line the previous May, and massed troops momentarily on the Czech border, until a partial mobilization by the Czech army coupled with the threat of British intervention made him briefly withdraw and offer to negotiate the question of Sudeten autonomy. Now, Sudeten leader Henlein seemed to be

stonewalling in negotiations with the Czechs overseen by the British, while
the Berlin government voiced almost daily protests against one outrage after
another supposedly perpetuated against the Sudeten Germans by the people
Hitler called "the Czech occupiers." With all this going on, the ambassador
speculated that Joe would be in for interesting times come September when
he was scheduled to spend a few weeks interning for William Bullitt, American ambassador to France, before beginning a tour of Europe.

.   .   .

A SOMEWHAT BORED Jack accompanied his father to Aberdeen, Scotland, during the last week of August. There the ambassador helped
dedicate a memorial to Samuel Seabury, first bishop of the Anglican Communion in the United States. A Connecticut priest of the Church of England, Seabury had been a loud and unapologetic loyalist during the
Revolutionary War but transformed himself into a reconciled American pa-
triot thereafter. Educated in medicine at Yale and the University of Edin-
burgh, Seabury found himself elected bishop of Connecticut and Rhode
Island in 1783. Church proprietors subsequently sent him to ask for conse-
cration from the bishops of the Episcopal Church in Scotland, who, unlike
their counterparts in England, did not demand that Anglican-American
prelates take an oath of allegiance to the British king. The bishop and bishop
coadjutor of Aberdeen, together with the bishop of Ross and Caithness, con-
secrated Seabury on November 14, 1784.

Many in the press commented on the irony of sending a papist to Scotland, a key battleground of the Reformation, to honor one of the founding
fathers of Protestant America. (The following spring, with criticism of
Kennedy and his isolationism on the rise, the ambassador would be heckled
with shouts of "no-popery" while receiving an honorary degree from Edin-
burgh University.) The bulk of Kennedy's Seabury speech—which he sent,
as usual, to Hull for approval—was nothing more than a benign and generally uninspired appreciation of the American clergyman. Just one small slice
of Kennedy's originally planned remarks departed from the topic at hand to
address more timely matters. Citing Seabury as a man of peace, the ambassador proposed to say: "I should like to ask you all if you know of any dis-
pute or controversy existing in the world which is worth the life of your son,
or of anyone else's son? Perhaps I am not well informed of the terrifically vi-

tal forces underlying all the unrest in the world, but for the life of me I cannot see anything involved which could be remotely considered worth shedding blood for. . . ."

Neither Secretary Hull nor FDR fancied Kennedy's implication. FDR went so far as to parody Kennedy's key phrase in conversation with Morgenthau, insisting that what the ambassador had meant to say was "I can't for the life of me understand why anyone would want to go to war to save the Czechs." At the time Hull and Roosevelt reviewed the draft for Kennedy's Seabury speech, Hitler had already given the order to assemble ninety-six divisions (one and a half million men) on the Czech border and laid down a deadline of October 1 for settlement of the Sudeten question to Germany's satisfaction. Britain's position was a bad one. France had committed herself by treaty to step in should Germany invade Czechoslovakia, after which the British would be bound morally, ethically, and politically to do the same.

On orders from Hull, Kennedy deleted the offending prose from his Seabury talk. Nevertheless—as the ambassador restated to Jack shortly before the boy boarded a ship back to the States for the start of his junior year—he remained unequivocal in his bias against confronting the Nazis. As usual, Kennedy saw things in entirely economic rather than moral terms. He summarized his simplistic view of the world situation to all who would hear him out. War, if it came, would undermine the capitalistic infrastructure of the Western world. Destruction of the major trading cities of Europe, combined with the collectivist initiatives in which all countries at war would have to engage, would strain capitalism to the breaking point. At the end of all the battles, there would simply be left a vast economic wasteland, a world of rubble poised for Communism to take root after the death of the capitalist world. The great fortunes, including Joe's, would be worthless. And his pampered children would be cast among the rabble. This, said Joe, would be the result of confronting the Nazis. Only by appeasing them when it came to Czechoslovakia and other "disposable countries"—and perhaps one day uniting with them against Soviet Russia—could the wealth of the world be saved.

Kennedy met on August 30 with one of the two men (the other being FDR) he believed best positioned to preserve civilization. Calling at 10 Downing Street, Kennedy found Prime Minister Chamberlain looking "quite unwell" and sounding "very much disturbed about the situation in Czechoslovakia." As he reported via confidential cable to Hull, the PM had reliable information that "Herr Hitler has made up his mind to peacefully take Czechoslovakia if possible, but with arms if necessary." Chamberlain said his intelligence indicated that Hitler, though prepared to fight, did not believe he would have to. Kennedy asked Chamberlain flat out whether he had as yet made up his mind to go to war to protect Czech territory in the event the French did so, to which Chamberlain replied "that he was very much afraid that they might be forced into it but . . . he had an agreement with France that they would not declare war before consulting Great Britain." Chamberlain told Kennedy he regarded war "as about an even chance." Still, Kennedy told Hull, "even if Herr Hitler strikes, my own belief is that [Chamberlain's] influence will be to keep the French out. . . . Today Chamberlain is still the best bet in Europe against war, but he is a very sick-looking man. . . ."

Kennedy saw Halifax the next morning. The foreign minister shared Chamberlain's grim view of the situation. Halifax said talks between Czech president Edvard Bènes and Sudeten leader Henlein had stalled. At the same time, British popular sentiment remained overwhelmingly against going to war for the Czechs. "The Foreign Secretary," Kennedy wrote Hull, "says that the French do not want to fight either. The Foreign Secretary asked me what American reaction would be if the Germans invaded Czechoslovakia, with the Czechs fighting them, and Great Britain did not go along. I told him a great deal would depend on the attitude the President would take as to whether he thought Great Britain should be encouraged to fight or whether he would contend that they should stay out of war until the last possible minute. The Foreign Secretary said he would keep in touch with me on this problem because obviously they cannot prepare for this emergency without tipping their hand to the Germans." When Kennedy asked Halifax if he thought the Germans were bluffing, Halifax replied that he did not think it was "quite a bluff. He thinks that Herr Hitler hopes to get all he wants without a fight and that by taking advantage of the situation as he thinks he sees it, it might be as good a time as any to march."

In reporting his conversation with Halifax, Kennedy went on to ask Hull for an answer to Halifax's query. What was U.S. policy likely to be in the event the British declined to oppose with force a German invasion of

Czech territory? Hull replied that it "would not be practicable to be . . . spe-cific as to our reaction in hypothetical circumstances." Hull said further that recent public statements made by both himself and the president—state-ments insisting on the territorial integrity of the Czech Republic—put the administration's current policy as completely as was necessary or, for that matter, prudent.

.   .   .

ROOSEVELT BECAME UPSET on August 31 when Hearst's *Boston Her-ald* published an exclusive front-page interview in which Kennedy asked Americans to remain calm in the face of the intensifying Czech crisis and to "keep cool—things aren't as bad as they may seem." Roosevelt did not appreciate his ambassador's making unauthorized analyses of the inter-national situation for domestic consumption. "Frankly," Roosevelt wrote Hull, "I think Joe Kennedy's attention should be called to this. . . . If all of our fifty-five or sixty Ambassadors and Ministers were to send exclusive sto-ries to specially chosen newspapers in the United States, your department might just as well close shop." Both Hull and Roosevelt wound up censuring Kennedy sharply in separate communiqués.

Nevertheless, Kennedy did not refrain from sending further messages home via the press; and it is interesting, in retrospect, to watch Kennedy's panic over Czechoslovakia evolve through the prism of these public utter-ances. Where Kennedy had called for calm at the end of August, he was sending quite a different signal by September 14, when he gave an interview to DeWitt Mackenzie of the *Washington Star*. Mackenzie wrote: "[Kennedy] believes it his business in the first place to throw his whole weight into an effort to assure peace. Beyond that, he is anxious to get the dictators and the democracies together to work out ways and means to avert the economic disaster for which, in his belief, the world is now coasting straight and fast. . . . He says he is scared and I can believe that, for he frightened me."

Indeed, all of Europe had been frightened by provocative remarks voiced by Goering and Hitler during a series of rallies at Nuremberg just a few days before. In the course of several torch-lit, hate-filled evenings laced with fevered Nazi rhetoric, Goering pronounced the Czechs "a miserable pygmy race without culture" who had lately been busy oppressing "a cul-tured people," the Sudeten Germans, aided and abetted by "Moscow and the eternal mask of the Jew devil." Promising prompt deliverance for the Sudeten Germans, Hitler announced emphatically on September 12 that "if these tortured creatures cannot obtain their rights and assistance by themselves they can obtain it from us."

. . .

As ANNOYING AS Roosevelt found Kennedy's incessant chatter to the press, he was even more put out by the ambassador's increasing penchant for attempting to shape, rather than articulate, U.S. foreign policy in the face of the developing crisis. Roosevelt had for months been walking a rhetorical tightrope in his dealings with the British, encouraging Chamberlain to mark the Czech border as the place where appeasement would end while at the same time not promising direct U.S. aid in the event of hostilities.

Restrained by the terms of the Neutrality Act of 1935—which forbade arms sales to belligerents in foreign wars to which the United States was not a party—FDR relied on smoke, mirrors, and diplomatic doublespeak to keep the British hope for American intervention alive. He therefore became deeply angered when Kennedy—without authority from the administration and despite Hull's precise command that vague remarks made by himself and Roosevelt be left to stand on their own—momentarily shattered the State Department's carefully crafted ambiguity. Hull's diary shows September 20 as the day FDR learned through backdoor diplomatic channels of Kennedy's latest faux pas: his unauthorized assurance to Halifax that if war broke out over Czechoslovakia the United States would most certainly remain neutral. Britain, Kennedy had told Halifax, should make a settlement with Hitler on Czechoslovakia rather than face the full might of German militarism without American backup.

Hull instantly sent a strongly worded cable ordering Kennedy to avoid rash, impromptu, and inaccurate remarks such as the type reported: remarks that only served to defeat the carefully calibrated effect of tightly scripted statements by the secretary and the president. Roosevelt himself summoned the British ambassador, Ronald Lindsay, to the White House for a private chat, after which Lindsay cabled Chamberlain his strong impression that compromise on the Czech issue was most definitely *not* recommended by Washington. Very shortly, FDR's friends Robert Kintner and Joseph Alsop (the latter a distant cousin to the president) reported "on the highest authority" in the *Washington Evening Star* that Ambassador Kennedy was on the outs with Roosevelt. "While Kennedy is loved in London, he is no longer popular at the White House. The President knows of his private talk, resents it, and rebukes it when he can."

. . .

KENNEDY MET WITH Chamberlain on September 14. "He felt it absolutely imperative . . ." Kennedy wrote Hull after the meeting, "to send a message last night to Hitler and ask if he would see him and go over the [Czech] situation. . . . He feels that Hitler cannot refuse to see him. . . ." Chamberlain told Kennedy he planned, first, to offer Hitler immediate local autonomy in the Sudetenland in exchange for immediate German demobilization, this to be followed in five years by either elections in the Sudetenland or international arbitration of borders to reunite the Sudetens with Germany, whichever the Sudeten Germans preferred.

"If," Kennedy reported to Hull, "the German Chancellor completely repudiates that on the ground that he wants immediate action, the Prime Minister will suggest that it might possibly be done in six months. The great trouble with this is that Herr Hitler will be winning a victory without bloodshed [thus making] the next crisis whenever and about whatever it comes, much easier for him to win out. This is realized by Mr. Chamberlain. . . ." It was clear, however, that Chamberlain was simply not prepared to go to war for Czechoslovakia. He showed every sign of being a desperate man greatly relieved when a message arrived from Hitler, inviting him to Germany the next day. "He will tell the German Chancellor," Kennedy reported to the State Department, "that he has come to try to formulate a settlement for world policy and that Czechoslovakia is after all a small incident in that big cause."

Chamberlain departed London for Berchtesgaden on the 15th and returned on the 18th with an agreement that amounted to little more than surrender. Meeting with Kennedy on the 19th, Chamberlain outlined a plan calling for the transfer to Germany of all areas in Czechoslovakia where ethnic Germans dominated the population: in other words, the partition of the Czech Republic. "The whole plan," Kennedy wrote Hull, "has been objected to by some members of the British Cabinet and Chamberlain appreciates that the rape of Czechoslovakia is going to be put on his shoulders. Nevertheless, since war is the only alternative, he says he can see no justification in fighting for a cause which would have to be settled after the war was over along more or less the same lines as he is trying to settle it at the present time." The assumption that the Germans would be the inevitable victors in any military altercation with the democracies *always* formed a key part of Chamberlain's—and, for that matter, Kennedy's—logic.

Chamberlain planned to return to Germany on the 22nd to finalize the agreement. In the meantime, British and French ministers conferred to decide exactly which Czech districts would be surrendered. The Czechs, in turn, found themselves informed that Britain and France would guarantee the borders of the newly configured Czechoslovakian state, but that if the Czechs refused to surrender the contested districts they would be left to fight Germany on their own.

While the Czechs grimly prepared for partition, Britain—which had been poised on the brink of war—relaxed and rejoiced. Kennedy commented that "there was little doubt the country as a whole stood behind Chamberlain. It was evident in the throngs gathered in Parliament Square and in the streets converging on Whitehall." Joining in the air of celebration, Kick traveled to Scotland for the last fortnight of the Scottish Season. Rose soon went to Scotland as well, booking rooms at the Gleneagles Hotel in Perth and accepting an invitation to attend the launching of the *Queen Elizabeth* with the queen and the two royal princesses. The younger Kennedy children, who had been dispatched to Cork, Ireland, as a precaution against the sudden outbreak of war and the bombing of British towns and cities, now returned to London. It seemed, on the face of things, that Europe had been pulled from the precipice. Only a few voices in the British wilderness questioned Chamberlain's wisdom in giving in to the Nazis. Churchill commented dryly (and realistically) that security could not be obtained by throwing a small state to the wolves; to think otherwise was a fatal delusion.

Britain's cumulative sigh of relief became a gasp on the 22nd, when—meeting with Chamberlain at Godesberg presumably to dot the *i*'s of the Berchtesgaden agreement—Hitler demanded more. Chamberlain had worked industriously over the past week to set up an international oversight commission for the Sudeten transfer. Now Hitler insisted the Sudetenland be handed over promptly and completely by October 1 with no international commissions or other such nonsense. He also required the recognition of other nationalities subjugated by the Czechs. In short, the Führer demanded the immediate partition of an even larger area of Czechoslovakia. When Chamberlain requested settlement of the issue through an independent international commission, Hitler responded petulantly by moving up his deadline to September 28. In conference on the 23rd at 10 Downing Street, Chamberlain futilely urged acquiescence to the new Nazi demands. Key members of his cabinet—among them Halifax and First Lord of the Admiralty Alfred Duff Cooper—refused to go along. France in turn mobilized and joined Czechoslovakia in rejecting Hitler's so-called Godesberg Memo.

"All over London," Kennedy recalled, "people were being fitted for gasmasks. In the churches, in the theaters, at the sportsmatches, announcements were made of the depots to which they should go. A motor van slowly cruised through Grosvenor Square with a loud speaker attachment urging people not to delay in getting their masks. It carried posters pleading for more recruits for the air protection services." Workmen at Buckingham Palace labored to reinforce the walls of the royal air raid shelter. Across from the ambassador's residence, volunteers worked night and day digging trenches in the gardens of Hyde Park. Hospitals discharged all but the most critically ill patients in anticipation of the fifty thousand casualties forecast to result from the first few days of German air attacks. Amid all this, the Kennedys once more made plans to remove their children from England, this time to the United States. The ambassador ordered their things packed, and asked Rose to come home from Scotland to supervise arrangements. Writing to Krock, the ambassador said fatalistically that he was generally "very blue" and "starting to think about sending Rose and the children back to America and stay here alone for how long God only knows. Maybe never see them again."

Speaking to the country on the 26th, Chamberlain called it "horrible, fantastic, [and] incredible" that the people of Great Britain "should be digging trenches and trying on gas masks here because of a quarrel in a far-away country between people of whom we know nothing. . . . I am myself a man of peace to the depths of my soul. Armed conflict between nations is a nightmare to me; but if I were convinced that any nation had made up its mind to dominate the world by fear of its force, I should feel that it must be resisted.

Under such a domination life for people who live in liberty would not be worth living; but war is a fearful thing, and we must be very clear, before we embark on it, that it is really the great issues that are at stake, and that the call to risk everything in their defense, when all the consequences are weighted, is irresistible. . . . I shall not give up the hope of a peaceful solution, or abandon my efforts for peace, as long as any chance for peace remains. I would not hesitate to pay even a third visit to Germany, if I thought it would do any good. But at this moment I see nothing further that I can usefully do in the way of mediation."

Despite the ambassador's request that they return to London, Kick and her mother were still in Scotland—Kick attending the Perth Races and her mother playing golf—on the 28th, the day of Hitler's 2-p.m. deadline for agreement on Czechoslovakia. That afternoon the ambassador sat in the packed diplomatic gallery of Parliament, listening to the grim Chamberlain address the House of Commons. Chamberlain explained how that morning he'd directed a last appeal to Hitler in hopes of avoiding war. Ministers from France and Italy sat near Kennedy, as did Jan Masaryk, Czech minister and son of the man widely recognized as the George Washington of the Czech Republic. Chamberlain spoke slowly and deliberately—approaching the prospect of war with a weary, halting, but inevitable rhetorical cadence— until at one point he was interrupted and handed a note. The room remained hushed as Chamberlain read, shook his head as if in disbelief, and then looked around for a moment, smiling. All was not lost. At least not yet. "I have now been informed," Chamberlain announced, his voice suddenly stronger, "by Herr Hitler that he invites me to meet him at Munich tomorrow morning. He has also invited Signor Mussolini and Monsieur Daladier. Signor Mussolini has accepted and I have no doubt Monsieur Daladier will also accept. I need not say what my answer will be."

The hall erupted with applause: a standing ovation of relief. Only a minority in the body—Winston Churchill, Duff Cooper, Anthony Eden, and Jan Masaryk among them—recognized the obvious problem with the meeting Chamberlain anticipated so happily. The proposed conference would determine the future of Czechoslovakia, yet the president of the Czech Republic had not even been invited to sit at the table with Hitler, Mussolini, Daladier, and Chamberlain. Later, Kennedy and Masaryk shared a cab back to their adjacent embassies on Grosvenor Square. "I hope this doesn't mean they are going to cut us up and sell us out," said Masaryk. Kennedy somberly told Masaryk he had no idea what the future held. He was much more animated, however, once he'd said his goodbyes to the Czech. The ambassador was all smiles inside the embassy. "Well boys," he announced delightedly to no one in particular, "the war is off."

The British PM traveled immediately to Munich, from which he returned a few days later waving a piece of paper, triumphantly declaring he had achieved "peace in our time." Hitler had agreed he would never wage war on Great Britain. In return, the British would make Czechoslovakia hand over not only the Sudetenland, but also the heavily fortified Czech borders (thus, though no one said it, leaving the country's interior defenseless against attack). While *The Spectator* nominated Chamberlain for a Nobel Peace Prize and Ambassador Kennedy hailed him as the greatest statesman of the age, Winston Churchill editorialized that Britain had "sustained a total and unmitigated defeat" in signing the Munich Pact. Just as he'd threatened, Hitler's troops still marched into the Sudetenland on October 1: but now with a veneer of legality, and without firing a shot.

Back in London, Ambassador Kennedy told his children to unpack their bags.

7

Unrelenting Antagonism

WHILE KICK HEARD Chamberlain extolled by her father as a visionary political genius, she got a very different read from Billy Hartington and his friends. They complained about how Chamberlain had "rolled over" for Hitler and talked about Chamberlain's much ballyhooed "peace with honor" as though it represented one of the most shameful episodes in British history. Young men like Ormsby-Gore and Hartington, from aristocratic families with notable military traditions, took pride in Britain's succession of wars—wars without which the wealth, stability, and greatness of the British Empire would have been impossible to achieve. For them and most members of their class, the only peace worth having was one with justice and security; and the Munich Pact was shockingly devoid of either element. This particular peace, achieved through the sacrifice of Britain's ally Czechoslovakia, seemed remarkably ignoble.

Joe and Rose sat in the gallery of Parliament when Alfred Duff Cooper, first lord of the admiralty, who had resigned from Chamberlain's cabinet over the Munich Pact, stood to explain his reasons in detail. The issue, insisted Cooper, was not so much peace or Czechoslovakia as it was whether Germany should be allowed "in disregard of treaty obligations, of the laws of nations and the decrees of morality, to dominate by brutal force the Continent of Europe." In resigning, said Cooper, "I have ruined, perhaps, my political career. But that is little matter: I have retained something which is to me of greater value—I can still walk about the world with my head erect." Despite Cooper's passionate remarks against the pact, the House of Commons voted with Chamberlain three to one, endorsing the agreement. Shortly after the vote, Kennedy came upon Czech minister Masaryk walking in Hyde Park. "Isn't it wonderful," said Joe. "Isn't *what* wonderful?" asked Masaryk. "Munich, of course."

Kennedy made his first post-Munich public statement on appeasement when addressing the members of the Navy League at their Trafalgar Day Dinner, held that year on October 19. He had run the speech by his cohorts in the State Department, but on a last-minute basis that did not allow them time to go through it properly. Jay Pierrepont Moffat recorded in his diary for the 17th: "Kennedy sent in a speech he is planning to make to the Navy League tomorrow night. He had spent about ten days on it and wanted us to vet it in one. A large part of it is an endorsement of the Chamberlain philosophy . . . but being expressly advanced as the Ambassador's personal views there was nothing to do but pass it." What was more, FDR and Hull had recently made a tactical decision to let Kennedy hang himself with his own words. Joe's Trafalgar Day speech made a good start toward this end, especially when he said: "It is true that the democratic and dictator countries have important and fundamental divergencies of outlook, which in certain areas go deeper than politics. But there is simply no sense, common or otherwise, in letting these differences grow into unrelenting antagonism. After all, we have to live together in the same world, whether we like it or not."

It seemed Kennedy had chosen the anniversary of Britain's greatest victory to urge her surrender. Numerous American newspapers immediately editorialized against the ambassador's statement. Columnists Drew Pearson and Robert Allen accused Kennedy of catering to the Cliveden set. Several Jewish organizations that had formally considered backing Kennedy for president now announced they would not. "For Mr. Kennedy to propose," said the *New York Post*, "that the U.S. make a friend of a man who boasts that he is out to destroy democracy, religion and all the other principles which free Americans hold dear . . . that passes understanding." The *New York Herald Tribune*'s Walter Lippmann also chimed in, pointing out that "amateur and temporary diplomats take their speeches very seriously. Ambassadors of this type soon tend to become each a little state department with a little foreign policy of their own."

"I wonder if Joe Kennedy understands the implications of public talk by an American Ambassador," Kennedy's onetime friend Felix Frankfurter asked Roosevelt, "and realizes the discouragement to right things and the encouragement to wrong things that he may, however unwittingly, give. . . . Such public approval of dictatorships, in part, even, plays precisely into their hands in that it helps to debilitate confidence in the democratic way of life. . . ." Within days, Roosevelt made a speech obliquely criticizing Kennedy and his remarks. Saying he did not want recent statements by high-ranking State Department officials to be misunderstood, Roosevelt roundly denounced Hitler and his habit of negotiating by threat of war. Reading between the lines, most observers realized Kennedy had been repudiated. Kennedy said later that Roosevelt had stabbed him in the back.

Traveling in Eastern Europe after having finished his several weeks of apprenticeship to Bullitt in Paris, Joe Jr. penned a rough draft for a rebuttal to Lippmann: "Mr. Lippman article shows the natural Jewish reaction to the speech of the ambassadors calling for some kind of cooperation between the democratic and fascists nations. . . . If the duty of an ambassador is to merely report the policies of the government to which he is accredited, and to make no effort to make his ideas felt, I suggest that the Ambassadors of the U.S. should be some unemployed office boy, who could ably transmit the releases of the foreign government to his own government."

Elsewhere Joe Jr. wrote that his father didn't like the idea of "taking orders and working for hours trying to keep things out of his speeches which an Ambassador shouldn't say." The ambassador would later claim that 75 percent of the attacks made on him after the Trafalgar Day speech emanated from "a number of Jewish publishers and writers. . . . The tactics of this group may some day be analyzed. Some of them in their zeal did not hesitate to resort to slander and falsehood to achieve their aims." He told his eldest son that in the light of the media attacks he would give up the ambassadorship in a moment were it not for the benefits he and Jack and Kick were getting from it, and the benefits Eunice would get when she came out the following spring. He added that what he disliked most about the job was having to put up with "Jewish columnists" in the States who criticized him with no good reason. "The papers have made up a pile of lies about him," wrote Joe Jr., "and he can't do anything about it but claims that he is going to let a few blasts when he gets back there. . . ."

Visiting Oxford not long after the Trafalgar speech, Ambassador Kennedy received a cool reception from members of the United States Society, a student group composed mostly of Americans in residence at various Oxford colleges. "Foolishly, he [Kennedy] had no prepared speech," recalled Philip Kaiser, one of the students. "Instead, he boldly announced that he would make no preliminary remarks and was ready to devote all his time to answering questions. We couldn't resist this opportunity to bloody him. It was no secret that Kennedy strongly supported Chamberlain's appeasement policy and favored Franco in Spain, which most of us deplored. Kennedy arrogantly emphasized his position in his replies to the first few questions, and we reacted by prodding him with one sharp query after another, adding provocative supplementaries whenever we felt his responses were unsatisfactory." Another American student recalled, "I was embarrassed for the country. Here was our chief representative, casually defending Franco and supporting Chamberlain as if there were no other conceivable view. And sitting at his feet were two of his teenage daughters, loudly chomping gum. It was all tasteless."

Shortly after the Oxford visit, Kennedy learned through contacts at the British Foreign Office about preparations for a royal visit to the United States. "I am somewhat embarrassed . . ." he wrote Hull. "I hear [through the Foreign Office] about Lindsay's dispatches and of the discussions that are taking place between the President and Lindsay. . . . If the President wanted me to be aware of any discussions he is having I suppose he would inform me, but I would know nothing about the King's trip whatsoever if I were not advised by the Foreign Office." He told Hull he made a habit of giving the British the impression, erroneous, that he was fully briefed, because otherwise his "contacts and prestige" would be seriously jeopardized. "Possibly nothing can be done about this and although it is difficult I can continue to look like a dummy and carry on the best I can."

Kennedy had few illusions about where he stood with the administration. "I don't know who spread poison around the White House as far as I am concerned," he wrote New York *Daily News* Washington correspondent Doris Fleeson, "but when I heard, the other night, from my father-in-law that somebody had just been in to see him and told him that Missy LeHand was saying very unkind things about me, I practically gave up. I thought Missy knew me well enough to know that I don't shift like the wind and that anything I have to say I say to the parties concerned. However, this is really the only news I had that got me down. What anybody else on that Executive Staff feels interests me not one damn bit." He was cavalier. He told London friends that Washington was very far away, and that it was very easy to forget what people there might be thinking or saying about him. He was happily busy, he said, with the active social life of balls and galas that so delighted Mrs. Kennedy.

Joe and Rose enjoyed the hospitality of one of London's finest homes—a small palace owned by a cousin to the king—on the evening of November 9. On the same night, only a few hundred miles away in the ghettoes of Germany, Austria, and Bohemia, Nazi thugs torched hundreds of synagogues, plundered and burned thousands of Jewish homes, and murdered and raped at random: all with government approval. This was Kristallnacht—the Night of Broken Glass. Writing to Lindbergh shortly thereafter, Kennedy seemed more concerned about the political ramifications stemming from high-profile, violent anti-Semitism than he was about the actual predicament of the Jews. ". . . Isn't there some way," he wrote the aviator, "to persuade [the Nazis] it is on a situation like this that the whole program of saving western civilization might hinge? It is more and more difficult for those seeking peaceful solutions to advocate any plan when the papers are filled with such horror." Kennedy's chief fear about Kristallnacht was that by hardening antifascist sentiment in the West it would jeopardize the fragile peace for which he was willing to compromise everything.

In the wake of Kristallnacht, Kennedy briefly dabbled with a scheme to remove the Jews in German-controlled territory to other countries. His own government offered only a lukewarm response. People close to the president voiced skepticism, especially after Henry Luce's *Life* magazine breathlessly reported that if successful, the "Kennedy Plan" would "add new luster to a reputation that may well carry Joseph Patrick Kennedy into the White House." Kennedy's idea soon sank of its own weight when the ambassador learned what the Intergovernmental Committee on Refugees had realized months before. No countries were willing to sign on as hosts to large populations of European Jewry, least of all the United States. In a cable to Hull,

Kennedy admitted he shared a fear recently voiced by Halifax: that a successful program to settle Austrian, Bohemian, and German Jews would prompt other countries to "get rid of theirs as well," thus overwhelming potential host countries.

.   .   .

Writing from Harvard after the ambassador's disastrous Trafalgar Day speech, Jack tried to lift his father's spirits with as optimistic a read as possible on U.S. reaction. "While [the speech] seemed unpopular with the Jews, etc.," Jack commented, "it was considered to be very good by everyone who wasn't bitterly anti-fascist." He added that his Winthrop House roommates—Macdonald and two other Harvard football greats, Ben Smith and Charlie Houghton—thought the ambassador's remarks inspired and wonderful. Only their black valet, George Taylor, voiced some reservations and was generally "with the Jews."

The sloppiest of George Taylor's wards—the young man named Kennedy who insisted on strewing his clothes across the floors of his suite—was this term far more attentive to his studies than he'd ever been before. "I don't think," Torb Macdonald recalled many years later, "[Jack] really got interested in the intellectual side of academic life until perhaps his junior year when war seemed to bring a lot of us, especially Jack, a realization that it wasn't all fun and games, and that life was about to get very real and earnest." The dark prospect of war aside, Jack was more happily motivated by another possibility. Dean Chester Hanfod had agreed to consider granting Jack leave for independent study in Europe come spring, provided Jack acquit himself well in six courses, as opposed to the normal four, during the autumn term. With London to look forward to, Jack focused diligently on all his courses, most of these embracing his main interests of politics and history.

In between his studies, Jack still found time to play. Visiting New York for a weekend in October, he was pleasantly caught off-guard by several Kennedy-family references in the play Leave It to Me, a comedy about an American ambassadorial family posted to Russia. At one point the ambassador's wife, speaking of her five daughters, said that if she'd had four more her husband would have been assigned to London. Later in the play, during a big celebration in the middle of Red Square honoring the ambassador, the same character was made to say, "I bet the Kennedys are boiling!" Jack told his parents, "It's pretty funny and jokes about us get by far the biggest laughs, whatever that signifies."

Jack's date for the play—as well as for several Harvard football games that autumn—was a girl he'd lately stolen (as was his habit) from a good friend. Beautiful, brainy, and filched from Chuck Houghton, Frances Ann Cannon was the scion of a prominent North Carolina family noted for their many cotton and wool mills. Unlike the whores Jack patronized, the occasional talented amateurs, and the typical "upright" girls he usually escorted to social functions, Frances Ann seemed to be someone he actually respected. All his friends of the period—Houghton, Macdonald, and Smith among them—agreed later that he was truly in love with Frances Ann. He wanted to marry her, this despite her Protestant background and her parents' noticeable lack of enthusiasm at the prospect of a Catholic son-in-law. In addition to being attractive and clever, Frances Ann had also been around. She'd graduated from the academically prestigious Sarah Lawrence College. She had great talent as a writer. And she possessed an extensive knowledge of current affairs. Frances Ann had even been presented at the British court in 1937, just one year before Jack's father slammed the door on debutantes from the American mainland.

Jack did not mention the Protestant Frances Ann in letters to his parents. He did, however, talk about her to his father when the ambassador arrived back in the States that December, leaving the rest of the family in Europe, where they would spend Christmas at St. Moritz.

.   .   .

THE AMBASSADOR'S FRIEND Boake Carter used his daily column to predict a stormy confrontation between the president and his returning ambassador. "The White House," wrote Carter, "has on its hands a fighting Irishman with blazing eyes and a determination to strip the bandages of deceit, innuendo and misrepresentation bound around the eyes of American citizens." Upon his departure from Liverpool, Kennedy told reporters: "I am going home to face the President and tell him what I think—and what I think won't please him." Arriving in New York on December 15, he was immediately asked what he thought of Hitler. "Come and see me the day I resign," he answered during a brief interview published in the next day's *New York Times*.

A few Roosevelt intimates, among them Henry Morgenthau, urged FDR to fire his ambassador in short order. Postmaster General and Democratic National Committee chairman Jim Farley built up Morgenthau's hopes when he told him Roosevelt was "terribly peeved with Joe. . . . When Joe comes back, that will probably be the beginning of the end." Timing, however, was everything. Speaking many years later, James Roosevelt recalled that by the end of 1938, "Father knew that Kennedy had to go. . . . [But he] did not want to make the change. He wanted it to evolve on its own." FDR told a somewhat deflated Morgenthau there was no point in discharging Kennedy just yet. Why create an even more vocal enemy when instead Kennedy might still be used to advance the agenda of the administration?

Thus FDR was nothing short of charming when Kennedy came to the White House. Kennedy in turn seemed relieved to find the president friendly and apparently earnest in wanting his ambassador's opinion on the situation in Europe. In a circuitous route through a two-hour discussion, the president suggested the only way to keep the United States out of the imminent war was to make her strong and thus unapproachable by would-be combatants. By the end of their conversation, Kennedy found himself agreeing the United States must rearm. More astonishing—to himself as well as others—Kennedy agreed it would be desirable to repeal (or at least revise) the Neutrality Act, for which he had long been a steadfast advocate, in order to give Britain and France the resources necessary to stop German aggression before it threatened the United States. Kennedy even promised Roosevelt he would talk to his friend Morgan banker Thomas Lamont about consolidating financial and manufacturing interests to back the cause of rearmament.

Over Christmas at Palm Beach, the ambassador entertained houseguests Walter Winchell, Arthur Krock, and Boake Carter. (Hearing of this gathering of journalists, Henry Ehrlich, Washington correspondent for the *Boston Herald*, published a piece in which he referred to the Kennedy home as "a virtual publicity bureau" and predicted the ambassador's imminent reentrance into presidential politics.) Kennedy worked the phones from his tropical poolside throughout the holiday, speaking to many contacts across the country, among them anti-Semitic radio priest Father Charles Coughlin (who would shortly go on the air to assert that the Rothschilds had financed the murder of Abraham Lincoln as part of a supposed plot to maximize the

influence of international Jewish banking interests in the United States). After his conversations with Coughlin and others like him, the ambassador told
Jack he was more convinced than ever that Americans as a whole still stood
strongly, unshakably, for isolation.

Although gathering his intelligence from very different quarters, FDR
nevertheless shared Kennedy's analysis of popular sentiment. This was why
he posited rearmament not as a preparation for war, but as a tool for enforcing isolationism and protecting the United States from involvement in European hostilities. It was also why he sought Kennedy as an ally. FDR knew
that with so noted a dove as Kennedy in his corner he could easily fend off
the very real and very on-target suspicions of isolationists that he was secretly a hawk, privately convinced of the bankruptcy of appeasement, and
bent on using any popular argument he could to prepare for war. That January, FDR called Kennedy to Washington from Palm Beach to join William
Bullitt in testifying for rearmament and repeal or revision of the Neutrality
Act before secret sessions of the Senate and House Military Affairs Committees.

While quite aware that he and FDR cherished fundamentally different
objectives, Kennedy nevertheless believed sincerely that the United States
must bulk up its military strength. He told Boake Carter that FDR might
very well be trying to build an interventionist America. Still, that was no reason why Joe and other workers for peace should not help facilitate the establishment of arms, armies, and fleets for their own agenda: fortress
America.

Interestingly, in a memorandum to Roosevelt, Kennedy would shortly
reiterate his previously stated view that to successfully fight fascism abroad
the United States would need to adopt fascist methods at home. Kennedy
reasoned that the Herculean effort to arm the United States against the
coming world cataclysm would require nothing less than a government-
controlled economy, extensive taxes, and a degree of regimentation that
would "inevitably mean the destruction of the American form of Government as at present conceived."

· · ·

THE AMBASSADOR departed for England on February 9, telling reporters at the pier that his son Jack would follow him in about two

weeks. (By the original plan, both father and son were to have embarked together on the 24th. It was FDR himself who insisted on the ambassador's
earlier departure, publicly citing urgent business in London but in fact just
wanting to get Kennedy out of the States and away from the journalist
friends who were again touting Kennedy as a serious contender for the
Democratic nomination.)

As all the reporters—both friendly and otherwise—were quick to observe, the departing ambassador seemed intent on emphasizing his independence from FDR. Boake Carter reported that Kennedy was proud of
having "bucked the State Department and Mr. Roosevelt, who is of course
the State Department." Carter hinted FDR had secretly hoped Kennedy
would resign, but that Kennedy had refused to be baited into such a move.
Instead he would defiantly stay on, if only to prevent the appointment of an
interventionist "marionette" to his post. "He feels," wrote Carter, "that he
can serve America, not Mr. Roosevelt, better by sticking than in any other
job."

Privately, however, the ambassador was not so sure he wanted to remain
at his post. He might very well prefer to get back to the States, there to pursue business interests and perhaps—though even Kennedy himself by now
thought it unlikely—the White House. Speaking confidentially to Princeton University's board of governors on behalf of Kennedy, Arthur Krock advised them the ambassador would likely resign in June 1939 and could
return at that time to accept an honorary degree if one was offered (one
wasn't). Drew Pearson also picked up hints, telling a friend he understood
Kennedy "wants to get out but Roosevelt wants him to stay because he'd
rather have Joe in England than here on his neck."

. . .

JACK PERFORMED WELL on his midterm exams—in fact, with distinction. This caused Dean Hanford to approve Jack's application for a half
year's leave abroad. Jack received the good news during the second week of
February while at the Mayo Clinic for what he called his ten-thousand-mile
tune-up. Once tuned, he retreated to the Palm Beach mansion, where—his
father now gone—he entertained Frances Ann for a few idyllic days. Subsequently, when the couple visited New Orleans shortly before Jack's scheduled February 24 departure for Europe, Frances Ann did not give Jack the

answer he wanted or expected when he asked her to marry him. Slipping easily into the past tense, she told him it had been a great romance, but her mother and father would simply never tolerate a Catholic son-in-law. And that, said Frances Ann quite matter-of-factly, was that.

The conversation—Jack's first encounter with bare-knuckled, undisguised, full-bore anti-Catholic bigotry after a lifetime of more subtle snubs—really "rocked him," recalled Torb Macdonald. "Jack wasn't a guy who heard the word *no* a great deal. He really wanted Frances Ann. And to have all that fall apart over somebody having some kind of an idea about not liking his religion, that was a real shocker and I think it influenced how he reacted to some other things that came up later, especially Kick's marriage to Billy Hartington."

Getting ready to board his boat for England, Jack told friends less close than Macdonald that he and Frances Ann had put their relationship on hold. Across the Atlantic, big brother Joe scoffingly told associates Jack would arrive shortly "to begin his education." In fact, Jack's education was already well underway.

8

An Era Ending

DURING A VISIT to Cliveden in late February of 1939, Ambassador Kennedy stood in Nancy Astor's ornate drawing room and—surrounded by distinguished guests—read aloud a letter from a precocious and confident young American happily trapped in a Madrid under siege. Writing from amid the mortared ruins of the once-great city, Joe Jr. spoke of the repression of the Catholic Church by the Loyalist forces then holding the embattled town, and of his adventures with Catholic fifth columnists who worked secretly to advance the cause of Franco behind enemy lines.

He recounted how he'd attended a mass held under the protective cover of drawn drapes in a private household; and he vividly narrated the murder of priests. ". . . today, here in this shattered city," he wrote, "religion must hide and be furtive in disguise, hemmed in by fears on every hand." None of the ambassador's listeners—not Lady Astor nor Charles and Anne Lindbergh, not Geoffrey Dawson, nor even Prime Minister Chamberlain— found anything irregular or unlikely in Joe Jr.'s pro-fascist interpretation, which Anne Lindbergh later praised in her diary as a particularly insightful analysis of Spain's tangled situation. The Loyalists, it seemed, killed only priests, while Franco's fascists, by implication, killed only priest-killers.

For all his evident pride when reading Joe Jr.'s war letters to groups such as that gathered at Cliveden, the ambassador had not wanted his son to go to Spain, had explicitly denied him permission to do so, and was dumbfounded when confronted with the fact of Joe Jr.'s arrival at the battlefront. "Sorry I missed you," read the cable the ambassador received upon his return to the embassy on February 16. "Arrived safely Valencia. Going to Madrid tonight. Regards Joe." As both son and father knew, had the boy not conveniently *missed* the ambassador he would not have been taking any trip at all.

There was reason for Ambassador Kennedy to be concerned. Back in 1937, Kennedy had joined with other prominent American Catholics in insisting that the Neutrality Act of 1935 be extended to cover countries in the midst of civil wars; he'd likewise been conspicuous the previous May in lobbying to keep the 1937 amendment regarding civil wars in place. (The American embargo hurt the Loyalists but not Franco, who received most of his arms from Italy.) He had, as we have seen, recently endorsed the repeal and/or revision of the Neutrality Act with regard to Britain in testimony before closed sessions of the House and Senate Military Affairs Committees. Still, he'd not gone anywhere near advocating a change in U.S. policy vis-à-vis Spain. Now the ambassador feared that if Joe Jr. fell into the hands of the Loyalists (liberals and Communists of various stripes and flavors) they might very well take revenge on his son and namesake.

The risks seemed very real and very high. As Joe Jr. arrived in Spain, Franco's insurgent Nationalists continued to make dramatic inroads. Nevertheless, the Republicans still dominated the third of the country embracing the cities of Madrid and Valencia—the two places Joe most wanted to visit. To top it all off, the young man traveled now without immunity, having swapped his diplomatic passport for a standard one during a brief stopover in Paris. On the line of the new passport designated to note the holder's profession, Joe wrote "journalist."

The ambassador should not have been surprised by Joe Jr.'s attraction to the fatal ground of war-torn Spain. The same young man who had so often bloodied himself on the football and rugby field—and who had most recently tempted death in a bobsled at St. Moritz shortly before breaking his arm in a reckless skiing mishap—had long seemed compulsively drawn to physical danger in a way that gave his father pause. (Fascinated with violence and mortal risks, Joe was at the same time, like Jack, quite stoic in the face of personal pain. "Louella," he'd whispered over the telephone to the Kennedy nanny immediately after suffering the compound fracture of his arm at St. Moritz, "I need a Band-Aid." When Hennessey, a trained nurse, saw the wound for herself she immediately applied a pressure dressing and set off with Joe to the nearest hospital, three hours away by sleigh. "Joe," she told his biographer, Hank Searls, many years later, ". . . had this high threshold for pain, and he never complained except afterwards, he'd say 'Look at this! It sure looks awful, doesn't it?' ")

Arriving at the devastated port of Valencia on February 15, Joe found utter destruction in the area immediately surrounding the harbor: the prime target for Franco's bombers. "Every house," he wrote, "within a radius of half a mile is a litter of wreckage. . . . It's like a deserted village that's been battered to death by bombs." And still more bombs could be counted on. It was just, wrote Joe, "plain suicide" to remain there any length of time. Dockworkers commanded triple their regular salaries to stay on under fire. A few old women sat hunched around the entrance to a shallow bomb shelter—a *refugio*—and Joe wondered why they lingered here. Away from the port—in the nonstrategic and infrequently bombed countryside—most buildings still stood tall. Joe was walking here with a junior official of the American consulate when the man, detecting an all too familiar sound in the distance, announced, "Here they come!" Sirens sounded a moment later. Joe heard the fire of antiaircraft guns, and watched the puffs of their exploding shells show white against the blue sky. He likewise saw the little black specks of the planes keep coming on, untouched by the firing, and pass peacefully overhead on their way to the harbor. "The noise was terrific" when they began dropping their bombs. "It made our ears ache. The buildings vibrated like drums. The planes must have been lost in the sun or hidden by high clouds for we didn't catch another glimpse of them. I'd have felt more comfortable knowing where they were."

When he turned up at the United States embassy in the bombed-out city of Madrid on the 16th, he did not find any other Americans in residence. Ambassador Claude Gernade Bowers had relocated across the French border on Thanksgiving of 1936, when Nationalist conquest of Madrid had seemed imminent. "A skinny Spanish chap named Ugarde is in charge," Joe wrote. "He's kind of bald and about thirty, I'd say. Only a foreign clerk before the outbreak of the revolt, he suddenly found himself looking after all the Americans left in Madrid. . . . Now, in his semi-ambassadorial position, he handles all Embassy matters. . . ." Ugarde and other Spanish employees had moved into the safety of the embassy two years before with their families, establishing a small, self-sufficient community of which Joe now became a part.

Sheep grazed on the lawn behind the locked gates. Hens and a pig and some "refugee cows"—left by a farmer who feared they'd otherwise be confiscated by the government—also found sanctuary, the hens roosting on the roof. The embassy car went out each day in quest of any food other than the regulation diet of lentils and salt fish. The car often had to travel as far as 250 miles into the country to find fresh meat and vegetables. Food queues on the streets reminded Joe of Russia, where he'd visited with Laski in 1934. "Everybody's hungry all the time. The amount of food rationed out isn't nearly enough. . . ." Heating fuel was also in short supply. People ripped apart benches along the streets and used them for firewood. "Today I saw them chopping down a beautiful tree on one of the main streets. When it fell, about fifty people let out a screech and rushed for it, some with tiny hatchets."

Joe was still in Madrid nearly a month later when Franco's Nationalists began to advance on the capital and Loyalist commander Colonel Segismundo Casado López, unwilling to continue his losing struggle, instigated a coup against Prime Minister Juan Negrín. "We awoke to find soldiers on every street corner," he wrote his father on March 8. "It appeared the city was under complete military control and the war was over. The soldiers inspected all documents, picking up bearers identified as Communists. By mid-day they had about 1,200 in jail." Not far from the embassy, some seventy Communists took control of the Ministerial Building at gunpoint, seized hostages, and barricaded themselves in. Meanwhile, fascists congratulated themselves on the ease with which the Casado takeover had been accomplished. Everyone seemed relieved to see soldiers in the streets. "I am sure most people thought the war was over in spite of a declaration by Casado that the Loyalists will fight until they get a worthy peace. Crowds of people chased after newspaper boys and the price of a paper rose to four cigarettes." That night, Joe heard the sound of gunfire. In the morning, he and his embassy cohorts found two corpses just outside the gates.

.   .   .

OUR DAYS LATER, on the morning of March 12, the ambassador was
hoping in vain for Joe Jr. to appear at quite a different spot: the Vatican.
He had sent his son an urgent message several days before, telling him in no
uncertain terms to come here, to this ancient spot, to be a part of Church
history in the making. One wonders if the son's absence (and silence) seemed
at all ominous to the father who stood outside St. Peter's, waiting with other
dignitaries to file in for the coronation of Pope Pius XII. Whatever
Kennedy's thoughts as he fell into line with uncovered head in the shadow of
the vast basilica, they were interrupted shortly by a greeting from a lowly
papal chamberlain. The man who stuck out his hand looked distinctly un-
Italian and vaguely familiar. A contemporary of Joe's at Harvard and also the
son of former Boston mayor Nathan Matthews, Vatican librarian Sullivan
Amory Matthews at first seemed insulted when Kennedy failed to recognize
him.

Matthews would have to forgive this, the ambassador explained. These
last few days had passed in a whirlwind of activity. His wife had been away
in distant Egypt—just concluding an extensive solo tour of the Riviera,
Genoa, Naples, Athens, Turkey, and Palestine—when they'd received word
their old acquaintance Eugenio Cardinal Pacelli, whom they'd entertained
at their home in New York, would be the next pope. Appointed FDR's official representatives to the coronation, the ambassador and his wife barely
had time to get themselves here—she traveling from Egypt, he from London. Kennedy and his second-eldest son, Jack, were just arrived from Paris,
where Kennedy had been required at a series of meetings with the French
ministers. The balance of the Kennedy children—all except for Joe, and all
around here somewhere—had come on a different schedule, riding on the
same train as the Duke of Norfolk, the highest-ranking Catholic peer in the
British realm. The ambassador confessed that given his present state of exhaustion he'd probably fail to recognize a few of his own offspring before
the day was out; thus Papal Chamberlain Matthews should not feel slighted.

Entering St. Peter's, Kennedy noticed Italian foreign minister Galleazzo
Ciano (Count of Cortellazzo, son-in-law to Mussolini) greeting people with
the fascist salute as he strolled through the massive church, the seat of world
Catholicism. (He was amused, later, when Ciano complained about being
placed somewhere behind the Duke of Norfolk in the procession of ambassadors and ministers. This, Ciano insisted, was an insult to all of Italy.)

Kennedy saw Ciano giving the fascist salute yet again outside, when the new pope and his distinguished guests went on the roof to greet the enormous crowd in Vatican Square. "A more pompous ass I have never met in my life," he wrote later.

Joe, Rose, and the children enjoyed a private audience with the pope the next morning, the children carrying a large assortment of religious trinkets and rosary beads to be blessed by the Holy Father. ". . . the family came in and all knelt and kissed the ring," recalled Kennedy, "and he talked with Rose and remembered Teddy. . . . Said Teddy was a smart boy. Then he walked over to the table, a thing a Pope never does, and got a white box with a rosary which he gave to Rose with his blessing. . . . He then gave rosaries in white casing to all the children." When their fifteen minutes were up, the Kennedys knelt for the pope's blessing. The pope had not yet gotten used to using the royal "we" and "us." "Pray for me," he said as the family withdrew. Later that same day, Jack expressed annoyance at having had his picture snapped by journalists as he bent to kiss the ring of a cardinal. According to his father, he muttered angrily that if the photo ever appeared in the United States it would mean "good-bye to Martin Luther [that is, Frances Ann] Cannon."

Rose, anxious not to miss a long-standing appointment with her Paris dressmaker, did not attend two days later when Teddy received his First Communion from the hands of the pope. With Jack, Eunice, Pat, and the ambassador looking on, the pope served mass in the same tiny chapel he had used in his previous position as Vatican secretary of state. His valet acted as altar boy. "I hope you will always be good and pious as you are today," he told Teddy at the end of the mass. Then he took off his vestments and knelt down to pray, timing his prayers with a little watch that he pulled from his pocket. It seemed "funny" to the ambassador that the pope should be timing his prayers, and he was amused when a papal aid confirmed that the pope was in the habit of praying for a precisely set amount of time—to the minute—every day. "He is awe-inspiring," Kennedy wrote in his diary, "majestic, kindness personified and with the humility of God."

. . .

HITLER'S TROOPS marched into Czechoslovakia just one day after the pope's coronation. The stage had been set just a few weeks earlier, when Chamberlain repudiated Britain's previous guarantee of Czech bor-

ders as stated in the eight-month-old Munich Pact. ("I have the evening papers in front of me with their headlines, 'Chamberlain washes his hands,' "
FDR told Bullitt. "You know the last well-known man about whom that was
said?" In the wake of the invasion, when Nancy Astor rose on the floor of
Parliament to ask whether the British government would protest Germany's
action, one of her fellow Conservatives shouted: "You caused it yourself!")

In the tradition of Pilate and Chamberlain, the pope likewise washed
his hands.

As Kennedy well knew, his old friend the new pope had a long history
of acquiescence to both Mussolini and Hitler. It must be mentioned that
Pacelli, who had served as papal nuncio in Munich and Berlin before his appointment as Vatican secretary of state in 1929, was a vehement anti-Semite
who would, in the coming years just as he had previously, say and do little to
stop the march of European totalitarianism. Mussolini's 1935 invasion of
Ethiopia went uncondemned by the Holy See. Indeed, it seemed enough for
Pacelli—just as it was, in essence, enough for Kennedy—that Hitler, Mussolini, and Franco stood at odds with world Communism. That feeling of
solidarity was a large part of the reason why, in 1933, Secretary of State
Pacelli had negotiated his Reich Concordat with Adolf Hitler. The Concordat granted to the papacy the power to impose Church law on German
Catholics. It also gave significant privileges to Catholic schools and clergy
in Germany, while at the same time closing Catholic newspapers and dis-
banding the German Catholics' primary political party. "The abdication of
German political Catholicism in 1933," writes John Cornwell in his study
Hitler's Pope, "negotiated and imposed from the Vatican by Pacelli with the
agreement of Pope Pius XI, ensured that Nazism could rise unopposed by
the most powerful Catholic community in the world—a reverse of the situation sixty years earlier, when German Catholics combated and defeated
Bismarck's Kulturkampf persecutions from the grass roots." Hitler is on
record as telling his cabinet the Concordat "gave Germany an opportunity
and created an area of trust that was particularly significant in the developing
struggle against international Jewry."

Interestingly, Kennedy's diary notes for the day of the Czech invasion
make no mention of Czechoslovakia at all, but are instead laced with narra-
tions of his family's audience with the pope, a subsequent visit to the papal
summer residence, and a diplomatic dinner hosted by William Phillips, U.S.
ambassador to Italy, where Kennedy sat next to Count Ciano's wife (the

daughter of Mussolini). There, somewhere in between the soup and the dessert, the Countess leaned over to Kennedy and told him pointedly that "she could not see any reason for the democracies fighting Fascist Italy. Fascism suited Italy, having lasted for seventeen years, and had been of great benefit to the Italians. . . . Secondly, she said that after all if the United States, France and England all stuck together, there was nothing left for the Duce to do but play along with Hitler for his own protection. Third, she made it very clear by implication that the Italians were deeply concerned over the loss of the friendship of America and since there are a number of enthusiasts for America around Mussolini, I believe there is a good deal in what she said." (Italy and Germany would sign a formal agreement of military alliance two months later, on May 22.)

·   ·   ·

Not only did Pacelli make no public statement on Hitler's invasion of Czechoslovakia, he also had nothing to say when the dictator annexed Memel, the Lithuanian port, on March 22. He was equally silent two weeks later when a bellicose Hitler shrilly demanded the Poles return the port city of Danzig and the Polish corridor to German control.

Dominated by a large German population, Danzig had since 1919 been a "free city" under the control of the League of Nations. The corridor—a strip of land twenty to seventy miles wide giving Poland access to the Baltic Sea—lay along the lower course of the Vistula River in West Prussia and the province of Posen, both of which were transferred to Poland from the defeated Germany by the terms of the Treaty of Versailles. Poland subsequently developed the port of Gdynia as an alternative to Danzig. Now Hitler was demanding the cession of Danzig and the creation of extraterritorial German highways across the corridor connecting to East Prussia.

Many in diplomatic circles viewed Hitler's demand as a provocation carefully calculated to incite war. Hitler expected and hoped for the Poles to deny him Danzig. Hitler watchers on both sides of the Atlantic quickly realized the Führer would much rather have an excuse for righteous warfare, via which he might take all of Poland, than the peaceful surrender of one little port. And Hitler was bound to get what he wanted, for the Poles were not inclined to surrender.

Ambassador Kennedy would recall that after the Czech invasion, Chamberlain "felt not only a sense of national but also a personal grievance against Hitler. . . ." During a meeting with Kennedy, Chamberlain opened a map to illustrate his various policies, adopted and abandoned throughout the course of the previous year, for stopping German expansion. The map was heavily overwritten: a mess of many crudely drawn lines that had at various times briefly defined the extent of German-held territory. "As I left," recalled Kennedy, the PM folded the map together "and wryly commented, 'If this continues much longer, I will need a new map.' " Speaking to Parliament on March 31, Chamberlain contemplated the latest target for Hitler's aggression and, at last, drew a real line in the sand. He told the members of the House of Commons that in the event of a German attack on Poland, "His Majesty's government would feel themselves bound at once to lend the Polish government all support in their power."

. . .

JOE JR. STOOD BY—a pleased observer—as Nationalist troops entered the city of Madrid on March 28, two days after Casado's surrender. Shortly before noon a large car drove by the embassy, its occupants waving the Nationalist flag and yelling "Viva Franco!" Soon Nationalist flags seemed to be everywhere and smiling people started wandering about, greeting each other with the fascist salute. "The city came to life," wrote Joe, "with parades, flags, shawls hung from windows and balconies, pretty girls appearing from nowhere, crowds hanging onto the sides of cars, women and men weeping with joy. We were touched by the expressiveness in their voices and the look in their eyes, by occasional sad faces, by a woman in black holding two children with a bitter look in her face." In the wake of the Nationalist victory, the pope telegraphed his warmest congratulations to Franco.

This, the last of many letters sent by Joe from Madrid, was also the most eloquent. The ambassador, for one, saw something in it. Once Joe Jr. returned to London at the start of April, the ambassador suggested they use Joe's correspondence as the basis for a book about the closing of the Spanish Civil War—a firsthand account by a Harvard-trained American observer. Someone who has written a book, the father told the son, picks up a type and degree of prestige that otherwise just can't be had. The letters, however, were unpublishable as they stood. They needed extensive expansion and editing for clarity. Harvey Klemmer—the embassy aide, publicist, and speechwriter who had been with the ambassador since Maritime Commission days—got this assignment along with a promise that in exchange for his efforts the ambassador would put all of Klemmer's children through college. By the time Klemmer finished the volume a year later, pro-fascist reporting would be out of vogue, the book unpublishable, and Klemmer on his own when it came to paying for Princeton.

.   .   .

K LEMMER RECEIVED his assignment on April 7—Good Friday. The Italians marched into Albania one day later. Shortly thereafter, on the 11th, Lord Halifax sent a message to FDR. It would be terribly convenient, said Halifax, if the U.S. fleet happened to find its way to the Pacific, where it might bolster the minimal presence of the Royal Navy, the bulk of the British fleet being otherwise engaged in the Mediterranean—there to discourage the Italians from extending their invasion of Albania into Greece and Turkey. FDR responded on the 14th by ordering the U.S. fleet to reassemble in the desired quarter. At the same time, FDR issued an explicit appeal for peace addressed directly to both Hitler and Mussolini. In his public letter the president reminded the German and Italian leaders that because of their recent acts of aggression, "throughout the world hundreds of millions of human beings are living today in constant fear of a new war." Roosevelt challenged the dictators to give explicit assurances they would refrain from further territorial grabs for a period of at least ten years. In London, Churchill, rising on the floor of Parliament, implored Chamberlain to accept a plan recently proposed by Russia: that Britain, France, Russia, Poland, Rumania, and Turkey ban together to create a defensive cordon around the Reich. Chamberlain, however, eschewed the idea of an alliance with the Bolsheviks, and said he did not like the idea of nations forming blocs opposed to one another.

The fleet, Roosevelt's peace message, and the Russian proposal were central topics of conversation a few days later when the Kennedys spent their second and last weekend with the king and queen at Windsor. Chamberlain, also a guest, greeted Kennedy effusively and said, "Well, that was a great job Roosevelt did, the message and order to the Navy." The king in turn announced he looked forward to thanking FDR personally during his and the queen's forthcoming visit to the United States. Contemplating this journey, the queen laughed about the possibility of being trapped in the United States or Canada in the event of war.

During lunch on Saturday, Princess Elizabeth discovered a ladybug on the table. Ladybugs were good luck, she said, so Mr. Chamberlain ought to have it. "It came down on a gold spoon," recalled Kennedy, "one from another, and I handed it to the Queen and then she tried to tip it out on the Prime Minister's shoulder. . . . the bug refused to stay, but after many attempts finally did and then went slowly up." The queen shortly removed the ladybug, however, when—good luck or not—Chamberlain complained that it was making him nervous and would probably go down his neck.

· · ·

JACK MET THE king and queen about this time at a court levee, where he appeared in silk knee breeches just like those his father refused to wear. After being presented to their royal highnesses, he shared tea with Princess Elizabeth. "She is still pretty young but starting to look like a looker nonetheless," he wrote a friend back in the States. "I think she rather liked me and now I wouldn't be surprised if she has a thing for me. The knee breeches are cut tight to show off my crotch at its best, and the uniform—worn by everyone but Dad at these Court functions—seems to have caught the polite eye of the young heir. I will, of course, still remember all my common friends back home once I am tapped for prince consort. Count on it. I may even find jobs for some of you. The Keeper of the Royal Hounds seems a plum job. Perhaps Billings would be interested."

The court levee took place amid Jack's few weeks of service as his father's confidential secretary and companion: the same shoes filled by Joe Jr. through the previous summer. He told friends he was feeling quite important going to work at the embassy each morning in his new cutaway. He was at this task for just about a month before his departure, in early April, on a "fact-finding" tour of Europe arranged by his father. Like that of his brother Joe, Jack's tour started with several weeks in the Paris embassy ostensibly assisting Ambassador William Bullitt. The ambassador's real assistant, Carmel Office, would remember Jack sitting in the office "listening to telegrams being read or even reading various things which were actually none of his business but since he was who he was we didn't throw him out." Quickly bored by all the documents he was not supposed to be seeing, Jack focused his energies on building an interesting life for himself outside the embassy walls. He enjoyed a brief affair with a former mistress to the Duke of Kent, spent a weekend skiing at Val d'Isere, and shortly—after Easter—escaped to the lush nightlife of the Riviera, where he'd had so much fun the summer before with Kick and Joe and Clai Pell.

With Kick off in London and Clai at Princeton, Jack searched Cannes for another playmate. He found one in a man who would one day serve his brother Bobby with distinction in the Justice Department before being elevated (by President Kennedy) to the Supreme Court. By all accounts Jack was actually awestruck—a rare event for our self-confident hero—when first introduced to football great and Rhodes scholar Byron "Whizzer" White. Then in the midst of a tour of Europe following Oxford's spring term, White was a certified celebrity who had earned the name "Whizzer" at Colorado State because of his propensity for whizzing by members of opposing teams and scoring touchdown after touchdown.

The same age as Jack, White had been born in Fort Collins. He worked in the sugar beet fields during his childhood, and experienced a public school education. He lettered in football, basketball, and baseball at Colorado State, was Phi Beta Kappa, and graduated first in the class of 1938, of which he was president. Colorado's team, the Buffaloes, went unbeaten in White's senior year. The six-foot-two-inch, 180-pound halfback led the nation in rushing (with 1,121 yards) and scoring (with 122 points). By the time Colorado played Rice University in the Cotton Bowl on New Year's Day, 1938, White was widely considered the most popular football player in the United States. When he subsequently signed to play with the Pittsburgh Steelers, his $15,800 contract made him the Depression era's highest-paid professional football player. White startled sports fans one year later when he quit pro ball to accept his Rhodes scholarship.

Kick Kennedy had met White during a reception held at Rhodes House, Oxford, earlier in the spring. She came away unimpressed by the self-made White, who she said was at a disadvantage because he "had not gone to an Eastern college." Not inclined to Kick's snobbishness, Jack found in White just the sort of friend and playfellow he wanted to cultivate. Of course, Jack had always enjoyed the company of football stars and had roomed at Harvard with three such heroes: Torbert Macdonald, Ben Smith, and Charlie Houghton. He had even more in common, however, with Whizzer. The two shared a certain shrewd, cynical brilliance. Both voiced open skepticism of authority and conventional wisdom. More important, both were bitterly pessimistic and felt as though they were experiencing the last good days the world was to know. White commented that as he traveled about Europe he believed he was witnessing "the sun setting on a golden age that would never recur." Looking back years later, Kennedy expressed the same view: "You had the feeling of an era ending, and everyone had a very good time at the end."

Jack showed Whizzer all of Cannes' high and low delights. The two spent several weeks together before White took off in the direction of Germany and Jack departed to continue the tour that would take him as far away as distant Palestine before he briefly returned to London in June.

Jack wrote his father from Palestine shortly after the British published their White Paper of May 17. This now notorious document expressed the British intention to eventually set up a single independent Palestine state with limited Jewish immigration to be allowed until 1944, and no further Jewish immigration thereafter except with Arab consent. The plan, Jack told his father, "just won't work." He wrote that he wanted to give his father his impressions of the situation in Palestine while they were still fresh on his mind, "though you undoubtedly, if I know the Jews, know the 'whole' story. . . . During the [First World] war, the British Government, desiring both the assistance of the Jews and the Arabs, made separate promises to both, one in the MacMahon, the other in the Balfour declaration. . . . In considering the whole question now, it is useless to discuss which has the 'fairer' claim." Jack noted the "fundamental objections" to the White Paper in both the Arab and Jewish camps which, "while they are not stated publicly, are nevertheless . . . important. On the Jewish side, there is the desire for complete domination, with Jerusalem as the capital of their new land of milk and honey, with the right to colonize in Trans-Jordan." For their part, the Arabs "realize their [the Jews'] superiority and fear it." Jack added that the sympathy "of the people on the spot seems to be with the Arabs," in part because "the Jews have had, at least in some of their leaders, an unfortunately arrogant, uncompromising attitude."

.   .   .

WHIZZER WHITE had been among the Oxford students so profoundly underwhelmed by Ambassador Kennedy's performance the previous autumn. As both Whizzer and Jack must have been aware, the recent events in Czechoslovakia, Lithuania, and Albania had significantly lowered the par value of Kennedy's political stock. Seen in the light of Hitler's

latest outrages, Kennedy's penchant for appeasement seemed even more un-
generous and amoral than before. "Criticism of me had begun to grow in
the United States," the ambassador would recall. The State Department no
longer allowed him to make any speeches other than "talking about flowers,
birds and trees . . . but I did not want war." Aware that Roosevelt now routinely bypassed him in favor of direct communications with Chamberlain,
Halifax, and other British leaders, Kennedy nevertheless attempted to remain a "player" on the world stage. In so doing, he recklessly embarked on
one of the most foolish and self-destructive chapters in his ambassadorship.

For Joe, the problem of non-Bolshevik Europe remained—despite all
evidence to the contrary—economic rather than moral: a question of arbi-
trating supply and demand, achieving balanced budgets, and developing affluent markets. So far as Kennedy and many other American businessmen
were concerned, simple prosperity could be counted on to heal all the Western world's ills. Thus Kennedy became quickly enthusiastic when James
Mooney of General Motors—a fellow Irish-American Catholic millionaire—stopped in London that April after meetings with high-ranking Nazi
officials in Berlin and sought Kennedy's aid in securing a large American
loan to help underwrite Goering's Four-Year Plan. Amazingly, given the
Nazis' recent territorial aggressions, the ambassador told Mooney he would
do all he could to help the unlikely proposal come to fruition. For starters,
he agreed to meet in London on May 9 with the American-educated German economist Helmuth Wohlthat, then working as a special assistant to
Goering. (The two men hit it off. In fact, they got along so well that they
would continue to socialize for many years after the conclusion of World
War II.) When FDR heard of Kennedy's unauthorized encounter with
Goering's aide, he immediately and expressly forbade his ambassador to have
anything more to do with Wohlthat, or to try in any way to advance the
German gold loan request.

FDR grew even more angry when onetime Kennedy friend Felix Frankfurter, returning from a trip to England, told Harold Ickes he'd heard the
ambassador denounce FDR more than once in the drawing rooms of London, and that Kennedy was "perfectly certain he will be the compromise
candidate for President on the Democratic ticket next year." Kennedy did
not help himself when he told a reporter for the London publication *The
Week* that "the Democratic [party] policy of the United States is a Jewish
production" and "Roosevelt will fall in 1940."

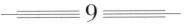

9

Upstart Ignoramus

Anxious for distraction during the spring of 1939, Ambassador Kennedy used his Hollywood contacts to get advance prints of new films. Kick often invited friends—among them Billy Hartington and several of his college chums—for private screenings. The ambassador grew annoyed on one occasion, during a film about the Great War, when he heard the young men speak with excitement about the likely coming fight with Germany—all of them apparently eager to get into battle. Their enthusiasm seemed to press a button in him, and he lost his cool. "See that?" he shouted during a scene showing dozens of Brit soldiers dead in their trenches. "That's what you'll look like if you go to war with Germany!" An awkward silence followed, and Kick wound up apologizing for her father.

Save for such moments as this, Kick and the other Kennedy women lived a life far removed from the realities of politics and international tensions through early 1939. In the course of one typical week, Kick and Eunice attended the London premier of *Wuthering Heights*, played tennis with movie star Spencer Tracy, and got fitted for the dresses in which they would assay the upcoming London Season. This was seventeen-year-old Eunice's year to "come out." The ambassador planned a gala for June 22 to rival that thrown for Kick and Rosemary the year before. (The highlight of Eunice's

Season—after her own coming out—was a June weekend spent at Blenheim Palace for a ball to present Lady Sara Spencer Churchill. Following the precedent set by Kick the previous year, Eunice traveled to Blenheim and other such destinations with her own personal maid.)

The youngest children continued their daily rounds at their various schools, the girls still at Roehampton and Bobby and Teddy commuting to the Sloane Street School for Boys. Sitting at an adjacent table when the king and queen came for dinner on May 4, Bobby and Teddy were too awestruck to be anything but well behaved. (During the meal, the queen asked Rose if she got up in the morning to see the boys off to their school. Rose answered that she most certainly did not. Then, to Rose's astonishment and humiliation, the queen announced that she usually emerged from her room, albeit half asleep, to bid the princesses good morning, and then went back to bed again.) Rose served the royal couple Virginia ham followed by strawberry shortcake—American fare designed to help the king and queen prepare for their upcoming visit to the United States. (A few weeks later, on the lawn of his home at Hyde Park, New York, President Roosevelt gave their royal highnesses hot dogs cooked on a barbecue.)

The Kennedys and the royal couple saw each other just one more time before the king and queen departed. They did not sit together, and had no chance to chat, on May 9 during a dinner held at Nancy Astor's London townhouse. "I went down to dinner with the Duke of Devonshire, Under-Secretary of State for Dominion Affairs," wrote Rose, dryly cataloging the presence of Billy Hartington's father without any further comment. She was, in fact, well aware, and increasingly disapproving, of Kick's flirtation with Billy.

Jack, in turn, rather liked Billy and was happy to spend time with him that June during a brief visit to London in the midst of his Continental wanderings. He did not, however, invite Hartington when several Kennedys—among them Kick—went to West London to watch Torb Macdonald race as a sprinter with the All-American team. As Jack well knew, Macdonald still nursed his old infatuation with Kick and would therefore not appreciate Hartington's presence.

After the competition, Torb delightedly accepted an invitation to stay at the ambassador's residence, where he could be close to the object of his desires. When Jack shortly asked Torb to join him on his continuing explorations of Europe—and even offered to help underwrite his friend's expenses—Macdonald had to think twice before accepting the offer, which would carry him away from Kick. However, the girl's frequent departures, and her announcement that she would soon join Joe Jr. and Hugh Fraser on an excursion to Madrid, seem to have cinched the deal for Torb. If he could not spend time with his favorite Kennedy—Kick—he'd resort to his usual fallback position and hang around with the runner-up. Torb and Jack started for Paris at the beginning of July and from there headed into Germany.

"I recall very well indeed," Macdonald told an interviewer years later, "the Ambassador saying—calling us in and saying—when we were in Germany, no matter what happened, not to cause any trouble and to bend over backwards to stay out of trouble. . . . He indicated that [the Germans] were very tough and paid no attention to laws and rules, and, if anything happened, just to back away." It is interesting, given this parental injunction, that Jack returned to the Munich Hofbrau House where he and Billings had been so annoyed by German bravado the year before. At first nervous and unhappy at being surrounded by belligerent, beer-swilling brownshirts, Macdonald was subsequently pleased when Jack encountered a familiar, friendly face in a far corner of the tavern.

After bouncing around different corners of Europe for several weeks, Whizzer White had decided to spend the summer in Munich reading Roman law and trying to improve his German. He recalled: "There were a couple of German fellows I horsed around with, and much of the time we would hang around the Hofbrau House, where a lot of American tourists used to go. Most of the young Germans I knew had already been in the army and were subject to recall. Naturally, there was a great deal of debating about war, because it was after the Munich settlement and on everybody's mind. When a couple of those German guys got recalled, that was a pretty good sign that the war was about to start."

White and Macdonald—the two football stars from modest circumstances—hit it off instantly. "We got along very well, all three of us," Macdonald remembered, "so we decided to take a tour of the city." They drove a car that had been lent to White by a British friend. ". . . we went by this monument to some beer hall hero, Worst Hessel or something, and we slowed down to take a look. They had a flame burning and they started to yell and at that time I didn't know who Worst Hessel was. . . ." The monument was to one Horst Wessel, a Nazi killed by Communists in 1930 and consequently transformed by Joseph Goebbels's propaganda machine into a secular saint of National Socialism. When Whizzer, Jack, and Torb cruised casually up to the martyr's eternal flame in a car bearing British license plates, they were subjected to some rough heckling and soon found themselves pelted with stones and bricks. "We were yelling back and they started throwing bricks at the car," Macdonald recounted. "So we drove the car away for a while, and I turned to Jack and said, 'What in the hell is wrong with them, what's this all about? We weren't doing anything, I mean, we weren't agitating people or doing anything.' . . . And this is the first time I ever heard Jack say it: he said, 'You know, how can we avoid having a world war if this is the way these people feel?' "

Leaving White behind in Munich, Jack and Torb journeyed to Italy and thence back to Paris, where, in early August, they hired a car and began to drive to Ambassador Kennedy's rented villa on the Riviera. They were halfway to Antibes when their car—driven by Jack at a high rate of speed—suddenly went off a shoulder, flipped upside down, and skidded thirty feet. Miraculously, both Jack and Torb walked away from the wreck, but Jack left it to Torb to pick up their belongings scattered along the highway. He found he could not bend over. His back, never good, was now instantly much worse.

Arriving at Cannes, Jack and Torb moved into a house that though large was already crowded with the presence of the ambassador, Rose, and most of the children. The only two missing were Rosemary (at her school in England) and Joe Jr. (on the road somewhere in Austria or Germany after having deposited Kick at Cannes following their visit with Hugh Fraser to Madrid).

Torb found Kick distracted, distant, and—worst of all—disinterested when he tried to romance her by the pool and on the beach. Her thoughts, it seemed, were elsewhere. She told her mother quite emphatically more than once, within hearing of both Jack and Torb, that she did not even want to be there. Rose insisted she stay, however, and spend time with the family rather than return to England and attend the enormous two-day party (August 15–16) being staged at Chatsworth by the Duke and Duchess of Devonshire to celebrate Billy Hartington's coming of age.

Billy had reached his maturity, twenty-one, the previous December, but festivities had been delayed out of respect for his recently deceased grandfather. The guest list for the Chatsworth celebration, numbering over two thousand, included not only titled aristocrats but also the Cavendishes' many tenants and employees. Far away from Chatsworth, on the lush French shoreline, neither Torb nor Jack, nor even Kick's good friend and houseguest Janie Kenyon-Slaney, could rouse her from her sulking. Her pout turned momentarily into a smile, however, on the 16th, when a Boston newspaper—perhaps erroneously, perhaps not—reported her and Billy's secret engagement: a rumor her father immediately denied.

Bored with Kick's dour mood, Jack and Torb had already taken off by the time the engagement story hit. They were in Vienna on the 14th, where Torb said his goodbyes to Jack and boarded a train for Budapest. Jack in turn traveled to Berlin by way of Nazi-controlled Prague: a city in crisis that the U.S. State Department had declared off-limits to U.S. tourists. Foreign Service Officer George F. Kennan recalled: "No trains were running, no planes were flying, no frontier stations existed. Yet in the midst of this confusion we received a telegram from the Embassy in London, the sense of which was that our Ambassador there, Mr. Joseph Kennedy, had chosen this time to send one of his young sons on a fact-finding tour around Europe, and it was up to us to find a means of getting him across the border and through the German lines so that he could include in his itinerary a visit to Prague. . . . We were furious. Joe Kennedy was not exactly known as a friend of the career services, and many of us, from what we had heard about him, cordially reciprocated this lack of enthusiasm. His son had no official status and was, in our eyes, obviously an upstart and ignoramus."

Something of a puritan, Kennan objected not only to the inopportune timing of Jack's visit but also to the young man's casual elegance, his propensity for nightlife, and his flirtatious nature. Still, though definitely a playboy, and certainly pampered and spoiled, Jack was by no standard an ignoramus. As we've already seen in previous letters quoted, Jack's jottings of this period reveal a serious, pragmatic student of current affairs. He was remarkably astute, for example, in writing to Lem Billings about the Danzig question:

It's been damn interesting and was up in Danzig for a couple of days. Danzig is completely Nazified, much heiling of Hitler, etc.

Talked with the Nazi heads and all the consuls up there. The situation there is complicated but roughly here it is:

1st. The question of Danzig and the corridor are inseparable. [The Germans] feel that both must be returned. If this is done then Poland is cut off completely from the sea.

If [the Poles] return just Danzig . . . [the Germans] could thus control Polish trade, as by means of guns they could so dominate Gdynia (see map) that they could scare all the Jew merchants into shooting their trade thru Danzig. However, aside from the dollar + chits angle—which is only secondary—there is the question of principle. The Germans don't give a good god damn what happens to Poland's trade—and they told me frankly that the best thing for Poland would be to come into a customs union with Germany. . . .

Poland is determined not to give up Danzig and you can take it as official that Poland will not give up Danzig and 2nd that she will not give Germany extra-territoriality rights in the corridor for the highways. She will offer compromises but never give up. What Germany will do if she decides to go to war—will be to try to put Poland in the position of being aggressor—and then go to work. Poland has an army of 4,000,000 who are damn good—but poorly equipped. The roads are bad however and can be destroyed which will nullify Germany's mechanical advantage and it takes one and a half to twice as many men to attack as to defend but remember France can't help, due to the Siegfried line in the west and England's fleet will be of little assistance, so Poland will be alone. But they are tough here and whether they can get help or not they will fight over Danzig—as they regard it first as symbolic + 2nd as the keystone.

An imperfect, hand-drawn map accompanied the letter. Beneath the rough outline of land and sea, Jack wrote: "The German fleet can blow up Gdynia while the Polish guns from Hell [an appropriately named peninsula north of Danzig] will blow up Danzig. Troops will come in from German + East Prussia and cut Poland off from the sea. This is very rough, and its impossible to set down the whole thing on paper but you can get an idea of what it is. Would suggest your reading Buelle's *Poland—Key to Europe*. Remember, however, the Poles are not Czechs + *they will fight*."

By contrast, Joe Jr.'s letters and diaries of the same period contain considerably less in the way of pragmatic insight. Ever the realist, Jack methodically and dispassionately analyzed the facts of the political and military situation in Europe as he found them. Joe, on the other hand, refused to take off the blinders bequeathed to him by his father. "Before Mr. Hull and Mr. Roosevelt ask me to go over and fight because an American ship is sunk or some tourist is killed by the Germans," he wrote in his travel diary, "I want them to answer me the following questions. What do they think would be the economic and political effect of German domination of Europe and having licked England and France? How much trade would we lose and how would it effect us? . . . Would the break up of the British Empire in itself be most dangerous for [us] or could we still retain our trading position to Germany after such break? . . . Do we want to get frightfully aroused by the treatment of the Jews when Cat[holics] and others were murdered more cruelly in Russia and in Republican Spain and not a word of protest came?"

.   .   .

It is unclear whether the upstart ignoramus and his brother Joe actually intended to rendezvous with each other in Berlin at the end of August, but rendezvous they did. Both were registered at the Hotel Excelsior on the 21st, the day Hitler and Stalin stunned the world by announcing the Nazi-Soviet Pact. The public text of the pact read as little more than a standard agreement of nonaggression and neutrality. As Chamberlain and FDR might well have guessed, however, the pact also contained a secret protocol that in effect partitioned not only Poland but also much of Eastern Europe. The Soviets were to take Finland, Estonia, Latvia, and Bessarabia, while the Nazis would get everything to the west of these regions, including Lithuania.

It is impossible to tell from the sole written record—a diary note made by his brother—whether Jack tagged along on the afternoon of the 21st when Joe Jr. went to visit Unity Mitford, the fourth daughter of Lord Redesdale. Like her sister Diane, Unity had long ago embraced fascism as a concept and Hitler as an ideal. (Diane had married Sir Oswald Mosley—the scion of an impoverished aristocratic household and leader of the British Union of Fascists—in Germany in 1938. The couple's reception had been held at the home of Joseph Goebbels. Hitler himself attended.) Two other sisters, Nancy and Jessica, espoused socialism and Communism, respectively, while only Pamela joined Kick's friend Debo—the girlfriend of Billy Hartington's brother, Andrew Cavendish—in loyalty to the class and system in which the Mitfords had been raised.

Although the Mitfords boasted an ancient lineage, their title was barely two generations old. More important, the family stood on the verge of financial collapse in the late 1930s. In fact, the House of Lord Redesdale rode the very cutting edge of the British aristocracy's steady decline, and all the Mitford children had grown up warily cognizant of the fact that they would be forced, come adulthood, to make their own way in the world without inherited wealth. Aspiring writer Nancy Mitford chronicled part of the British aristocracy's demise during the late thirties when she edited two volumes telling the story of one branch of her forebears, the Stanleys, once among the largest landholders in Cheshire. "Alderly," Nancy wrote, "where they lived for five hundred years, sees them no more—the house has been pulled down, and the estate is a dormitory suburb of Manchester."

While Nancy and Jessica Mitford reacted to the slow liquidation of the aristocracy with a move to the left, Diane and Unity took the same phenomena as impetus for their move to the far right. Having resided in Germany for five years, Unity Mitford proudly announced herself a committed Nazi who frankly worshiped Adolf Hitler, her longtime friend. (Commenting on Unity, sister Nancy called her "Head of bone and heart of stone.") Hitler told reporters the blond-headed Unity was "the perfect Aryan type," but Joe considered her fat and commented in his diary on her bad teeth. Neither did she impress him with her personality. "[She] seems," he wrote, "to be in a state of high nervous tension in which she has no great interest in other things but thinks only of the Führer and his work." She constantly referred to the German leader as "the Führer," and looked askance at Joe when he called the dictator "Hitler"—"as though I was taking his name in vain. . . . She is the most fervent Nazi imaginable, and is probably in love with Hitler." Later that same day—or perhaps at the same time his brother chatted with Mitford—Jack visited the United States embassy, where Captain Alan Kirk—the American chargé d'affaires, Joe Kennedy's former naval attaché, and a man who would figure again in the life of Jack Kennedy—handed him a note that was "eyes only" for his father. The note told the elder Kennedy to count on war within a week now that the Nazis no longer had to look over their shoulders at what the Soviets were up to.

The man for whom Kirk's note was intended had been relaxing with his family at Cannes up until the 21st. Ambassador Kennedy returned to London that afternoon nearly immediately after hearing of the agreement between the Nazis and the Russians, leaving Rose and the children behind. Calling at 10 Downing Street, Kennedy found Chamberlain depressed, downcast, and spiritually beaten. The pact, the PM explained, meant the imminent and inevitable invasion of Poland followed by the war he had struggled for so long to avoid. He shook his head no when Kennedy, characteristically, suggested he try making further concessions to Hitler. "I have done everything that I can think of, Joe," he said, "but it looks as if all my work has been of no avail. I can't fly again; that was good only once. . . . The thing that is frightful is the futility of it all. The Poles can't be saved. All that the English can do is to wage a war of revenge that will mean the entire destruction of Europe." Returning from this meeting, Kennedy almost immediately wired Hull with the suggestion that FDR lean on the Polish leadership to compromise.

Cabling Rose on the 22nd, the ambassador told her to gather the family, leave France, and get back to London on the fastest possible schedule. Kick and her houseguest Janie Kenyon-Slaney were still in their tennis whites when, on the 23rd, they joined Rose, Louella Hennessey, and the children on the train that would take them to Paris and thence to the Channel ferry. At first Kick and Janie cracked jokes about the absurdity of the evacuation. They stopped laughing, however, when they began to pass trainloads of French troops heading inland toward Poland. They arrived in London on the 24th, the same day the ambassador issued a statement suggesting that all Americans without urgent business in England return home ASAP. "Accommodations are now available on most vessels," he wrote. "The same may not be true in another day or two."

Kennedy visited Downing Street again on the 25th, at which time he was shown a secret communiqué from Sir Neville Henderson, the British ambassador to Berlin, in which Henderson quoted Hitler as saying it was useless for the British to make an issue of Poland, since he and the Russians had already agreed "to cut it up." When asked by Chamberlain and Halifax what he thought should be their next step, Kennedy revealed yet again his fundamental misunderstanding of the historical forces and national ambitions at work in Europe. Mistaking Hitler's thirst for power and territorial advantage with a thirst for economic advantage, Kennedy—by his own account—told Chamberlain: "You have to make your solution more attractive to Germany than what she is trying now to get out of Poland. Do it this way. Propose a general settlement that will bring Germany economic benefits more important than the territorial annexation of Danzig. Get the United States now to say what they would be willing to do in the cause of international peace and prosperity. After all, the United States will be the largest beneficiary of such a move. To put in a billion or two now will be worth it, for if it works we will get it back and more."

At a meeting a few days later, the 31st, Chamberlain—apparently either forgetting the gist of Henderson's cable or lapsing into unreality—said the whole crisis could be short-circuited if only the Poles could be convinced to be "reasonable" on the topic of Danzig and the corridor. (Acting on a suggestion from Kennedy, the British had—according to the ambassador—"belatedly [and] almost hysterically" endeavored to persuade the Poles to let Chamberlain and Halifax do their negotiating for them. The Poles, quite likely recalling what happened to the Czechs when they granted Chamberlain similar license, refused to go along.) In any event, the Poles were not in a mood to negotiate. "The unfortunate thing is," Chamberlain had told Kennedy earlier that same day, ". . . there is a great body of opinion in England, headed by men like Churchill and Eden, who are telling the Poles to give up nothing. . . . They are wrong. If they persist, it will mean war."

10

Fortune Subsiding

JACK CAUGHT A FLIGHT out of Berlin on the 23rd. Joe, however, remained in the German capital for several days, seemingly fascinated by the sudden and rapid mobilization of the Reich, the staunch comradeship of the people, and the Wagnerian rhetoric of the Nazi leaders. He departed on September 1, the same day 1.8 million German troops invaded Poland on three fronts: from East Prussia in the north, Germany in the west, and Slovakia in the south. The Germans sent 2,600 tanks against Poland's 180, and more than 2,000 aircraft against Poland's total of 420 fighters. The Luftwaffe bombed not only towns and cities, but also fleeing refugees. The Poles in turn rushed to get their army into the field—something they'd refrained from doing sooner because of Chamberlain's insistence that a full Polish mobilization would be viewed by Hitler as provocative and aggressive.

Now, with Hitler being quite provocative, the world watched and waited for Britain and France to honor their previous guarantees of Polish borders. The invasion had gone on for thirty-eight hours when, in the House of Commons, acting Labour Party leader Arthur Greenwood and Liberal Party leader Sir Archibald Henry Macdonald Sinclair rose to query Britain's delay in formally taking Poland's side. Chamberlain, meanwhile, searched frantically for a way to disavow Britain's obligation to Poland and thus take one giant step back from the precipice. With Kennedy's encouragement, the PM briefly tinkered with a plan for a five-power conference (headed by Mussolini) to arbitrate the Danzig question and, in essence, sanction Hitler's incursion. Thus, in the tradition of Munich, Chamberlain grasped for yet one more ignoble peace. This plan fell through, however, in the early morning of the 3rd, at which point Chamberlain had no choice but to send Hitler an unambiguous ultimatum. A communiqué went out assuring the Führer of war with Britain in the absence of Hitler's immediate withdrawal from Poland, the Nazis' announcement of same to be issued no later than 11 a.m. London time.

Early on the 3rd—a Sunday—"Ding Dong" Jack told the ambassador of some young British fliers he'd met at a bar the night before, all of them disgusted with Chamberlain's hesitation in the face of German aggression. "These boys and all the rest of the country and those smart people in the USA who wanted England to fight will soon see what Chamberlain was trying to save them from," the ambassador wrote in his diary. Learning from British officials of Chamberlain's last-minute communiqué, and also that Chamberlain would broadcast to the nation at 11:15 a.m., Kennedy decided to skip 11-a.m. mass. Rose, characteristically, opted to go to church. She would later comment on the noticeable absence of men from the service, and the overabundance of women.

Kennedy telephoned Chamberlain just a few minutes after the broadcast, in which the PM finally conceded that war was at hand. Their talk was brief, the PM expressing his sadness over his failed efforts to win peace for the world. "The Prime Minister," Kennedy wired Hull shortly thereafter, "has just broadcast that no undertaking having been received from the German government to withdraw its troops from Poland, Great Britain is in consequence at war with Germany."

As if on cue, the practical realities of war began to make themselves felt just moments after Kennedy dictated his cable to the secretary of state. The ambassador, his wife, and the eldest children were dressing to go hear Chamberlain address Parliament when an air raid siren began to sound. Kennedy immediately issued orders for the staff to leave the Princes Gate residence and go across the street to the store of the society dressmaker Molyneaux, who had a sizable basement. (There was no basement or bomb shelter of any size at the ambassador's residence, funds for same having been recently denied by Assistant Secretary of State George Messersmith.)

There, at Molyneaux's, they crouched for a dismal and tense half hour— no enemy planes swooping, no bombs falling—until the siren at last sounded all clear, freeing the ambassador and his family to rush down to Parliament. We have a photograph of Joe Jr., Jack, and Kick walking briskly toward the House of Commons, where they, along with Mrs. Kennedy, would sit in the Strangers' Gallery to hear Chamberlain's formal declaration of war. They were taking their seats—and the ambassador was just in the process of joining his fellow diplomats—at 12:05 when another air raid warning came. "We all went down to [the] shelter in [the] House of Parliament," the ambassador recalled. "This [warning] proved to be very short and the *all clear* whistle came quickly and we all marched back." The ambassador missed most of Chamberlain's remarks, however, because a parliamentary attendant summoned him to take a call from FDR's assistant, Missy LeHand, who asked him to call the president that afternoon.

Kennedy returned to his seat just in time to hear Chamberlain announce his regret over his many miscalculations with regard to Hitler. "Everything that I have worked for, everything that I have hoped for, everything that I have believed in during my public life has crashed in ruins." The prime minister also had one other thing to announce: the formation of a war cabinet to include Winston Churchill as first lord of the admiralty.

Leaving Parliament, Kennedy bumped into Conservative MP and sometime journalist Arthur Beverly Baxter, who mentioned that his wife and children were in Canada and that he intended to leave them there. Lady Astor, who overheard the conversation, complained after Baxter had left that he should make his family come to England and suffer the same dangers and face the same hardships as everyone else. Astor, Kennedy reported to his diary, was sobbing as she said it, and complained out loud about the prospect of losing her five sons. Subsequently, Kennedy returned to Princes Gate with the family, listened to a speech by the king supporting Chamberlain, and telephoned Hull and the president, in that order.

The phone call to FDR did not go well. As Roosevelt made a point of informing Joseph Alsop, Kennedy sounded very much like a blubbering child during their brief exchange. Recounting the conversation for his friend and cousin, FDR mimicked Kennedy's distraught, sobbing, hysterical repetition of the phrase "It's the end of the world, the end of everything." (Interestingly, at just about the same time on the same day, Unity Mitford contemplated the advent of war with similar distress. Unstable to begin with, Mitford simply could not abide the thought of war between her homeland and her idealized Aryan nation. During the same hour Kennedy made his tear-filled report to his president, Mitford took a gun from a drawer in her Berlin apartment, put it to her head, and pulled the trigger. The bullet lodged in her skull but failed to kill. She would be returned to England through neutral channels in 1940 and would eventually die from complications of the wound in 1948, at the age of thirty-three.)

Others, weary after struggling against the possibility of war for so long, now embraced the fight, glad for the new challenges it would offer. Halifax was one of these. Writing to Hull on the 4th, Kennedy reported Halifax's comment that the impending fight "reminded him of a dream he once had in which he was being tried for murder. When he was finally convicted and found guilty he was surprised at the feeling of relief that came over him. Now it was very much the same. He had planned in every way to stave off a world war and had worked himself into a sad state of health. Now that he had failed he found himself refreshed for the new struggle."

In the same dispatch, Kennedy told Hull the Allies had thus far refrained from bombing Germany or its occupied territories and were "very carefully watching to not give the Germans an opportunity to say that the British are killing women and children first and Germany is finally forced to fight back. . . . In the first bombings on the Western Front, the British feel there is great danger [of offending] world public opinion, particularly the United States. . . . As a matter of fact, I think a good deal of this war's strategy is directed with one eye toward the United States." Thus the British refrained, wrote Kennedy, despite pressure to do otherwise from the French, who, unlike the British, were currently "leaning on the Siegfried line" with two million men.

As Kennedy perhaps knew, Britain had secretly promised the Poles they would only have to fight a defensive campaign for two weeks, during which the Allies would supposedly gather their forces and prepare to attack German forces in Poland from the west. In point of fact, the schedule for Britain's mobilization was based on British intelligence indicating the Poles could only hold out for a maximum of two weeks. The maneuvering of

Chamberlain's government was entirely cynical. When September 14 came and went with the beleaguered Polish troops still standing, Chamberlain continued to hold back, intent on not shedding British blood in defense of what he openly called the lost cause of Poland.

One is tempted to wonder how lost it really was, and what might have happened had the British and French forces come to Poland's aid in a timely manner. Despite Hitler's "Blitzkrieg" tactics and a secondary invasion by Germany's ally Russia from the east on the 17th, the outgunned and out-manned Poles would manage to hold out for a full month before finally capitulating. In that time they would inflict more damage on the Germans than the British and French combined in the year 1940. In the end, the Poles would make Hitler pay dearly for his conquest of their country. Poland would wind up costing the Nazis fifty thousand men, 697 planes, and 993 tanks and armored cars. (Jack Kennedy could not have been more correct when he'd told Lem Billings: "Remember . . . the Poles are not Czechs + *they will fight.*")

·   ·   ·

FOR ALL OF CHAMBERLAIN'S concern about public relations, it was the Germans who scraped heavily against the side of world opinion when they inadvertently killed their first British and American civilians during the first twenty-four hours of the war. Ambassador Kennedy was in bed at two-thirty on the morning of the 4th when his phone rang. An anonymous voice from the British Foreign Office informed the groggy diplomat that the British liner *Athenia*, bound for Canada from Glasgow, had been torpedoed and sunk approximately two hundred miles west of the Hebrides. The ship carried 1,347 souls, among them 311 Americans. Of the 118 dead, twenty-eight carried U.S. passports. (As Allied investigators would discover after the war, the sinking of the *Athenia* was not a provocation but rather a mistake. German submariners thought they were shooting torpedoes at one of the Royal Navy's auxiliary cruisers.)

"We spent a rainy, cold night in lifeboats," remembers one American woman who, as a nineteen-year-old student from Iowa State University, survived the tragedy. "Many hours passed before a British destroyer came out of the fog to rescue us. Our boat had been leaking, and we'd been using our shoes to bail water. It was a very rough few hours and we were all considerably shaken, considerably frightened, and very, very tired. We were at Glasgow a good day or more before anyone from the U.S. Embassy came, and then it was this kid who looked younger than I was."

It is unclear why Ambassador Kennedy chose to send twenty-two-year-old Jack to look after the interests of the *Athenia*'s 283 American survivors. Jack looked eighteen, possessed no authority to speak or act for the United States government, and had no experience in dealing with such matters. Many survivors did not know at first what to make of the lad whom the London *Daily Telegraph & Morning Post* identified inaccurately as "the 18-year-old son of the United States Ambassador." Jack arrived in Glasgow on the 7th to face what the *Telegraph* called "a determined audience of his fellow Americans who had survived the torpedoing" and to hear "their polite but firm demands for some assurance of adequate protection when, next week, they sail for home in a specially chartered freighter now on its way from New York."

All went reasonably well until Jack, as instructed, informed the group they would not have convoy protection on the American vessel now scheduled to bear them home. Many of Jack's listeners—according to the *Telegraph* reporter—became highly annoyed when they heard the "schoolboy" who had been sent to tend to their wants explain "that President Roosevelt had said there was no need for a convoy, as American ships would not be attacked." An American observer described their reaction as "a storm of protest burst[ing] from the refugees. . . . Many Americans, still bearing bruises, burns and other traces of their ordeal on the *Athenia*, began to shout, 'You can't trust the German Navy! You can't trust the German government!' "

By all accounts, Jack remained calm, eloquent, and confident in the face of these protests. In fact, more than one journalist commented on Jack's grace under pressure—not to mention the charm, courtesy, and genuine concern with which he dealt with the survivors. The reporter for the London *Evening News* dubbed Jack an "Ambassador of mercy" who "spent one of the busiest days of his young life today, going from hotels to hospitals in Glasgow, visiting the *Athenia*'s American survivors. His boyish charm and natural kindliness persuaded those who he had come to comfort that America was indeed keeping a benevolent and watchful eye on them. . . . Mr. Kennedy displayed a wisdom and sympathy of a man twice his age."

This gracious young man's father would later claim in his memoirs that he had personally rejected the survivors' "impossible and unnecessary" request for a convoy. Documents from the time, however, tell a different tale. On the advice of his son, the ambassador in fact encouraged Cordell Hull to supply the requested naval escort, if only for PR purposes. "Yesterday my son Jack went up to Glasgow to contact the people rescued from the *Athenia*," he wrote Hull on the 8th. "He came back with the very definite impression that they are in a terrible state of nerves and that to put them on a ship going back to America for seven days without a convoy or some kind of protection would land them back in New York in such a state that the publicity and criticism of the Government would be unbelievable. Also remember that a great deal of attention is being paid to these people and they are beginning to feel terribly important and they are having an awful lot to say, most of which the censor is not permitting to go through, particularly criticism of our Government."

Jack spent the next two weeks before his return to Harvard working diligently in the interest of the *Athenia* survivors, doing his best to tend to their needs as graciously and promptly as possible. In this he found himself frequently at odds with the embassy's career bureaucrats, through whom the paperwork of repatriation needed to flow. He quickly came to loathe what he characterized as their "grudging, mindless, mechanized approach" to the business of helping people.

· · ·

WITH THE ADVENT OF WAR, the formerly raucous and brilliant London of the luminous night changed dramatically and immediately, becoming the far more subdued London of the hushed blackout. A frustrated and annoyed Kick—about to be sent home and profoundly unhappy about it—wandered through that absolute darkness during one of the few evenings she had left in Great Britain, then went home to record the stroll in her diary. Walking in the pitch black, she bumped against a lamppost beside which lurked a steel-helmeted blackout warden, his gas mask slung over his shoulder. Little green crosses winked dimly in the mist at intersections, where she crossed carefully, watching out for the few cars that prowled about the town with veiled headlamps. The once luminous Piccadilly and Leicester Squares were now completely dark, their theaters and restaurants surrounded by sandbags. Beautiful Kensington Gardens wore a bracelet of trenches filled at night with soldiers who pointed various gadgets up toward the stars, their ambition to detect incoming enemy aircraft as early as possible. It was, Kick wrote, "a new London, a London that looks like Barcelona before the bombs fell."

Joe Jr. returned to the embassy with a black eye after a similar excursion. No one believed his explanation—that he had walked into a lamppost—until the next morning when the paper ran a story about hundreds bumping into trees, falling off curbs, and being hit by autos. When the first nighttime air raid siren sounded, Kick jumped out of bed, seized her gas mask, and, "offering my soul to the Lord, ran downstairs where the rest of the family stood ordering one another about, and trying at the same time to put on gas masks." Joined by their servants, the Kennedys went across the street to the Molyneaux establishment. Air raid wardens ran about the streets, issuing orders and rushing people into shelters. "After 40 minutes the *all-clear* signal sounded and everyone murmured a prayer of thanks," Kick wrote. "An auxiliary fireman said that planes had been seen off the East coast, which later turned out to be English."

As the nightly blackouts began, so too did the evacuations from London and other major population centers. All together more than 750,000 schoolchildren and teachers joined in the evacuation, along with nearly 500,000 mothers with children under five, 11,000 expectant mothers, and 7,000 of the blind and otherwise infirm. Jack spent the better part of a day at Euston Station, witnessing the often wrenching farewells between youngsters and their parents. "The big men of Berlin and London sit and confidently give their orders," he wrote, "and it is these kids—so far as I can see—who are among the first casualties, emotionally at least. Someday the children of Berlin will be loaded on to trains for their safety, and the big men on both sides will be just as culpable."

It seemed all of London took notice on the 5th, when President Roosevelt—as required by American law—activated the arms embargo provision stipulated in the Neutrality Act, forbidding the sale of American arms to belligerents. "[The British] feel . . ." Ambassador Kennedy wrote FDR on the 10th, "that America has talked a lot about her sympathies, but, when called on for action, have only given assistance to Britain's enemy." Still, said Kennedy, "I think that we will have to exercise the greatest caution. . . . Because, of course, [England] wants to drag us in. And my own impression is that if by any chance she should succeed, the burden will be placed more completely on our shoulders by 100% than it was in 1917."

The ambassador visited with the king and queen on the 9th, and met with Home Secretary Sir Samuel Hoare later the next day. The king—as Kennedy reported in a joint dispatch to Hull and FDR dated the 11th—was worried about the fact that "within a relatively brief period, possibly three or four weeks, Poland will have been liquidated by Herr Hitler and then certainly a proposal will be made by him [Hitler] to France and England to put a stop to this war and to arrive at some understanding." Hoare said he was concerned with the very same issue. "He [Hoare] is positively of the opinion that the gravest fact confronting the world today will be the proposal to abandon the fight which he feels will without question be presented within the next month or so by the Reich to Britain."

As Hoare advised Kennedy, if the ruling party considered any sort of understanding with the Reich it would most likely mean that the party would be put out of power. Still, if war continued and the present government was maintained on a war basis, it would eventually—in Kennedy's view—lead to the complete social, financial, and economic breakdown of Great Britain. With the PM in no position politically to make peace with Hitler, there might soon, wrote Kennedy, "be a point when the President himself may work out plans for world peace. Now this opportunity may never arise, but as a fairly practical fellow all my life, I believe that it is entirely conceivable that the President can get himself in a spot where he can save the world. . . ." In short, the United States was in the ideal position to sell out Great Britain and force her into peacemaking mode by withholding economic support.

FDR told Jim Farley the ambassador had just sent him the "silliest message" he had ever received. The President was more specific in the comments he addressed to Henry Morgenthau, Jr.: "Joe has been an appeaser and will always be an appeaser. . . . If Germany and Italy made a good peace offer tomorrow, Joe would start working on the King and his friend the Queen and from there on down to get everybody to accept it." (It was in fact not likely the ambassador could sway the king, who wrote him on the 12th: "As I see it, the USA, France and the British Empire are the three really free peoples in the world, and two of these great democracies are now fighting against all that we three countries hate and detest, Hitler and his Nazi regime and all that it stands for.")

Back in the States, Hull responded to Kennedy's dispatch for both himself and Roosevelt: "This Government, so long as the present European conditions continue, sees no opportunity nor occasion for any peace move to be introduced by the President of the United States. The people of the United States would not support any move for peace initiated by this Government that would consolidate or make possible a survival of a regime of force and aggression." Two days later, on the 13th, Roosevelt summoned Congress to convene on September 21 for a special session to consider revision of the Neutrality Act to allow arms sales to the United Kingdom. Writing to King George VI of Roosevelt's action, Kennedy the diplomat said it reflected what "many" Americans wanted: "to help England and France economically, but not to send American troops to Europe."

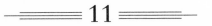

11

A Combination of
the Holy Ghost and
Jack Dempsey

AMBASSADOR KENNEDY booked Rose, Kick, Eunice, and Bobby to embark for New York aboard the U.S. liner *Washington* on September 12. (They found conditions on board cramped and uncomfortable. "People are sleeping in the lounge, swimming pool, gymnasium, in fact everywhere thinkable . . ." Eunice wrote her father. "Nobody has their bags, and Kick and I wear the same costume for breakfast, lunch, and supper but then, so does everybody else. . . .") The rest of the younger children followed a few days later on another U.S.-flagged ship, accompanied by Louella Hennessey. During a goodbye party at the embassy, Kennedy made a few brief remarks, proposed a toast, and then predicted England was going to be badly thrashed. Joe Jr.—scheduled to start shortly at Harvard Law School—set off on the British ship *Mauretania* as part of a convoy on the 18th, the same day German and Soviet forces met up at Brest-Litovsk in Poland. Perhaps shaken by his conversations with *Athenia* survivors, Jack, on his way back to Harvard for his senior year, chose to avoid the chilly waters of the Atlantic altogether and took Pan Am's new flying boat, the *Yankee Clipper*, to New York on the 19th.

Once Jack was gone, only Rosemary, the Moores, and the ambassador remained behind—the Moores in their little cottage, and Rosemary at her school in Hereford, now with a full-time companion, Dorothy Gibbs. "She is much happier when she sees the children [her brothers and sisters] just casually," Joe wrote Rose at about this time. "For everyone peace of mind, particularly hers, she shouldn't go on vacation or anything else with them. . . . She must never be at home for her sake as well as everyone else's." Over the previous year Rosemary had become increasingly frustrated, upset, and depressed in the company of her energetic family. Unable to keep up with the fast-paced gaiety of her brothers and sisters, Rosemary frequently lapsed into prolonged sulks punctuated by violent outbursts. As a consequence, she had hardly been in the company of the family at all since the previous Christmas at St. Moritz.

Although he did not frequently avail himself, Kennedy had ample opportunity to visit his daughter. Wary of the threat of bombing, the ambassador now all but abandoned the London house and spent the majority of his evenings at Wall Hall, Watford, an old abbey not far from Rosemary's school that the J. P. Morgan family had restored years before and then given, along with the Knightsbridge residence, to the U.S. government for the use of American ambassadors. A limo carried him to and from the London embassy, and now the same British newspapers that had greeted the Kennedys so fondly a year and a half earlier dryly noted not only the family's fast exit but also the ambassador's own equally swift removal to the hinterlands.

Other American diplomats found themselves closer to the firing line. When Kennedy dialed up the embassy in Paris on the 17th, Bullitt reported he'd just spoken to Anthony Drexel Biddle, U.S. ambassador in Poland, who had described terrible bombing and several close calls for him and his wife, the copper heiress and occasional journalist Margaret Thompson Shulze Biddle. Bullitt sounded ready to go to war against both the Germans and the Russians, and equally likely to wage war on Lindbergh, who, back in Washington, was actively lobbying against Roosevelt's proposed change in the Neutrality Act. "That son of a bitch," said Bullitt. "He wants to be the Führer in the U.S." Bullitt added that if there wound up being a filibuster of the measure—as threatened by Senator William Borah and other isolationists—he'd go home and "stop at nothing" to get it through. "You've never seen me in a fight. I'll lay that opposition low. I'll drag Borah's prostate over the front page of the papers." When an assistant took the phone away from Bullitt, Joe commented: "Your boss is quite excited." "He'll cool down," replied the aide.

"I talk to Bullitt occasionally," Joe wrote Rose soon after. "He is more rattle-brained than ever. His judgment is pathetic and I am afraid of his influence on FDR because they think alike on many things." In the same letter, Joe told Rose he was taking pains to get all the departments of the embassy organized to function efficiently without him. "So around Dec. 1 you might suggest to Johnny Burns he might drop a line to Franklin that he should send for me to come home. After all Joe Grew came home from Japan when Hell was popping in the Far East. . . ."

· · ·

THE WAR STOPPED FOR A TIME, and seemed to hover in a state of suspended animation, after the fall of Poland in early October. The Führer's troops stood poised on the Maginot Line, the "invulnerable" groundworks erected by France along the German border, but the Germans showed no immediate signs of belligerency toward either France or England. Advocates for peace took heart when the Germans refrained from amassing troops on either the Belgian or the Dutch border. Air raids upon London—always a threat—did not materialize. Still, Europe was at war, despite the lull that everyone knew could not last forever.

"England and France can't quit," Kennedy wrote FDR at the end of September, "whether they would like to or not and I am convinced, because I live here, that England will go down fighting. Unfortunately, I am one who does not believe that is going to do the slightest bit of good in this case." Kennedy told FDR that the idea France and England—particularly England—were opposing Germany for the sake of Poland was a ruse. The truth of the matter, so far as Kennedy saw it, was that the British were fighting the Huns "just as they fought them twenty-five years ago" simply because "forty-five million Britons controlling the greatest far-flung maritime empire in the world and eighty million Germans dominating continental Europe haven't learned to live together peacefully."

The difference this time was that England was bankrupt politically and economically: the empire on the ropes. What was more, Kennedy did not see the current war changing the direction of what he viewed as Britain's inevitable diminution. "England passed her peak as a world power some years ago and has been steadily on the decline. War, regardless of the outcome, will merely hasten the process." After it was all over, no matter who won, "democracy as we now conceive it in the United States will not exist in France and England. . . ." The ambassador's recommendation? Since Britain did not stand a "Chinaman's chance" against Hitler, Americans should act without "sentimentality and look to our own vital interests." In the end, a new Great Britain dominated by Nazi Germany would wind up consuming as much in the way of American goods as the old, archaic Britain ruled by the Crown and an inefficient Parliament. The revised Britain might even be an improvement, as it would not include men like Churchill, the new first lord of the admiralty in Chamberlain's war cabinet, who—as Kennedy told Rose in a private note—had "energy and brains but *no* judgment."

Kennedy became enraged when, in early October, he found himself relegated to the role of messenger boy between FDR and the man with no judgment. A sealed diplomatic pouch arrived at the embassy from the president, with orders that it be delivered unopened to the honorable Mr. Churchill. A day later, Churchill summoned Kennedy to the Admiralty, where he read him FDR's note. Roosevelt expressed his delight with Churchill's appointment and invited the first lord to use the American diplomatic pouch should he ever want to send the president "something personal." This, Kennedy fumed in his diary, was an example of Roosevelt's "conniving mind. . . . It's a rotten way to treat his Ambassador and I think shows him up to the other people. I am disgusted."

Kennedy came away from his meeting with Churchill carrying one sentence to be transmitted to FDR: "The Naval person will not fail to avail himself of the invitation and he is honored by the message." He also came away with a reinforced negative image of Churchill, who had spent a great amount of time during the meeting paying lip service to neutrality and the importance of keeping the United States out of the war. "I can't help feeling he's not on the level," Kennedy wrote in his diary. "He is just an actor and a politician. He always impressed me that he'd blow up the American Embassy and say it was the Germans if it would get the U.S. in. . . . I don't trust him."

Neither, of course, did Kennedy trust Roosevelt, nor Roosevelt him. Both, however, still pretended to hold the other in high regard, and each continued to try to use and influence the other. When Kennedy's friend the press baron Lord Beaverbrook called at the White House, FDR made a point of complimenting the ambassador for his smarts and fortitude, knowing full well his comments would get back to Kennedy. "Incidentally," the ambassador wrote FDR on November 3, "Beaverbrook told me in his conversations with you, you were most complimentary in discussing me and I am deeply grateful to you for this. One's influence in this Country is primarily dependent on how they think one stands with the President." Kennedy, in turn, enthusiastically endorsed Beaverbrook's opinion that "only one man can save the world, not only in attaining peace, but in planning for the future, and that man is yourself. . . . at the minute, you are a combination of the Holy Ghost and Jack Dempsey."

One's influence in this Country is primarily dependent on how they think one stands with the President. Whether he realized it or not, Joe Kennedy's influence in the British corridors of power was now virtually nonexistent. Even Chamberlain claimed to be outraged by Kennedy's defeatist views as so frequently uttered and just as frequently noted by informants and eavesdroppers for Whitehall, which now kept close tabs on the ambassador. The Foreign Office minute books began to fill with the collected remarks of the American envoy. The contents of the minute books—these "Kennediana" as some Foreign Office staffers dubbed the prose—would remain classified for thirty-five years.

In one of the most damning of a dozen or more damning entries, Charles Peake of the Foreign Office transcribed a conversation with American reporter William Hillman—a close Kennedy associate—who described Kennedy as a "a professing Catholic who loathed Hitler and Hitlerism almost, though perhaps not quite as much as he loathed Bolshevism. . . . He was not amenable to reason, his argument being that Hitler and the Nazis could not have lasted forever and that there was bound to be a change in regime in Germany one day if we had only let it alone." On another page, John Balfour wrote: "I wish that I could resist the feeling that Mr. Kennedy is thinking all the time about (1) his own financial position, and (2) his political future." The minute books contain Kennedy's *bon voyage* party prognostication that Britain would be badly thrashed, and numerous accounts of similar utterances made to Britons high and low. Alongside this catalog of undiplomatic utterances, Foreign Office officials penned their comments and suggestions on how to deal with the American emissary, who they now saw as a threat to British hopes for American cooperation and support.

Some Foreign Office officials thought a complaint should be made to Roosevelt through Lord Lothian, the new British ambassador to Washington who had just succeeded Lindsay. Sir Berkeley Gage disagreed. "A complaint might make him shut up," wrote Gage, "but in that case we shall neither know what he is thinking nor what he is telling the U.S. Government." Whitehall eventually sent Lothian several quotes from Kennedy's conversations in October. "Kennedy has been adopting a most defeatist attitude in his talk with a number of private individuals," wrote a Foreign Office staffer. "The general line which he takes in these conversations as reported to us is that Great Britain is certain to be defeated in the war, particularly on account of her financial weakness." While not instructing Lothian to say anything to FDR yet, the ambassador's superiors put him on notice this might be necessary in the future. The whole exchange must have been an interesting one for Lothian. A longtime appeaser whose home, Blickling Hall in Suffolk, had sometimes been called "the second Cliveden," Lothian was a friend of Kennedy's and a man who believed Britain should energetically pursue a separate negotiated peace with Hitler on the fastest possible schedule, leaving the balance of Europe to fend for itself.

. . .

JOE JR. SETTLED IN at Cambridge at the end of September to begin the big grind of first-year Harvard Law School. He took rooms (for $50 a month) in the Bay State Apartments at 1572 Massachusetts Avenue, and promptly recruited the first two of what would prove a succession of roommates. Howard Clarke, one alum of Joe's apartment who went on to become president of American Express, recalled him as "Goodlooking, articulate, attractive, energetic. A very tough guy. Just a little bit unfeeling; he wouldn't have been elected the most popular man in our class." Another roommate, Tom Bilodeau, remembered Joe as tightfisted and brusque, with an annoying need to set and enforce household agendas, schedules, and rules. A third graduate of the Bay State Apartments, Tom Killefer, recollected Joe's working like a slave to keep up with the work at Harvard Law School, where he just barely held his own despite constant tutoring from his father's good friend Judge John J. Burns.

Shortly after the start of classes, Joe went on a popular local radio program to describe his experiences in Spain, the blackout, and the ongoing evacuation of Londoners to the countryside. He wrote his father that nearly everyone he encountered seemed against American entry in the war, with the one exception being his cousin Joey Gargan—the son of his mother's sister, Agnes Fitzgerald Gargan—"for he is afraid that the Russo-Germ combination will be too strong and if they get beaten he says that these German and Russians organizations here will really do a job on us."

As Joe well knew, his father had been silent on FDR's call for revising the Neutrality Act. Although not wildly enthusiastic about the idea, Kennedy bit his tongue and thus gave tacit support to FDR's request despite his fears that Britain was a lost cause with or without American arms and despite the fact that she looked likely to be unable to pay for most arms delivered. Joe Jr., on the other hand, supported the notion of repeal more energetically. He believed a strengthened Britain would be able to negotiate better with Hitler, build a firmer peace, and thus insulate the United States more reliably for the long term. Writing to the ambassador, he noted a recent radio address by Father Coughlin, who "condemned the empirical designs of England and France and said why should we fight so they could preserve their ill-gotten gains. He has flooded the Congressmen with telegrams against the repeal of the embargo [revision of the Neutrality Act] for he says this would be the first step in involving us. I think a lot of people don't understand the bill and a lot of people have been able to capitalize on it by stating that the repeal of the embargo would involve us in war."

Joe Jr. became the first of the younger generation of Kennedys to see print in anything other than a campus publication when *The Atlantic Monthly* published one of his letters from Spain. Dressed up by ghostwriter Klemmer, the item appeared in the "Under Thirty" section of the October issue. Not to be outdone, Jack got into print about the same time with an anonymous editorial for the *Harvard Crimson* on the most relevant of topics: "Peace in Our Time." Jack's piece echoed what he'd been hearing from his father for months. "There is every possibility," he wrote, "almost a probability, of English defeat. At the best, Britain can expect destruction of all her industrial concentrations and the loss of the tremendous store of invested wealth she has been amassing ever since Drake brought home the Golden Hind. At the worst she can expect extreme political and economic humiliation. Peace is wisest by far, peace based on a solid reality."

Like his father, Jack saw FDR as the one person on the planet best posi-

tioned to foster a peace between the British and the Nazis. Incorrectly characterizing the British and the Germans as both being "painfully eager to end
the fight after the first preliminary round," Jack said it would be "the sad-
dest event in all history if their peace hopes were frustrated merely because
neither is in a position to make direct overtures. Obviously there must be a
third power to bring them together, and just as obviously, the President of
the United States is in the most logical position to act." FDR should move
forward to make the peace, Jack argued, even though it would involve "considerable concessions to Hitlerdom"—a puppet Poland and a free economic
hand for the Nazis in Eastern Europe. It would be worth it, however, if it
would induce Hitler to disarm. Then "Hitlerism—gangsterism as a diplomatic weapon—would be gone, and Europe could once more breathe easy.
The British and French empires would be reasonably intact. And there
would be peace for our time." Jack's naiveté in thinking Hitler could ever be
induced to disarm was rivaled, perhaps, only by Chamberlain's naiveté at
Munich.

"Everyone here is still ready to fight till the last Englishman," Jack
wrote his father, "but most people have a fatalist attitude about America getting in before it is over—which is quite dangerous." He made it plain that
he thought revision of the Neutrality Act a bad idea because the Brits were
just too poor to pay for the arms they needed—and too unlikely of success to
be extended credit. Jack did not buy FDR's argument that keeping America
out of the war meant keeping the democracies of Europe strong, as a buffer
between the United States and Hitler. That, he told Torb, was what the Atlantic Ocean was for. Nevertheless, anticipating eventual repeal of the arms
embargo despite his and others' arguments against it, Jack speculated in the
shares of American defense contractors, hoping for a windfall as soon as the
law changed.

Everyone here is still ready to fight till the last Englishman. Strolling about
the Harvard campus that autumn of 1939, both Joe Jr. and Jack found themselves surrounded by isolationist sentiment on the part of their fellow students. A Harvard Student Union survey published on November 10
indicated 95 percent of eighteen hundred undergraduates polled were
against immediate American entry into the war, while 78 percent wanted the
United States to refrain from entering the war even if France and England
were defeated. Still, only a very small number endorsed the United States'
engaging in direct peace negotiations with Hitler.

Faculty sentiment went 180 degrees the other way. Harvard president James B. Conant expressed the dominant sentiment of virtually all of Harvard's leading professors when he called for aid to the Allies. One of Jack's favorite teachers, the venerable political scientist Payson Wild, used the *Crimson* to publish an editorial in support of the Neutrality Act revision, insisting the United States would be able to stay out of the war only if European democracies held their own.

Jack's workload that semester—four courses addressing the principles of politics, international law, comparative politics (focusing on constitutional government vs. dictatorship), and modern imperialism—seemed timely to say the least. With European tensions increasing every day, the theories propounded in Harvard classrooms by Payson Wild and other informed sources did much to engage and enlarge Jack's thinking.

Toward the end of the semester, in a thirty-five-page paper on the League of Nations, the author of "Peace in Our Time" seemed to recant nearly completely the assumptions that had provided the basis for his editorial published two months earlier. Jack condemned Britain's "failure to utter one word of disapproval" after Hitler's annexation of Austria, and said Chamberlain's policy of "localizing the danger spots has seemed to mean giving to Germany what twenty million people gave their lives to prevent in the four years following 1914." Jack said Britain's policy toward the League—though perhaps justified from the point of view of her immediate national interests—was ultimately flawed as it resulted in a "denial of justice" to weak states and peoples, most notably the Czechs. He ascribed most of the blame for British policy on the Conservatives of the upper class, "a propertied class which has never entertained any sympathy for [Russia] since it became Bolshevist. . . . Fear of an invasion of Communist ideas has prevented England from collaborating with Russia in international affairs."

Shortly after completing his paper on the League, Jack finalized the topic he would attack in his senior honors thesis that spring. Jack proposed to analyze Britain's foreign policy since 1931 with specific reference to class influences on the development of that foreign policy.

Whatever Jack's thoughts on international relations and the need to contain Hitler, he must have been convinced—for the moment at least—that he would not personally play a part in any impending warfare. He remained a basket case physically, and told friends he did not imagine he would be very tempting bait for draft boards. His longtime problem back had been made much worse by the car accident in France. He was now forced to wear a special corset in order to give himself enough support to stand straight. All his other chronic maladies continued as well, and he remained on a carefully contrived cycle of prescription medications that he swallowed and injected daily, with religious dedication, on a precisely outlined schedule.

Nevertheless, despite his health problems, he still managed to chase skirts with great regularity. Frances Ann formally broke it off with him shortly after his return to the States in order to marry writer John Hersey, but Jack quickly dug up a host of substitutes. For good respectable company (i.e., public dates at football games and posh New York and Boston night-clubs), he most often resorted to Charlotte Macdonald, a Catholic and a good friend of Kick's from Noroton. For other pleasures, he migrated toward models and actresses, all of whom he ran through rather quickly and virtually none of whom he introduced to his family. As Jack's skill at cultivating talented amateurs increased, so did his need for professional prostitutes decline. He dated good Catholic girls for show and bad girls—regardless of their theological bent—for fun. The same went for many of his friends. "Get something that likes lovin'," he wrote Kick's occasional date Lem Billings, "preferably therefore not Kick this weekend."

Kept from Billy Hartington by the whole distance of the Atlantic Ocean, Kick casually dated an assortment of young men, among them Yale junior George Mead, Jr. (heir to the Mead Paper fortune and an old friend of both Kick's and Jack's from the days of their childhood summers on Cape Cod). She also saw Joe Jr.'s roommate Tom Killefer, Winthrop Rockefeller, and even (briefly) Peter Grace. ("He's just the same . . ." she wrote her father.) Her taste ran to "jocks," and she was nothing if not fickle. She was known to arrive at a nightspot with one date and unhesitatingly leave with another. In short, she treated her beaus just as cavalierly as her father and brothers did their girls. The only difference was Kick's allegiance to the tenets of her Catholic faith. She made it clear to all suitors that sex was *verboten*.

Having been rejected by the academically ambitious Sarah Lawrence (Frances Ann's alma mater), Kick enrolled instead at Finch—a junior college that at the time ranked just one rung above a finishing school. Here she studied art, design, and home economics with other wealthy young ladies of limited academic potential. She spent most weekends—especially autumn home-game weekends—up at Harvard. On other weekends her brothers would come down to Bronxville and the three Kennedys, joined by an assortment of friends that often included Charlotte Macdonald, entertained themselves till all hours at such nightspots as the Stork Club and the Persian Room at the Plaza Hotel. "This party is probably going to stop very quickly very soon," Jack wrote at the time, "but for now we've got to enjoy as much as we can. Who knows what tomorrow is going to throw at us? We get a little closer to war every day, it seems to me. What will Hitler do once Congress overturns the Neutrality amendment and we start sending arms to our limy cousins?"

. . .

COMPROMISE ON THE Neutrality Act took the form of a revision to the law allowing arms sales to belligerents, but only on a cash-and-carry basis, this stipulation reflecting growing doubts of Britain's solvency. Chamberlain unwittingly thanked Ambassador Kennedy for his efforts—which had been minimal—on behalf of the Neutrality Act revision once the measure became law. FDR signed the revision on November 4 following much bitter debate in Congress. In a diary note penned after his meeting with Chamberlain on the 8th, Kennedy recorded not only Chamberlain's remarks on the Neutrality Act but also the prime minister's comments on Churchill, whom Chamberlain saw as being after his job. "He thinks [Churchill] is better in the Cabinet than out. Easier to handle. . . . He felt people were getting on to Churchill. He couldn't keep up this high pace all the time." On another front, both Kennedy and Chamberlain—perhaps grasping at straws—took heart from a rumor Kennedy had recently heard from the apostolic delegate's secretary. It appeared Mussolini had returned to the Catholic Church. Both men agreed—unrealistically—that Mussolini's new reverence would necessarily make him adopt an antagonistic attitude toward ungodly nations.

Kennedy said much the same thing to the king and queen three weeks later, on the 28th, when they hosted him for a private goodbye luncheon shortly before he traveled home for the holidays. The king, dressed in an admiral's uniform, "didn't look well," remembered Kennedy. "[He] was thin and drawn, and stuttered more than I had ever seen him." As usual, Kennedy refrained when the king and queen ordered up sherry before the meal.

When the king, jokingly, asked Kennedy whether he'd yet taken to drink, the ambassador answered "No, but the temptation is becoming greater every day." The queen said she regretted some of Charles Lindbergh's recent rhetoric in the States. In lobbying against the Neutrality Act revision, the aviator had lapsed into attacks on the monarchy as an institution. "I stuck up for Lindbergh," Kennedy noted in his diary. "[I said] he was honest and not pro-Nazi."

Kennedy found himself once again refusing liquor during a visit to Churchill at the Admiralty later the same day. "[He] asked me to have a whiskey and soda," Kennedy noted disapprovingly. "I declined. He acted like he wanted one." The two men briefly discussed a recent idea of Kennedy's: for U.S. ships to take over English lines between nonbelligerent ports, thus enabling British imports to get as close to Britain as possible without being subject to German attack. "Like getting wheat in Australia and taking it to Halifax, dropping there and reloading on British boats . . . [Churchill] is heartily in accord." Kennedy told Churchill he would mention the plan to FDR.

Later in their discussion, Churchill openly speculated on the likelihood of the Soviets invading Finland: a prognostication that, ironically, found fulfillment just one day later when the Soviets crossed the Finnish border in flagrant violation of the nonaggression pact signed by the two countries in 1932. Finally, at the conclusion of their meeting, Churchill mentioned a British desire to mine Norwegian territorial waters against German shipping. Churchill said he wanted Roosevelt's quiet approval before proceeding, asked Kennedy to make the appropriate overture, and said he would refrain should the president think such an act would cause too much of an uproar in the United States. Kennedy—pleased the message was being conveyed through him rather than via sealed diplomatic pouch—told Churchill that should FDR give the plan a thumbs up, he'd cable the Admiralty saying "Eunice would like to go to party." If thumbs down, then Eunice would be staying home.

All in all—in the wake of his conversations with Beaverbrook and Churchill—the ambassador had every reason to feel a bit less isolated, and a bit more like a player, when he embarked for the United States on the 30th. And this, evidently, was exactly how Roosevelt and Churchill wanted him to feel. FDR had told Morgenthau several weeks previously that Kennedy needed some "plates to keep spinning on sticks" in order to stop him from being a pest. And Churchill told associates he believed an enthusiastically busy Kennedy would be preferable to an indignant and destructive Kennedy. The first lord harbored no illusions about the ambassador's biases. Hearing tell of Kennedy's various forecasts of doom for Great Britain, Churchill was overheard to respond: "Supposing, as I do not for one moment suppose, that Mr. Kennedy were correct in his tragic utterance, then I for one would willingly lay down my life in combat rather than, in fear of defeat, surrender to the menaces of these most sinister men."

Having traveled from Britain to Lisbon on the 30th, Kennedy then flew across the Atlantic aboard the *Dixie Clipper* bound from Lisbon to Port Washington, New York, on December 6. Rose stood by to greet him when he landed. "The London Embassy," reported the *New York Times*, "announced on November 23rd that Mr. Kennedy had been called home by the State Department in Washington, D.C., for consultation on the European situation. It was also known that the envoy was anxious to get home for the Christmas holiday." In his unpublished "Diplomatic Memoirs," Kennedy wrote of this time: "There was only one thing I really wanted to do, and that was to have at least two weeks in Palm Beach. Then I would not have to be on guard. I could read detective stories and sleep and swim and sleep again." To the reporters who greeted him at the airport, Kennedy intimated that he hoped to retire from public life in the near future. "I'm all through," he said. "This is my last public job. I'm going to spend the next five years watching my family grow up." As for the upcoming presidential campaign, Kennedy told the gentlemen of the press he hadn't "any idea" whether he'd play a role or not.

Charades

O N H I S W A Y in to the White House for an early-morning meeting on December 8, Kennedy surprised reporters by endorsing FDR for an unprecedented third term (an idea even the president himself had not broached publicly). Going inside, Kennedy followed a butler to the president's private quarters, where Roosevelt sat propped up in bed. After shaking Kennedy's hand, FDR leaned back against his pillows and drew deeply on a cigarette. He thanked the ambassador for his endorsement but pooh-poohed the notion of a third term. He told Kennedy point-blank he would not run, and seemed genuinely tired as he said it.

"He didn't flash the way he used to," Kennedy recalled. Roosevelt insisted he needed at least one year's rest. "That's what you need, too," said the president. "You may think you're resting, but the subconscious idea of bombings, wars, etc. is going on in your brain all the time." FDR told Kennedy categorically he would not stand for reelection unless he found the country at war before his term ended, in which case he would persevere. He went on to please Kennedy by castigating Churchill: "I always disliked him since the time I went to England in 1917 or 1918. At a dinner I attended he acted like a stinker." Likewise FDR said of England and the English, "I'm willing to help them all I can but don't want them to play me for a sucker."

Roosevelt said he agreed with Kennedy's proposal for shipping. He also gave the green light to Churchill's plans for mines off Norway, saying that since he—as under secretary of the navy—had personally approved doing the same thing during the last war he did not have much grounds now for saying no. FDR noted laconically that Norway's protest in 1917 had been perfunctory; the same was likely to be true in 1940. "I took this as a go-ahead," wrote Kennedy, "and so cabled Churchill in the code we agreed upon." Eunice was going to a party, whether she knew it or not. Kennedy briefed Hull on Churchill's mining plan during a meeting a few hours later. The secretary of state "brushed off the mention of [himself] as candidate for President but impressed me he was a candidate."

Like the majority of Roosevelt's advisers and intimates, Kennedy did not see FDR's hesitancy with regard to a third term for what it was: a charade—part of a carefully calculated effort to force a draft at the summer convention. As has been pointed out by Michael Beschloss and other historians, the enormously popular president sought at this moment to sow confusion on political waters by encouraging a host of likely Democrats—among them Harry Hopkins, Cordell Hull, Alben Barkley, Henry Wallace, Harold Ickes, and even Jim Farley (who had served as FDR's campaign manager in '32 and '36)—to enter the race while at the same time refusing to make an emphatic public statement as to whether he would or would not run himself. In private conversations with all these gentlemen, FDR repeatedly used the prospect of war as the single thing that might distract him from retirement.

Following his talk with FDR, Kennedy briefly toyed once again with his own presidential prospects. Going to Boston for a short visit, he arranged for his Lahey Clinic doctors to diagnose him as suffering from chronic exhaustion and insist that he rest at Palm Beach well into February. At the same time, the ambassador instructed his cousin Joe Kane to file nomination papers for the Massachusetts primary scheduled to take place April 30. This Kane did, somewhat reluctantly, while at the same time warning the ambassador to make sure FDR was out of the race before going public with his bid. Kane told Joe there was no opposing Roosevelt, who enjoyed historically high bipartisan approval ratings and was viewed as nothing less than a god within the party. As both Kennedy and Kane knew, Jim Farley had plans to declare himself a candidate and was actively agitating for FDR to announce his withdrawal from public life. If Roosevelt ultimately chose to remain in the arena, Farley would be ruined. What was more, as Kennedy observed, "Farley's efforts to force Roosevelt to . . . retire from the scene were clearly annoying him."

If Kennedy did run, it would be on a platform contrived to seduce the country's enormous isolationist majority. With an eye toward this majority, Kennedy delivered an impromptu—and profoundly isolationist—speech on the 10th at the old East Boston church where he had once served as altar boy. "The talk that I gave was extemporaneous," he told a reporter shortly thereafter. In other words, his speech had not been cleared with the State Department. ". . . I pointed out that America's sporting instinct might well incline her to resent an unfair and immoral thing but that this was not America's war." There was no economic, financial, or social reason to justify the United States' becoming involved militarily. "As you love America," said the ambassador, "don't let anything that comes out of any country in this world make you believe that you can make the situation one whit better by getting into the war. There's no place in the fight for us. It is going to be bad enough as it is."

Kennedy's audience, the men of the Catholic Holy Name Society, greeted his antiwar message with enthusiasm. Editorial writers for British newspapers did not, although Sir Alexander Cadogan of the Foreign Office thought Kennedy's remarks restrained considering what the ambassador had been muttering all over London for the past three months. Commenting on Kennedy's speech in the Whitehall minute books, he wrote: "I should not have been surprised by worse." The Foreign Office's chief American adviser in London viewed Kennedy's comments more emphatically: "Mr. Kennedy is a very foul specimen of a double-crosser and defeatist. He thinks of nothing but lining his own pockets. I hope the war will at least see the elimination of his type. I suppose we will have to have him back, but once back he will be estimated at his true value."

· · ·

"ALTHOUGH I HAD made it clear to the press that I intended to support Mr. Roosevelt for a third term," Kennedy wrote in his unpublished memoirs, "the President's hesitation to declare himself on this issue kept [alive] the press's interest in other candidates in the ranks of the Democratic Party who might be presidential timber." Once again, as during the Christmas before, Kennedy gathered friends and accomplices around him at Palm

Beach to consider his next move. In addition to Krock and other journalists, the party this year included newly named Supreme Court justice William O. Douglas, British ambassador Lord Lothian, and—somewhat surprisingly—Under Secretary of State Sumner Welles.

Welles hailed from the highest level of the Eastern aristocracy. As a boy, he'd served as a page at the wedding of Franklin and Eleanor Roosevelt. He later attended Groton and Harvard. Welles entered the Foreign Service in 1915, became chief of the State Department's Latin American Division at the tender age of twenty-eight, and gained appointment as under secretary of state in 1937.

Welles would be forced to resign in 1943 as the result of a homosexual scandal. Now at the height of his political powers and prestige, Welles visited Palm Beach with several purposes. Officially, Welles sought to brief Kennedy on upcoming visits to Berlin, Rome, Paris, and London during which he, Welles, would assess the views of German, Italian, French, and British officials as to the likelihood of concluding a just and permanent peace. Unofficially, he participated in lengthy brainstorming sessions and joined the chorus of those who advised Kennedy to stay far away from the 1940 presidential race.

Upon his return to Washington, Welles made sure to inform FDR of Kennedy's disinclination to run in the absence of an unqualified Rooseveltian withdrawal from the contest. With that knowledge in hand, FDR must have been amusing himself during the second week of February 1940 when he encouraged the ambassador to enter the Massachusetts primary. (Indeed, the White House may well have been the source for the news story with which Kennedy found himself blindsided on February 12. "Kennedy may be candidate," declared an extra edition of the *Boston Post*.) Meeting with Kennedy the same day, FDR suggested that Farley, who had declared his Massachusetts candidacy on February 10, had interloped on Kennedy's territory and wouldn't stand a chance against the ambassador in a Boston race. Still, Kennedy wrote later, "I could see that [FDR] had not resolved for himself the question as to whether he himself would run for a third term." He also had a nagging, and probably correct, feeling that FDR would only like to see him in the Massachusetts contest in order to block Farley's bid and slow down the postmaster general's momentum. Given this, Kennedy informed Roosevelt in no uncertain terms that he would not be a candidate.

He subsequently told the press the same thing, and prepared to depart for London (via Naples) aboard the American-flagged *Manhattan* bound out of New York on February 24. He did not look forward to the return. He complained to associates that all the pleasures of London he'd once shared with his family had now been replaced by nothing but discomforts and uncertainties he was forced to confront alone. He did not want to be seen as running from his post just as things in Europe reached their boiling point. Still, he definitely wanted *out*. He confided to his family and closest friends that he would resign the first moment he could do so without criticism. Psychologically, however, he had already moved on.

Harboring no immediate political ambition—either to continue as ambassador or to seek the presidency—Kennedy relaxed and was not quite as careful as he should have been in making public statements. Or perhaps, in his current mood of feeling himself done with politics generally, he was hoping that in speaking in an outrageous enough manner he might be asked to leave his London assignment sooner rather than later. In Washington just a few days before embarking for London, Kennedy visited the offices of the State Department and there chanced upon William Bullitt—on leave from Paris—in the midst of an interview with Joseph Patterson and Doris Fleeson of the New York *Daily News*. Bullitt later told Harold Ickes of his outrage when he heard Kennedy tell the reporters "that Germany would win, that everything in France and England would go to hell, and that his one interest was in saving his money for his children." Bullitt said Kennedy seemed "abysmally ignorant on foreign affairs" and was furthermore a fool, as a sitting administration official, to share such "idiotic candor" with journalists.

. . .

KENNEDY ENGAGED another journalist—the not-yet-Catholicized Clare Boothe Luce—with even more candor. When Joe departed for Naples aboard the *Manhattan*, Clare went with him. It is not clear exactly when Kennedy first became smitten with the beautiful and brilliant wife of Time-Life publisher Henry R. Luce, but it is likely the two had been conducting an affair for several weeks before they boarded the ship. Kennedy and Clare spent every night together during the voyage across, and would continue the relationship briefly thereafter, Joe joining Clare in Paris for several nights in early April, and she making visits to him in Britain. (Indeed,

Clare would find ample time for Kennedy in the midst of researching her assignment for *Life*: a commentary on the European scene destined to became the book *Europe in Spring*.) As Kennedy probably knew, Clare's husband, Henry, was at the same time enjoying an affair with Lady Jean Campbell, Lord Beaverbrook's beautiful granddaughter.

The *Manhattan* arrived at Naples on March 4. Kennedy encountered Sumner Welles two days later on a train bound from Milan to Paris. The under secretary had been to see Hitler the week before and had just concluded discussions in Rome with Mussolini. Welles told Kennedy he'd been impressed with Mussolini and his apparent desire for peace. He hadn't cared for Hitler, but nevertheless thought the Führer seemed willing to strive for a reasonable solution to current problems. Kennedy in turn told Welles of his desire to get out of his ambassadorship, if this could be done gracefully. He said he missed his wife and family, and that the job was no longer the challenge it had once been. (Still, he was not sure what he'd do once his stint in London came to an end. ". . . knowing myself as I do," he wrote Rose, "when I've been home 6 months I'll want to get going again. Maybe old age and a bad stomach will change me. I don't know. I guess I'm a restless soul: Some people call it ambition. I guess I'm just *nuts!*")

Welles and Kennedy parted company in Paris on the morning of the 7th, Welles moving into the American embassy for a round of talks with French leaders, Kennedy catching a plane to London. Arriving at Heston Airport, the ambassador confronted a large crowd of reporters and photographers. Asked to comment on the state of isolationist feeling in the United States, Kennedy answered: "If you mean by isolation[ist feeling] a desire to keep out of war I should say that it is definitely stronger. I think it is stronger because the [American] people understand the war less and less as they go along." As Kennedy recalled in his unpublished "Diplomatic Memoirs," his comments made as he got off the plane at Heston "which I believe correctly summarized American thinking at that time, were not received graciously by the British press. In fact, the press lashed out at me quite bitterly. [Arthur] Beverly Baxter, writing in the *Sunday Graphic* and confusing my function as the American Ambassador to Britain with that of Lothian as the British Ambassador to the United States, bitterly criticized me for not telling the American Public what I believed the British war aims to be. Others reiterated Baxter's criticism and it soon became evident that a coolness had developed towards me in those circles, official and otherwise, whose use for America was to embroil her in the war."

Baxter had used his column in the *Sunday Graphic* to demand to know why the American ambassador did not use his time home "to tell the people of the USA the truth about the war." And the truth, Baxter insisted, was that Great Britain had come to the point of war in order that "your children and my children and the children of every country may live in a world where there is decency and light instead of the darkness of war and scientific barbarism. Because of the sacrifice of the young men of France and Britain, our sons and daughters shall not see the Gestapo or the concentration camp, the fouling of the young mind, the setting of son against father, the enslavement of the soul and the end of individual liberty. They shall not see the night replace the day nor civilization turn back to the ages of cruelty and ignorance. . . . That is what this war is about."

The social atmosphere in London—already quite chilly for Kennedy upon his departure at the end of November—now became arctic. Even Nancy Astor made herself scarce. "I don't think any of the children should come over," he wrote Rose. "They have friends here now, but you would be surprised how much anti-American they have become and if the war gets worse which I am still convinced it will, unless Welles & Roosevelt pull off a miracle, I am sure they will all hate us more. So for Kick to see her old friends and get into a discussion about U.S. and the war might undo all the pleasant memories she has." It was right at this time that a British Foreign Office official summarized the unofficial view of his government when he said Kennedy had returned to London "not because he wants to or because the President or State Department have the slightest degree of confidence in him, but in order to get him out of the way." Embassy staff told Kennedy that he was an object of ridicule by many Londoners—criticized for having evacuated his family and taken himself to the countryside, out of harm's way.

Kennedy did, indeed, remain anxious to be away from what he called the "massive target" of London. It was, after all, just a matter of time before bombs started to fall. Yet he'd by now grown a bit tired of Wall Court. In the place of Morgan's rural outpost, he now began to use St. Leonard's in Windsor, a sixty-room country estate owned and lent by American automotive heir Horace Dodge, Jr., where Rosemary occasionally joined him. As Kennedy contemplated his own permanent departure from England, he briefly considered leaving Rosemary behind at her school, where she seemed to be happier, and to do better socially, than she had at any other institution to date. "I had a talk with Mother Isabel about her staying here," he wrote Rose on March 20, "and Mother Isabel says she is already working on it and she is selling Rose the idea to stay. So depending on what happens here I think we can work that out. I invited her in to Claridge's to have lunch with me Tuesday. . . . She looked fine and got along OK. I really don't have any trouble with her when she is alone. She's not 100% of course, but no real difficulty."

· · ·

JOE JR.'S CLASSMATE, friend, and sometime roommate Tom Killifer recalled that Joe had to "work like a slave" to keep up with things at Harvard Law School. In addition to being tutored by Judge Burns, Joe bought notes for classes on Harvard Square's "black market" for such items and actively participated in a rather intense study group along with classmates Tom Bilodeau and Charles Garabedian. Bilodeau remembered Joe as "increasingly overwhelmed academically" and "increasing jealous" of what he perceived to be Jack's easy successes, academic and otherwise. "Joe told me once he thought Jack had some sort of lucky charm," Bilodeau remembered. "But he said the luck wouldn't last forever, and Jack would be sunk in the long run, once genuine effort was called for. He was clearly disapproving of Jack's relaxed attitude, and at the same time envious of how Jack's successes tended to pile up despite Jack's casual approach."

Unlike Jack, Joe religiously showed up for Sunday dinner with his Fitzgerald grandparents at their apartment in the Bellevue Hotel, near the Massachusetts State House. There he routinely found himself grilled with a succession of queries as to Jack's progress, Jack's likes and dislikes, and Jack's prospects for the future. Jack's perennial absence from their table, Joe observed dryly to Bilodeau, had evidently caused the grandparents' hearts to grow quite fond toward him. Joe speculated that he should perhaps try the "absentee grandson" approach and see where it would get him.

Bilodeau recalled Joe complaining, after hearing Jack speak extemporaneously and brilliantly at a Harvard meeting, that Jack had been blessed "with the golden tongue" while he, Joe, seemed condemned to freeze up and be struck mute before crowds. Full of grand ideas, he was nevertheless

clumsy at conveying them. Killifer was not surprised when Joe shortly enrolled himself for night classes at Staley's School of the Spoken Word.

Always willing to describe Jack's lax approach to studies for any authority figure in the family who might have an interest, Joe did not hesitate to
inform his father of the slapdash manner in which Jack had composed his
thesis. "Jack rushed madly around the last week with his thesis and finally
with the aid of five stenographers the last day got it in under the wire," Joe
wrote on St. Patrick's Day. "I read it before he had finished it up and it
seemed to represent a lot of work but did not prove anything." Now that the
project was done, Jack was ready—reported his older brother—"to run for
Florida" for spring break.

. . .

ENTITLED "APPEASEMENT AT MUNICH" and based largely on research conducted by James Seymour, press attaché at the embassy in
London, Jack's 150-page thesis made two key arguments. First, said Jack (apparently repudiating the lead argument of his League of Nations paper from
earlier in the year), British leaders Baldwin and Chamberlain were *not* at
fault for appeasing Hitler. They'd had no choice, since history had set them
up in a situation where they had no arms in readiness with which to combat
the threat of German and Italian expansion. Secondly, Jack contended that it
was the inherent slowness and inefficiency of democracy—and most explicitly the profound antimilitaristic bias of the working classes—that caused
this situation. Jack concluded by assessing democracy itself as a weak gov-
ernmental foundation from which to launch a serious national security program. He further implied that dictatorships were inherently more efficient
than democracies in carrying out armament programs and arriving at viable
long-term plans for defense. By implication, Jack's thesis endorsed what the
ambassador had been telling FDR for a year: that the United States would
ultimately have to adopt fascist policies in order to get on the war footing
necessary to oppose fascism abroad.

It has been widely reported (in Rose Kennedy's *Times to Remember*,
Doris Kearns Goodwin's *The Fitzgeralds and the Kennedys*, and even Thomas
C. Reeves's critical *A Question of Character*) that Jack received *magna cum
laude* recognition for "Appeasement at Munich." This, however, is not so.
Only one of Jack's professors, Henry A. Yeomans, recommended *magna cum*

laude. The other faculty reader, Carl Friedrich, knocked the grade down to *cum laude*: the same recognition Joe Jr. had received for his own honors thesis several years before. In reducing Jack's grade, Friedrich complained that Jack's fundamental premise was never fully analyzed and commented that the thesis itself was much "too long, wordy, [and] repetitious." Friedrich also described Jack's paper as being flawed by poor English diction and numerous typographical errors.

Sending his father a copy of the thesis at the start of April, Jack reported that Krock had read it and felt it should be published. Krock—who noted the thesis would need substantial revision and polishing before publication—had even suggested a title: *Why England Slept*, a play on the title of Churchill's *While England Slept*. Jack was all for the idea, and hoped to get the book published in short order, by May or June. "I suppose the best plan," he wrote his father, "is that someone [there] looks it over, suggests new ideas or how it can be improved, and then send it back and I will work on it with someone around here as regards getting my English polished up. I think the best plan would be to air-mail it as I should try and get it published as soon as possible [and] get it out before the issue becomes too dead and, 2nd, before everyone goes away for the summer. I should like to get something in the conclusion about the best policy for America as learn't from a study of Britain's experience but of course don't want to take sides too much. Is 'Why England Slept' OK for a title—and will Churchill mind? What should I do about a publisher—keep Krock's agent or can you fix it?" Meanwhile he applied to and was accepted by the law school at Yale: an institution he preferred over the law school at Harvard simply because it would get him away from his easily rankled and intensely competitive older brother.

· · ·

Letters Kick received from her friends in London cataloged a war that was, quite simply, a bore. The blackout ruled, and nightlife remained the most immediate casualty. Severe rationing of foodstuffs—and a shortage of booze—did not do much to improve the situation. Virtually all the young British men of Kick's acquaintance had been called up for training. Stationed at Alton in southern England through late 1939 and early 1940, Billy served as a reserve officer with the Coldstream Guards. Many of Kick's debutante girlfriends also wound up in uniforms of one stripe or another. Sally Norton traded her ball gown for a boiler suit and took a job in an airplane factory outside London, where she helped manufacture a small RAF bomber called the Hurricane. Sally worked twelve-hour days with a brief teatime and a one-hour lunch break. As a special treat, a swing band rolled in to provide entertainment during the Wednesday lunch.

Perhaps sensing that *real* war was not far off, several of Kick's London friends planned weddings. Sissy Lloyd-Thomas and David Ormsby-Gore— she Catholic and he Anglican—threw religious caution to the wind and (to Nancy Astor's horror) became engaged. Debo Mitford and Billy Harting- ton's brother Andrew also set a date for marriage. Billy, meanwhile, had been seen sporting around with Sally Norton and with his old girlfriend from Ox- ford days, Irene Haig. Kick prayed these flirtations would not turn serious, and counted the days until May, when Billy would trade the romantic haz- ards of London for the military hazards of Europe, shipping out to France with the British Expeditionary Force.

13

Jackals and Betrayers

WELLES ARRIVED IN London from Paris during the fourth week of March. Kennedy considered Welles's mission little more than an exercise in diplomatic smoke and mirrors: a consciously doomed project positioned to appease those who thought FDR a hawk. In London, Welles and Kennedy held several conferences with Chamberlain, Halifax, Churchill, Eden, and other British leaders. When Chamberlain threw a dinner for Welles at 10 Downing Street, Kennedy announced jokingly during a toast that before leaving America he'd given Secretary Hull an important warning. Were Kennedy's ocean liner to be blown to bits in the mid-Atlantic, the president should in no way consider the event a cause for entering the war. "I thought this would give me some protection against Churchill placing a bomb on the ship," quipped Kennedy with First Lord Churchill looking on.

Visiting with Halifax on March 28, a few days after the Downing Street dinner, Kennedy noted Halifax's comment that he pictured Roosevelt as a man with too much class to put immediate political convenience before the good of humanity. When queried as to whether he thought FDR would go for a third term, Kennedy repeated what the president had told him in December. The British government, in Kennedy's estimation, clearly wanted

FDR to continue in office. He reported to his diary that Churchill and Halifax—both quietly confident—acted as though they had private advice Roosevelt would run again.

Welles had barely gotten back to the States when the Germans entered
Denmark and Norway on April 9. Denmark fell within twenty-four hours
and Hitler promptly occupied Copenhagen. He in turn installed a puppet
government in Norway under former Norwegian minister of defense Major Vikdum Quisling. Norway's legitimate rulers, meanwhile, retreated to
Oslo. All along the coast, Norwegian and British battleships found themselves decisively and repeatedly turned back by Nazi guns, suffering heavy
losses. "The Norwegian invasion by Hitler was a staggering blow to the
British," Joe wrote Rose, "although, strangely enough when it happened,
Churchill and others were rather optimistic in thinking that Hitler had over-
stepped himself." They'd since learned different. "The Germans are demon-
strating that control of the air from their bases in Denmark is a very
important factor in maintaining supremacy in Norway. The British have
landed men and supplies and they haven't the airplanes to protect them and,
as a matter of fact, they haven't many aircraft guns to help them, so the German air force is continuously attacking the transports and the troops and
their supplies as fast as they are landed. The result of this is that the British
are not making a very good job of it."

The ambassador probably did not know—and likely would not have
cared—that his onetime Harvard classmate Kermit Roosevelt, aged fifty,
served with distinction in the Brits' futile attempt to liberate Norway.
Theodore Roosevelt's second-eldest son had volunteered that spring and received a commission as an officer in the British army through the influence
of his friend Churchill. Interestingly, Kermit—a member of Harvard's elite
Porcellian Club and someone who'd never been a friend of Kennedy's during their undergraduate days—had adopted a similar policy during World
War I: fighting with British forces in North Africa until his reluctant country finally decided to join in. (Kennedy, on the other hand, had taken great
pains to avoid what he called "the sucker's game" of military service during
World War I, quitting several lucrative banking posts to take a relatively
low-paying job as manager in one of Charles Schwab's shipyards at Fore
River, where the real remuneration was getting out of the draft.)

· · ·

"BADLY THRASHED" just as Kennedy had once foretold they would be, the British withdrew from the Norwegian coast during the first week of May. In the wake of this defeat, Kennedy wrote in his diary about the undercurrent of despair he sensed in London and commented on the hopelessness of England's task.

Surprisingly, it was just at this tense moment that Kick asked her father for permission to come back to England. "I got a letter from Kick the other day," Billy Hartington wrote Sally Norton from France. "She seemed doubtful if she would be coming over this summer as apparently her father doesn't want her to because he thinks there is too much anti-American feeling in England." Jack wrote his father from Harvard in order to plead Kick's cause and, to a lesser extent, his own: "I gathered from your last letter to Mother that you did not think it too advisable for us to come over for the summer. I should like to come very much if there is anything of interest going on—otherwise I shall stay & sail at the Cape. Kick is very keen to go over—and I wouldn't think the anti-American feeling would hurt her like it might us—due to her being a girl—especially as it would show that we hadn't merely left England when it got unpleasant."

Neither journey was to be. Things grew even more unpleasant—and Kick's prospects for a swift return to Great Britain even bleaker—early in the second week of May, when the Germans did an end run around the Maginot Line, attacking Belgium, Luxembourg, and Holland. French forces and British troops (Billy Hartington among them) found themselves quickly put into retreat by the advancing Germans. These latest military moves on the part of the Nazis coincided with the final downfall of the Chamberlain government and the formation of a new coalition, headed by Churchill as prime minister. In the end, not even Nancy Astor—whom Sir Stafford Cripps had recently referred to on the floor of the House of Commons as "the honourable member from Berlin"—voted to preserve the Chamberlain government.

Meeting with Prime Minister Churchill on May 14, Kennedy noted with disapproval that Britain's new leader—who had not yet moved into 10 Downing Street—continued to hoard a large cache of liquor in his office at the Admiralty House. Churchill drank a whiskey and soda—not his first that day, Kennedy surmised—as they chatted. Kennedy talked with Churchill for more than an hour, and later sent a hurried dispatch to FDR and Hull:

Tomorrow morning [Churchill] is sending you a message saying that he considers the chances of the Allies winning is slight with the [likely] entrance of Italy. The German push he said is showing great power and the French are definitely worried although they are holding tonight. The French are calling for more British troops at once but the Prime Minister is not willing to send more from England at present for the reason that he is convinced the England will be vigorously attacked within a month. He needs help badly is the reason for the message to you. I inquired what the United States could do to help that wouldn't leave us holding the bag for a war which the Allies expected to lose; that if we had to fight it seemed to me that we would do better fighting in our own backyard. "You know our strength," I said. If we wanted to help all we can, what could we do? You don't need credit or money now; the bulk of our Navy is in the Pacific Ocean, our army is not up to requirements and we haven't sufficient airplanes for our own use. So what could we do if this is going to be a quick war all over in a few months? It was his intention, he said, to ask for whatever airplanes we could spare right now and the loan of 30 or 40 of our old destroyers. Regardless of what Germany does to England and France, he said, England will never give up so long as he remains in power in public life, even if England were burnt to the ground; he said "Why the Government will move, take the fleet with it to Canada and fight on." . . . Mr. Churchill called in Eden [newly appointed secretary of state for war] and the first Lord of the Admiralty [actually, newly appointed secretary of state for air] Sinclair and they are very low tonight although they are tough and mean to fight.

Kennedy visited Chamberlain—a heartbroken and physically savaged man suffering from an as yet undiagnosed cancer—on the 16th. Churchill had asked the former PM to stay on as lord president, but there was nevertheless some real question as to whether Chamberlain should play a role in the new government, what with so many of Churchill's allies accusing Chamberlain of almost criminal negligence in failing to rearm. Kennedy commented that Chamberlain did not seem bitter, only brokenhearted. In the course of their conversation, Kennedy mentioned Jack's plan to make his thesis into a book. Ironically, Chamberlain seemed very interested in the

proposed volume—addressing, as it did, why he and England had slept—
and requested that the ambassador get him a copy when it became available.

While Kennedy and Chamberlain talked, Churchill flew to Paris,
where, Kennedy reported to FDR and Hull, "the situation is deadly acute."
Churchill's agenda, according to Kennedy, was to "try and strengthen the
French morale." The French, the ambassador reported, seemed hardly to
be fighting at all. "The President might start considering, assuming that the
French do not stiffen up, what he can do to save an Allied debacle." Most of
the high-ranking British officials Kennedy spoke to blamed the French funk
on air bombardment of the civilian population. "The Ruhr was bombed last
night by the English and today there was a row in the Cabinet over the sending of more planes to France. It was Churchill's wish to send a substantial
number of squadrons though this would leave the position rather precari-
ous here. A compromise was finally reached on sending four squadrons.
Some people in the Government feel that this was too many at this time
since the Germans will definitely return last night's engagement unless they
decide to finish off their present job in Belgium and later on take care of
England."

FDR addressed both houses of Congress on the same day and—citing a
recently published government report summarizing the country's calami-
tously bad defense posture as of spring 1940—insisted that they vote him
$286 million to be used to shore up American defenses against attack. Point-
ing out the lack of preparedness that had enabled such rapid German conquest of so much of the European continent, Roosevelt asked for the large
infusion of cash in order to dramatically accelerate rearmament programs
already in progress under the aegis of the army, navy, and marine corps.
FDR said, too, that industrial capacity must be expanded. He proposed that
the nation be tooled to produce at least fifty thousand fighter planes a year.
FDR's request received immediate and overwhelming support. "Rarely, if
ever before," wrote a reporter for the *New York Times*, "has Mr. Roosevelt
received such an ovation as that which greeted his appearance before the
joint session of Congress." (Within weeks, shortly after the collapse of
France, Congress would vote FDR even more preparedness money: $4 bil-
lion for the construction of a two-ocean navy of seven battleships, eighteen
aircraft carriers, twenty-seven cruisers, 115 destroyers, and forty-three submarines.)

"Everyone is unanimous in thinking that Roosevelt made a marvelous speech," Joe Jr. wrote his father. "Some wonder what we are going to do with 50,000 planes, and suspect that it is Roosevelt's intention to get the country into war immediately after the election, whereas to others it is a natural defensive measure. . . . Also the change in attitude toward the war has been remarkable. Overnight the people turned strongly sympathetic to the Allies, and now many people are saying that they would just as soon go to war, and that they will have to go anyway and why not now." Some of the job of rebuilding the defense program would be right up his father's alley, and might—Joe speculated—make a good excuse for the administration to bring the ambassador back home.

The more immediate problem for at least one Kennedy—Kick, who with genuine horror read daily accounts of the fierce fighting on the ground in Belgium—was just how one Billy Hartington, lieutenant of the Coldstream Guards, would find his way back to *his* home in one piece. The Germans advanced through Belgium to Abbeville on France's north coast in only five days, cutting off British and French forces to the north from those in the south. "The situation is terrible," the ambassador wrote his wife on May 20, "unless the French can push to the sea and with the British who are falling back from their position [and] stop this drive of the Germans, I think the jig is up. The situation is more than critical. It means a terrible finish for the Allies." He said he planned to get Rosemary and the Moores out of England as soon as possible, via either Ireland or Lisbon. "We will be in for a terrific bombing pretty soon and I'll do better if I just have myself to look after. The English will fight to the end but I just don't think they can stand up to the [expected] bombing indefinitely."

In short order, during the first few days of that grim June of 1940, Lieutenant Billy Hartington and his men—beaten back to the coast at Dunkirk along with 330,000 other British Expeditionary Force and French First Army soldiers—had to be rescued by the now legendary "Mosquito Armada" of destroyers, ferries, dinghies, and pleasure craft that rushed across the Channel to retrieve the exhausted and famished armies. Following the rescue, Churchill took to the airwaves to declare Dunkirk a victory, and to sound a strong note of defiance. "We shall fight on the beaches, we shall fight on the landing-grounds, we shall fight in the fields and in the streets, we shall fight in the hills. We shall never surrender." Later, off the air and off the record, Churchill elaborated to radio commentator Edward R. Murrow: "And if they do come, we shall hit them on the head with beer bottles, for that is all we shall have to fight them with." The Luftwaffe began bombing Paris on June 3. Two days later, German ground forces launched an offensive between Laon and the coast, initiating the Battle of France.

Citing the need to strike while the anvil of Europe was hot, Ambassador Kennedy encouraged Jack to find a publisher for *Why England Slept* as quickly as possible. While thus stroking Jack, the old man did not fail to pay attention to Joe Jr. In letter after letter, the ambassador congratulated his eldest son not only on the respectable grades he garnered in his first year at Harvard Law, but also his successful candidacy as a Farley delegate in Boston. "Grandpa thought I did quite well . . ." Joe had written his father shortly after emerging victorious from the little election on April 30. One of two endorsed candidates in a field of six running for two convention delegate slots, Joe came in second after John Brennan, his running mate on the endorsed ticket. In the process he beat Dan Coakley, an old political nemesis of his Grandfather Fitzgerald's.

"I had been hoping and praying that I would be back so that I could be with you on your twenty-fifth birthday," the ambassador wrote Joe on June 6, almost two months before the event, "because on that day you take over your interest in the [Kennedy Family] Trust and you become owner of a considerable amount of securities and money. In addition to that you are now arriving at the point where you have a responsibility to the family. Of course I am completely confident nothing is going to happen to me in this mess, but one can never be sure, and you don't know what a satisfaction it is for me to know that you have come along so well. . . ." The ambassador said he looked forward to getting to the Cape sooner rather than later. He wanted to be away from London, away from the war, and away from Churchill, whose cavalier attitude toward the approaching apocalypse he abhorred and whom—ironically—he was about to start seeing more of.

·   ·   ·

WHAT IS THE OLD SAYING? *Be careful what you wish for.* No one was more surprised than the ambassador when FDR suddenly put him back into diplomatic play. With events in France coming to a head and Churchill actively agitating for America to enter the war, FDR took his ambassador off the shelf and activated him, albeit briefly, as a buffer between the White House and the British PM. Thus Churchill and Kennedy scheduled their first meeting in nearly a month for the evening of June 11. Norway had finally surrendered on the 9th, and Italy had declared war on Britain and France on the 10th.

"[I made an appointment] for 6 PM tonight," Kennedy recorded in his diary on the 11th. "This morning it was moved to 7 PM and subsequently canceled. In talking to Beaverbrook [now serving as Churchill's new minister for aircraft production], I expressed my resentment at this because I feel it was personal." Perhaps at the intercession of Beaverbrook, Churchill rescheduled the meeting for 7:30 p.m.

Greeting Kennedy, Churchill offered a highball, which the ambassador brusquely declined. Sipping on his own drink, Churchill launched into a prolonged denunciation of Mussolini—calling him the "jackal and betrayer of all things good and fair" for his decision to team with Hitler in the savaging of Europe. Churchill told Kennedy that Reynaud, the French premier, had assured him the French would not quit even if Paris fell. And fall it would. The British, said Churchill, had no help to send. "We can't give them anything that will take away our capacity to make war," he told Kennedy. Still, said Churchill, "Hitler has not won this war until he conquers us. Nothing else matters. . . . We'll hold out until after your election and then expect you'll come in. I'll fight them from Canada. I'll never give up the fleet. Maybe some other government may."

Churchill said he did not see how the United States could not come into the war once France fell and the American people saw England being bombarded. In the meantime, said the PM, how about some destroyers? Kennedy noted that Churchill's briefing—though lush with heroic rhetoric and cagey requests—was remarkably short on substance as to Britain's immediate plans. The following morning—just as the Germans broke through the French line along the Marne, having already crossed the Seine in their push toward Paris—Churchill sent a terse note to FDR via diplomatic pouch saying he was "worried about Ireland. An American Squadron at Berehaven would do no end of good I am sure."

The squadron was not to be sent. However, addressing the graduating class of the University of Virginia just two days earlier—the 10th—FDR had condemned Mussolini for turning against Britain and France, and repeated his call for immediate rearmament and the need for substantive, material assistance to the Allies. The French government was forced to move from Paris to Tours on the 11th, and would move again to Bordeaux on the 13th. On that same day, in response to a direct appeal from Reynaud to provide ships and materials for the Allied cause, FDR cabled the French premier: "Your message . . . has moved me very deeply. As I have already stated to you and to Mr. Churchill, this Government is doing everything in its power to make available to the Allied Governments the material they so urgently require and our efforts to do still more are being redoubled."

FDR sent Kennedy a copy of the message and directed him to deliver it to Churchill. Kennedy arranged an appointment for late in the evening of the 13th. Going to the Admiralty House at 9:30 p.m., Kennedy found Churchill just returned from a flying visit to Tours, where he'd been accompanied by Beaverbrook, Halifax, Secretary of War Anthony Eden, and General Sir John Greer Dill. The five had met there with Reynaud, Marshal Pétain, and General Maxime Weygand, the former chief of staff to the French army who had succeeded Gamelin as Allied commander in chief on May 19.

Beaverbrook told Kennedy later, confidentially, that Reynaud had looked a broken man. His expression had seemed a mask of defeat, and he was about to move his government (as mentioned earlier, to Bordeaux) to keep it well ahead of the advancing Germans. Not looking much better than Reynaud, Weygand had surprised the Brits by insisting on the need for an armistice and saying the French army simply could not hold out any longer.

Purporting to give Kennedy a detailed account of the trip and meeting, Churchill skipped the dour details Beaverbrook had quietly confided. He instead lapsed once more into heroic hyperbole. Churchill said the French— though thoroughly thrashed on the land—would never give up their fleet. They would turn pirates before that or, to save the French people from further punishment, they might scuttle their ships. Both Churchill and Halifax said they regarded the latter event as a distinct possibility.

Churchill became visibly excited when Kennedy read him the text of FDR's message to Reynaud. He then read it himself several times. It was Kennedy's impression that Churchill was greatly moved by the sentiment of the message (or possibly by the champagne he had been drinking). Churchill told Kennedy he would immediately send Reynaud his interpretation of Roosevelt's words, which Churchill took as a firm offer of help.

Later that evening, after presenting the message to his cabinet, Churchill asked Kennedy to request FDR's permission to publish his words and thereby hearten the resolve of the beleaguered French. In fact, Churchill insisted Kennedy telephone FDR directly, and was chagrined when FDR hesitated to authorize publication. Cabling FDR later, Kennedy agreed with the president's reluctance and added: ". . . I realize the tragedy of the present moment and how important it is for the success of these poor people that their morale should be bucked up. . . . I nevertheless see in the message a great danger as a commitment at a later date." As FDR had told Kennedy on the phone, Hull saw the same danger.

Kennedy handed Churchill a wire the next day, the 14th, expressing FDR's formal decision. "As I asked Ambassador Kennedy last night to inform you," wrote FDR, "my message of yesterday's date addressed to the French Prime Minister was in no sense intended to commit and did not commit the Government to military participation in support of Allied governments." Only Congress had the constitutional right to make such commitments. For that reason, FDR would not permit the message to be published.

Churchill was made glum by the news, and said that if the remarks could not be published—and if the United States was truly not willing to commit to aiding the French in significant ways—then all would be lost on the Continent. Kennedy confided to his diary that he thought all was going to be lost there anyway, and that he was sure the publication of FDR's message to Reynaud would have done little except delay the inevitable and prolong the suffering of the French. Churchill was not very much heartened by further word FDR sent via Kennedy that if the French fleet broke away from a defeated France, the United States would see to it that they were fed and supplied. Paris fell that afternoon.

Reynaud's coalition—based now in Bordeaux—collapsed on the 16th. French president Lebrun asked Marshal Philippe Pétain to form a new government. Just hours before his coalition imploded, Reynaud cabled Halifax to ask if the British would agree to the French making a separate peace. The French, in turn, would promise not to allow their fleet to fall into German hands. To this the British responded that before making peace—neither government used the term "surrender"—the French must order their fleet to sail at once for British ports. They were, in turn, to instruct their air force to depart France for either England or North Africa. And they were likewise to command all French infantry divisions abroad to remain loyal to the Allies. Churchill also told Reynaud to evacuate to London all representatives of the legitimate Polish, Czech, and Belgian governments then finding sanctuary in France.

Brigadier General Charles de Gaulle, whom Reynaud had appointed under secretary of state for defense and war two and a half weeks previously, arrived in Britain on the 17th to form a French government in exile. Five days later, on the 20th, Marshal Pétain signed an armistice with Germany. Kennedy decided quickly that he did not care for de Gaulle, who seemed to be very much in tune with Churchill: both of them thoroughly and—to Kennedy—*absurdly* upbeat.

As Kennedy observed, even Beaverbrook had begun to participate in what the ambassador considered an exercise in denial. Kennedy cabled Hull that Beaverbrook "seemed very optimistic about the production of airplanes, saying last week was the biggest week in England and that he was not at all worried. He said if the Germans had come over three or four weeks ago and knocked out the Derby works, they would have ruined their production, but now they have managed to spread it around, so they can't be knocked out quickly. He didn't talk like his old self. He talked as a Minister of the Churchill Government should, I suppose, and seemed to be doing his best to sell me on the idea that things were still all right. . . ."

Unable to get hold of FDR, who had no good news to give Churchill and therefore continued to make himself unreachable for the short term, Churchill rang Kennedy late at night three days after the French surrender. Still displaying steadfast optimism, Churchill urged American recognition for de Gaulle's provisional French government in exile and once again inquired as to the status of his request for battleships. "We have to get those," he told Kennedy, "because if we don't, we will all go down the drain together, because if we are not successful, you will be taking orders from the Germans unless you have the British fleet to support you."

14

Dummy

D URING HIS LAST weeks at Harvard in the spring of 1940, Jack
Kennedy organized a student committee to help the Red Cross
raise funds to aid European refugees. "The desperate need of Europe's invaded population requires no more argument than the familiar facts
reported in the daily papers," he told a reporter for the *Boston Herald*. "In
making this appeal to Harvard students, the committee knows that many of
them are low on funds at the end of the college year. I feel, however, that
students can and should be given an opportunity to contribute." The drive
raised $1,700.

Jack formally jumped on the rearmament bandwagon—and turned
completely away from the young man who had composed "Peace in Our
Time" the previous October—with a letter published in the *Crimson* on
June 9.

In an editorial on Friday, May 31, attacking President Conant's
speech, you stated that "there is no surer way to war, and a terribly
destructive one, than to arm as we are doing." This point of view
seems to overlook the very valuable lesson of England's experience

during the last decade. In no other country was this idea that arma-ments are the prime cause of war more firmly held. Lord Grey's statement in 1914—"the enormous growth of armaments in Eu-rope, the sense of insecurity and fear caused by them, it was these that made war inevitable"—was quoted again and again by success-ful opponents of British rearmament. Senator Borah expressed the equivalent American opinion, in voting against the naval appropri-ations bill of 1938 when he said, "one nation putting out a program, another putting out a program to meet the program and soon there is war."

If anyone should ask why Britain is so badly prepared for this war or why America's defenses were found to be in such shocking condition in the May investigations, this attitude toward arma-ments is a substantial answer. The failure to build up her arma-ments has not saved England from war, and may cost her one.

Are we in America to let that lesson go unlearned?

Jack's evolving view on the need for preparedness stemmed directly from his ongoing work to shape the scattered "Appeasement at Munich" into a publishable, book-length study. The more he considered the complex roots—and now obvious failure—of British appeasement, the more he came to realize the need to back diplomacy with genuine military strength and to negotiate from a position of power. "I have come down to New York on the book which is running into some snags," he wrote his father that June, shortly after his graduation. "Harpers felt that France's quick defeat has changed the interest. My stuff (what happened in the past) is not of such in-terest as what is going to happen in the future. . . . I have changed it consid-erably. It is now about 210 pages where formerly it was only 150, and I have tried to make it more readable. Luce was very nice and is going to do the foreword."

Jack based much of his revision not only on comments from the editors at Harper Brothers, but also on a memorandum drafted by Jim Seymour at the London embassy containing a digest of criticisms from Harold Nicol-son, Laski, and others in the British intelligentsia to whom the ambassador had circulated the original thesis. Years later, a host of writers—among them Blair Clark and the London embassy's Harvey Klemmer—claimed credit for transforming Jack's mishmash of a thesis into a best-selling book. In fact they had nothing to do with it. The evidence (in the form of many drafts edited and overwritten in Jack's hand) shows JFK cobbled together the book largely on his own. Krock offered a few revisions, but not many. "I can't say that I did more than polish it and amend it here and there," he remembered, "because it was very, very definitely [Jack's] own product."

Harpers felt that France's quick defeat has changed the interest. In fact, Harper Brothers had rejected the manuscript—offered by agent Gertrude Algase for a mere $250 advance—outright. In doing so the Harper Brothers editors wrote Algase that "the disastrous turn of events in France has, we think, so shocked and shaken people in this country that, in our judgment, it would be practically impossible to get attention for any historical survey as this, even though the period covered is a very recent one. Events which preceded the outbreak of the war now seem to have occurred years ago, so rapidly has history moved since May 10th. Also, the collapse of France has made only one question seem important in people's minds, namely, what will England do now? And of course as a corollary to that, what will we do? In the face of this grave crisis, nothing else seems important."

It is important to realize that what Harper Brothers saw and rejected was the thesis "Appeasement at Munich." Harcourt—the next house to turn down the project—reviewed the same prose. Jack honed his manuscript, rewrote many drafts, and changed the focus and analysis significantly before allowing Algase to send the book out to yet another publisher. Among the most important of Jack's changes—triggered by a comment in Seymour's memo—was to remove some of the blame he'd previously placed on the isolationist bent of the British working classes and return it to the shoulders of such leaders as Baldwin and Chamberlain. Changed too was Jack's vision of democracy as an inefficient platform from which to mount a national defense strategy. Now he said quite the opposite, calling on Americans to make of their democracy the robust and effective power that it could and should be. "Any system of government will work when everything is going well," he wrote. "It's the system that functions in the pinches that survives."

Finally—and most important—Jack drafted a new conclusion for his book, a conclusion defined by a strident call for American preparedness not unlike the one he'd published in the *Crimson*. The result was a manuscript strong enough that Wilfred Funk, proprietor of a small New York imprint bearing his name, decided Jack's book was well worth signing. Excited by Jack's subject and the way he treated that subject, Funk nevertheless forecast modest sales: just three to five thousand copies. He scheduled publication for July 24: late enough to allow time for a rush printing, but early enough to allow his young author a few weeks to do publicity before reporting to Yale Law School in September.

Henry Luce seemed hesitant at first when Joseph Kennedy asked him to read and comment on Jack's book. He didn't expect much, and was surprised when he came away impressed. "England . . . stood alone," he recalled later, "and the popular tendency was to put all the blame on the so-called appeasers, namely Mr. Chamberlain and the Tory appeasers, the Cliveden Set." *Why England Slept*, however, took a more subtle view "and showed that the blame [for the failed policy of appeasement] would have to be shared quite generally by nearly all aspects of British opinion, including the Labor Party." Luce believed the book held important lessons for the United States, but in his foreword he took Jack's thesis—that rearmament was necessary to avoid war—one step further and implied that simple rearmament without tandem psychological and political preparation for battle would not be enough.

"America will never be ready for any war," Luce insisted in the belligerent, hastily composed essay, "not in one year nor in two nor in twenty—never until she makes up her mind that there is going to be a war. . . . Until that moment America will lose many wars—all the wars she does not fight. Or, if she doesn't actually lose it, she will win the last battle only at an appalling cost of blood and treasure." Luce argued that all the preparedness in the world would be useless if perceived of as being only theoretical. "A boxer cannot work himself into proper psychological and physical condition for a fight that he seriously believes will never come off." Still, though Luce argued the United States must be prepared both physically and psychologically to war against Hitler in defense of the American mainland, he at the same time railed against the notion that the United States should intervene in the European hostilities on behalf of Britain.

· · ·

AMBASSADOR KENNEDY evacuated Rosemary and the Moores from Britain at the start of the summer, and Rosemary wound up briefly re-

united with her brothers and sisters at Hyannis before being sent to a school
for the mentally handicapped in Washington, D.C.

Early July on the Cape proved idyllic, despite Europe's distant trauma.
The family saw a lot of Torb Macdonald, who—looking forward to Harvard
Law School in the fall and dedicating his summer to playing semipro football with the Eastern Shore League—stopped by often to visit with Jack and
ogle Kick. Jack, in turn, relaxed, anticipated the publication of his book on
the 24th, and looked forward to Yale. Joe—Jack reported in a letter dated
July 7—"busily comes and goes, quite distracted and involved but no-one
can ever tell quite what with. He goes to the Democratic Convention in a
few days, after that to Wisconsin to see Tom Schriber [an old friend from
Choate], and then to California. So maybe all that will calm him down. He
seems quite content with his 72 from Harvard Law but it still strikes me as
just a 72."

Jack's friend Chuck Spalding, who spent several days visiting the
Kennedys at Hyannis during the first week of July, later spoke of the great
energy and activity that permeated the household. "Jack was autographing
[advance] copies of *Why England Slept* while Grandfather Fitzgerald was
reading to him a political story from a newspaper. Young Joe was telling
about something that happened to him in Russia. [I also remember] Mrs.
Kennedy on the phone with Cardinal Spellman, . . . Bobby trying to get
everyone to play charades, next thing all of us choosing sides in touch football, Kathleen calling the plays on our side. Conversation at dinner ranged
from war and Washington politics to books, sports and show business."

In between calling football plays, racing sailboats, and fending off romantic advances from Torb Macdonald, Kick practiced bandage-making at
a makeshift Red Cross headquarters across the street from Hyannis's pic-
turesque St. Francis Xavier Church. She also knitted a scarf for Billy and
spent a great deal of time helping plan an October luncheon and fashion
show to benefit the Allied Relief Fund, a charity to aid British seamen dis-
abled in the war. (These were more numerous every day. Over one half of
Great Britain's destroyers would be sunk by the end of August.)

She missed London desperately. "Thanks a lot Daddy," she'd written
shortly after arriving back in New York the previous September, "for giving
me one of the greatest experiences anyone could have had. I know it will
have great effect on everything I do from here on in." Unlike her father, she

repeatedly expressed faith that the British would endure. "At the moment," she wrote him, "it looks as if the Germans will be in England before you receive this letter. In fact from the reports here they are just about taking over Claridge's now. I still keep telling everyone 'the British lose the battles but they win the wars.' " When a vote was taken at Finch that spring as to whether the United States should intervene on behalf of Britain, only Kick and one other girl voted yes, the balance of the student body going the other way.

. . .

HAVING JUST INSTALLED Republican Henry Stimson as secretary of war, Roosevelt in turn gave Republican Frank Knox (former publisher of the *Chicago Daily News* and a veteran of Theodore Roosevelt's Rough Riders) the appointment as secretary of the navy. FDR likewise informed his closest advisers that he was in the early stages of establishing what might well, if need be, become his bipartisan war cabinet in the event that hostilities ripened. In anticipation of the fight that loomed on the horizon, FDR further decided to start building direct lines of communication between his new appointees and their counterparts in Britain, yet again bypassing Kennedy. FDR told Morgenthau he did not trust his ambassador's estimates of British strength, manpower, and will. He said he needed an informed, unbiased appraisal of Britain's capacity to repulse Hitler's attacks, or her lack thereof, and that he'd never get an accurate judgment out of the gloomy, defeatist Kennedy.

As might have been expected, Ambassador Kennedy took it as a slight— not to mention "the height of nonsense and a blow to good organization"— when the president dispatched Colonel William "Wild Bill" Donovan to London in July. An old Republican friend of FDR's who would shortly found the OSS, Donovan brought along with him Edgar Mowrer, a highly respected foreign correspondent in the employ of Navy Secretary Knox. "I will render any service I can to Colonel Donovan, whom I know and like," Kennedy told Hull. But as for Mowrer, "we don't need a newspaperman to make this investigation for the government and it is most embarrassing to me. I think he should be called off the complete assignment." (Donovan and Mowrer subsequently told FDR that Great Britain looked likely to be able to turn Hitler back. "I hope that at Washington they have got the Ambassador's number!" John Balfour jotted happily in the Whitehall minute books once Donovan's and Mowrer's verdict became known.)

While the ambassador rather sourly squired Donovan and Mowrer around Britain—where they inspected RAF bases, met the king, and spoke with everyone from enlisted men to diplomats, laborers to lords—Joe Jr. briefly made headlines at the Democratic convention, held in Chicago during the second week of July. In the process, he also made a good start toward nationalizing his local Cambridge reputation as a sometimes reckless, always obstinate, and frequently self-destructive individualist. Few were surprised by FDR's last-minute, furtively laconic announcement that he would be open to the idea of a third term. Many expressed astonishment, however, when Postmaster Farley refused to withdraw his name in the face of FDR's sudden availability. And no one much doubted the eventual outcome of what ensued: a heated scramble to woo Farley delegates and assure Roosevelt's unanimous nomination on the first ballot. When William "Onions" Burke, chairman of the Massachusetts delegation, rallied his delegates to switch to FDR, only one—Joseph P. Kennedy, Jr.—refused to go along. When Roosevelt operatives called the ambassador in London and asked him to reason with his son, Kennedy refused. And when the roll call was taken, Joe Jr. joined seventy-one other delegates in voting for Farley, the balance of the convention (946 votes) going solidly for Roosevelt. Subsequently Farley withdrew not only from the convention, but from his chairmanship of the Democratic Party.

Back on the Cape, Jack read press accounts of Joe's escapade and, speaking to friends, questioned the wisdom of his brother's futile gesture against Roosevelt. Joe Jr. had lately been telling people that he one day hoped to be president. With that in mind, why make powerful enemies within the party just for the sake of remaining loyal to Farley's doomed candidacy? Jack—ever the pragmatist—said it just did not make sense. (Jack told friends it was likely a case of Rooseveltian retribution a few weeks later when, after the ambassador's name came up as a possible replacement for Farley as Democratic National Committee chairman, the president personally called London to tell Kennedy the job would not be his.)

Whatever FDR thought of the two Joe Kennedys, he made a point of congratulating Jack upon the publication of *Why England Slept* at the end of July. FDR wrote Jack that he thought the book (which he'd evidently read thoroughly) quite lucid and penetrating, and "a great argument for acting and speaking from a position of strength at all times."

Others agreed. Reviewing the book for the *New York Sun*, John Wheeler-Bennett applauded Jack for not writing as "the son of the ambassador . . . but with becoming modesty, as a young man of intelligence, forming his opinions for himself, sifting his evidence and finally evolving a political and psychological analysis of rare penetration, with an immensely appealing quality of freshness and breadth of understanding." (Another critic, while applauding Jack and his book, went so far as to suggest the volume might well have been titled *Why Daddy Slept*.) The *New York Times*, the *San Francisco Chronicle*, Luce's *Time* magazine, the *New York Tribune*, and many other newspapers and magazines joined the *New York Sun* in singing Jack's praises. The reviews sparked sales so high as to place *Why England Slept* on best-seller lists across the country for many weeks.

There is no evidence for (and no truth to) the tale, told so many times, that Ambassador Kennedy bought thousands of copies of *Why England Slept* and tucked them away in the basement of his Hyannis home in order to guarantee the book's "best-seller" status. He did not need to. Bookstores sold out Funk's first edition of 3,500 copies in the first two days after publication. The book was to sell more than 40,000 copies in 1940 alone, earning both Jack and his publisher a tidy sum. The torrent of favorable reviews and outstanding sales more than counterbalanced the opinion voiced by Laski in a letter the ambassador never bothered to show Jack. Professor Laski condemned *Why England Slept* as a "very immature" work containing "no real structure" and dwelling "almost wholly on the surface of things." Dozens of leading American critics—some, but by no means the majority, under the influence of the ambassador and his friends—plainly disagreed.

The sales for *Why England Slept* reflected Jack's focused effort to synthesize the many aspects of his complex analysis in an interesting and engaging manner; the sales also reflected world events that could not have dovetailed more neatly with the book's publication, reinforcing Jack's message of preparedness as nothing else could. German planes began a succession of small probing attacks on British shipping in the English Channel and the outer Thames Estuary on July 10—the date many historians cite as the first day of the Battle of Britain. They also made occasional bombing forays into Portsmouth, Falmouth, Swansea, Newcastle, and Merseyside. The

Luftwaffe began bombing RAF airfields in southern and southeastern England on August 8, less than two weeks after the publication date for *Why England Slept*. Concentrated daylight bombing of London—the first phase of the Blitz—would commence on September 7.

· · ·

In London, Ambassador Kennedy seemed an unlikely publicist for a book condemning appeasement as a concept. On the one hand he enthusiastically gave copies of Jack's tome to every prominent Brit he knew. On the other he routinely assured the State Department of Britain's imminent defeat, and urged the king and queen to send their children and gold to Canada. It was about this time that the *New Statesman* described Kennedy as "a self-centered, frightened rich man who thinks only in terms of money." As the editors pointed out, Kennedy the investor seemed to be hoarding stock in firms doing business with the Nazis while at the same time divesting equities in British firms.

Writing Bobby in mid-July, Kennedy predicted that Hitler would try to choke off Britain and win a surrender on the fastest possible schedule. He calculated that the Nazis would be wary of letting Britain endure beyond the autumn elections in the States, after which it would be likely the United States might rush to Britain's side with significant aid. "The English people," he wrote his son, "have been led to believe that England is a fortress, well protected, and that the Germans can never successfully get here because of the strength of the British Navy and because of the great number of men they have under arms here. On top of that, they have been led to believe that their air force can take care of any attacks that Hitler can make. Personally I am of the opinion that is the spot against which he will make his great drive. If he can beat the Air Force, the Navy and the Army will not be of great value to England. So we are like the fellow sitting in the theater waiting for the curtain to go up. We should know very soon."

"Saw Joe Kennedy," the mortally ill Chamberlain wrote in his diary in mid-July. "[He] says everyone in the USA thinks we shall be beaten before the end of the month." The ambassador told the truth: a recent poll indicated more than two-thirds of all Americans believed Britain doomed to defeat and the United States doomed to an eventual war of self-defense.

· · ·

JOE JR. VISITED for a few days with his old Choate friend Tom Schriber in Wisconsin after the debacle at the Democratic convention. He then headed out to California. William Randolph Hearst, Jr.—son of his father's newspaper publisher friend—hosted Joe for a week at Wyntoon, the Hearst family's beautiful ranch on the McCloud River, not far from Mount Shasta. Hearst later claimed that during the visit Joe developed a schoolboy crush on the publishing heir's wife, Lorelle, a former dancer with the Ziegfeld Follies and subsequently a journalist. Perhaps to show off for Lorelle, Joe insisted on diving into the frigid McCloud, which found its source in the ice-cave region of the Shasta National Forest. Joe took several plunges before returning to mock Hearst, who'd refrained after explaining he'd been warned away from the cold river ever since childhood.

Joe left the lush atmosphere of Wyntoon at the end of the first week of August and (probably for effect, since he had plenty of money) hitchhiked to the modest Hermosa Beach home of his law school friend Tom Killifer. Both Killifer's mother and father—the latter a former pro baseball player who now held a modest job managing a farm team, the Hollywood Stars—enjoyed Joe very much. Though not Catholic themselves, they admired his fervent piety and his frequent trips (once again, hitchhiking) to the local Catholic church. "He just loved to go to church," Mrs. Killifer told Joe's biographer Hank Searls many years later. "He'd come back just beaming. He'd say, 'It just makes me feel so good.' I had a hard time remembering to serve him fish on Friday and sometimes he'd forget and eat a hamburger on the beach, but no matter how late he was out on Saturday night, he was right up and going to church." Most days, Joe lounged on the beach and waited for Tom to wrap up his job as assistant at a local law firm, after which the two young men would enjoy the beach and the ladies to be found there.

When Tom's father spotted a newspaper profile of Jack Kennedy, the young author of the surprise best-seller *Why England Slept*, he clipped the piece and told Joe it must be nice to have such an up-and-comer for a brother. Joe in turn explained that Jack's book really wasn't much and had been accomplished with a lot of help from professionals. Joe made scathing comments as he scanned the profile, and became especially critical when he read the line "Young Kennedy pleads for immediate conscription to prepare the United States for defense." Joe said he hoped he and Tom would be well clear of law school before conscription ever came to pass, if indeed it had to come to pass. At the same time, Joe acknowledged the likelihood of war.

The two young men, Killifer and Kennedy, packed up together at the start of September to head back to Harvard. They departed California by plane just as Joe received word that Jack—the young up-and-comer who seemed so enthusiastic about the idea of a draft—had been taken to the hospital. After spending several days at the Lahey Clinic in Boston toward the end of August, Jack was now being dispatched to the Mayo Clinic for what Joe must have at first assumed was treatment for the usual complaints. In fact—and this would not come out until many years later—Jack had been diagnosed with venereal disease: gonorrhea complicated by painful post-gonococcal urethritis. Jack shortly complained to his brother in a letter about the pain that accompanied urination, and bitterly repeated the doctors' grim word that though the gonorrhea itself could be cured with sulfonamides, the urethritis would be his companion for life. On top of his new affliction, his old symptoms still plagued him and proved just as much a puzzle to the Mayo doctors now as they had several years before.

In the end, the VD and his other ailments conspired to keep Jack from starting law school at Yale, where his doctors predicted he'd find himself exhausted in no time. The *Boston Herald* noted on September 10: "John F. Kennedy, 23, second oldest son of Ambassador to Great Britain, Joseph P. Kennedy, will not enter Yale Law School this fall as originally planned, he disclosed tonight. Planning to remain at the family's summer home here for another fortnight, young Kennedy said he had no definite plans for the future. He expects to travel and will probably spend part of the winter in the West. . . . He plans to enter Yale Law School next fall."

. . .

FDR DID NOT APPRISE Ambassador Kennedy of his new secret proposal to the Brits for what would come to be known as Lend-Lease. FDR's ingenious policy-idea included trading a large number of mothballed World War I battleships to the cash-strapped British in return for ninety-nine-year leases on military bases located in Great Britain. In this way, FDR proposed to get around the cash-and-carry stipulation in the 1939 revision to the Neutrality Act. Negotiations held at the British embassy in London bypassed Kennedy, who was further humiliated to learn from Whitehall,

rather than from Washington, of a special presidential commission led by
Admiral Robert Ghormley arriving in London in late August. In a huff, he
threatened Hull with resignation but then backed down. He explained to
Lord Halifax that with the Battle of Britain now fully engaged, he worried
about how it would look if he walked out now "under the threat of bombing." This, he told Halifax, was the only reason he was hanging on. Kennedy
made sure to be equally blunt in his frosty communiqué to FDR dated August 27, 1940:

> Regarding our last telephonic conversation . . . You were kind in
> saying that the people in the United States [felt] that their interests
> were being well protected here and that it was important for the
> morale of the English that I remain here.
>
> Regarding the negotiation of destroyers and bases, I am sure
> you must be aware of the very embarrassing situation I feel myself
> in in this connection. While realizing that Washington handled the
> matter entirely, on the other hand I can find no commonsense ex-
> planation when I consider the amount of information furnished to
> the British Ambassador in Washington by the British Government
> and the lack of information furnished to me on matters of vital im-
> portance to me. I would have no knowledge whatsoever of the situ-
> ation had it not been for the fact that the Prime Minister had seen
> fit to send some cables back through me and also has furnished me
> with supplementary data. You may properly say there is no reason
> for my knowing anything about it but if I am not acquainted with
> facts of vital importance to both countries I fail to see how I can
> function with any degree of efficiency. Mowrer and Donovan who
> were appointed only recently on special missions and two Gener-
> als and an Admiral were assigned without consulting me and the
> event was known in important British circles even before I was in-
> formed. Rarely, as a matter of fact, am I ever advised when impor-
> tant conversations are held in Washington with the British
> Ambassador. While vice versa Lothian is informed by his govern-
> ment in all talks or events of which there is a mutual importance.
> Of course it has been impossible for me to make any contribution to
> the destroyer-bases discussion seeing as I do not know any of the

facts, except second hand, but there was a possibility that I might have been able to make some contribution.

I have been fairly active in any enterprise which I have taken up for the last twenty-five years. Frankly and honestly I do not enjoy being a dummy. I am very unhappy about the whole position and of course there is always the alternative of resigning, which I would not hesitate to do if conditions were not as they are.

15

"Democracy Is All Finished in England"

As required by statute, Joe Jr. registered for the draft just three weeks into his second year at Harvard Law School, where he'd recently been joined by first-year student Torbert Macdonald. Across the country, seventeen million other young men between the ages of eighteen and thirty-five—brother Jack among them—did the same. Joe Jr. wrote a friend, "I have become one of Roosevelt's several million numbers, and am not enthusiastic about said designation. If it starts to really look like war, I doubt if I'll wait for the draft and will instead sign up for whatever service I think might suit me best, perhaps the Navy Air Corps.—an option many fellows around here [Harvard] are talking about. I've always fancied the idea of flying; and I've never fancied the idea of crawling with rifle and bayonet through European mud." Jack seemed equally restive under the prospect of the draft. "I don't like the idea of being summoned," he wrote, "and at the same time I don't like the idea that, once summoned, I may have to sit things out because of my many legendary physical shortcomings (none between legs). With a little careful planning our man Jack can probably—when the time comes—provide some useful service and do so on his own terms, don't you think?"

Jack submitted his 3×5 card to the draft board in Palo Alto, California, where he'd decided to spend the autumn auditing classes at the Stanford School of Business Administration. Living at first in the sumptuous President Hotel and later in a small rented cottage, Jack drove his new car (a green Buick convertible bought with some of his proceeds from *Why England Slept*) around town at very high speeds, but complained that driving made his back hurt even more than usual. He slept on a plywood bedboard, insisted on making love with his dates on top so as not to exacerbate his back problem, and sunbathed constantly in the belief that a tan made him look healthy. (Without a tan he continued—as he had for years—to present a jaundiced yellow complexion that made him appear, he said, "like a Jap.")

He had come to Stanford at the suggestion of Joe's law school roommate, Killifer, an alum who said the area's warm, dry climate might prove the perfect balm for Jack's many ailments. On top of the allure of the climate, Stanford's luxurious campus resembled a country club. Student facilities included one of the most beautiful of all Pacific Coast golf courses. Two thousand coeds completed the appeal.

People who knew Jack at Stanford recall him as having been, at turns, bossy and personable, arrogant and charming, vulgar and cultured. Something of a mini-celebrity in the wake of *Why England Slept*, Jack generally presented a more sophisticated front than most other young men on campus. At a school where drinking constituted a large part of the culture, Jack's incessant sobriety—enforced as much by his father's example as by the quirks of his troublesome stomach—made him stand out still more. His auditor's status gave him the luxury of drifting in and out of classes, coming and going on a random schedule improvised to accommodate the demands of his health and social life. He quickly took to skipping the business lectures—which plainly bored him—in favor of dropping in on courses concerning political science and history.

Although a favorite of Stanford coeds, Jack made few friends at the university—a place infested by Republicans. Indeed, Jack quickly found himself isolated by his Democratic credentials and the FDR button he insisted on wearing everywhere he went. Most everyone he met, meanwhile, wore a button supporting Republican presidential candidate Wendell Willkie.

Jack encountered one—and only one—true comrade at Stanford. Henry James was not a member of the notable clan suggested by his name. A Yale-educated Catholic grad student—and a New York native—James exhibited just the right combination of smarts, charm, and cynicism for Jack to find him appealing. James and Kennedy went to football games together and talked a lot about their shared religion. Kennedy told James he had a hard time believing most of the tenets of the Catholic faith, and that the mass bored him. Still, he said he intended to hold on to his Catholic affiliation, if only for secular reasons. He enjoyed walking through the commonly Protestant world cloaked in all his Catholic uniqueness almost as much as he enjoyed traipsing about Republican Stanford wearing his FDR button.

Jack became unique in an altogether different way on October 29. He was likely still asleep—or at least in bed—on that morning when, far away from Stanford, a blindfolded Henry Stimson reached down into a huge glass bowl to select the first draft lottery slips. The eighteenth slip extracted bore the serial number 2748. "The holder of 2748 for the Palo Alto area," reported the *Stanford Daily*, "is Jack Kennedy, son of Joseph P. Kennedy, U.S. Ambassador to the Court of St. James's, and student at Stanford Business School. Young Kennedy is the author of a recent best-seller on the conditions of England before the outbreak of World War II." In the event of a call-up, Jack could count on being among the first summoned.

Writing to facetiously congratulate Jack on his luck in the lottery, Torb said it was about time Jack got down on his knees and thanked God for his bum stomach. Lem Billings—now working for Coca-Cola in Connecticut—proffered similar advice: Jack should stay out of the sun, since henceforth yellow might prove a most stylish color. Another friend wrote that he'd seen Jack's picture, and mention of his draft status, in a Movietone newsreel. Jack himself seemed less worried about his selection than he was about the attendant publicity. There had been enough in the press about how the Kennedys, exemplified by the ambassador, were cowards. "This draft has caused me a bit of concern," he told Billings. "They will never take me into the Army—and yet if I don't [go in], it will look quite bad." He told another friend he was thinking about "the unhappy political future awaiting anyone who is even suspected of being a slacker. I'd ideally, in the long run, like to find some way to get into uniform even though I know Uncle Sam will never put this broken body in between himself and any serious adversary."

. . .

BACK IN BRONXVILLE, Kick started another dull semester at Finch and worried over reports that Billy—now stationed with his Coldstream

Guards unit at Elstree—was being seen more and more frequently in the company of Sally Norton. Bored with factory work and fluent in German, Sally had recently accepted a job translating documents for MI6 (British intelligence). Much to Kick's chagrin, this relaxed, London-based assignment left Sally with increased time for socializing. As Kick heard through intermediaries, Billy and Sally spent a lot of time at London haunts—now tightly cloaked in the blackout—that Kick knew well: the Mirabelle, the Café de Paris, and the 400. The couple continued to make their rounds of the dimmed London clubs even after September 30, when Hitler (having failed to knock out the RAF during what had been nearly a month of daylight bombing) switched to nighttime raids. In fact, Billy and Sally were only a few blocks away—on their way to the spot—when the Café de Paris became ground zero for a German bomb in early October. The orchestra members and most of the couples on the dance floor died in the explosion; Sally and Billy pulled up in their cab to the sight of the wounded being dragged from the burning nightclub. The Cavendishes' London townhouse—happily empty at the time—sustained a direct hit several evenings later.

Kick sorely wished it were she dodging bombs with Billy, but her father would have no part of exposing her to such risk. "There has been plenty of bombing going on . . . and they are dropping them all 'round 14 Princes Gate," the ambassador wrote Eunice. "Last night they dropped one in the pool of Buckingham Palace. . . . The prospect of bombing every night is driving [the British] frantic. I don't know where it is all going to end but everything I see confirms what I always thought, that it ought never to have started." He wrote Jean, as well, with more bombing-related news. "The house . . . that I live in is such a bright color that the Air Ministry came in the other day and said it was such a perfect landmark for the German aeroplanes that it will have to be camouflaged, so they are trying to fix it up before the new moon. From that you can see all the problems that one has over here during the terrible war that this is."

With his usual nose for a good story, Kennedy summoned the press when authorities found the initials "JPK" inscribed on an unexploded German bomb not far away from the house at St. Leonard's. Newspapers around the world carried a photograph of Kennedy standing beside the German incendiary. The caption declared him "America's Most Bombed Ambassador." (It seemed Kennedy had not chosen his woodland hideaway carefully

enough. Dodge's house at St. Leonard's lurked quite near a number of targets the Germans found attractive: several factories and an airstrip.) The
ambassador recalled after the war that he "wasn't very cordial" when FDR
telephoned in mid-September of 1940 "and said perfunctorily that he hoped
we were all right. . . . For ten days there had been continual bombing and at
night the anti-aircraft barrage made sleep impossible."

"The people here keep saying their chin is up and that they can't be
beaten," he wrote Jack, "but the people who have had any experience with
these bombings don't like it at all. After all, it remained for London to receive the worst bombing since Rotterdam and remember that this city is attempting to function while all this is going on, whereas Warsaw and
Rotterdam were evacuated. . . . I can see evidences of some people beginning to break down. Herschel Johnson was almost killed Sunday night when
the house next door to him was blown right off the map. The Natural History Museum in Kensington was practically gutted by bombs and fire Sunday night, so all in all, Jack, it is a great experience. The only thing I am
afraid of is that I won't be able to live long enough to tell all that I see and
feel about this crisis. When I hear these mental midgets (USA) talking about
my desire for appeasement and being critical of it, my blood fairly boils.
What is this war going to prove? And what is it going to do to civilization?
The answer to the first question is nothing; and to the second I shudder even
to think about it."

While Ambassador Kennedy still defended his utterances of the previous year, others who had once stood with him—among them Nancy Astor—
now came out and admitted their error in supporting the chimeras of
appeasement and disarmament. Nevertheless, Kennedy continued to inun-
date Hull and FDR with defeatist cables and memoranda. "To enter this
war," he wrote Hull, "imagining for a minute that the English have anything
to offer in the line of leadership or productive capacity in industry that could
be of the slightest value to us, would be a complete misapprehension."
While commentators such as Edward R. Murrow chronicled and applauded
the steely determination of the British to survive and endure against Germany's attacks, Kennedy saw things quite differently, telling FDR that "if
the English people thought there was a chance of peace on any decent terms
an upheaval against the Government might come."

For himself, Kennedy wanted nothing so much as to simply come home. The bombing rattled him, and he continued to resent the indignity of being bypassed in exchanges between the United States and Britain. Back in Washington, FDR told intimates he had no intention of summoning Kennedy before the election. "The President," reported Joe Alsop and Bob Kintner in their syndicated column published October 7, "regards Kennedy as likely to do less harm in London than in New York." Alsop and Kintner said Roosevelt thought that if Kennedy was permitted to return to the United States he would "reduce large numbers of leaders of opinion to such a state of hopeless blue funk that our foreign policy will be half-immobilized by fear. In short, the President has repeatedly urged Kennedy to remain in London in order to keep him quiet." The reporters said FDR feared Kennedy would voice "his opinions to every available American listener the instant he got through customs." In London, Kennedy bragged to Beaverbrook that were he home he could "put twenty-five million votes behind Wendell Willkie to throw Roosevelt out," and intimated that Henry and Clare Luce (the latter still Kennedy's mistress whenever time and geography permitted) had suggested he resign his post, return to the States, and do just that.

The British ambassador to the United States received an urgent communiqué from Halifax just three days after the article by Alsop and Kintner. The foreign secretary reported a conversation during which Kennedy told him he'd sent an article to the United States that would appear in an unnamed prestigious publication—most likely Henry Luce's *Time*—in the days immediately before the election, if "by some accident" Kennedy was not able to get home before then. "When I asked him what would be the main burden of his song, he gave me to understand it would be an indictment of President Roosevelt's administration. . . . He is plainly a very disappointed and rather embittered man." "The article which Mr. Kennedy has written," reported a Foreign Office memorandum, "is due to appear four days before the election [scheduled for November 5] in order to damage Mr. Roosevelt's cause." The Foreign Office understood that "Mr. Kennedy has decided to ally himself with Mr. Roosevelt's opponent Mr. Willkie" and feared that Kennedy's piece would prove "sensational and influential" once published.

With Roosevelt and Willkie in a statistical dead heat for the popular vote, both FDR and the British government agreed it best to make sure Kennedy's piece did not see print. Thus Cordell Hull authorized Kennedy's recall in a memo issued October 11, and Kennedy boarded a Pan Am flying boat to Lisbon eleven days later. When Kennedy's plane landed in Lisbon, he received a message asking that he report directly to the White House upon his arrival in the States and that he make no statements to newsmen along the way. The message, Kennedy said in his unpublished memoirs, left him feeling "indignant." Kennedy had originally expected to be in New York by the 23rd, but bad weather forced lengthy layovers first at Horta and then Bermuda. Kennedy received further urgent messages from the White House at each stop.

Late in the morning of Sunday, the 27th, shortly before getting on the plane that would finally take him from Bermuda to New York, Kennedy managed to place a call to the White House. "Ah, Joe. It is good to hear your voice," said FDR, two congressmen looking on. "Please come to the White House tonight for a little family dinner. I'm dying to talk to you." The men sitting with the president—Speaker of the House Sam Rayburn and an awestruck young Texas congressman by the name of Lyndon Johnson— watched the smiling FDR draw a finger across his throat as he uttered the words "I'm dying to talk to you."

Kennedy disembarked from his plane around two-thirty that afternoon carrying a souvenir British air raid siren he would use in future years to summon his children and grandchildren for meals at Hyannis. Reporters pressing their noses against the Pan Am VIP lounge's glass windows saw him raise and wave the siren as if in greeting to Rose and his daughters, who stood to one side of the lounge. Then he did the same in the direction of Henry and Clare Luce, standing at the opposite side of the room. In between these two polarities gathered a small army of Foreign Service officers led by Robert Stewart, head of the British Empire desk at the State Department, and Max Truitt, an old Kennedy colleague from the Maritime Commission. Stewart handed Kennedy two envelopes. The first contained a handwritten note from FDR formally inviting Joe and Rose to spend the night at the White House. The second bore a letter from Senator James Byrnes of South Carolina, a Kennedy friend, emphasizing the necessity for Kennedy's immediate compliance with the presidential request.

In a quick huddle away from Stewart and Truitt, the Luces urged Kennedy to refuse the White House invitation and immediately endorse Willkie, as he had evidently suggested to them he might in previous conversations. Rose, however, would have none of this. She insisted that she and Joe were duty-bound to honor the president's invitation. Later, on their flight down to Washington, Rose uncharacteristically argued with her husband about his evident plan to resign his post and abandon the Democrats. In a conversation overheard by Arthur Krock, Rose said Kennedy would be writing himself down "as an ingrate in the view of many people" if he resigned now, after all FDR had done for him.

At the White House during several hours of intense discussion in the presence of Senator Byrnes and Byrnes's wife, FDR heard Kennedy's complaints and then emphasized three points in response. First of all, FDR denied any involvement in freezing Kennedy out of the diplomatic process, claiming he had expected the State Department to keep the ambassador in touch and in play. Secondly, he suggested that so long as Kennedy proved himself a continually reliable team player, his future in the Democratic Party would be bright. In fact, Kennedy would be an extremely likely contender for the 1944 presidential nomination. Lastly, the president warned his ambassador that by throwing over his party now he would mark himself forever as a "Judas"—and the stigma would attach itself not just to him, but to his offspring. Byrnes, in turn, suggested that he thought it would be a splendid idea if Kennedy would go on the radio the following Tuesday (one week before the election) and endorse FDR, thus clearing away the "illusion" of any unpleasantness or disagreement between himself and Roosevelt.

Willkie supporters shortly became elated when they heard Kennedy would make a nationwide broadcast to the nation. They were also pleased when given to understand that Kennedy had refused an offer to accompany FDR on the presidential train to New York on Monday. Clare and Henry Luce in particular took heart in the news that Kennedy had chosen to fly back to Manhattan late Sunday evening, shunning an invitation to spend the night at the White House. There was yet another good sign for Republicans the following night when Kennedy failed to appear at a large FDR rally in Madison Square Garden, leaving an empty seat on the stage beside a formerly belligerent outcast, Jim Farley. Both the Willkie people and, ironically, analysts for London's Foreign Office ignored one key bit of data when they deduced Kennedy would use his Tuesday speech to endorse the Republican candidate. Unlike her husband, Mrs. Kennedy spent Sunday night at the White House and seemed both charmed and charming as she boarded the presidential train for New York the next day.

In his memoirs, Kennedy recalled that he'd refused to share Roosevelt's train to New York because "if I did that, my attitude would be perfectly plain to everyone and there would be no surprise [when he made his Tuesday speech]; in fact, it would definitely leave an impression that I was not likely to go against [Roosevelt]." Alternatively, it is possible that when Kennedy left the White House on Sunday night he was still not sure which way he would go or—at least—how he would explain to his mistress that he would not, after all, be rushing to aid her candidate. (Subsequently, trying to put the best face on his change of heart, he would lie to the Luces and say FDR had pledged to back Joe Jr. should the young man seek the governorship of Massachusetts in 1942—a most unlikely possibility.)

"On Sunday," said Kennedy on the evening of the 29th, enunciating slowly and carefully into the microphone for a nationwide broadcast he had paid for out of his own pocket, "I returned from war-torn Europe to the peaceful shores of our beloved country renewed by my conviction that this country must and will stay out of war. . . . Unfortunately, during the political campaign, there has arisen the charge that the President of the United States is trying to involve this country in the world war. Such a charge is *false*." Given the grave crises confronting the United States and the world, the ambassador said, now was not the time to turn away from the great wisdom and seasoned experience of a proven leader. In endorsing FDR, Kennedy said he spoke with his full heart and soul, for "after all, I have a great stake in this country. My wife and I have given nine hostages to fortune. Our children and your children are more important than anything else in the world. The kind of America that they and their children will inherit is a grave concern to us all." Kennedy did not mention—and perhaps did not yet realize—that the draft serial number for one of his hostages to fortune, twenty-two-year-old Jack, had been drawn in Stimson's lottery that very morning.

Knowing full well what Kennedy's true feelings were, his air force attaché Colonel Raymond Lee said he considered the speech proof positive that "Kennedy has no depth of political philosophy" and "is exactly the opportunist that everyone now thinks he is." Meanwhile Democrats nationwide rejoiced in Kennedy's remarks, delighting in the ringing endorsement for FDR and his policies as voiced by a major national figure with impeccable noninterventionist credentials. The Democratic National Committee took out advertisements in all the leading newspapers coast to coast quoting key portions of Kennedy's remarks. "This one simple, sincere statement by Ambassador Joe Kennedy smashed into smithereens Wendell Willkie's brutal charge that President Roosevelt is planning to send our boys to England. . . . For months on end, Joe Kennedy remained at his post in London, braving the fire and bombs and death to perform his duty to the American people and the land that he loves. . . . And then Joe Kennedy boarded an airplane and flew home—to tell the American people the truth!"

FDR came to Boston for a Halloween rally a few days after Kennedy's speech, which, from appearances, seemed to have atoned for one of the gravest of recent Kennedy family sins. FDR astonished bystanders when he invited both Honey Fitz and Joe Jr.—the latter, as the reader will recall, the most obstinate of Farley delegates at the Chicago convention several months earlier—to ride with him from South Station to the Boston Garden, where the three rendezvoused with Ambassador Kennedy in front of thousands of cheering Roosevelt supporters. FDR told the crowd he was delighted to "welcome back to the shores of America that Boston boy, beloved by all of Boston and a lot of other places, my Ambassador to the Court of St. James's, Joe Kennedy." Later in his speech, FDR played to Boston's generally isolationist Irish-Catholic Democrats—and to Kennedy—when he promised: "Your boys are not going to be sent to any foreign wars!"

FDR swept 449 electoral votes to Willkie's 82 on election day. Ambassador Kennedy visited the White House the next morning to offer both his congratulations and his resignation. FDR did not try to talk Kennedy out of his decision, but got Joe to agree to keep his resignation secret until a new ambassador could be found. According to Kennedy's memoir of the meeting—the only account we have—the two men talked a bit about world affairs, FDR emphatically agreeing that the United States must stay out of the war. Later in the chat as described by Kennedy, the president did not utter a word of protest when his ambassador said Roosevelt would either go down as the greatest president in history "or the greatest horse's ass."

Kennedy seemed in a confident and jubilant frame of mind several days later when Louis Lyons of the *Boston Globe* and two journalists from the *St. Louis Post-Dispatch* interviewed him at his suite in Boston's Ritz-Carlton Hotel. During their ninety-minute discussion—which the ambassador later claimed he'd believed to be largely off the record—Kennedy made a number of startling statements which wound up being published on the morning of

November 10 right beside the announcement of Neville Chamberlain's death. "Democracy is all finished in England," said Kennedy. "It may [also] be here. Because it comes to a question of feeding people. It's all an economic question. I told the President last Sunday, 'Don't send me fifty admirals and generals. Send me a dozen real economists.' It's the loss of our foreign trade that's going to change our form of government." He said he'd supported Roosevelt because he was "the only man who can control the groups who have to be brought along in what's ahead of us. . . . I mean the have-nots. They haven't any stake of ownership."

Kansas editor William Allen White—a founding member of the Committee to Defend America by Aiding the Allies—told FDR he must publicly condemn Kennedy as nothing less than an enemy of democracy. The *New York Times* chastised Kennedy for his "unguarded talk," while the *Herald Tribune* flatly asserted Americans would only breathe easy once Kennedy was removed from office. Walter Lippmann dryly observed that if Kennedy thought "democracy is finished because it is making these extraordinary sacrifices to save itself from destruction, he is of course entitled to his opinion, and even in England, where democracy is supposed to be finished, his opinion will be published."

Indeed it was, and both the British public and their leadership expressed outrage over Kennedy's premature obituary for their nation, culture, and history. "We can forgive wrongheadedness, but not bad faith," wrote George Murray in the London *Daily Mail*. "How little you know us after all. . . . Your three years as Ambassador have given you no insight into the character and traditions of the British people. Plainly you know nothing of their fierce championship of freedom." Speaking at the Tomb of the Unknown Soldier on Armistice Day, the day after Kennedy's remarks appeared in the press, Roosevelt did not mention Kennedy by name but seemed to repudiate the ambassador's remarks when he told his listeners the United States was obligated to always do all it could to defend democracy at home and abroad.

Controversy followed Kennedy to California, where, on the 13th, he made more incendiary remarks at a luncheon hosted by Harry Warner, Sam Goldwyn, and Louis B. Mayer. One guest, Douglas Fairbanks, Jr., subsequently chronicled Kennedy's comments in an unsolicited memorandum to President Roosevelt. Fairbanks reported Kennedy's opinion that "the Lindbergh appeasement groups are not so far off the mark when they suggest that this country can reconcile itself to whomever wins the war and adjust our trade and lives accordingly." Fairbanks also told FDR that Kennedy had insisted to his Jewish film mogul friends that "the Jews were on the spot and they should stop making anti-Nazi pictures or using the film medium to promote or show sympathy to the cause of the democracies versus the dictators." It seemed to the actor that Kennedy had been "violently influenced by strong Catholic appeasement groups and is in favor of a negotiated peace." (Darryl Zanuck of Twentieth Century Fox subsequently told Joe Alsop that Kennedy was trying to "scare the Jews out of the film business so that he can get back into it.") Fairbanks added in his memorandum to Roosevelt that he did not like to "tattle" but did so because "many people are beginning to feel that because [Kennedy] is still accredited to you as Ambassador . . . he is voicing new Administration thoughts. On the other hand, there are many of us who do not, can not, and will not believe that that is so."

Fairbanks need not have written. By the time his memo arrived, FDR had already read in the newspapers about his outgoing ambassador's impromptu speech. He was also getting other scandalous reports. While visiting at William Randolph Hearst's Wyntoon, where Joe Jr. had been a guest the previous summer, Kennedy bumped into FDR's daughter Anna and her husband, John Boettiger, both of them Hearst employees. Boettiger later wrote FDR: "After our talk with Joe in California, both Anna and I were considerably worried about what we thought were Fascist leanings." (In fact, though he did not tell his father-in-law, Boettiger and Kennedy had nearly come to blows when Boettiger confronted Kennedy with his many reported anti-Rooseveltian remarks. At least this was the memory of Marion Davies, Hearst's longtime mistress and a witness to the meeting.) Roosevelt subsequently told his son-in-law he was not sure what to do with Kennedy, and thought he should spend a little time with his old ally to see if he could not be brought around. After all, Roosevelt was only weeks away from taking his Lend-Lease proposal to the public; and Kennedy would, as usual, be better to have as a friend than an enemy.

FDR arranged a meeting at Hyde Park on the Saturday after Thanksgiving, and invited Kennedy to spend the night. Eleanor Roosevelt made small talk with Kennedy as she and a Secret Service man drove him up to the house from the train station at nearby Rhinecliff. At the house, Kennedy and

Roosevelt spent no more than ten minutes alone together before Eleanor received word through a servant she was wanted in FDR's study. Smiling cheerfully, FDR invited Kennedy to step out of the room for a moment. Then, turning back to Eleanor, he dropped his mask and said: "I never want to see that son of a bitch again as long as I live. Take his resignation and get him out of here!"

Eleanor said later she'd never remembered seeing her husband so mad. Now she reminded him that Kennedy had already been invited for the weekend. Besides, guests were on their way for lunch and the next train wouldn't depart for several hours. "Then you drive him around Hyde Park," insisted FDR, "give him a sandwich, and put him on that train!" Trying to make the best of the situation, Eleanor lunched with Kennedy at her Val-Kill cottage and there began to understand FDR's furor as she listened to Joe go on and on about Germany's indomitable and undefeatable power and how futile it was to try to hold out against totalitarianism: the unstoppable wave of the future. Dropping Kennedy off at the train later that afternoon, Eleanor gave thanks that what she would later call "the most dreadful four hours of my life" had finally come to an end.

. . .

THE AMBASSADOR stopped at the White House on December 1 to formally and publicly hand in his resignation. Speaking to reporters as he left the Executive Mansion, Kennedy said he would now give his full attention to keeping the United States out of the war. Several weeks later, Harold Ickes noted that Kennedy was "an outstanding example of what the President can do in the way of an appointment when he is at his worst. Despite the fact that Kennedy was nothing but a stock market gambler, with no political background and no social outlook, the President brought him here to make him chairman of the SEC. There he did everything he could for the stock market gamblers. Kennedy made a stiff fight to become Secretary of the Treasury and Morgenthau blocked him there. Against a less stubborn man than Morgenthau, or one less close to the President, he might have won. As a consolation prize, the President sent him to the Court of St. James's. . . . Now he is back here undertaking to sabotage the President's foreign policy."

Pearl Harbor was just one year away. FDR announced his Lend-Lease bill on the 17th. In addition to the battleship-for-lease swap, the bill also gave the president broad powers to authorize many other types and varieties of aid to Britain, and to provide naval protection to merchant ships delivering supplies across the North Atlantic. Almost immediately, Joe Kennedy expressed reservations about Lend-Lease in a letter read on the floor of the House of Representatives by Congressman Louis Ludlow. Congressman Ludlow had recently authored legislation—narrowly defeated by just one vote—requiring a national referendum in order to declare war. "While our own defenses are weak, we are limited as to what we can do for Britain, even though we want to," wrote Kennedy. America's primary task was to defend herself rather than others. Kennedy demurred when offered the chairmanship of America First in mid-December, refusing the job on grounds that he was still officially an ambassador of the United States, if only in name, until Congress confirmed a replacement.

He became annoyed, two days before the end of 1940, when he heard what he thought was an unmistakable reference to himself as he sat by his radio in Palm Beach. In what was to become known as the "Arsenal of Democracy" speech, FDR said that never before since Jamestown and Plymouth Rock had American civilization been so near to disaster. FDR warned of "unwitting" highly placed Americans who were busy advancing foreign, anti-Democratic agendas, spreading defeatism, and fostering cynicism among the American public. "The experience of the past two years has proven beyond doubt that no nation can appease the Nazis," said Roosevelt. This, he declared, was a lesson yet to be learned by the "American appeasers" who insisted that "the Axis powers are going to win anyway, that all this bloodshed in the world can be saved, that the United States might just as well throw its influence into the scale of a dictated peace, and get the best out of it that we can. They call it a 'negotiated peace.' Nonsense! Is it a negotiated peace if a gang of outlaws surrounds your community and on threat of extermination makes you pay tribute to save your own skins?"

·   ·   ·

KENNEDY CLUNG TO HIS diplomatic title. His children, going forward, always referred to him as "the ambassador" in talks with non-Kennedys. Rose used the same term when speaking to friends and staff. Thus, in the pages that follow as in life, Kennedy remains "the ambassador" in name if not in truth.

=== 16 ===

Neither One Thing
nor Another

THE RADIO IN THE PARLOR of the Palm Beach mansion crackled once again with the voice of FDR on the evening of January 6, 1941, when the president enumerated the Four Freedoms in his State of the Union address and called upon Americans to be wary of the type of peace routinely dictated by tyrants—a peace from which no one could realistically expect the emergence of "international generosity, or return of true independence, or world disarmament, or freedom of expression, or freedom of religion—or even good business. . . . We must always be wary of those who with sounding brass and tinkling cymbal preach the 'ism' of appeasement." The ambassador's wife and others, including Jack, noted with some surprise the old man's lack of anger as he listened to FDR's remarks. They were even more surprised when they heard the ambassador speculate out loud, later in the evening, on the possibility that he might still play a role in the Roosevelt presidency. It seemed that—policy aside—he actually didn't like the idea of being denied a place on FDR's team.

A week later, flying from Palm Beach to New York, the ambassador serendipitously found himself seated beside naval officer Franklin Delano Roosevelt, Jr., to whom Kennedy loudly complained about FDR's inept advisers, all of them too blind to see that England should be forced to make peace with Germany. At one point Kennedy became so agitated and loud that another passenger asked him to quiet down. Upon receiving agreement from young Roosevelt that the gentleman's accent sounded British, Kennedy sneered: "I hate all those God-damned Englishmen from Churchill on down." (The passenger in question subsequently reported Kennedy's remark to British intelligence, which in turn reported it to Whitehall.)

Later in the flight, Kennedy mentioned Wendell Willkie's recent endorsement of Lend-Lease, and speculated that Republicans would likely be in the market for a high-profile Democrat to denounce the measure and counterbalance Willkie's desertion. The next day, the 14th, Kennedy telephoned Sumner Welles and told him he'd accepted an invitation from Rep. Hamilton Fish (R-NY)—FDR's own congressman—to testify one week hence before the House Foreign Relations Committee on the topic of the Lend-Lease bill. While he had Welles on the phone, Kennedy also mentioned one other item: his intention to go on the radio the following Saturday, the 18th, to answer what he characterized as recent unfair criticisms of himself in public remarks by the president, and to give his views on current issues.

After consulting with FDR, Welles called Kennedy back on the 15th and—as Kennedy no doubt expected—invited the former ambassador to Washington for a meeting with the president. Kennedy met with Welles early in the morning of the 16th and subsequently went to the White House at ten-fifteen to see FDR. Interestingly, in what was either a gesture of familiarity, a sign of disrespect, or an intriguing combination of both, Roosevelt received Kennedy in one of the bathrooms of the family quarters. Wearing gray pajamas, FDR sat in his wheelchair and shaved himself while Kennedy perched uncomfortably on the lid of FDR's closed toilet and complained, once again, about his recent treatment. Most hurtful, Kennedy said, were FDR's veiled allusions to him in speeches. Kennedy insisted he was not "unwitting," and that when it came to relations between the United States and Germany, he was not an appeaser. Kennedy further told FDR he was all for aid to Britain short of going to war, but questioned the broad powers granted to the president under the terms of the Lend-Lease bill as presently drafted. To this FDR said he would be willing to entertain an amendment offered in recent days permitting a joint committee of the House and Senate

Joe Kennedy, Jr., playing football as a Harvard freshman, 1934.
Tenacious but untalented.

Joseph P. Kennedy, Sr., newly appointed ambassador to the Court of St. James's, and James Roosevelt in Joe's stateroom aboard the *Manhattan*, February 23, 1938. Roosevelt had come to see Kennedy off.

Joe and Rose outside the London embassy, March 16, 1938.

Kick, Rosemary, and Rose dressed for presentation at court in the spring of 1938. All eyes were on Kick.

Ambassador Joseph P. Kennedy, Sr., leaves 10 Downing Street after a visit with Prime Minister Neville Chamberlain on August 30, 1938, just as events in Czechoslovakia were coming to a head.

Rose (right) at an embassy luncheon, 1938.

Joe Kennedy, Jr., at the Harvard graduation his father boycotted. Jack won the McMillan Cup for Harvard that same day—thus accidentally stealing Joe's thunder.

Jack, the ambassador, and Joe Jr. aboard the *Normandie*, June 28, 1938.
The ambassador smiles, but at the same time quietly fumes over
reporters' questions about the propriety of his relationship with James
Roosevelt.

Jack Kennedy in Jerusalem, 1939.

Joe Kennedy, Jr., at St. Moritz,
Christmas, 1938.

September 3, 1939: Joe Jr., Kick, and Jack walking to Parliament, where they will hear Neville Chamberlain declare war on Germany. They'd experienced their first air raid warning just moments before.

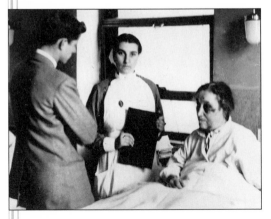

Jack in Glasgow with one of the *Athenia*'s American survivors on September 7, just four days after the British declaration of war. A reporter for the *London Evening News* dubbed Jack an "ambassador of mercy" who "spent one of the busiest days of his young life today, going from hotels to hospitals in Glasgow, visiting the *Athenia*'s American survivors. His boyish charm and natural kindliness persuaded those whom he had come to comfort that America was indeed keeping a benevolent and watchful eye on them . . . Mr. Kennedy displayed a wisdom and sympathy of a man twice his age."

Jack in graduation gown— June 1940. Note the dirty saddle shoes.

Rose meets Joe as he disembarks from the *Dixie Clipper* out of Lisbon at Port Washington, New York, on December 6, 1939.

Joe Kennedy, Jr., with grandfather, Boston's irrepressible John "Honey Fitz" Fitzgerald, and uncle Henry Fitzgerald at about the time Joe ran for a spot as a Farley delegate.

Ensign Joseph P. Kennedy, Jr., receives his commission from his father. The ambassador broke down in tears while addressing Joe's Jacksonville graduating class.

Jack and other PT boat trainees at Melville (Portsmouth), Rhode Island. Jack is the seventh man from the right in the top row. The PT training base at Melville provided mediocre training. Jack later said it was appropriate: "Mediocre training for mediocre boats."

Ensign John F. Kennedy, circa 1942.

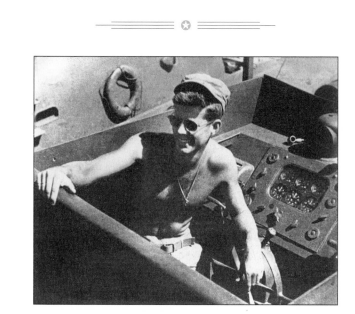

Jack at the helm of PT 109.

Jack and some of his crew aboard PT 109 in July 1943, just one month before their ordeal.

Aerial view of Tulagi.

Jack and friends at Tulagi, autumn 1943. Left to right:
Jim Reed, Jack Kennedy, and Red Fay, with Barney Ross
sitting behind Jack.

February 2, 1944: Jack lounges with a cigar at Palm Beach.

Joe Kennedy, Jr., ready to fly at Dunkeswell, April 1944.

Joe Kennedy, Jr., aloft in his Liberator.

Kick and Billy on the day she lapsed into mortal sin: May 6, 1944. Joe Jr. and the Duchess of Devonshire stand behind the newlyweds. Joe said this photograph would "finish" him in Boston.

The Marchioness and Marquess of Hartington.

Jack receives his Navy and Marine Corps medal at Chelsea Naval Hospital—June 1944. He said he thought Kick's recent marriage should make him "some kind of lord or something."

Jack entertains PT buddies and girlfriends at Hyannis on Labor Day weekend, 1944. The ambassador will shortly lean out of his upstairs window and castigate the revelers for enjoying themselves so soon after Joe Jr.'s tragedy. "Jack," he'll say, "don't you and your friends have any respect for your dead brother?"

Kathleen on that same Labor Day weekend, 1944.
Jack insisted on referring to her as "Your Ladyship."
Her husband would be dead in under a week.

Joe Jr. finally gets his medal in a posthumous ceremony. Rose receives the Navy Cross as the ambassador, Eunice, Ted, Bobby, and Jean look on in the autumn of 1944. Joe Jr. was dead four months when this picture was taken and Billy Hartington three. The Kennedy clan's part in the war was now over.

The family at the launching of the *Joseph P. Kennedy, Jr.*, July 26, 1945. Bobby served on the *Kennedy* as a radioman during the destroyer's first year of service. The *Kennedy* later played a key role in President John F. Kennedy's blockade of Cuba during the Missile Crisis. The ship is now open to the public at the Battleship Cove Museum in Fall River, Massachusetts—an institution that also houses two vintage World War II–era PT boats.

to be kept posted as to what was going on—but that there could be no power sharing. All final authority would have to remain with the chief executive.

Later in the talk, Kennedy noted that many choice jobs in FDR's cabinet had gone to Republicans like Stimson and Knox rather than to good Democrats (such as himself) who had been with FDR through all his campaigns. FDR replied that he needed good administrators, and for some reason the majority of these seemed to be in the Republican camp. Toward the end of the conversation, FDR dangled the possibility of Kennedy in the role of special emissary to Eire, sent with a portfolio that would include handling delicate negotiations toward securing British naval and air bases on the Irish coast. "He told me he would like to have a long talk with me about the Irish situation," Kennedy recorded in his diary, "repeating that [Sumner] Welles insisted that I was the only one who could straighten it out."

Given the possibility of rejoining the Rooseveltian fold as special emissary, Kennedy acted as FDR must have assumed he would and watered down his radio address, especially with regards to Lend-Lease. Indeed, more than a few notations in the Whitehall minute books for January 18 expressed pleasant surprise at Kennedy's remarks as broadcast on the NBC Red network. If Kennedy's speech did not constitute a ringing endorsement for Roosevelt's proposal, neither did it constitute an outright denunciation. (Columnist Dorothy Thompson said the speech exasperated her and that Kennedy had out-Hamleted Hamlet during his thirty minutes of fence-sitting by seeking "to be *and* not to be.")

"Many Americans," Kennedy told his radio listeners, "including myself, have been subjected to deliberate smear campaigns—merely because we differed from an articulate minority. A favorite device of an aggressive minority is to call any American questioning the likelihood of a British victory an apostle of gloom—a defeatist. . . . Another label used as a smear against certain citizens who favor keeping America out of the war is the word appeaser. . . . If by that word, now possessed of hateful implications, it is charged that I advocate a deal with the dictators contrary to the British desires, or that I advocate placing any trust or confidence in their promises, the charge is false and malicious. . . . But if I am called an appeaser because I oppose the entrance of this country into the present war, I cheerfully plead guilty."

Kennedy went on to say that he backed aid to Britain—perhaps even

Lend-Lease—so long as it was viewed correctly for what it was: a play for time with which the United States might rearm, render herself invulnerable, and thus spare herself participation in the war. He was, he said, concerned about the momentous powers reserved for the president by the Lend-Lease legislation—powers that would allow the president to usurp even the Congress in key budgetary and regulatory matters—and hoped that the president and Congress would work together to come up with "less drastic ways of meeting the problem of adequate authority for the President." He was, however, "a great believer in centralized responsibility and therefore believe in conferring all powers necessary to carry out that emergency."

America Firsters came away disappointed and surprised by Kennedy's tepid remarks. Hamilton Fish and other congressional enemies of Lend-Lease seemed equally unhappy a few days later—on the 21st, one day after FDR's third inaugural—when the man whom they'd hoped would be their star witness failed in the course of five hours' testimony to utter even one specific criticism of the measure. Instead Joe referred them—again and again—to his remarks made on the radio. When asked whether he worried whether the broad executive powers included in Lend-Lease might eventually lead to a dictatorship, Kennedy replied simply: "I would not want to answer that question." Journalist Raymond Clapper wrote that Kennedy had made "almost as good a witness for the Administration as for the opposition."

In the end, the episode left Kennedy finally and totally alienated from the one political group with which he had the greatest affinity: the America Firsters, who would never wholly trust him again. Meanwhile Roosevelt—who had never trusted Kennedy anyway—unceremoniously and completely dropped his former ambassador the moment he no longer posed a threat to the Lend-Lease program. Kennedy's mission to Ireland never materialized. From here on in, Joseph P. Kennedy, Sr., would officially be out in the cold: a cold that would slowly enter his bones and make him a very bitter man.

. . .

BACK IN BOSTON, Joe Jr. actively agitated against Lend-Lease all through the winter and early spring—this despite the fact that he'd previously spoken in favor of a like-minded measure, revision of the Neutrality Act. At a meeting held in Cambridge on December 30, Joe Jr. cofounded

Harvard's Committee Against Military Intervention in Europe, an endeavor in which he was joined by Langdon Marvin, Jr., godson to the president. Quentin Roosevelt II—son of Theodore Roosevelt, Jr., and namesake for another Roosevelt, his father's youngest brother, shot down over France in July 1918—served as another charter member.

Giving a speech at Harvard's Ford Hall Forum on January 6, Joe bashed Lend-Lease as a concept, arguing that the United States could not afford to prop up an unbankable Great Britain. At the same time, however, he said he thought it likely FDR's plan would wind up being enacted. If that came to pass, said Joe, Americans would have no other choice than to unite behind the decision and prepare to play an ever more active role in the war. That, he made clear, was certainly what he intended to do. (He shared Jack's sensitivity to charges that the Kennedys—especially the ambassador—were "chicken." He told a friend that in some moods he looked forward to war as an opportunity to "prove wrong all those who have cast aspersions on the intestinal fortitude of various Kennedys, old and young.")

Jack kept his rhetorical distance from the Lend-Lease debate. Although making no public statement on the subject, he stood privately in favor of the measure and urged his father to do the same in a series of letters written shortly before the senior Kennedy's radio address. Tellingly, Jack had spent a week the previous December attending a decidedly antifascist and rabidly interventionist conference sponsored by the Institute of World Affairs at Riverside, California, where he served as secretary for four of the conference's round-table discussions. In his eloquent summaries of these proceedings we see him repeatedly home in on the idea of collective security—the foundation for FDR's Lend-Lease rubric. "There is a real feeling here," he wrote a sympathetic friend from the floor of the conference, "that outright and total support for Great Britain is not only preferable but essential for long-term survival and stability here in the States. There is near unanimity that we have no choice now but to make ourselves, and our friends, strong."

He himself, however, seemed anything but strong. Dr. Sara Jordan of the Lahey Clinic examined him on December 20 and, alarmed by a sudden and significant weight loss, insisted that after Christmas he enter New England Baptist Hospital for further tests. He was confined to the hospital that January when he penned an editorial for the *New York Journal-American* on the topic "Should Ireland give naval and air bases to England?" Published on February 2, 1941, the article by the author of *Why England Slept* suggested that Eire, in her refusal to allow British military operations within her borders, slept "the same sleep that brought England to the brink of disaster." Jack insisted that if Britain fell, then Eire would "quickly follow in the tragic path of Norway, Holland, Belgium, Denmark, and other small countries who thought their neutrality would preserve their independence." Indeed, the pragmatic Jack denied there could actually be some such thing as "neutrality" in the world of 1941. At the same time, he recognized and acknowledged the roots of Eire's reluctance to give aid to the English. He recalled for his readers how Churchill as minister of war under Lloyd George had set the Black and Tans loose on the Irish for three long years and how, during the World War, Irish regiments had been delegated first "over the top" in battle after battle lest large numbers of well-trained Irish soldiers return to their troubled homeland after the war. Still, he wondered whether all that history meant a thing in the face of Hitler.

After his hospital stay, Jack made a short journey to Bermuda and later—in mid-May—flew off to South America, where his mother and Eunice were already touring. He spent a lot of time visiting churches and chatting with papal nuncios on those rare occasions when he arranged to be in the same city as his mother and sister. During the balance of his trip he explored the sex districts of Rio and other exotic ports of call. He also, however, did some research of a more serious nature—learning all he could about the geopolitics of Argentina and Brazil. Speaking in Brookline that same spring, Joe Jr. had suggested confidently that the United States could defend itself quite nicely against Hitler so long as it had strong South American bases from which to enforce the Monroe Doctrine. Down in Rio just a few weeks later, at a dinner hosted by the American embassy, Jack heard the Brazilian foreign minister announce candidly that the position and alliances of his country "would be strongly influenced by which side won the victory abroad." Arriving in Argentina a few days after the embassy dinner, Jack encountered a population that seemed ardently pro-Nazi. So much, he thought to himself, for strong South American bases.

· · ·

L END-LEASE BECAME LAW in mid-March. On May 26—the same day Jack flew from Brazil to Argentina—FDR declared a state of "unlimited national emergency" and invoked special powers to allow him to "repel any and all acts or threats of aggression directed toward any part of the western hemisphere." The following evening, during a "Fireside Chat" from the White House, FDR emphasized to Americans what he called "the first and fundamental fact" that "what started as a European war has developed, as the Nazis always intended it should develop, into a world war for world dominion. Adolf Hitler never considered the domination of Europe an end in itself. European conquest was but a step toward ultimate goals in all the other continents. It is unmistakably apparent to all of us that, unless the advance of Hitlerism is forcibly checked now, the Western Hemisphere will be within range of the Nazi weapons of destruction."

FDR predicted that the Nazis intended to "treat the Latin American nations as they are now treating the Balkans. They plan then to strangle the United States of America and the Dominion of Canada." He reminded his listeners that the Nazis at that moment possessed the armed power and the territorial thrust to quickly occupy not only Spain, Portugal, and French North Africa should they choose to do so, but also the Atlantic fortress of Dakar and island outposts of the New World: the Azores and Cape Verde Islands. "These Cape Verde Islands are only seven hours distance from Brazil by bomber or troop-carrying planes. They dominate shipping routes to and from the South Atlantic. The war is approaching the brink of the Western Hemisphere itself. It is coming very close to home." In short, the wolf was at the door.

Speaking at a Notre Dame commencement not long after, the ambassador called FDR's May 26 proclamation "a most historic and most solemn pronouncement" to which there could be but one response: "unlimited loyalty." Even Kick, luxuriating at Palm Beach, where she'd recently enrolled in a typing and stenography course at the local community college, sensed war on the horizon. "Everyone feels that we are in the war although there has been no official declaration," she wrote a London friend. "Of course we have gone so far it is silly to think of turning back. The only possible way we can get the tools to you is by convoys and once one of the convoys gets sunk we will be forced to declare war. Everyone is getting ready for the defense of the cities from air-raids. . . . We do live in upsetting times. There is so little, if anything these days that is a sure thing. I suppose it seems funny for me to say this when we haven't begun to feel the horrors and uncertainties of real war. But sometimes I feel that almost anything is better than an existence that is neither one thing or another."

During his two weeks in Argentina at the end of May and the start of June, Jack spent a great deal of time with his brother Joe's old cronies, Bebe and Chiquita Carcano, whose father, the former Argentine ambassador to London, now resided in Paris, where he served as Argentine minister to Vichy France. Jack made a visit of several days to Francisco de Vittoria, the Carcano family's vast ranch in Córdoba, during which he struck up a brief but passionate romance with Bebe, the eldest of the girls, and went on several hunting expeditions with Michael Carcano, a brother. (The younger daughter, Chiquita, eventually married John Jacob Astor V. Lady Astor boycotted the wedding and, reportedly, never forgave her son for marrying a Catholic.) At some point during his stay at the ranch, Jack nonchalantly informed Mrs. Carcano he would one day be president of the United States. This is the first record we have of such an utterance.

From Argentina, Jack traveled on his own through Uruguay and Chile, then boarded the S.S. *Santa Lucia* bound from Valparaiso to New York via Peru, Ecuador, Colombia, and the Panama Canal on June 10. He was still at sea when the Nazis invaded Russia on the 21st.

═══ 17 ═══

The Most Dangerous
Thing There Is

ACING A CALL-UP in the summer and likely assignment to the infantry, Joe Jr. volunteered within days of Roosevelt's May 26 declaration, signing up for something he much preferred over the idea of the army: the Naval Aviation Cadet Program of the U.S. Naval Reserves. "Wouldn't you know it?" the ambassador moaned. "Naval aviation: the most dangerous thing there is!" Joe Sr. soon offered Junior an alternative "safe" assignment working for Captain Alan Kirk, the father's former London naval attaché, who now commanded the Office of Naval Intelligence (ONI) in Washington, but the son refused. He was, he told a friend, intent on showing the world that the Kennedys were not afraid of anything. At the same time, he was enthusiastic about joining a fighting force that he believed could yet—if formidable and efficient enough—serve to keep the United States out of war.

Reporters on the scene said the twenty-five-year-old seemed genuinely happy—his face full of eager expectation (and perhaps relief after having survived another year at Harvard Law, to which he hoped, eventually, to return)—when he queued up at the end of June to be inducted with the

187

president's son John and several other would-be aviators from Harvard Yard. Shown into the lobby of the navy's downtown Boston recruiting office at 150 Conway Street, Joe and his cohorts formed into several ragged lines, raised their right hands, and in unison repeated the oath by which they became seamen second class—pay rate $21 per month.

An official navy bus carried Joe and the others from Conway Street to their first assignment: Squantum Naval Air Base just south of Boston at Quincy, not far from the Fore River Shipyard where Joe's father had worked as a manager during World War I in order to avoid the draft. Here, for the next month, Joe and his colleagues confronted a tough program specifically designed to winnow out the physically weak, the academically slow, and the psychologically vulnerable—all of whom would be assigned alternative duties at the end of July while the stronger candidates moved on to an even more demanding program: ground school and flight training at Jacksonville, Florida.

Joe and his associates spent a grueling twelve hours or more every day combining strenuous physical training with ambitious, fast-moving classroom work in the areas of navigation and flight theory. Each man realized he was competing with his brethren for the few choice spots in the Jacksonville program. It was whispered that Squantum averaged a 50 percent attrition rate—not unlike Harvard Law School. (Navy regulars called Squantum and places like it "elimination bases" or "E-bases.") Joe appears to have accepted and mastered every challenge. He seemed as intent on his studies at Squantum as he'd ever been at Harvard or Choate. A friend remembered him, in the midst of a few hours' leave, taking out his practice keyboard and working out messages in Morse code while walking up Commonwealth Avenue.

Like all the other new recruits, Joe took his initial flight training in a little Stearman Kaydet biplane. Flying with an instructor, he slowly learned to work the stick (which reminded him of a sailboat's tiller) and read the pulse of the rudder as it pulsated through the pedals at his feet. (In a letter to his father, Joe explained that the plane's nickname—Yellow Peril—had nothing to do with the Japanese and everything to do with the yellow aircraft's sometimes tricky ground-handling characteristics.) Joe logged ten hours bumping up and down amid the thermals above Boston and the Cape—always with his coach at his side. Then finally, after several weeks, he received permission to solo once around the Squantum field: a prerequisite for Jacksonville. When Joe arrived in Jacksonville at the start of August, he carried with him a flight-time record that indicated ten hours of dual flight and a full five minutes of solo.

Situated along the west bank of the St. Johns River about twenty minutes from downtown, the Naval Air Station Jacksonville had been in existence less than a year. Here at Jacksonville, Joe's odds became a bit better than they'd been up at Squantum. Jacksonville policy called for flunking out just one of every three cadet candidates. Still, Joe wrote his parents about his doubts that he'd make it through. About 80 percent of his classmates—sent from a variety of E-bases across the country—seemed to have quite a bit of flying experience behind them. If Joe survived the many rounds of eliminations and lasted to the end, he'd spend about ten months total at Jacksonville before graduating and getting his golden wings in May.

Joe and his cohorts received absolutely no leaves during their first weeks at Jacksonville. Joe sat through eight hours of classes every day studying the history, traditions, and protocols of the navy. He told his father he found the degree of difficulty in the coursework low, but the volume staggering. His life became, for a time, a grim routine of banal rituals: Reveille at 5 a.m. then calisthenics in the dark outside the barracks, followed by breakfast served from steam tables in the mess hall, and then the day's classwork followed by drill instruction. On Fridays one swabbed the barracks and prepared for Saturday morning's inspection, that inspection followed by a dress parade review in the blazing sun of the Jacksonville forenoon. At least, he wrote his parents, he enjoyed the company of his brave companions in the program, many from Ivy League schools and one of them his old pal Tom Killifer, who arrived at Jacksonville after surviving a California-based equivalent to the Squantum E-base.

At the end of September, as Kennedy and Killifer pinned on the tiny gold cadet anchors that signified them as full-fledged naval air cadets, they congratulated each other not only on their new prestige but their new pay rate, now more than tripled to the princely sum of $75 per month. The dignities of cadet status also included evening passes till 11 p.m. every second night and a move out of the bunkhouse barracks to semiprivate quarters. Joe drew Bill Ash, a "cadet officer" a few steps ahead of him in the Jacksonville program, as roommate. The two got on well. In other words, Ash did not mind when Joe started a floating blackjack game that quite often floated into their room whenever Joe's partner in the enterprise—Phil Kind, a Jewish cadet from Philadelphia—could not host it in his.

Once he'd made cadet, Joe faced a daunting six-week gauntlet—Ground School. Joe's Ground School work involved the study of aircraft engines, aircraft structures, communications, and advanced navigation. He put a particular focus on bringing up his Morse code speed, and he earned stellar grades in the use of international signal flags, semaphore, and airplane blinker. While he'd once thought he'd like to fly a fighter—perhaps a single-seater Wildcat or a three-man torpedo plane—he had by now decided he'd rather serve as patrol plane commander (PPC) over long ocean reaches on a multiengine flying boat. For the moment, however, he flew nowhere but from class to class, and often did that by the seat of his pants. (He had not gotten into the air since Squantum and would not be allowed back into the cockpit until after he'd successfully wrapped up his six weeks of Ground School.)

His Las Vegas–style after-hours entrepreneurship aside, Joe remained devout. He cultivated a strong golf friendship with the base chaplain, Father Maurice Sheehy, who also served as the naval air station's public relations officer and edited the station newspaper (to which Joe contributed). He ran for and—since he was the only candidate—won the presidency of the naval air station's Holy Name Society. In this capacity he rather delightedly took on the task of waking Catholics well before reveille and dragging them to daily mass. When some refused to rise, he poured water on their heads—for the good of their immortal souls, he explained to Sheehy. Surely it was better to suffer for a moment with a bit of dampness than to be tormented forever by the fires of hell. When he accidentally woke several Jews using what he termed "the hydro-redemption" method, they complained and Father Sheehy told Joe to watch himself. "Don't they have souls?" Kennedy asked ruefully. "Aren't you interested in saving them?" Sheehy shook his head and suggested Joe was unlikely to win any converts by dousing people with water at five in the morning.

·   ·   ·

JOE WAS SOMEWHAT deflated at the time of his advance to cadet status in late September to find himself immediately outranked by his brother

Jack, who received a commission as an ensign in the U.S. Naval Reserve on the 25th of that month. The younger brother had already beat Joe to the punch in writing a book. Now Jack outpaced Joe in the race for stripes and seemed to do so almost effortlessly.

There are hints that Jack did not enjoy these victories. More than aware of Joe's strong competitive instinct and penchant for brooding insecurity, Jack was at the same time wary of upsetting what observers outside the family often referred to as the Kennedys' "hierarchical" family structure. Nevertheless, he liked to travel at his own rate of speed without worrying about how his activities might affect the status of his precariously positioned elder brother. Thus he often sought different roads from those traveled by Joe just so as to avoid what might appear to others—or to Joe himself—as direct challenges to Joe's superiority.

That's why Jack had thought of Yale Law School over Harvard. It is also why his first choice for military service was not the navy but the army. Confronting a draft call-up after his return from South America, Jack had endeavored in July to volunteer for the army's Officer Candidate School. He was not surprised, however, when army doctors rejected him as 4-F. The army physicians specifically cited his bad back in their paperwork, but also noted his other ailments: asthma, VD, ulcers, and the adrenal problem not even they could put a name to.

Jack could easily, at this point, have accepted a summer job at a Boston bank where his father had influence—Columbia Trust—and entered Yale Law School in the autumn, leaving the world and the increasingly likely war to explode without him. But he did not want that. "I am rapidly reaching a point where every one of my peers will be in uniform," he wrote a friend, "and I do not intend to be the only one among them wearing coward's tweeds. I am sure there is somewhere where I can make a contribution in all this, despite whatever glaring physical deficiencies might be in evidence on my illustrious person." It was likely in this spirit that he queried Captain Kirk as to the availability of the ONI job previously set aside for brother Joe, and subsequently sought Kirk's aid in slipping past navy doctors. Kirk, who during his tenure in London had headed an inquiry into the 1939 sinking of the *Athenia*, knew Jack well, respected him, and believed he'd be an asset in the ONI's Washington office, where physical endurance counted for little and brains (which he said were in short supply) for a lot.

Kirk arranged for the Boston Naval Medical Board to give Jack a cursory examination on August 5, after which the candidate underwent several weeks of investigation by the Office of Naval Intelligence. ONI researchers checked FBI and police records for any indiscretions, and Jack supplied a long list of prominent friends to be interviewed as references. Judge John Burns told investigators that "John" was "a very unusual youngster. He has good judgment, a keen intellect and a great reputation everywhere. Most boys with prominent parents get an inflated opinion of themselves, but John has never been that way. He is regular all the way through and shows definite signs of great character. I cannot recommend him too highly." Another friend, the Kennedys' Cape Cod neighbor Jack Daly, touted Jack as a boy with "a very active mind" and—of dubious interest to investigators—"a damn good sailor." Summarizing their investigations of the young candidate, Lieutenant Commander J. A. Johnson and Lieutenant Carl Sternfelt described him quite accurately as "an exceptionally brilliant student" with "unusual qualities and a definite future in whatever he undertakes."

With his commission in hand as of September 25, Jack was made to wait several weeks "on inactive service" before finally receiving his orders to report to Washington. He used the time to best advantage: sailing and socializing. "Macdonald came down to crew for me in a regatta," he wrote on October 9 to his old sailing chum Cam Newberry, now in the army. Macdonald was not a natural sailor. "[He] caught a quick load and rolled gently over-board and had to be retrieved at a crucial point in the race. Kick has gone to Washington where she is now secy. of the editor of the *Times Herald*—a very interesting fall both for her and the editor—who, I understand, dictates at a furious rate in the happy belief that Kick can take shorthand."

. . .

KICK HAD MOVED to Washington during early September at the behest of Page Huidekopor, her old friend from the London embassy. After having spent the previous year as researcher/secretary for *Times Herald* editor Frank Waldrop, Page had now been promoted and made a reporter in the city room. She suggested Kick as her replacement. Like Page before her, Kick received a salary of $20 per week. Kick was at her job several days before Waldrop realized he had hired the daughter of the ex-ambassador.

Profoundly conservative and isolationist, the *Times Herald* was also somewhat mercurial in that it slavishly reflected the wandering and usually short-lived enthusiasms of its publisher, the legendary Washington hostess Eleanor "Cissy" Patterson. Nevertheless, Kick seemed to thrive at the paper and made a number of friends. These included a former Miss Denmark and sometime roommate of Page's by the name of Inga Arvad. Inga's beat on the paper included writing a daily column in which she chronicled the comings and goings of second- and third-echelon government officials. Glamorous, blond, and seven years older than Kick, Inga had married an Egyptian diplomat when still quite young and later became the wife of Hungarian filmmaker and explorer Paul Fejos, from whom she was separated by the time she and Kick became friendly in mid-1941. Inga had studied briefly at Columbia University's School of Journalism toward the end of 1940, and had come to the *Times Herald* based on a recommendation by Arthur Krock, who subsequently admitted he'd been impressed more by her looks than her prose.

Kick joined Page and Inga in a social set of young people that included Claiborne Pell (recently enlisted in the U.S. Coast Guard), George Mead (now a marine stationed at nearby Quantico), a young Swiss diplomat by the name of Samuel Campiche, and Dick Bolling, the nephew of Woodrow Wilson. The clique's regular rounds included weekly touch football games held Saturday afternoons on the playing field of Georgetown High School. Campiche and Pell recall their group as epitomized by affluence and, according to Pell, "too much smarts for our own good. We were all very aware politically, very perceptive, very sharp. We had a good sense of what was ahead for our country and our world. We knew pretty well that the cataclysm was inevitable. I think we felt we were the butt of a cruel joke being played by the gods. We were young and well and wealthy in a world that was about to go up in smoke. So, there was an element of not giving a damn for convention, and just living for the moment." Campiche recalls of the circle: "We let our hair down. There was lots of drinking. Lots of sex. No one knew what the future held, so we enjoyed while we could. The only girl we had around who did not fool around was Kick. A very good Catholic, that girl; very reserved."

"I have just had lunch with Dinah Brand [Nancy Astor's niece and an old friend from London] and I am nearly going mad," Kick wrote her father on the 20th. "[Dinah] said that everyone [in London] . . . sent all sorts of messages to me and that there [has] just never been such a missed girl as I am. I am so anxious to go back that I can hardly sit still. I received a letter from Andrew and Debo [Billy Hartington's brother Andrew Cavendish and his new wife, the former Deborah Mitford] pleading with me to come back and save Billy from Sally Norton who apparently has got him in the bag. No one wants him to marry her and all told Dinah to go tell me to come back and save him. Apparently they are going to announce it. . . . I haven't heard from him for simply ages and that no doubt is the reason." A few days later she wrote her father again, this time with a certain forlorn matter-of-factness. "Received letter from Billy last night. He said he was engaged and that apparently he had quite a tough time with his parents as they did not think the Nortons were respectable enough. The Duchess and Mrs. Norton had a tremendous fight but things have settled down and they are going to announce it in Dec."

· · ·

JACK REPORTED FOR DUTY at the Office of Naval Intelligence, Washington, on October 27, 1941, just a few days after Kick received her shattering news. Ironically, Jack missed Captain Kirk by several weeks, Kirk having received orders at the end of September to assume command of a destroyer squadron escorting convoys to Iceland. Jack quickly felt at home, however, amid the sharp ex-journalists who formed the bulk of the staff in his department. His compatriots showed him the ropes, and Jack was soon at work preparing intelligence bulletins and briefing information for Secretary of the Navy Frank Knox, Under Secretary James Forrestal, the navy chief of staff, and other top officials. "There were six of us in the room—a plain room with metal desks," one of Jack's coworkers at ONI would recall. "Our job was to prepare three intelligence bulletins: a daily bulletin for the Secretary of the Navy and other top people, which was a summary of key developments; another daily bulletin—a four-page leaflet type of thing—which was less sensitive and more widely circulated to shore stations and ships at sea; and a weekly four-page bulletin. . . . We all had typewriters at our desks and spent most of the day writing, condensing, editing. . . . I remember Kennedy quite well. He was a man of high intelligence with a facile wit—a good writing hand. He also had a heavy social life."

Jack's heavy social life included several evenings at the home of *Times Herald* publisher Cissy Patterson, where, on one memorable night (November 10), he joined James Forrestal and journalist Herbert B. Swope in arguing American foreign policy with Senator Burton K. Wheeler, an isolationist and a good friend of the ambassador's. Wheeler insisted, as Jack recalled, "there was not a real emergency here now—no one could possibly invade this country. With our strong air force we were invulnerable, no matter what happened to the British Fleet. He was very much against the Lend-Lease policy. . . ." (Jack commented later that Wheeler reminded him of some of the British aristocrats he'd met at the home of Nancy Astor several years earlier, and written about in *Why England Slept*. He penned a quick character sketch depicting Wheeler, jotted down their conversation, and noted dryly that he hoped he would not be needing the notes toward a follow-up volume on why America slept.)

During the debate across Cissy Patterson's dining-room table, Jack chimed in to agree when Forrestal insisted the United States must become "the dominant power of the 20th century." Forrestal said that Wheeler and other isolationists had built up Hitler in their minds, and in the minds of many Americans nationwide, as "an invincible force," but that Hitler was "tired, strained. We would have to fight him some day—it was best to take him on now, while we had allies. The job had to be done—Senator Wheeler was living in an idealistic world—a fool's paradise." The attack on Pearl Harbor was less than a month away.

Jack may well have been content with the prospect of war on the horizon, but he was not content to spend very much of the precious time before Armageddon with the likes of Burton Wheeler. Thus his evenings at Mrs. Patterson's were few, and Jack soon began spending the majority of his time with Kick and her circle, of which he quickly became the center of attention. He occasionally hosted the group in his little apartment at Dorchester House on Sixteenth Street, NW. More often the gang congregated at Kick's even smaller place not far away. It was here, very early during his time in Washington, that Jack met Inga Arvad—whom he would soon nickname "Inga Binga." Jack found himself instantly attracted to the beautiful woman several years his senior; she was similarly drawn to him. They were already deep into their affair when she profiled him in her *Times Herald* column at the end of November.

> An old Scandinavian proverb says the apple doesn't fall far from the tree. No better American proof can be found than John F. Kennedy. If former Ambassador Joe Kennedy has a brilliant mind (not even his political enemies will deny the fact), charm galore, and a certain

way of walking into the hearts of people with wooden shoes on, then son No. 2 has inherited more than his due. The 24 years of Jack's existence on our planet have proved that here is really a boy with a future.

Young Kennedy—don't call him that, he will resent it greatly—did more than boot the football about at Harvard. He was extremely popular. Graduated cum laude, was a class officer, sailed on the intercollegiate sailing team during his sophomore year, and most important, wrote a thesis.

Arthur Krock from the *New York Times* read it and suggested it be put in a book. Henry Luce of *Time, Fortune* and *Life*, must have thought the same because he wrote the foreword, and by putting in 12 hours a day, cooled off with as many showers, Jack polished it off during the summer and the much praised book, *Why England Slept*, was the result.

It sold like wildfire.

How, exactly, does wildfire sell? Jack usually answered mixed metaphors with unmerciful sarcasm, but one guesses that in this instance he let Inga's rhetorical slip go unpunished.

.   .   .

KICK, TOO, let a bit of romance into her life. Quite likely feeling cheated over the loss of Billy, she now for the first time since England struck up a relationship that was something more than a flirtation. Thirty years of age to Kick's twenty-one, John White enjoyed a large reputation around Washington as a star feature writer for the *Times Herald*. White exhibited a Mencken-like editorial ferocity, often writing five or more wry columns on any given day, all published under various pseudonyms. Sarcastic and cynical, White had been disowned by his father, a stern Southern Episcopal priest who objected to John's belligerent flouting of traditional values. (One of White's first encounters with Kick involved a loud argument over birth control. In line with the teachings of her church, Kick equated contraception with murder. White responded by saying the Church espoused this item of dogma solely to keep membership up and collection baskets full.)

Despite the bumpy start of their birth-control debate, White and Kick nevertheless clicked. She spent a great amount of time at the "cave," White's name for the Georgetown basement apartment he rented from his older sister Patsy and her husband, anthropologist Henry Field, a scion of the Marshall Field family. Here White and Kick drank wine and held many spirited discussions—most of them centering around Kick's fidelity to the Catholic Church. White made it his mission to try to question Kick's belief system at every turn, hoping to help it collapse and thus, in his view, set Kick free. (Of course—as White told Kick's biographer Lynne McTaggart many years later—he hoped that once Kick had shed the medieval strictures of Roman Catholicism she would likewise shed her clothes and thereafter share not only his cynicism, but his bed.)

In addition to freeing Kick from her church and her virginity, White also hoped to liberate her from her clan. White could not believe it when, early in his relationship with Kick, he learned the ambassador had run a background check on him. Kick, in turn, seemed resigned to such intrusions. In fact she told White point-blank that whenever she or one of her sisters started dating someone new, they were obliged to inform their father, who could then be counted on to do a little homework. If a suitor did not pass muster, then the ambassador would immediately order him dropped. When White expressed astonishment that he had "passed muster," Kick laughed and said: "Oh, Daddy considers you frivolous but harmless."

Uncomfortable with Kick's family and religion, White also pronounced himself wary of such friends as Sam Campiche, George Mead, and Pell. The few members of the crowd whom White genuinely seemed to like included Chuck Spalding (a friend of Mead's from Yale whose family owned a home not far from that of the Kennedys' in Palm Beach) and Jack, whose native intelligence and ironic wit the reporter found appealing. The rest he thought without depth, overburdened with charm, and too much infatuated with the veneer of style. In short, he did not think them terribly clever. They in turn viewed White as sullen and hypercritical.

.   .   .

BY ALL ACCOUNTS, Rose and Joseph Kennedy discouraged Jack and Kick from visiting their twenty-three-year-old sister Rosemary, a student at a Washington convent school for the mentally handicapped. Joe Sr.

had long been of the opinion that Rosemary's times spent with her talented and vibrant brothers and sisters only served to make the girl realize all that she lacked, and inspire in her a furor and rebelliousness that her parents found repulsive. Lately, Rosemary's situation had gotten worse when the girl—experiencing the sudden onset of long-delayed puberty—found herself befuddled by frustrations far more profound than those posed by her inability to crew in a sailboat race or succeed on the tennis court. She was now at times violent and verbally abusive. Of even more concern, she'd begun slipping away from her school, and had been found on more than one occasion wandering the streets of Washington alone, late at night. In her nightmares, the girl's mother saw visions of her attractive daughter made pregnant by a stranger encountered on the street.

The ambassador—perhaps in concert with his wife, perhaps not—chose a drastic means for correcting his daughter's erratic behavior. Widely and appropriately out of favor today, the prefrontal lobotomy was, in the early 1940s, hailed as a pioneering new surgical innovation providing nothing short of a miracle cure for mentally unstable or deficient patients suffering from extreme worry, depression, and frustration, as well as those manifesting violent antisocial behavior. "These unfortunates," announced Marguerite Clark in the March 1941 edition of *The American Mercury*, "may, in some cases, be brought back to useful life by the surgical removal of the frontal lobes of the brain. When worry leads to agitated depression, violence or gloomy silence, surgeons can remove the patients' cares . . . by removing that part of the brain concerned with the future." At the time, little attention was paid to the fact that the frontal lobes are the places in the brain where personality lurks, and without them one is little more than a sleep-walker, an automaton.

With respected physicians from Washington's St. Elizabeth's Hospital advising him to lobotomize his daughter, and respected magazines like *The American Mercury* hailing the lobotomy as a new wonder of medical science, Joseph Kennedy most certainly believed he was obtaining for his daughter the best medicine money could buy when, in the autumn of 1941, he authorized that the procedure be performed on Rosemary at St. Elizabeth's. "The operation eliminated the violence . . ." wrote Rose years later, "but it also had the effect of leaving Rosemary permanently incapacitated. She lost everything that had been gained during the years by her own gallant efforts and our loving efforts for her. She had no possibility of ever again being able to function in a viable way in the world at large." It was, Rose wrote, "the first of the tragedies that were to befall us."

Previous writers have been nearly unanimous in vouching for an unlikely scenario. According to virtually all authorized and unauthorized biographies of the Kennedys, none of Rosemary's brothers or sisters—*nor even her mother*—were ever informed of Rosemary's surgery or its terrible result. According to the popularly accepted version, Joe Kennedy made the decision to lobotomize on his own and then successfully kept his family in the dark about what he'd done to his daughter, insisting it would be best for Rosemary henceforward if she did not see her siblings or her mother. We are asked to believe that none of Joe's smart, inquisitive children—nor even his wife, Rosemary's mother—ever questioned why the girl who had been an integral, if slow, part of their family for more than two decades had now to be banished from their midst forever. (What mother accepts without question a decision that she may not see one of her own children again for decades, if at all?)

If we believe the version, and Rose's first-person testimony as presented in Doris Kearns Goodwin's *The Fitzgeralds and the Kennedys*, Rose herself only discovered the true facts of Rosemary's situation after her husband was immobilized by a stroke in the early 1960s and she by default took up correspondence with Rosemary's longtime caregivers at St. Coletta's Convent, Jefferson, Wisconsin. Rose herself, however, said something quite different in her own memoir, in which she suggested her involvement in the decision to lobotomize: "Joe and I brought the most eminent medical specialists into consult, and the advice, finally, was that Rosemary should undergo a certain form of neurosurgery."

Whatever the truth about what Rose knew and when she knew it, Jack—at least—learned of Rosemary's surgery, and its result, soon after it happened. Evidence shows he was significantly affected by the tragedy. It is doubtful Jack got true details about Rosemary from his father or mother. More likely he made his own inquiries and got his information from staff at the hospital where Rosemary's mind was wiped clean. The logistics would have been simple enough, and Jack's interest likely enough.

Writing to a friend shortly after Rosemary's surgery, Jack hinted at Rosemary's predicament and explained that his sister's tragedy "has returned to the surface of my character, and confirmed that vital part of me, that has always been, at heart, a fatalist." This fatalism, said Jack, "has in turn made me confront unavoidable facts, grim realities, and awful possibilities about the times in which we find ourselves abandoned. It has also made me realize something more simple. Father does not always know best." Jack had taken to sometimes calling himself an existentialist. He told associates he'd finally lost his religion completely, but hoped the lapse would prove temporary. He still attended mass. He wrote Billings that where faith no longer lingered, hope endured. After Rosemary's lobotomy, he felt he'd been knocked off his already shaky spiritual moorings. He claimed to be certain of "nothing, absolutely nothing." His whole world seemed to have come unglued. Like life itself, the war seemed not only inevitable but also absurd. Faith—like glamour—was, for the moment at least, a thing of the past. Both the world and Rosemary were broken in ways Father couldn't fix.

. . .

Jack and Lem Billings spent the morning of Sunday, December 7, playing touch football with strangers on the lawn near the Washington Monument. "I particularly disliked to play with people I didn't know," recalled the nearsighted and unathletic Billings. But Jack enjoyed nothing "better on a Sunday than to find a touch game and ask if we could play. One team would pick me—and I wasn't half as good as he was. It didn't take them long to figure this out—I hated that! Anyway, on that particular Sunday . . . we'd just finished the game and were driving back to his apartment. All of a sudden the news came over his car radio that the Japanese had attacked Pearl Harbor."

18

Backwater

O N THE SNOWY AFTERNOON of December 12, *Times Herald* editor Frank Waldrop escorted two young ladies out of the newspaper's downtown office and ushered them several blocks to the FBI
field bureau in the Panama Railroad Office Building on Lafayette Square.
The two women—once roommates, once the closest of friends—exchanged
no pleasantries during the trek, and indeed seemed intent on keeping Waldrop between them. After it was all over, those who knew them both said
what lay at the bottom of the episode was jealousy over Jack Kennedy. Still,
Jack's name appeared nowhere in the memorandum—entitled "Mrs. Paul
Fejos, alias Inga Arvad"—that landed on J. Edgar Hoover's desk the next
morning.

> On the afternoon of December 12, 1941, Mr. Frank Waldrop, edi-
> tor of the Washington *Times Herald* called at this office with Miss
> P. Huidekoper, a reporter of that paper, and Inga Arvad, columnist
> for the *Times Herald*. . . . Briefly, Miss Huidekoper several days ago
> stated to Miss Kathleen Kennedy, a reporter on the *Times Herald*
> and daughter of former Ambassador Kennedy, that she would not

be surprised if Inga Arvad was a spy for some foreign power. She
remarked to Miss Kennedy that one of her friends had been going
through some old Berlin newspapers and had noted a picture of
Inga Arvad taken with Hitler at the Olympic games in Berlin. . . .
Miss Kennedy, a very close friend of Inga Arvad, told her of Miss
Huidekoper's statement.

Miss Arvad then contacted Mrs. Patterson and complained
about such rumors. Mrs. Patterson was quite worried about this
matter, stating to Miss Arvad that it might reflect unfavorably upon
the *Times Herald*, an isolationist paper, if it became known that they
had been employing a person suspected of being a spy; however,
Mrs. Patterson professed to have complete faith in Miss Arvad and
instructed Mr. Waldrop to take both of the young women to the
Federal Bureau of Investigation, so that a complete report might be
made.

[While admitting her past associations with prominent Nazis,
Miss Arvad states that she] detests the German people and their
form of government and, if necessary, will bring suit against Miss
Huidekoper to clear her name.

Subsequent investigations by the FBI revealed the sum of Inga's story.
As it turned out, Inga had made extensive visits to Berlin throughout the late
1930s (culminating in 1940) on assignment for various Danish newspapers.
In the course of her sojourns in the city she had become friendly with a
number of high-ranking Nazi officials. She'd been a guest at Hermann
Goering's wedding and even viewed some of the 1936 Berlin Olympic
Games from Hitler's private box, where her photo had been snapped. Perhaps more troubling for FBI investigators, Inga had more recently been mistress to Axel Wenner-Gren, a German industrialist suspected of using his
yacht (the *Southern Cross*, purchased from Howard Hughes) to help refuel
Nazi submarines in the Gulf of Mexico.

Wenner-Gren had underwritten numerous documentary-film expeditions for Inga's husband, Paul Fejos. He also owned his own bank in the Ba-
hamas and was known to have laundered money for the Duke of Windsor
(a Nazi sympathizer who thereby circumvented strict British currency re-
strictions). As for Inga, one of her former classmates at the Columbia School

of Journalism told investigators that she was "very pro-Nazi" and "made no secret of her views. . . . She used to object to the fact that we had several Jewish members in our class. She called them 'Chews.' Those God-damned 'Chews.' That was her accent." Still—as an outspoken supporter of the Nazis and a personal acquaintance of Hitler—she was the least likely of spies.

Subsequent surveillance by the frequently witless FBI failed to identify the young man—code-named "Jack"—who so often spent the night at Inga's Washington apartment. Nevertheless, once Inga's background became known, her beau received many warnings from friends and family to stay away from her. She could, Jack's friends speculated, prove fatal to his career in naval intelligence. On top of that, Inga's estranged and unpredictable husband, Fejos, twenty years Jack's senior, appeared unwilling to let her go without a fight. Fejos set private eyes on Inga and Jack and even made a threatening personal visit to Ambassador Kennedy.

The ambassador soon came to suspect Fejos as Walter Winchell's source for a column published on January 12, 1942, in which he wrote: "One of Ex-Ambassador Kennedy's eligible sons is the target of a Washington gal columnist's affections. So much so that she has consulted her barrister about divorcing her exploring groom. Pa Kennedy no like." The ambassador—recalled Frank Waldrop—"came boiling down" to Washington on the heels of Winchell's piece, "and I sat in on one of the head butting sessions with his children." The ambassador insisted Jack drop Arvad, and Jack refused. His sister Kick took his side, saying love was all that mattered, that love conquered all. The father in turn raged at their questioning of his authority in such matters. Jack said he wanted to marry Inga. "Damn it Jack," said the father, "she's *already* married." Jack replied defiantly that he did not care.

Reading Winchell's piece, J. Edgar Hoover immediately sized up the situation his muddling agents had not as yet been able to figure out. It was just a matter of days before Jack received an abrupt transfer to the ONI field office in the Sixth Naval District, Charleston, South Carolina, where a less sensitive job waited. Kick subsequently moved into Jack's old rooms at the Dorchester, these being far more comfortable and plush than her previous digs.

Inga was placed under FBI "technical surveillance" several days before she arrived in Charleston for the first of several weekend visits on the 24th.

She checked into the Fort Sumter Hotel, right up the street from Jack's rooms in a private brick house on Murray Boulevard, and neither she nor Jack was seen outside the hotel for the duration of the weekend. "Inga returned with an infected throat," Kick wrote Jack shortly after. "Torb and I want to know what you do to girls that causes TB or infected throats or causes them to marry someone else. The doctor advised her to retire to bed but she refused and is now in the pink of condition."

Torb had arrived in town on the heels of Jack's departure, his mission to avoid the draft by finding either a civilian government job with a deferment or a cush officer's assignment without the threat of overseas service. Astonishingly—given her present situation—Inga suggested the FBI as a viable option. "She toted Torb around to see some guy [her attorney, Lyle O'Rourke] yesterday who used to be in the FBI but is now an independent lawyer," Kick told Jack in her letter. "Of course Macdonald doesn't have any idea what he wants to do. If he is looking for an easy job the FBI certainly isn't the spot. . . ."

Evidence suggests that the weekend of the 24th included a lengthy discussion between Arvad and Kennedy on the subject of whether or not they should continue their relationship. Her letter to Jack on January 26 smacks of ambiguity:

> He wants fame, the money—and what rarely goes with fame—happiness. He strives hard himself. More than any boy in the same cottonwool-position. He is a credit to the family and to his country. He is so big and strong, and when you talk to him or see him you always have the impression that his big white teeth are ready to bite off a huge hunk of life. There is determination in his green Irish eyes. He has two backbones: His own and his fathers. Somehow he has hit the bulls-eye in every respect. "He can't fail" I have said to myself very often. I love him more than anything else or anybody in the world.
>
> It is funny. In reality, we are so well matched. Only because I have done some foolish things must I say to myself "NO." At last I realize that it is true "We pay for everything in life."
>
> . . . Plan your life as you want it. Go up the steps of fame. But—pause now and then to make sure that you are accompanied

by happiness. Stop and ask yourself "Does it sing inside me today." If that is gone, look around and don't take another step till you are certain life is as you will and want it. And wherever in the world I may be, drop in. I think I shall always know the right thing for you to do. Not because of brains. Not because of knowledge. But because there are things deeper and more genuine.

"Distrust is a very funny thing, isn't it?" she wrote him one day later, on the 27th. "I knew when Kick got a letter from you today why you haven't written to me. There was a peculiar feeling at the realization that the person I love most in the world is afraid of me. Not of me directly but of the actions I might take some day. I know who prompted you to believe or rather disbelieve in me, but still I dislike it. However I am not going to try and make you change—it would be without result anyway—because big Joe has a stronger hand than I." When she heard that Torb had chatted with Jack on the phone, she grilled him on what the ensign might be thinking and feeling. "[I] saw Inga . . ." Torb wrote Kennedy, "[and] had a long chat with her on our only subject. [I] controlled my nausea long enough to do a good journeyman job. She either is crazy about you or is fooling a lot of people. How was he—What did he say, etc., etc. I lied as usual, Kennedy. . . ."

Inga returned to Charleston on Friday, February 6, and registered once more at the Fort Sumter under the name Barbara White. FBI agents spotted the couple leaving their room several times for meals and tailed them on Sunday morning when Jack—feeling confused and low—dragged the bemused Inga to the ritualistic comfort of the mass. ("You always say you have faith," she wrote him a few days later. "Sometimes I wonder if you believe it yourself. To me it seems that the faith you are born with is an empty one. The one you acquire later in life, when God has risen the curtain and showed you life, showed you all its beauties and many of its miseries—well, if you have faith then—that is worth something.")

Writing their report about Inga's weekend, the agents stated that from a listening device planted in the room they'd deduced that "Kennedy and Mrs. Fejos engaged in sexual intercourse on a number of occasions while she was occupying room 132 at the Fort Sumter Hotel." About the same time, back in Washington, another FBI operative overheard Kick explain to a friend her father's vehement opposition to Jack's marrying Arvad. According to

Kick, the ambassador did not like the idea of Arvad's previous marriages and the implications this would have for Jack as a Catholic. Speaking to Eddie Moore at about the same time, the ambassador said his objection to Arvad hinged on the fact that friends of Hitler were likely to prove a liability in the long run if allowed to marry into the family. He also suspected that Inga might be something of a gold digger. (It appears that sometime during the first week of February, Ambassador Kennedy discussed both these theories with his son, who now responded more cautiously than before, saying he quite likely would not marry Inga but saw no reason why he could not continue to have some fun with her.)

Jack subsequently told friends he was completely in love with Arvad and wanted her desperately—though perhaps no longer as a wife. At the same time he remained a pragmatist and, in some moods, said that he should put as much distance as possible between himself and the Danish beauty. He confessed to Macdonald that having his name associated with Arvad's could have a very bad impact on his career now and in the future, and that Inga seemed not to have any respect for this fact. (When Jack informed Inga he was being investigated because of his association with her, she rejoiced and predicted he would "soon be kicked out" of the navy. He, in turn, answered ruefully that there was "more truth than poetry" to Inga's statement.) He became increasingly concerned early in the second week of February when *Life* magazine—its owner, Luce, still annoyed with Jack's father for deserting the Willkie cause—threatened to run a piece about him and his now notorious girlfriend. And he was further harried when he discovered an operative for navy security copying his personal mail. He would, of course, have been even more upset if he realized—as the FBI knew already and Kick would soon learn—that Inga had been two-timing him for several weeks with an old Danish boyfriend, Nils Blok.

The frustrated and nervous Jack Kennedy wanted three things desperately: Inga, the absence of publicity, and a fresh assignment. "My plans are as usual varied and interesting," he told Billings that February, "as I have a number of irons in the fire. One is an assignment to Pearl Harbor—the other to a battleship—both of which will probably fall flat on their arse but both of which make interesting conversation. . . ." He told friends he absolutely hated Charleston, which he viewed as a provincial backwater compared to Washington. He likewise hated his new job translating incoming ciphered messages for the base commander. Jack, recalled Billings, "wasn't happy at all in what he was doing. . . . He was very frustrated. . . . it just seemed to him a waste of time. . . . At the time there was nothing he could do about it. He was very frustrated and unhappy." "Have I discussed Southerners with you?" he asked in one letter. "It's not so much that they say 'hear' after every God damned remark—'now come and see us Kennedy, hear'— but it is the abots and oots—and all the rest of the shit that convinces me we should have let their bootucks go [at the time of the Civil War]."

. . .

To what can we ascribe Jack's intense and out-of-character loyalty to Inga—a loyalty he initially clung to despite so many obvious obstacles? He'd for so long viewed most of the women he'd met as disposable, and even seems to have given up Frances Ann Cannon (whom he'd told friends he loved and wanted to marry) with relative ease after she refused him. At the same time, he had no stronger a track record than any of his siblings when it came to denying the wishes of his father: something he now did with a vengeance by continuing to see Inga.

Perhaps it was the timing of things, on the heels of Rosemary's tragedy, that made Jack search for something deeper in a relationship and in turn made that relationship harder to give up. Perhaps the timing also made him less likely to take advice from the man, his father, on whose authority the lobotomy had been performed. In any event, a situation arose where it would take something more than Jack's own most sensible instincts, and something more than his father's insistence, to separate him from Inga.

We don't know exactly how Kick became aware of Inga's cheating on Jack, but it happened sometime during the second week of February. The revelation changed her perspective on the wisdom of Jack's affair. "Kathleen," Inga wrote Jack, "[is] sweet. I love her for admitting that what really gets her goat is that she is jealous of me. My God. What I give you—if I give you anything—and what I take—which is plenty—that is something she couldn't do for you anyway. But she is young and as yet intolerant. She is more afraid of the pain that I shall cause you in the future, than she is concerned with the happiness we may enjoy at present." Staying with her parents at Palm Beach for the week after Valentine's Day—during which General Percival surrendered the British garrison at Singapore to the Japa-

nese—Kick filled her father in on Inga's "other man." Kick had no way of
knowing that at the same time Arvad—conflicted—was debating which of
her two lovers to marry, Kennedy or Blok. The Dane finally decided in favor
of Kennedy, who as yet had not heard about the existence of his rival.

Jack and Inga tried to avoid the now obvious surveillance at Fort Sumter
when she arrived on Friday, February 21. They did not, however, outma-
neuver the FBI for long. Their room at Charleston's Francis Marion Hotel,
just a few blocks away, received listening devices while they breakfasted
downstairs on Saturday morning. Thus we know much of the conversation
that weekend involved Inga trying to lure Jack into marriage. Inga raised the
possibility of annulments (she'd be needing two of them) as the perfect cure
for religious difficulties. She also voiced her perhaps contrived fear that she
might be pregnant. Jack, however, did not rise to the bait. A few days later,
on Friday the 27th, he spoke to his father at length on the telephone and
learned of Mr. Blok. He traveled to Washington the next day, spent what he
thought would be one last night with Inga, and formally broke off the relationship on the afternoon of Sunday, February 29. "I may as well admit," she
wrote him a week later, "that since that famous Sunday evening I have been
totally dead inside."

If not dead inside himself, Jack certainly became increasingly bored and
gloomy. The news of the war did not help. The Japanese had already taken
Malaya, Thailand, Wake Island, Hong Kong, and the Dutch East Indies by
that first week in March, when the Allies surrendered 100,000 American,
British, and Dutch troops at Java. Jack also noted General MacArthur's escape from Corregidor Island, just off the embattled Bataan Peninsula, on a
PT boat during the night of March 11. Jack was still talking a lot about the
rescue of MacArthur and his family by Bataan's Motor Torpedo Boat
Squadron 3, commanded by Lieutenant Commander John Duncan Bulkeley, five weeks later when Bataan fell and 75,000 Americans became prisoners of war. The PT boats seemed, from a distance, to offer the only good
news out of the Pacific. Of course it didn't help Jack's spirits that his morbid
father made a religion of passing on every bit of defeatist gossip and commentary he could find.

"The newspapers still go on printing headlines that say Victory," Jack
wrote sourly to his old Choate classmate Rip Horton, "and a news-story that
stinks of defeat. I suppose that a lot of the trouble comes from the fact that

nobody knows exactly what the hell the war is all about. There's still too great an impression that we're embarked on a lofty crusade for the Four Freedoms, not a bitter savage back-to-the-wall fight for our survival. Because that's what its turning into. I really think now that we will be either defeated—that is, we will make a compromise peace, [and] by compromise I mean we will settle for the US's territorial integrity—or we will fight a war that will take eight or ten years, a war that will make any resemblance between our democratic life as we know it today and our life then purely coincidental. . . . The lineup for this war is not drawn definitely—there'll be some changes made. You could write another version of *An American Tragedy*. The very definition of tragedy in Greek means that the disaster in the last act is inevitable and inherent in the attitude of those who are involved. Now, I don't mean that we inevitably are going to watch the *American Tragedy* on a larger scale than Mr. Dreiser played with. The reason we're not witnessing a true tragedy is that we can do something that the Greeks couldn't—we can prevent the gloomy ending—it isn't inevitable—something can be done, but before its ended it may call for us to be regimented to the point that [will] make the Nazis look like starry eyed individualists. If we decide that its worth it—what we're fighting for warrants the sacrifice—we'll win. Otherwise we won't. . . ."

. . .

"HAVE BEEN OFFERED commission in Navy," Macdonald wrote Jack at the start of February, "at rank of Lieutenant Junior Grade as assistant athletic director at Naval Flying Station at Pensacola—full ratings and pay etc. & exemption from draft. However, high draft number, 8900 out of 9300 to be called from Malden + local draft boards' statement they won't grab me till next April + varicose veins (you know I couldn't march, Jack) = indecision on taking the job as once in the Navy I'm good for the duration of the emergency. But as have been deferred from accepting the job till June am going to wait till then to see what Roosevelt's next act of aggression will be. After his speech last night am beginning to think the softest place I could be is a non-combatant officer at Pensacola (but not in the summer). God damn Hitler. God damn the English & double God damn Roosevelt."

Jack did not applaud Macdonald's reluctance when it came to the service. "Macdonald is up in Boston," he wrote Claiborne Pell, now engaged in dangerous convoy duty in the North Atlantic. "He is intent on finding himself a safe harbor state-side for the duration. A decade from now he will be able to tell his children he threw a football or pushed a pencil all through the war, and won't they be proud. He was never chicken-shit on the football field, and would have scoffed at the stuff it takes to run cross-country for Princeton, but when push came to shove you wound up in torpedo alley and he wound up in the whiner's corner." (Pell had been a cross-country star at Princeton.)

Despite Macdonald's carefully calculated plans to avoid risk to life or limb, he subsequently decided he'd be more than happy to go to war after enduring several weeks of utter tedium in the safe, noncombatant job he eventually negotiated for himself: clerk in the office of the Inspector of Naval Material, Boston. "I swear to God Kennedy I've worked like a damned nigger (pre 1865 vintage)," he wrote on March 9, "and have been so God damned tired that I go home & fall in bed, not that I'm tired literally, but that I know I will be at 7 am when that fucking alarm goes off. Life was never like this & for my dough they can have it." He was now, after laboring so hard to get safe duty stateside, considering applying for a post at sea because, he told Jack, he'd "just as soon drown as suffocate here beside this radiator for 3 years. . . . If you can arrange it why don't you go to sea with me as your valet or in charge of diet & we can involve ourselves in some feminine troubles in the lower color scheme. As a veteran habitué of the Balinese Room I figure a few days in Bali could get us in a lot of trouble (I hope). Seriously though . . . while I realize this war is no 'Great Adventure' or a Harvard/Yale game we might as well see what its like & not live the same sort of life we've lived in these troubled times. If we do we'll probably regret it later on." Macdonald would subsequently apply for a transfer to PT boats, and he and Jack would meet up again in short order.

Meanwhile their friend George Mead—the paper-company heir who had enlisted in the Marine Corps even before the war began—got word that he and all the other men of the 5th Marine Regiment would soon depart for the South Pacific. As soon as George received his orders, his mother scheduled a weekend-long party at the family's winter plantation in Aiken, South Carolina. She wanted, she said, her eldest son to have one more really good time before he went to war. Chuck Spalding, Jack Kennedy, Kick, and other friends—among them Lady Astor, then visiting relatives in Virginia—all gathered to wish George well. Sometime during the festivities Mead picked up a tape recorder and, pretending to be an interviewer asking questions of the famous news commentator H. V. Kaltenborn, asked: "Mr. Kaltenborn, do you think this is the beginning of the beginning or the end of the beginning or the beginning of the end?" Later on, talking confidentially to Jack and Chuck Spalding, Mead admitted he was frightened. Jack's advice: George should avoid thinking he was going to be killed, because those who fixated on the possibility were the ones, in his opinion, most likely to receive a free government headstone.

· · ·

WHILE JACK TRIED to learn to do without Inga, the ambassador tried once again to get a job from FDR. A telegram he'd sent the President on December 7, 1941—"Name the battle post. I'm yours to command"—had gone unanswered. "I don't want to appear in the role of a man looking for a job for the sake of getting an appointment," Kennedy told the president in a letter dated March 4, "but Joe and Jack are in the service and I feel that my experience in these critical times might be worth something in some position."

When FDR replied warily that he might be able to find him a post, Kennedy leaped at the opportunity and came immediately to Washington, arriving March 12. Simultaneously, according to the now standard choreography associated with Kennedy's successive bids for appointed office, Arthur Krock used his *New York Times* column to issue a call for Kennedy's return to public life. This time, however, the publicity backfired. After Krock's piece, the White House received hundreds of wires and letters denouncing Kennedy as a fool at best and a pro-fascist traitor at worst. As a result, FDR wound up offering the former ambassador a low-profile assignment advising on how to overcome bottlenecks in the building of destroyers—a position Kennedy declined. He may not have wanted to appear like a man looking for a job for the sake of getting an appointment, but he was quick to refuse when offered a position that lacked the dignity and importance he required. So much for "Name the battlefront. I'm yours to command." FDR had called Kennedy's bluff.

Animosity seemed to abound when it came to Kennedy, now a political untouchable. "A funny thing happened the other day," Kick wrote her parents on March 20. "A rather cultured gentleman called to give Mr. Waldrop an idea for a column. As Mr. Waldrop was busy on another phone I asked if I could take the message. The voice on the other end then proceeded to tell me that he had just learned that Supreme Court Justices (active and retired) do not pay any Federal Income Tax. (We have found this to be false.) I asked his name. He said that it didn't matter—it was just an old Irish name. I replied 'Tell me because I certainly have an Irish name.' He said, 'What is it?' 'Kennedy,' I answered. The voice continued, 'I've liked every Kennedy I've ever known except Joe Kennedy.' My ears perked up. 'Why don't you like him? I hear he's quite a nice guy.' With a bite in his voice the answer came from the other end, 'I know him; I went to college with him.' "

Ensign Jack visited Palm Beach in the company of his Stanford friend Henry James just a few days after the ambassador rejected Roosevelt's half-hearted job offer. Smart, confident, and not easily intimidated, James took an instant dislike to Jack's father, whom he quickly came to view as a despot torturing his sons and daughters, most of whom appeared frightened to death of him. James became indignant one afternoon when the ambassador chewed him and Jack out for arriving late to dinner. Unlike Jack and his siblings, the objective James shrewdly surmised the root of the ambassador's belligerence. This small circle of space, this dinner table overlooking the ocean, was one of the few tiny islands left in the world where the ridiculed and repudiated old man could exercise immediate and total power. James came away thinking the ambassador was not scary at all—just pathetic.

So too was Jack when it came to his physical health. Still "pessimistic on all fronts," Jack wrote a friend he felt "more scrawny and weak than usual" and that he had lately been harassed by intense pains in his spine and stomach. (Jack's superiors at Charleston had recently given him a score of 3.0, out of a possible 4.0, on his fitness report. They graded his job performance at the highest level of excellence, but docked him a full point because of his physical condition, most especially the problem with his back. Jack, wrote his Charleston commander, "has been greatly handicapped by trouble with his lower spine which will require long surgical attention.")

Citing his back condition, Jack arranged to take ten days' unpaid personal medical leave following his brief visit to Palm Beach. Experts at both the Mayo Clinic and Lahey Clinic studied him up and down and diagnosed chronic, recurrent dislocation of the right sacroiliac joint: a condition requiring surgical fusion of the joint. A few weeks later, physicians at the Charleston Naval Hospital—where Jack commenced a one-month incarceration on April 13—disagreed about the advisability of surgery as compared to physical therapy and drugs. Finally, Jack wound up ordered to the Chelsea Naval Hospital, Massachusetts, in mid-May, there to turn twenty-five and linger yet another month while doctors x-rayed, studied, and debated. He wrote Billings that he would enter the hospital a pauper and depart a man of means, since he would—like his brother before him—come into his share of the family trust upon reaching the quarter-century mark.

· · ·

JOE JR. TOOK NO particular notice of the PT that scooted MacArthur away from the embattled island of Corregidor on March 11 and landed him on the marginally safer island of Del Monte. He did, however, talk a great deal about the two B-17E Flying Fortresses which swept down on Del Monte a few days later to collect MacArthur and his party. He told Killifer he wished he'd been one of the pilots ferrying the general to Australia. He clearly envied those who were close to the firing line.

It had taken till mid-November for Joe to finally get up in the air above the golf courses of friendly Jacksonville. Once again he was in a Yellow Peril. He shared dual controls with his instructor until December 9—two days after the Japanese attack on Pearl Harbor—at which point his superiors approved him as "safe for primary solo." That is, his primary instruction ended on the 9th and he received approval to go on to basic pilot training, in which he was involved that spring while Bataan collapsed and Jack languished in his various hospital beds. Basic pilot training would, in turn, be followed by advanced pilot instruction and operational training, *if* Joe made the grade. His record in the air, however, left something to be desired. "This student does not absorb instruction readily," read one report. "He cannot remember things from one day to the next. . . . student does not look where he is going." On another day: "Student flies with head in cockpit too much. Student is afraid of inverted spins; consequently recovery uncertain." Translated this meant Joe spent too much time rationalizing and thinking out the mechanics of flight instead of feeling the plane beneath him and working with its flow. He needed more instinct and less intellect.

It was likely nervousness over not performing well that caused him to drop twenty pounds early in the new year. "I saw young Joe in Jacksonville last week," his father wrote a friend near the end of January, just as Jack's relationship with Inga became news for Winchell. "They are working them frightfully hard and he's quite thin, but he seems to be very happy and anxious to do his bit." In fact he was altogether too anxious. His anxiety only mounted when he graduated to the SNJ low-wing metal monoplane. He continued to draw questionable comments from his instructors, and soon—at the start of February—the Jacksonville flight surgeon ordered him to take a week off. He was—the surgeon noted on his record—"temporarily incapacitated" because of "accumulated stresses."

Friends who saw him at Palm Beach said he did not seem able to relax, so concerned was he about what he was missing back at Jacksonville and who might be pulling ahead of him in class standing. Things were slow to get better after his return when he began flying the PBY Catalina twin-engine patrol plane—a "flying boat"—off the St. Johns River. "Student is tense in cockpit. Did not perform cockpit check when I asked him. . . . Does not know course rules." In the end, he graduated seventy-seventh out of eighty-eight pilots in his class. Joe's final report from his last instructor described "Cadet Kennedy" as someone who had "a cheerful, co-operative disposition and a strong, forceful character. His handling of his regular and additional duties has been [only] satisfactory, but he is expected to improve considerably in this respect as he gains experience in the naval service."

Such were the mixed reviews that Joe Jr. took with him as he departed Jacksonville for operational training at Banana River, Florida, near Cocoa Beach, during the second week of May 1942, just a few days after his father addressed the graduating naval air cadets at Jacksonville. As many who witnessed the graduation recall, the ambassador became extremely emotional and broke down in the course of his remarks to the cadets. Writing later to base commander G. R. Fairlamb, he apologized for his performance, saying: "The sight of those boys moved me so deeply that I am afraid I did not do what I consider my customary job in speaking. It made me realize how unimportant everything and everybody is today compared to them."

Joe's graduation coincided with the Battle of the Coral Sea, a fight during which naval aviators showed for the first time what they were really made of. (It would, in fact, go down as the first naval engagement of history fought without opposing ships making contact. All the action happened in and from the air.) The fight had begun on May 4 when the naval fighters of Task Force 17 (commanded by Rear Admiral F. J. Fletcher) took off from the carrier *Yorktown* and bombed Japanese transports engaged in landing troops at tiny Tulagi Island, which with the larger Florida Island formed the southern edge of the Solomons. (An ungarrisoned but strategically important strip of land, Tulagi boasted a splendid port from which the Japanese would be well positioned to mount a thrust toward New Caledonia and New Zealand.) By the end of the 4th, the naval aviators had damaged several Japanese transports and sunk one destroyer. Subsequently, Fletcher's task force teamed up with Task Force 11 (commanded by Rear Admiral A. W. Fitch) and the carrier *Lexington* south of the Lousiades. The bulk of these combined units then moved northward in search of the enemy covering force that would, if left unhindered, occupy Port Moresby, New Guinea, in short order.

Early on the 7th, carrier aircraft located and sank the light carrier *Shoho*. They also damaged but did not succeed in sinking the carrier *Shokaku* the next day. At the same time, enemy planes damaged the *Yorktown* and set off uncontrollable fires on the *Lexington*, which caused her to be abandoned and sunk. In the end, the score for ships sunk or damaged favored the Japanese, and they maintained control of Tulagi, but the action of the navy fighters did at least cause the Japanese to give up on their attempt to occupy Port Moresby by sea. Still, the prospects for the Allies in the Pacific seemed bleak, given the overwhelming Japanese superiority in ships, planes, and men.

·   ·   ·

WHATEVER THE PROSPECTS for Allied victory in the Pacific, May saw a drastic improvement of Kick Kennedy's prospects for victory on a very different front. "I got an excited note from Debo yesterday," she wrote Jack on the 20th, "and another from Billy H. himself today: the wedding to Sally is off, says Billy, due to irreconcilable differences between the parents of the bride and the parents of the groom. Of course, I am infinitely happy about this for Billy's sake, and perhaps for my own. Time will tell." For now, however, Billy remained an entire dangerous ocean away.

=== 19 ===

Rather like Choate

THE FORMER naval air station at Banana River, where Joe Jr. spent that summer and autumn of 1942, is today part of the great Florida space center complex named for his brother.

Joe's operational training involved intensive work flying the luxurious yet sometimes idiosyncratic PBM Mariner float plane most often used for long-range submarine reconnaissance. Easily the most comfortable aircraft aloft short of the Pan Am Clipper, the Mariner featured bunks, a head, a refrigerator, and a complete galley. The plane had a total wingspan of 188 feet, measured just over 80 feet in length, and received its thrust from two 1,900-horsepower Wright R-2600 engines. Armaments included one .30-caliber plus five .50-caliber flexible machine guns, along with twelve 800-pound bombs. (These bombs could sometimes be replaced by torpedoes, of which the Mariner was equipped to carry two at a time.)

All this added up to a great deal of weight that made for slow, lumbering takeoffs out of the water and uncouth belly-whopper landings. Still, despite its heft, the Mariner flew considerably faster than most other aircraft in its class, getting about six knots additional speed (for an average of 211 mph) by virtue of its flexible "gull wing," which actually flapped like a gull approximately six feet up and down at the wingtip. Joe adapted quickly to the Mariner—which required not a lot in the way of piloting finesse—and seems to have passed muster at Banana River promptly enough. He gained more ease in the cockpit every day, and managed to navigate his way out of his operational training coursework by the end of July.

His next stop should have been assignment to an antisubmarine squadron. Joe, however, had other plans. He'd seen the life led by junior flight officers: days spent plotting fixes on maps, carrying the primary pilot commander's luggage, and fetching coffee. He did not want any of that, but he had only three hundred hours flight time and would need a thousand before he'd get a chance at command. With this in mind, he volunteered to serve for the duration of the year as an instructor at Banana River, teaching others to master the PBM Mariner in the same way he had. In the process he would accumulate the flight time needed for command pilot status. "At present I am teaching other young ensigns how to fly these planes," he wrote his sister Jean, "and my famous patience is sore-taxed. They pull some of the dumbest maneuvers possible, so as a result, you have to watch them every minute, which tires you a lot." In between flights, he put in extra shifts as duty officer and continued his friendship with Father Sheehy on golf links at both Banana River and Jacksonville. Also, much to his parents' displeasure, he briefly dated a Protestant. Of course, Protestantism was not on Joe and Rose's list of desirable characteristics for a daughter-in-law.

The ambassador used a long letter to lecture his son on the dire political ramifications likely to accompany marriage outside the faith. He directed Joe Jr.'s attention to the plight of Joe Casey, a current contender for the Democratic senatorial nomination in the Bay State. Casey was encountering severe headwinds, said the ambassador, largely because of his Protestant wife. The Catholic women voters—of which there were many in Boston—simply did not like it. "You wouldn't think this very important," he wrote, "but it definitely is, and I am thoroughly convinced that an Irish Catholic with a name like yours and with your record, married to an Irish Catholic girl, would be a push over in this state for political office. . . . It seems like a silly thing, but I can't impress it on you too strongly."

As both Joe Jr. and his father knew, Casey's chief rival for the Senate nomination was none other than Honey Fitz, who, at the age of seventy-nine and after many years of retirement, seemed to be running a strong race.

(Honey Fitz's campaign had been financed by his son-in-law, who told intimates he objected to Congressman Casey's long and loyal service to Franklin Roosevelt.) Honey Fitz would eventually lose to Casey in the primary, and thereby miss the chance to run against the grandson of his old rival, Senator Henry Cabot Lodge, in the November election. Happily, however, the old man concluded his career on a respectable note, polling 82,000 votes against Casey's 106,000. "I am awfully sorry to hear that Grandpa got beaten," Joe Jr. would write his father. "Maybe I'll get a shot at Casey when this thing is over."

· · ·

JACK SPENT a great amount of time during his second week at the Chelsea Naval Hospital (the first week of June) listening to radio reports about the Japanese naval advance on tiny Midway, an atoll in the western Aleutians. As Jack observed to his wardmates—some of whom soon grew tired of his running commentary on events in the Pacific—the Japanese not only wanted to overrun the atoll's strategically important airstrips but also probably hoped to draw out and destroy the U.S. Pacific Fleet's aircraft carrier strike forces.

Jack's fellow patients would remember him shouting and clapping his hands on June 3 when Midway-based aircraft located and attacked the Japanese Occupation Force six hundred miles to the west of the island. He seemed equally enthusiastic the following day when ground-based aircraft succeeded in turning back the Japanese carrier planes sent to destroy Midway's defensive installations. He wrote Inga—in Reno for a month securing a divorce from Fejos so that she might move to New York and marry Nils Blok—that the United States Navy seemed to have learned how to fight, and the Japanese had best get used to being outclassed if not outgunned. There is no record as to whether he took note, early on the 5th, of reports that said several Japanese aircraft carriers had shrugged off heroic but wholly ineffectual attacks mounted by PTs from Motor Torpedo Boat Squadron 8. But he is on record as having become exuberant a few hours later on the same day when radio reports said carrier-based dive-bombers from the *Yorktown*, *Hornet*, and *Enterprise* had hit and sunk the Japanese carriers *Akagi*, *Kaga*, *Soryu*, and *Hiryu*.

In addition to the carriers, the Japanese wound up sacrificing one heavy

cruiser, 258 aircraft, and a large percentage of their experienced carrier pilots. The United States, on the other hand, lost just forty shore-based planes
and ninety-two carrier aircraft along with the destroyer *Hammann* and the
carrier *Yorktown*, both the victims of a submarine attack. In the end, the Battle of Midway added up to a decisive victory—*the first*—for the Americans: a
victory that seemed to refresh Jack and pull him out of his post-Inga malaise.
He wrote Billings that things were looking up. He said he was feeling more
himself, and that he'd like nothing better than to get out to the Pacific and
contribute in a real way to the American effort in a war that suddenly seemed
winnable.

He became even more optimistic two weeks later, near the end of June,
when his doctors told him he did not need surgery for his back. His problem—they incorrectly observed—appeared to be nothing more than severe
muscle strain of a kind easily treated with exercise and muscle relaxants. Lem
Billings thought the news too good to be true. "I think it would be a mistake," he wrote, "to postpone your operation & take exercises instead. Of
course I don't know a damn thing about the circumstances, but to me, it
doesn't look like the best thing to do. As far as I can see you're merely
putting off the inevitable because you'll probably have to have the operation
sometime anyway. You'll just fool around for a couple of years with exercises—being still unable to do anything you want for fear of throwing it out
again."

A friend who met Jack on the street in Cambridge a few days after his
discharge from Chelsea recalled that he seemed nothing short of anxious to
get overseas and into action. Boston, of course, offered a different type of
action, which he seized upon during his few days of leave before returning to
Charleston. "I understand you and Bunny Waters are twosoming it," his
brother Joe wrote him, "and the bets are that there will be a threesome before long, and it won't be in bundling clothes but it will have a long beak and
a shotgun, and he will answer to the name of Jolson, after he has given you a
shot of lead up the ass. You have probably been given the setting of your
brother's station, through the enlightening letters to the Kennedy household, but Banana River speaks for itself, as does the town of Cocoa."

Stopping in Washington on his way back to South Carolina, Jack spoke
to a number of acquaintances—among them Under Secretary Forrestal—
about getting the training he needed for sea duty. "He has become disgusted

with the desk jobs," the ambassador wrote Joe Jr., "and as an awful lot of the fellows that he knows are in active service, and particularly with you in fleet service, he feels that he ought to be trying to do something. I quite understand his position, but I know his stomach and his back are real deterrents."

As a first step toward getting overseas, Jack joined a fellow ONI ensign, Fred Rosen, in seeking and receiving appointment to the Naval Reserve Midshipmans School at Northwestern University, near Chicago. Both Jack's and Fred's orders came through on July 22. They were to report to the Midshipmans School just five days later, the 27th. "[Jack] went through town and . . . he is going to active sea-duty," Inga—just back from Reno and preparing for her marriage to Blok—wrote a friend. "Only you know, his back—he looks like a limping monkey from behind. He can't walk at all. That's ridiculous, sending him off to sea duty."

Those who knew Jack best later speculated on his frantic urge to get into naval combat, all of them disagreeing as to his motivation. "I think," recalled Macdonald, "the break-up with Inga helped instill a certain 'I don't give a damn' mentality that made Jack want to go to the Pacific." Chuck Spalding suggested that Jack had decided to try to get to the Pacific in order to break faith with the father who would rather see him do anything but. And finally, Lem Billings offered (as was frequently his habit) the most complex and—in the opinion of this writer—likely explanation. "Jack always had something to prove, physically," Billings observed. "He was always so behind the eight-ball with his health, that he would engage in this bravado—right?—to overcompensate and prove he was fit when he really wasn't. So, he turns into a killer football player and he turns into a voracious womanizer, a stud. Then what's next? Well, of course, he turns into a voracious warrior, hungry for a fight. It was the logical next step given the times. Nothing surprising. I always thought it was kind of interesting that Jack read Hemingway an awful lot, with all those flawed heroes coming on strong: striving, enduring, spoiling for fights and for opportunities to prove themselves. That was Jack."

. . .

NORTHWESTERN'S Naval Reserve Midshipmans School offered two separate and distinct programs. One, based in Abbott Hall, was a three-month curriculum structured to take raw college recruits and turn them into qualified naval officers: so-called ninety-day wonders. The other, with offices and classrooms in Tower Hall, featured an even more vigorous *two*-month program in navigation, gunnery, semaphore, and command strategy. With nearly a year behind them already as commissioned ensigns, Jack and Fred Rosen wound up on the sixty-day-wonder track with all its frantic instruction, high demands, and sparse amenities. Their colleagues in the school were, as a reporter described them, "a cross-section of American manhood . . . former lawyers, chemists, steel workers, salesmen, economists, professors and teachers, insurance executives, authors, newspapermen, merchant skippers, an orchestra leader, a son of an admiral and a son of an able seaman, bankers and booksellers, a member of the New York Assembly and a scion of the aristocratic Cabots. . . ." In a note to Billings—now serving as an ambulance driver with Montgomery's Eighth Army in North Africa— Jack summed up his cohorts at Northwestern as simply "a good bunch."

"You are probably quite a bit leaner by now," he told Billings. "If you're not—I am. . . . sleeping eight in a room—and B.O. can be exceedingly dismal. This is certainly a different company I am working for now than before. The food is stinking—no fresh vegetables and the daily order of bologna is always pimento tinted. I'll go along with the Department a good distance in their drive for economy, but this concentrated drive to starve us to death will keep me off the editorial page just so long." He told Billings that many aspects of the school—including the lousy food—bore "a remarkable resemblance to Choate, and my record here is also exceedingly similar—being caught in bed one minute after reveille, etc. and other serious offenses like that." Actually, given the state of his back, he quit sleeping in his bed after just a few days and instead opted to lie on the long table set in the middle of the large, barrackslike dorm.

"They want me to conduct an [ecumenical] Bible class here every other Sunday for about ½ hour with the sailors," he wrote his mother. "Would you say that is un-Catholic? I have a feeling that dogma might say it was—but good works come under our obligations to the Catholic church. We're not a completely ritualistic, formalistic, hierarchical structure in which the Word, the truth, must only come down from the very top—a structure that allows for no individual interpretation—or are we?" As Jack knew well enough after many years of Catholic instruction, the Church was nothing if not a "formalistic, hierarchical structure" in which canon law was indeed dictated from the very top, the pope. His rhetorical question to the devout Rose could only have been contrived to ruffle her Romanist feathers.

. . .

IN THE WAKE of the Battle of Midway, the war in the Pacific entered a period of balance. The Japanese would never be able to replace the aircraft carriers, planes, and skilled pilots they'd lost the first week in June, while the United States would not gain a clear advantage until late 1943 with the arrival of the *Essex* and *Independence* class carriers and the new F6F Hellcat fighter.

As has been mentioned, the Japanese thought Tulagi the ideal jumping-off spot from which to invade New Caledonia and New Zealand, to the south. The Allies, on the other hand—specifically, Admiral Ernest King, chief of U.S. naval operations—saw the little island as the logical point of departure for a move up to Rabaul, near the northern tip of the Solomons. Both of these plans, however, required significant (and unavailable) support from fighter and bomber aircraft. In the aftermath of the Battle of Midway, neither the Japanese nor the Americans possessed enough carrier strength to make a difference. Also, each side's ground-based air reserves were poorly positioned vis-à-vis Tulagi. The nearest airstrip for the Japanese lay at Rabaul, 350 miles distant. And the Allies possessed no airfields nearer than Espíritu Santo, some 500 miles from Tulagi and the adjacent Florida Island (both of which presented terrains unsuitable for the construction of runways).

A shrewd observer of the Pacific war—of which he hoped to soon become a part—and a wily student of naval military strategy, Jack Kennedy coolly appraised the situation in the southern Solomons and did not express surprise when, early that summer, the Japanese began building airfields on Guadalcanal, an obscure and relatively flat island a few miles to the southwest of Tulagi. Nor was he surprised when, in August, the Allies endeavored to seize both Tulagi and Guadalcanal. The Tulagi base, protected by a small and evidently unenthusiastic Japanese garrison, fell almost immediately. Guadalcanal, however, was to be a different matter. Wave after wave of marines hit the beach without dislodging the Japanese. Jack read the action reports every day. Noting the presence of the 5th Marine Regiment on the Guadalcanal beachhead, Jack employed the symbolism of college varsity sports when he wrote Billings that he envied George Mead who "may have gotten his big 'S' in the recent Solomon Islands engagement."

. . .

JACK AND FRED ROSEN were halfway through their work at the rigorous Midshipmans School on the day in early September when Lieutenant Commander John Duncan Bulkeley—MacArthur's rescuer—came to visit. Bulkeley was nothing if not impressive: a bona fide war hero one step ahead of Audie Murphy in the fame game. The lieutenant commander's recent publicity had been virtually impossible to miss: a ticker-tape parade down Broadway, the Medal of Honor, dinner with the president, and a larger-than-life profile in William L. White's popular (but, as Jack would learn, highly romanticized) best-seller *They Were Expendable*.

Bulkeley had lately proved a huge draw on the war-bond circuit, where he loudly extolled the benefits of PTs. The war-bond crowds ate up Bulkeley's rhetoric, and purchased bonds with a vengeance wherever he appeared. Jack wrote at the time of their first meeting that he found Bulkeley "magnetic and charismatic. . . . this man is the real high priest and chief advocate for the independent, innovative naval action that can and must win this war." Likewise the gentleman who accompanied Bulkeley to Northwestern, Lieutenant Commander John Harllee, executive officer of the navy's new Motor Torpedo Boat Training School in the Melville section of Portsmouth, Rhode Island, seemed "sharp and exacting, a no-nonsense guy with whom one can do business."

The popular allure and glamour of the PT service was not to be denied; nor was the fact that the PTs represented the one opportunity the navy offered junior officers who sought to command their own vessels. Thus, there was never really any question for Jack when Bulkeley, after addressing 1,024 ensigns for about an hour, concluded by saying he needed fifty volunteers of "surpassing courage" to command PTs in the Pacific.

When Bulkeley asked those interested to step forward, Jack and exactly 1,023 of his classmates—every man in the auditorium—did so. "Those of you who want to come back after the war and raise families need not apply," Bulkeley announced with an impeccable sense of theater. "PT boat skippers are not coming back." Not long afterward, writing in one of her many round-robin letters to the scattered Kennedy clan, Rose noted that Jack appeared "quite ready to die for the USA in order to keep the Japanese and the Germans from becoming the dominant people on their respective continents, believing that sooner or later they would encroach upon ours. He also thinks it would be good for [brother] Joe's political career if he [Jack] died for the grand old flag, although I don't believe he feels that is absolutely necessary."

Of course, one glance at Jack's damning medical dossier from Chelsea Naval Hospital would have been enough to tell Bulkeley and Harllee that Jack could never measure up to the harsh physical requirements associated with service on the boats some called "Bucking Broncos." Astonishingly, however, neither Bulkeley nor Harllee consulted their volunteers' medical histories. They instead relied on very brief and very routine exams administered to all candidates on the spot at Northwestern. Jack's heart beat in a steady rhythm, his blood pressure registered normal, and his eyes appeared clear and healthy. He also interviewed well, displayed great wit and self-confidence, and had sailed since his early youth. Perhaps more important, Jack's father had lunched with Bulkeley just a few weeks before. "[The ambassador] had a lot of bitter things to say about the president," Bulkeley recalled. "[Ambassador] Kennedy . . . said that he thought Jack had the potential to be the president of the United States [and] he wanted Jack to get into PT boats for the publicity and so forth, to get the veteran's vote after the war." At the same time, Kennedy added that he hoped his son might eventually be sent someplace that "wasn't too deadly."

In the end, both Jack Kennedy and Fred Rosen received invitations to the Motor Torpedo Boat Training School at Melville, as did twenty other men from their class.

. . .

KICK SPENT MANY weekends in New York that summer of 1942 visiting John White, who—having entered the Marine Corps on May 12—wound up assigned to guard duty at the Brooklyn Navy Yard. Sampling the sights and sounds of the city, the couple continued their circumspect and (for White) highly frustrating relationship. They shared long days at Jones Beach and long platonic evenings in Kick's hotel room, her door cracked open for propriety's sake as they rehearsed the same old debates. Needless to say, Kick's virtue inevitably remained intact night after night, weekend after weekend. The couple nevertheless enjoyed their time together in New York, sipping Brandy Alexanders in the Rainbow Room, taking long walks in Central Park, and making several visits to the apartment on Riverside Drive where Inga now lived with her new husband. (Mr. Blok—to whom Inga would not remain married for long—appeared not to like having Kick around. White guessed he was afraid the girl might remind Inga of Jack. The two ladies, however, spoke not so much about Jack as about Inga's old column, "Did You Happen to See," now being written by a very pleased new cub reporter: Miss Kennedy herself.)

White thought it a healthy sign of rebellion when Kick invited him to spend Labor Day weekend at Hyannis. He strolled quite happily into the lion's den, not realizing what he was in for. Kick's grim and plainly disapproving parents barely spoke to him over the course of two days, while the younger Kennedys approached him as just one more unsuspecting outsider ripe for humiliation in a host of sports. White would recall years later that he'd never—in the course of a long life—been made to feel more uncomfortable or unwelcome. He breathed a sigh of relief when he and Kick departed on Monday night. The family chauffeur drove them to Providence, where they caught the Washington-bound train. They rode together as far as New York, where White disembarked.

Although neither at that moment planned for it to be so, Kick and John were kissing each other goodbye for the last time. He would shortly ship out for a base of operations in Northern Ireland. Their worlds would not again overlap and their correspondence would fall off. When he called her on September 23 for what he could not have realized would be their last conversation, she answered the phone in tears. She'd just gotten off the line with George Mead's mother, who had given her grim news. George had been killed a month before, on August 20. He had been leading his platoon forward across a beachhead at Guadalcanal when a Japanese bullet hit him square in the face. He died instantly, and his men buried him not far from where he fell.

"I've known Georgie almost longer than I've known anyone," Kick wrote Nancy Astor on the 24th. "It all seems so far away and terrible, and I know it is true; but still I can't quite get myself to believe that Georgie with all of his good spirit and all his potential is really gone, buried in some dirty sand on some island nobody ever cared about before all of this. I remembered him in my prayers at mass this morning. I lit a candle and I thought about how stupid it all seems. George was going to do great things. He had so much behind him in his family, and such smarts. It'll be a long time before I get used to the idea that I'll never see him smile again. I called Jack this morning and he just broke down when he heard the news. First he was crying and then he was just mad. He said he hoped he'd get a chance to pay some of what George got right back once he gets over there—if he gets over there. I sure hope he doesn't."

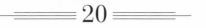

20

"Shafty" Kennedy

A s KICK TOLD Nancy Astor in her letter, Jack received word of
George's death on September 24. He graduated from the Naval Reserve Midshipmans School just three days later and advanced to the
rank of lieutenant, junior grade. (This once again put him in a position
where he outranked Joe, who was now an ensign.)

The new lieutenant (j.g.) spent most of the next week at Hyannis, with
all its memories of George, before reporting to the Motor Torpedo Boat
Squadron Training Center in Rhode Island on October 10. Kick came up
from Washington to join him, and it appears that brother and sister spent a
lot of time helping each other deal with the loss of their old friend. They
spent long hours strolling the beach they'd shared with Mead through so
many childhood summers, and they visited the little Catholic church up the
road, where at least one of them found solace. (A few weeks later, still in
mourning, Jack would stop in the graveyard of a church near Newport—the
tiny Episcopal chapel of St. Columba's not far from the Sakonnet River in
Middletown—and linger there with a new acquaintance: a girl from a
wealthy Newport family. She remembers him loitering amid the plots and
stopping at the grave of Hugo Koehler, who was stepfather to Claiborne Pell
and had died a few years earlier. Standing by Koehler's tombstone, Jack com-

mented that he hoped when his time came he would not have to die without religion. "But these things can't be faked," he added. "There's no bluffing.")

"Jack came home," the ambassador wrote Joe Jr., "and between you and me is having terrific trouble with his back. . . . I don't see how he can last a week in that tough grind of Torpedo Boats and what he wants to do, of course . . . is to be operated on and then have me fix it so he can get back in that service when he gets better. This will require considerable manipulation. . . ." Jack's ideal scenario proved impossible to arrange, however, and he began his training at Melville right on schedule just a few days later. He was barely two days into the program when, finding himself with a few hours' leave, he took off from the Melville base on an important errand. With Fred Rosen on hand to do the heavy lifting, Jack drove to a lumberyard, where he bought a large piece of plywood to place beneath the mattress on his bunk.

Like his father and older brother—both of whom said they had nothing against Jews but disliked "Kikes"—Jack had for a long time enjoyed friendships with Jews while at the same time engaging in fairly regular and routine verbal anti-Semitism. Like all his brothers and sisters, Jack had grown up listening to his father bad-mouth the Jews as a race in the presence of those few Jews (like Krock) whom the father accepted as his friends. And Jack had, by all accounts, never heard Krock or any of their father's Jewish protégés protest these remarks. Thus Jack presumed to engage in the same banter with his friend Rosen, the Jew from Georgia who had followed Jack from Charleston to Chicago and now to Melville. As Rosen explained it to Nigel Hamilton many years later, he put up good-naturedly with Jack's anti-Jewish remarks for many months until one night early in their time at Melville, when Kennedy uttered a particularly unattractive anti-Semitic slur, and Rosen announced that he would like it very much if Jack would just shut up. In the heated exchange that followed, Rosen persuaded Kennedy to recant the random, casual anti-Semitism on which he'd been weaned, and came away from the experience admiring Jack for his willingness to admit he was wrong.

The school to which Kennedy, Rosen, and their cohorts had been assigned took up a mile or more of Narragansett Bay shoreline on a natural harbor (Coggeshall Point) that today hosts the municipal docks for the town of Portsmouth. The school's physical plant comprised a cluster of ten PT boats, three unlovely piers, and some 286 hastily constructed Quonset huts, these serving as administrative offices, classrooms, dormitories, and workshops. A staff of forty-six officers and 187 enlisted men saw to the instruction of a student body that usually averaged 860 enlisted trainees and ninety student officers. This student population cycled through on a series of staggered eight-week schedules, with different freshman classes arriving and senior classes graduating every seven days.

Like other students, Jack did most of his training on one of the hundreds of Elco motor torpedo boats of the PT 103 class. These Elco boats—the first the company made—were the largest in size of the three types of PT boats built for the U.S. Navy during World War II. (In addition to the 103 class of Elco craft, the navy also inventoried slightly smaller, later PTs built not only by Elco but also by Higgins Industries of New Orleans and Huckins Yacht Corporation of Jacksonville. The school's fleet of boats included eight original-model Elco craft and two latter-day Higgins PTs.) Wooden-hulled and eighty feet long with a twenty-foot-eight-inch beam, the 103-class Elco boats were powered by three twelve-cylinder Packard gasoline engines generating a total of 4,500 horsepower for a designed speed of forty-one knots. The typical PT offered accommodations for three officers and up to fourteen men. (Crew sizes varied: either twelve or fourteen, but never thirteen, which PT sailors thought an unlucky number.) Each vessel represented a full-load displacement of fifty-six tons. Early Elco boats carried two 20mm guns (later replaced with one 40mm cannon), four .50-caliber machine guns, and several 21-inch torpedo tubes (later replaced with launching racks), along with depth charges, mine racks, and rocket launchers. Additionally, many PTs wound up being jury-rigged in the field to carry Army Air Force 37mm aircraft guns and even Japanese 23mm guns on their foredecks.

Jack would later complain bitterly about the twin inadequacies of PT boat design and the training offered those being asked to make do with that design. ("The first time I ever fired a torpedo was at the enemy!" Fred Rosen would recall. "I never fired once at Melville! We saw one fired: there were twenty-five of us on the boat, and we saw Green, who was the torpedo officer at the base, fire one. That was the extent of our torpedo training at Melville—and torpedoes were our main weapon!")

The anonymous author of the U.S. Navy's official, unpublished "Administrative History of PTs" would explain: "The Training Center . . . tried desperately to make each man a jack-of-all-trades. The result was inevitable: the caliber of men turned out was lowered by inefficient training." What was worse, New England waters proved hardly ideal for autumn and winter training. Weather often forced the cancellation of underway training, and this "could not be replaced by classroom work." The consequent effect was "a lack of proficiency in boat handling upon the part of personnel reporting to the operating squadrons. . . . Weather caused the cancellation of at least thirty percent of scheduled underway operations at Melville [and] climatic and sea conditions were the determining cause of Melville's failure as a shakedown base. . . . The crews were more concerned about hanging on and keeping warm than they were about learning their duties."

When Jack wasn't busy hanging on or trying to keep warm he learned—among other things—"not to believe everything one is told, *never* to believe government-sponsored publicity, and likewise not to believe everything one reads, especially words published in books entitled *They Were Expendable*." Jack was at Melville no more than two days before he figured out that both Bulkeley and William L. White's book had tended to exaggerate the value demonstrated by PT boats to date. In fact, as Jack entered the Motor Torpedo Boat School at Melville, the official count for Japanese vessels and planes destroyed by American PTs stood at zero.

As Jack was quick to observe, the sketchy syllabus for the Melville training program focused almost entirely on the severe deficiencies inherent in PT boats and how to minimize the risks associated with those deficiencies. Jack was warned to keep his boat concealed under cloak of darkness as much as possible, since three thousand gallons of gasoline contained within the thin plywood shell of a PT made for a tempting target. Jack's teachers also coached him in the unhappy fact that PT torpedoes, which traveled at a top speed of only twenty-eight knots, had thus far proved ineffective against faster-moving Japanese battleships, destroyers, and cruisers. "Add into that equation our frighteningly inaccurate deck guns," he wrote at about this time, "and you've really got something to laugh or cry about. Right now I'm thinking Mr. White should write a sequel to *They Were Expendable* and title it *They Are Useless*."

. . .

I NTERVIEWED MANY YEARS LATER, Lieutenant Commander Harllee recalled Jack Kennedy as "a sincere and hardworking student [who] showed particular aptitude in boat handling." Another contemporary from Melville days—a dirt-poor farmboy from the South with whom Jack would remain friends for the rest of his life—remembered Jack as being "receptive to everybody. I did not consider him a stuck-up individual, or superior in attitude. . . . he associated with people no matter who—and that was unusual. Here I was, a southerner, and all these other people from Harvard, Yale, and these other places would give me hell. . . . Now, Jack didn't do that. He respected people." At least smart people. While anyone with wit could, regardless of background, count on becoming fast friends with young JFK, he did not and never would suffer fools gladly.

On their days off, Jack and his friends from the base (including Fred Rosen and the sharecropper's son, Sim Efland, quoted above) entertained themselves variously in nearby Newport (at a bar called the Lobster Pot), at the Bacardi Room in Providence, or down at posh nightspots in New York. Some of Jack's Melville cronies from humble backgrounds still remember their first trips with him to such clubs as "21" and El Morocco—evenings routinely capped by mad dashes for the last train back to Rhode Island. Rosen later remembered nearly being killed in Jack's Buick not far from the railroad station at Kingston, Rhode Island, with Jack flooring it down Route 138 in a rush to get them back to Melville in time for reveille.

When not training or nightclubbing, Jack and his friends whiled away their time with incessant rounds of touch football. Regular players included Efland (who had coached for Tennessee), Johnny Iles (a football star from Louisiana State), "Jumping" Joe Atkinson (the former left guard and captain of Vanderbilt's distinguished 1941 football squad), Princeton lacrosse star Barney Ross, and Lennie Thom—a tall, blond 220-pound tackle from Ohio State. This core of crackerjack players shifted and changed as time progressed. With new students arriving and departing every week, team lineups proved quite fluid.

Jack had hoped to depart the increasingly frigid campus as part of the group he'd arrived with—joining Rosen, Efland, and others at the end of November on what he imagined would be a fast track to war. The navy, however, had other plans. "[Jack] was such an outstanding student," Harllee remembered, "that I selected him for assignment to the training squadron at

Melville. . . . As soon as he was selected to remain in the training squadron as an instructor he saw me and insisted that he be sent overseas to one of the squadrons in combat. . . . He felt there was no reason why he should be kept in the United States. . . . He was most insistent. He and I had some very hard words. . . ." Jack told a number of his friends that either his bad back, or his father's influence, or a combination of both had probably kept him from getting the combat assignment he wanted. He said he'd been "shafted." His complaint led quickly to a nickname: "Shafty."

"I got Torb in here yesterday," he wrote somewhat sourly to Billings on 19 November, "so he will be reporting in a week or so, and then I shall be around here instructing for a couple of months before leaving for someplace." At the same time he was taking "practical steps" to "get my prospects up to snuff and my ass out of Melville." The practical steps involved going immediately and aggressively over Harllee's head. He did not, however, request his father's help in getting assignment to the Pacific. In fact, he studiously avoided involving the ambassador, whom he suspected of influencing Harllee's initial decision to keep him stateside. Jack instead went to his Grandfather Fitzgerald and through him arranged an interview on November 29 with Senator David I. Walsh of Massachusetts, chairman of the Senate Naval Affairs Committee, who agreed to intercede with the Navy Department on Jack's behalf. Walsh promised to work as quickly as possible. Meanwhile Jack would just have to contend with his instructor duties as best he could.

Jack took command of PT 101, one of Melville's two late-model seventy-eight-foot Higgins PTs, on December 3. His mood—already good in the wake of Walsh's promise and a similarly positive reaction from Under Secretary Forrestal—improved even more during the second week of December. By all accounts, he absolutely delighted in daily action reports that brought word, at last, of actual, tangible PT boat successes in the Pacific. PT 59 sank a two-thousand-ton blockade-running submarine near the still-embattled Guadalcanal on the 9th. Then, on the 12th, three other PTs sank a new Japanese destroyer, the *Teruzuki*, in the same waters. Macdonald would recall Kennedy "ripping an operations manual to shreds and tossing the pieces around the Quonset like confetti. He seemed almost too exuberant: perhaps a bit relieved, like maybe he wasn't wasting his time after all and maybe there was something constructive to be done with the PTs: those boats he'd started to refer to, in some moods, as 'tin cans.' "

. . .

Paul B. Fay, Jr., still remembers how unimpressive Melville seemed at first and even second glance when he arrived there in early December. Nicknamed Red because of his bright shock of red hair, the freckled San Franciscan initially approached the school at Melville as he did most things: with the same cocky, sometimes acerbic, consummately know-it-all attitude he'd learned at the knee of his strong-willed, self-made, Irish Catholic father. Playing football with several new acquaintances in the cold twilight of his first day on the base, Fay did not immediately welcome the "skinny kid" who came up and asked to join the game. When perfunctorily told to go find another player to even out the squads, the kid produced a beefy friend whom Fay instantly selected for his team, unloading the "runt" to the opposing side.

The runt, Fay remembers, far "outclassed the heavier one, outran him—and certainly outtalked him. On the second play after he joined the game, he stopped everything and said we were not following the rules. I protested loudly but the other players, including some of those on my team, agreed with the skinny kid." Back in the huddle, Fay announced that he would cover the skinny kid for the rest of the game. "In the plays that followed, I saw nothing but elbows, shoulders and knees, and acquired a collection of bumps and bruises." One of Fay's teammates, the former Northwestern All-American Don Geyer, who'd also just arrived at Melville, repeatedly pointed out the inadequate job he was doing by asking, "Who's got the skinny kid?"

Fay and the skinny kid met again the next day when Fay—"full of attitude"—refused to get onto the youngster's Higgins PT as ordered and instead jumped aboard one of the Elco eighty-footers. "This," Fay freely admits, "caused considerable confusion, and delayed Lieutenant Kennedy, his crew and his group of students ten or fifteen minutes." When Fay returned to the base, he received word he was wanted in Kennedy's Quonset, pronto. Kennedy, Fay recalls, "chewed out my ass" for a good half hour. "If everybody behaved as irresponsibly as I had, he told me, the Japanese could be marching through Times Square within a few weeks. He was thinking of recommending that I be dropped from the Motor Torpedo Boat training because of my failure to follow orders. I practically got down on my knees to ask for a second chance, and he finally relented."

In the end, Fay and Kennedy—with their shared experience of domineering, multimillionaire Irish-Catholic fathers—would become fast friends. They were destined to overlap only a few weeks at Melville, but would meet again in the Solomons and remain on the best of terms for the rest of their lives. Fay would serve in the Kennedy administration as assistant secretary of the navy, and it would be he who would oversee the promotion of John Bulkeley to rear admiral in June of 1963.

.   .   .

Jack's initial ticket out of Melville came in the form of orders to conduct four PT boats—among them the 101—to a base in Jacksonville, Florida. Departing on January 8, Jack personally steered the 101 while ensigns and several enlisted men took turns at the helms of the other three boats. The little squadron made good time in Long Island Sound and later on the Intracoastal Waterway until day three, when, somewhere in Virginia, 101 ran aground, after which a towline became fast in her propellers. Jack dove into the cold water and cut the rope away. Then he waited—shivering belowdecks—for the incoming tide to lift 101 off the bottom. He became ill the following day—the 12th—somewhere near Morehead City, North Carolina. Doctors diagnosed his chills, temperature, and sweats as "gastro-enteritis, acute," and ordered bed rest. He felt better by the 16th, at which point he checked himself out of the hospital, jumped a train, and rejoined the Melville PT boats that had journeyed on to Jacksonville without him.

"I'm now on my way to war, or so they tell us," he wrote Billings in January, not long after a few days' leave spent at the mansion in Palm Beach. Joe Jr. came home at this time as well. The two brothers spent long hours by the pool smoking cigars and sharing stories of navy inefficiency. Those who were with them noticed the brothers seemed more comradely than they'd ever been before: more understanding of one another, more sympathetic, and more solicitous. Perhaps it was their *new* brotherhood—the brotherhood they shared as officers in the navy—that accounted for the change. Perhaps it was just the natural maturity that is bound to come upon all of us in good time, with or without war's sobering presence. Or perhaps it was their shared suspicion that their father, acting silently and through back-door channels, would likely do everything in his power to keep each of them in a condition they did not care for: the condition of safety.

Ensign Joe complained bitterly to Lieutenant (j.g.) Jack about his current situation. Joe did not care for his new orders detaching him from his transition training squadron at Banana River—where he'd finally managed to log one thousand hours flight time—to a safe and boring backwater. Joe said he absolutely hated the thought of going to San Juan, Puerto Rico, there to patrol for German submarines in waters where none had as yet been spotted. He'd requested Europe or the South Pacific; and he suspected (correctly) that the ambassador might have pulled a string or two to keep him in the Americas. Of course, Jack had harbored similar suspicions about his Melville instructorship.

. . .

JACK WOULD AGAIN sense the ambassador's influence a few weeks later when—on February 14—he received orders to report to a spot that promised the same amount of tedious safety that Puerto Rico had to offer: Panama. (To make things even more annoying for Jack, the Navy Department at about this same time ordered his old Melville exec, Harllee, to form a new squadron—12—destined for the South Pacific. Indeed, it seemed even the inept, barely trained, and entirely hesitant Macdonald would soon beat Jack to the front.)

"Having reached my limit on bullshit several months before the definitive word on Panama came down from on high," he wrote a friend, "I immediately appealed directly to various wise men (skipping JP, just like before) and also filled out the official form for change-of-assignment. The distinguished Senator Walsh shortly responded by obtaining some beautiful words on Navy Department letterhead that order my happy ass to the Solomon Islands: Motor Torpedo Boat Squadron Two. I haven't given JP the good word yet, and of course I think he was behind my indispensability as an instructor up at Melville. I don't know why he believes he needs to protect the Japs from Joe and I. What have they ever done for him?" Jack's new orders told him to "proceed via government or commercial air to the port in which the Commander Service Force, Pacific Subordinate Command may be and upon arrival report . . . for the first available transportation including government or commercial air to the port in which Motor Torpedo Boat Squadron Two may be and upon arrival report to the commanding officer of that squadron for duty."

. . .

JOE JR. AND TWO COLLEAGUES—Lieutenant (j.g.) Emerson G. Johnstone and Ensign S. V. McCormack A-V(N)—journeyed to the PBM
Squadron VP-203 at the Roosevelt Roads Naval Air Base, San Juan, Puerto
Rico, on January 20, 1943. Here—in one of the least interesting theaters the
Battle of the Atlantic had to offer—Joe would fester till April, obediently flying his Mariner and glumly scanning the placid horizon for German submarines that stubbornly refused to appear.

Joe's executive officer, Jim "Sunshine" Reedy, a former navy football
star, developed a quick affinity for the fresh young ensign who now commanded a fully operational Mariner for the very first time. Their friendship,
however, did not stop Reedy from quickly realizing Joe's shortcomings as a
leader of men. Reedy found himself frequently having to speak to Joe about
his methods of training and managing his crew. "He [Joe] stood for perfection in himself and expected the same from others," remembered Jack Deg-
man, an ordnanceman with VP-203. "This at times led to a strained relation
between him and his crew. At one time the relationship became so bad that
it came to the attention of the squadron skipper." In fact, Joe's record from
San Juan cites several reprimands stemming from the verbal abuse he routinely heaped on his subordinates.

"I thought he was a typical Harvard type, all stuck up," recalled William
Sherrill, a mechanic on Joe's Mariner. Another man, navigator Eugene Martin, from Indiana, quickly grew tired of Joe's curt orders on-duty and his
seeming lack of good fellowship off-duty, when Joe would rush by him without a word or sign of acknowledgment, as though they lived in different
worlds. "I seemed to be invisible to Joe," he recalled. "I had a feeling he
viewed me as 'the staff,' and I shouldn't have felt that way. He did not bring
out the best in us and he did not inspire a good *esprit de corps*." Joe's inept-
ness as a leader and motivator prompted wide dislike, and this in turn fos-
tered unfair rumors about Joe and his motivations. Enlisted men (and even
some officers) mumbled that Joe's influential father had pulled strings to get
him to the comfortable safety of San Juan—an exotic city of country clubs
and world-class hotels that could be quite accommodating to millionaire ensigns, if not to their impoverished crews. What the whisperers did not realize, of course, was that Joe would far rather have been in the war than in
Puerto Rico; and at least a part of the exasperation he directed at them was in
fact a reflection of his frustration at not being in the thick of things.

. . .

JACK KENNEDY DEPARTED for the thick of things out of San Francisco harbor on March 6, bound for the New Hebrides on the USS *Rochambeau*. Ironically, just as the *Rochambeau* slipped past Alcatraz, Jack found himself being introduced to Paul Pennoyer, a torpedo boat pilot and grandson of J. P. Morgan. Pennoyer, Jack told his parents in a letter, had "lived a good bit of his life out at Wall Hall" and had known a longtime butler there who—still in residence during the late 1930s—had proved haughty enough to intimidate even the Kennedys. "Evidently the whole Morgan family has lived in some awe of Butler Bengley," Jack wrote, "and [Pennoyer] was extremely interested in Bengley's reaction to the nine Kennedys."

Pennoyer's roommate on the *Rochambeau*, Ensign J. A. Reed, joined Pennoyer in striking up a friendship with Jack. "He had a certain aura of shyness about him," Reed recalled, "which in itself was rather engaging. I must say that my first, initial reaction to him was a pure one—that is to say, I was attracted to him as an individual, having absolutely no knowledge who he was." Another ensign, Edgar Stephens of Missouri, remembered that the *Rochambeau* "was very basic—no frills about it. We were assigned seats at the mess table, and I was assigned a seat next to Jack. He impressed me then as a real quiet, very nice person . . . the type of person who knew how to state a point concisely, and a man who, having chosen a position, would stand by it."

One of the *Rochambeau*'s navigators, a Cape Codder from Brewster whom Jack had never met before but guessed he had probably raced against on more than one occasion, enjoyed many "long and valuable chats with Jack and some of the others in the little group that formed. I remember one day in particular sitting with Jack and Paul [Pennoyer], quietly taking stock of all the naval pilots on their way to the Solomons. I remember us playing a macabre and perhaps grotesque game: looking over those pilots and guessing which ones looked more jittery and nervous than others. Jack pointed out the ones he thought, from the look of them, were most likely to 'get a government gravestone,' as he put it. He had a firm theory that those with a survivor's mentality would make it through, and those who didn't have a survivor's mentality were doomed. It was, so far as he was concerned, as simple as that. He said he'd had a friend who'd 'gone over shaky' and then died on Guadalcanal. And he told us in no uncertain terms that he was a survivor."

21

Tulagi

THE FIRST THING to greet Jack Kennedy in the South Pacific was not warfare, but nearly classic military inefficiency and extreme boredom. The *Rochambeau* arrived in the harbor at Espíritu Santo, New Hebrides, on March 16, after which she sat unapproached for a full two weeks while her captain and the harbormaster exchanged bureaucratic niceties. The formalities did not wrap up until April 1—April Fool's Day—at which point Kennedy and the rest of the *Rochambeau*'s human cargo finally received permission to disembark. Here, at Espíritu Santo, the trio of Kennedy, Pennoyer, and Reed parted company. Jack was to head across the Coral Sea in the direction of Guadalcanal. Reed and Pennoyer, meanwhile, had orders for Noumea in New Caledonia, where Harllee, Bulkeley, and other heroes (among them Torb Macdonald) had their base.

Jack witnessed his first action six days later, at what he'd thought would be the end of a tedious three-day journey on board the U.S. Navy's LST 449. (LST stood for Landing Ship Tank, but these vessels were generally referred to as Long Slow Targets by their crews.) As one of several naval officers being delivered to Solomon Islands assignments, Jack had no duties on deck as 449 approached the north coast of Guadalcanal. He was below in his bunk, reading, at 3 p.m. on the afternoon of April 7, when he suddenly felt the ship—packed with munitions—begin to make a series of sharp turns and pursue what felt like a zigzagging course. Intrigued, Jack pulled on his pants and went above.

Two and a half hours earlier—as 449 pushed past Togoma Point and across Iron Bottom Sound (so called because of the many Allied ships that lay there sunk)—the skipper had encountered a small fleet of American vessels and destroyers running in the opposite direction. They were all fleeing Tulagi harbor, some twenty miles from Guadalcanal, after having been warned of an incoming Japanese air strike. Soon the LST received a flash from the signal station at Koli Point reading "Condition Red," and the transport's commander, Lieutenant Carl S. Livingston, turned his vessel around, pointing her up through Lunga Roads and joining the other American ships at approximately 12:30 p.m.

Enemy planes did not come into sight until just before 3 p.m. when some of 449's crew spotted dots in the sky to the east over Cape Esperance, Guadalcanal. The dots—170 Japanese fighter planes flying out of Rabaul—appeared considerably larger just a few minutes later. Soon the men on deck could clearly differentiate the Japanese "Vals" from the "Zekes" as the planes peeled off to pursue their various assigned targets. Some of the planes headed in the direction of Henderson Field on Guadalcanal. Others swooped down toward the islands of Florida and Tulagi. And a few—perhaps nine or so—made a beeline for LST 449 and the next-nearest ship, the USS *Aaron Ward*, a *Bristol* class destroyer dispatched to give cover to the LST. It was now that Lieutenant Livingston—following instructions issued by the commander of the *Ward*—ordered his ship to undertake the zigzagging course, and now that Jack left his small cabin to investigate what was going on.

Jack had almost reached deck level when he felt 449 shudder beneath him. The ship listed twenty degrees to starboard and the stern momentarily lifted out of the water. Running on deck to the sound of guns blazing, Jack quickly took in the situation. A 500-pound bomb had just missed LST 449 and exploded in the water a mere ten feet off her port bow. Lieutenant Livingston, standing on the port wing of the bridge at the time of the explosion, had been hurled across to the starboard wing. It was there Jack saw him lying, his neck broken, as the enemy planes continued to home in on 449 and the *Aaron Ward*. A second bomb hit fifty feet off 449's port bow; then three more exploded quite close to the starboard side, causing considerable collateral damage: shattering lifeboats, bursting bulkheads, and destroying key electronics.

These were, however, mere cuts and bruises compared to the damage sustained by the *Ward*. A bomb exploded square atop her engine room, ripping her in two. Another, hitting in the water, tore holes in the *Ward*'s starboard side, allowing the forward fireroom to ship water rapidly. One more near miss holed the *Ward*'s port side, near the aft engine room. Smoke billowed from her deck, and flames leaped out of her companionways and hatches as the *Ward* began to go down. Lieutenant Livingston—still commanding, despite his broken neck—at first ordered LST 449 to start for the *Ward* and look for survivors. He only diverted when he saw two minesweepers move in and begin to tow the *Ward* toward a shoal near Tinete Point, where she could be safely beached. (They would not make it. The *Ward* was to sink, stern first, in forty fathoms of water just six hundred yards from the shoal and not far from Florida Island. Twenty-seven of her crew wound up dead or missing, fifty-nine wounded.) Looking out over the horizon, past the dying *Ward* and the minesweepers that struggled to help her, Jack saw the U.S. oil tanker *Kanawha* explode in flames after a direct hit.

Typically, Jack's description of the event says as much about his wit and attitude as it does about the battle. "As we were carrying fuel oil & bombs," he wrote Billings, "and on a boat that was a tub—I thought we might withdraw + return at some later date, but the Captain evidently thought he was in command of the *North Carolina* as he sailed right in. . . . During a lull in the battle—a Jap parachuted into the water—we went to pick him up as he floated along—and got within about 20 yds. of him. He suddenly through aside his life-jacket + pulled out a revolver and fired two shots at our bridge. I had been praising the Lord + passing the ammunition right alongside—but that slowed me a bit—the thought of him sitting in the water—battling an entire ship. We returned the fire with everything we had—the water boiled around him—but everyone was too surprised to shoot straight. Finally an old soldier standing next to me—picked up his rifle—fired once—and blew the top of his head off. He threw his arms up—plunged forward + sank—and we hauled our ass out of there. That was the start of a very interesting month—and it [the Japanese pilot's refusal to give in] brought home very strongly how long it is going to take to finish the war."

. . .

AFTER THE BATTLE, Jack's transport headed back to Espíritu Santo and did not return to Guadalcanal for another six days. The transport finally made Florida Island—home of "Calvertsville," the headquarters for Commander Allen P. Calvert, commanding officer of the local motor torpedo boat flotilla—on April 13. From there a little whaleboat rushed Jack across the small channel to Sesapi on the island of Tulagi, home for Motor Torpedo Boat Squadron 2. Johnny Iles, Joe Atkinson, Barney Ross, and other friends from Melville were there to greet him, and soon Jim Reed would transfer in from Noumea.

Initially assigned as temporary executive officer for PT 47—a recent-model seventy-seven-foot Elco boat—Jack assumed command of his own vessel, PT 109, on April 25.

Jack's PT was one of the squadron's two surviving eighty-foot Elco vessels from 1942. As such, it had no radar—a fact that would become very important one fateful night in the coming summer. Bryant Larson, the skipper Jack replaced, had seen the worst of the fighting around Guadalcanal. So had his men. So had his boat. All were in need of rest and repair. After a long and dangerous tour in a fragile wooden craft incapable of firing torpedoes at a speed Japanese ships could not outrun, Larson and his crew headed home. The only man left behind was Larson's executive officer, good old Lennie Thom from Melville, who'd preceded Jack to the South Pacific by several months. "Have my own boat now," Jack wrote his parents, "and have an executive officer, a 220-pound tackle from Ohio State—so when the next big drive comes—will be protected." And that was good, because the balance of Jack's crew seemed quite green overall: just like him. "I'd like to be confident they know the difference between firing a gun and winding their watch," he wrote ruefully to his parents, but he guessed they didn't.

The crew included three Massachusetts natives besides Jack: Charles "Bucky" Harris (twenty), an assembly-line worker from a tire factory in Watertown; Maurice Kowal (twenty-one), a toolmaker from Uxbridge; and Dorchester's William Johnston (thirty-three), who in civilian life drove a truck for Gulf Oil. Writing to Lem Billings, Jack ran down the names of the Massachusetts boys and then itemized the balance of the personnel on 109. He said he had already come to like and respect Pittsburgh steel inspector Edmund T. Drewitch (thirty), Miami cab driver Leon Drawdry (thirty), and Macon refrigeration engineer Andrew Jackson Kirksey (twenty-five). He also had seen enough to expect "good stuff" from New York factory worker John Maquire (twenty-six), Chicago jack-of-all-trades Edman Mauer (twenty-eight), and—as Jack described him, the "only enlisted seaman I feel I have to call 'sir' "—Patrick "Pop" McMahon (forty-one), former mechanic for the Detroit Street Railway Company, who came to 109 directly from the Navy Diesel School at the University of Missouri, where he'd ranked at the top of his class.

.   .   .

THE PORT AT SESAPI consisted of just one floating dry dock, a machinery shed, and a PT tender. Officers and seamen found shelter in scattered Quonset huts, thatched huts, and tents. As one old Sesapi hand would recall, the whole base could have fit on the flight deck of the carrier *Enterprise*. Although Jack and his roommates Thom and Iles bunked in huts of the type any Westerner might expect to see in the standard cliché picture of a South Pacific archipelago, tiny Tulagi was in fact littered with evidence of so-called civilization. Decrepit and abandoned roads, water towers, and even large Western-style homes covered Tulagi, which had once been the capital of the British Solomon Islands Protectorate. In fact, the place seemed a tropical ghost town version of Hyannis. Before the war, the soapmaker Lever Brothers had owned a string of plantations on Guadalcanal. Here—on smaller, more temperate, and less mosquito-ridden Tulagi—the Lever executives and overseers had maintained their homes and offices until they were run out by the invading Japanese.

The remaining shells of the Western-style structures could do nothing to improve the primitive conditions endured by Jack and his colleagues. Although spring was officially the "dry season," it still rained four or five hours every day. Green mold grew on Jack's clothes, his writing paper, his books, and the Victrola on which he liked to play one of the few records he'd packed with him: Frank Sinatra's "All or Nothing at All." He wrote Inga that the scene at Tulagi was very different from the one he'd imagined on his way over: his "greatly illusioned" dream "about spending the war sitting on some cool Pacific beach with a warm Pacific maiden stroking me gently but firmly, while her sister was out hunting my daily supply of bananas." Still, he admitted, "as I hear you saying, I asked for it honey and I'm getting it." He wrote Billings that regarding his "gut and back" it was "still not hooray— but I think it will hold out."

Native islanders—Melanesian cannibals—visited regularly. "We had one in today who told us about the last man he ate. 'Him Jap, him are good.' . . . They're smartening up lately. When the British were here they had them working for 17 cents a day but we treat them a heck of a lot better. 'English we no like' is their summation of the British Empire." Jack added that the Melanesian men loved to trade: "All they seem to want is a pipe and will give you canes, pineapples, anything, including a wife." Although we have no direct testimony on Jack's sexual activities at this time, we do know that many others in his squadron made frequent trades of Western articles in exchange for the attentions of Melanesian women: what the islanders called "pushy-pushy in the bushy."

·   ·   ·

109 HAD SEEN her share of the war and more. She was well worn, beaten up badly to both port and starboard, and infested with rats and cockroaches. Additionally, her three aero engines needed a complete overhaul before she could return to sea. Jack and his crew worked on aesthetics (cleaning and painting) while Sesapi's mechanics fixed the aeros. Johnston and Mauer, both of whom had served a few months on other PT boats and in that time encountered more than their share of stuck-up PT commanders, commented many years later about how surprised and impressed they'd been when Kennedy stripped down to shorts and worked beside his men, scraping and painting the bottom of the boat. As he worked, he spoke a bit wistfully about his little sailboat back home, *Victura*, and how he liked to take care of her himself: putting her in order every year, giving her the TLC she needed before she could give him her best.

It took several weeks of TLC to make the battered 109 seaworthy; both boat and crew were finally ready to pull patrol duty by mid-May. "We go out on patrol every other night," he explained to his parents, "and work on the boats in the day time." Luckily for the inexperienced men of the 109, there was very little Japanese naval activity around Tulagi in the spring of 1943. Thus 109's patrols amounted to little more than shakedown cruises: badly needed shakedown cruises. "On good nights it's beautiful," Jack wrote his parents, "the water is amazingly phosphorescent—flying fishes which shine like lights are zooming around and you usually get two or three porpoises who lodge right under the bow and no matter how fast the boat goes keep just about six inches ahead of the boat."

He much preferred those alternate evenings dedicated to peaceful patrols to those spent at Tulagi in total blackout, awaiting the inevitable and frequent Japanese air raids. The attacks from above unnerved him. He didn't like being at the mercy of the Japanese "Washing-Machine Charlies." Jack would curse and dive for cover at the first sound of their unsynchronized engines.

. . .

JACK WAS INTRIGUED when his father wrote of MacArthur's popularity in the States. "Here he has none," Jack replied. "[He] is, in fact, very, very unpopular. His nick-name is 'Dug-out-Doug' which seems to date back to the first invasion of Guadalcanal. The Army was supposed to come in and relieve the Marines after the beach-head had been established. In ninety-three days no Army. Rightly or wrongly (probably wrongly) MacArthur is blamed. He is said to have refused to send the Army in—'He sat down in his dugout in Australia,' (I am quoting all Navy and Marine personnel) and let the Marines take it. . . . There is no doubt that as men start to come back that 'Dug-out-Doug' will spread—and I think would probably kill him off. No one out here has the slightest interest in politics—they just want to get home—morning, noon, and night. They wouldn't give a damn whether they could vote or not and would probably vote for Roosevelt just because they knew his name."

He expected to be in for a long haul. His informed view from the front was that the fight in the Pacific would not end for at least another three years. Still, he was sure of Allied victory in the end. "Our stuff is better," he wrote his parents, "our pilots and planes are—everything considered—way ahead of theirs and our resources inexhaustible though this island to island stuff isn't the answer. If they do that the motto out here 'The Golden Gate by 48' won't even come true. A great hold-up seems to me to be the lackadaisical way they handle the unloading of ships. They sit in ports out here weeks at a time while they try to get enough Higgins boats to unload them. They ought to build their docks the first thing. They're losing ships, in effect, by what seems from the outside to be just inertia up high. Don't let any one sell the idea that everyone out here is hustling with the old American energy. They may be ready to give their blood but not their sweat, if they can help it, and usually they fix it so they can help it. They have brought back a lot of old Captains and Commanders from retirement and stuck them in as the heads of these ports and they give the impression of their brains being in their tails, as Honey Fitz would say. The ship I arrived on—no one in the port had the slightest idea it was coming. It had hundreds of men and it sat in the harbor for two weeks while signals were being exchanged. The one man, though, who has everyone's confidence is Halsey, he rates at the very top."

He told his dad to tell Joe not to be in too big a hurry to get into the war. "He is coming out eventually and will be here for a sufficiency and he will want to be back the day after he arrives, if he runs true to the form of every one else." And he informed Billings that he hoped himself to be home before Christmas: ". . . they have been pretty good about relieving us—as the work is fairly tough out here."

. . .

Jack's squadron commander, Allen Harris, gave the newcomer a stellar performance rating that May: a perfect 4.0 in shiphandling and a 3.9 for his ability to command. Young Kennedy, Harris concluded shortly before being transferred out of Tulagi, was a man who could be counted upon in a pinch. Harris's replacement at Motor Torpedo Boat Squadron 2— a young Annapolis graduate by the name of Alvin P. Cluster—arrived at the start of June. Cluster quickly came to like and respect Kennedy as much as Harris had. Twenty-six-year-old Jack and his new commander got along well. Cunning and skeptical of authority, Cluster scored points with Jack early in their relationship. Jack couldn't have agreed more when Cluster suggested the administrators of certain key and wholly inefficient navy bureaucracies might be in line for medals from Hirohito.

22

Life in Addition to
Fortune Knows God

O N A SUNDAY in mid-June of 1943, Jack and fellow Catholic Johnny Iles sat in a jeep at Tulagi talking about matters of faith. Jack told Iles what he'd told others many times before: that he had "lost his religion" but hoped to get it back. He said, perhaps jokingly, that he'd go see Fulton Sheen after he returned to the States and that Sheen would probably be able to fix things. As strikes from Japanese aircraft out of Rabaul and Bougainville became more frequent, Jack wrote his family he was grateful for their prayers but hoped they would not take it as lack of faith if he continued to duck. To his mother he joked: "You will be pleased to know that there is a priest nearby who has let all the natives go and is devoting all his energies to my salvation. I'm stringing along with him—but I'm not going over easy—I want him to work a bit so he'll appreciate it more when he finally has me in the front row every morning screaming *hallelujah*." Despite the bravado of letters home, his contemplation was often profound.

He made a point of visiting George Mead's last resting place on Guadalcanal: a mound of earth marked by an aluminum plate from a mess kit crudely inscribed with the words "Lt. George Mead USMC. Died Aug. 20.

A great leader of men—God bless him." Writing to his parents, Jack reported that he'd found Mead "buried near the beach where he fell—it was extremely sad." A short while after visiting Mead's grave, Jack got word that another friend, Aldie Howe, had died in action less than twenty miles away.

He was reading *Pilgrim's Way* that spring. Jack seemed mesmerized by, and talked incessantly to friends about, John Buchan's elegy for the fine crop of wellborn Brits—many of them friends of not only Buchan but also Billy Hartington's father—who had found meaning (and, too often, death) on the battlefields of World War I. Personally, Jack perhaps related most to the tale of Raymond Asquith—son of the famed Liberal prime minister—who in 1915 grew bored with a safe job in intelligence, volunteered for the front, and there reveled in "the mingled bondage and freedom of active service." Asquith died in the Battle of the Somme, 1916. "For the chosen few, like Raymond," wrote Buchan, who had known Asquith at Oxford, "there is no disillusionment. They march on into life with a boyish grace, and their high noon keeps all the freshness of the morning." In his own copy of *Pilgrim's Way*, Jack—perhaps thinking of Mead and Howe—circled a choice two lines of Buchan's tribute: "He loved his youth, and his youth has become eternal. Debonair and brilliant and brave, he is now part of that immortal England which knows not age or weariness or defeat."

·   ·   ·

Jack didn't drink because of his bad stomach, so he did not spend much time at what answered for Tulagi's officers' club. Sometimes referred to (laughingly) as the Royal Palm Club, this consisted of a tent where was served a mysterious alcoholic concoction incubated from the 190-proof fluid otherwise used to power torpedoes. He wrote his parents that every night at about seven-thirty the officers' club tent would "bulge" and several men would come "crashing out, blow their lunch and stagger off to bed. This torp juice, which is the most expendable item on the island, makes the prohibition stuff look like Haig and Haig. . . ." When a Melville friend by the name of Jerry O'Leary visited the island, Jack gave O'Leary his many unused liquor chits "and he polished off five scotches with no visible effect except he could hardly stand by the time I got him out." Instead of hitting the booze, Jack read a great deal, played cribbage, organized touch football games, and wrote many letters like this one to Kick:

. . . lying on a cool Pacific island with a warm Pacific maiden hunting bananas for me is definitely a bubble that has burst. You can't even swim—there's some sort of fungus in the water that grows out of your ears—which will be all I need, with pimples on my back— hair on my chest and fungus in my ears I ought to be a natural for the old sailors home in Chelsea, Mass.

I read in *Life* magazine an article by John Hersey on PTs out here. It didn't have the wild west stuff of *They Were Expendable*, but it was a much truer picture. The glamour of PTs just *isn't* except to an outsider. It's just a matter of night after night patrols at low speed in rough water—two hours on—then sacking out and going on again for another two hours. Even with that however it's a hell of a lot better than any other job in the Navy. . . . As a matter of fact this job is somewhat like sailing, in that we spend most of our time trying to get the boat running faster—although it isn't just to beat Daly for the Kennedy cup—it's the Kennedy tail this time.

Speaking of John Hersey I see his new book *Into the Valley* is doing well. He's sitting on top of the hill at this point—a best seller—my girl [Frances Ann Cannon]—two kids—big man on *Time*—while I'm the one that's down in the God damned valley. That I suppose is life in addition to fortune knows God, says I.

. . .

THE SISTER TO WHOM Jack wrote on June 3 finally got to England a few weeks later having—as she told a friend—"figured an angle" and (against her father's wishes) signed up for employment with the Red Cross. There was record heat on the day in late June when Kick and her fellow workers queued up at the Brooklyn Navy Yard to board the *Queen Mary*. Despite the weather, the ladies wore winter uniforms along with raincoats and helmets. They also carried gas masks, thirty-five-pound musette bags, and shoulder bags along with canteens and first-aid kits strapped to their waists. After waiting several hours for their papers to be checked, Kick and her colleagues marched up the gangway and located their quarters. (Kick found herself one of eight women assigned to a small, cramped four-bunk cabin. She wound up drawing straws to see whether she would sleep with the first or second shift.) In an odd implementation of the notion "ladies first," Kick and the other Red Cross women boarded twenty hours before departure.

They spent much of the intervening time either napping or gazing over the side as eighteen thousand troops slowly made their way onto the ship.

The soldiers were assigned sleeping spots in the hallways and on decks. "It really is the most pathetic looking sight in the world to see the way they are living," Kick wrote the family. The ship's passengers also included 160 army nurses—"a lot of tough babes"—and 300 officers. "Most of the Red Cross girls don't pay any attention to [the officers], as it certainly isn't any compliment to be sought after when the ratio is so uneven." Kick told Rose she would not recognize her old beloved *Queen Mary* in the ship's present incarnation as a troop transport. "The only lounge available to the officers is the one main one and you can imagine how crowded that is at all hours of the day. And the deck space is about 40 feet long for walking. I pace 400 or 500 times a day trying to eke a mile out of it."

Breakfast and dinner bells rang at 9 a.m. and 7 p.m., respectively. In between people kept themselves from getting too hungry by munching on crackers and chocolate, both plentiful. Kick attended Roman Catholic mass every afternoon—"a wartime measure," she wrote, "and guess where we have it—in the Synagogue. I have been serving Mass, as the soldiers didn't seem to show up. We are allowed to go to Communion then and yesterday we had Mass on the deck under the most crude circumstances." Kick thought the scarcity of people at mass surprising, given the constant threat of submarine attack. "About a half-hour after each sharp swerve we are informed that this good ship has just missed a sub. There's another one. It was probably about nine miles to starboard."

Kick landed in Glasgow on June 28 and, with the other Red Cross girls, marched aboard a troop train bound for London. Later, while her erstwhile comrades retreated to rather dismal suburban London quarters, Kick sought more elegant accommodations with friends. "At the moment I am sunning myself in the Gore's garden," she wrote Jack from Pimlico House, Hemel Hempstead, the home of David and Sylvia Ormsby-Gore. Married three years now, the couple had a small daughter and son. Just as the Anglican David (cousin to Billy Hartington) had promised the priest who had officiated at his marriage to the Catholic Sylvia, both children were being "raised Roman" even though the boy was heir to the Harlech barony. ("How could you?" Lady Astor is reported to have hissed, confronting David shortly after the marriage.)

"London seems quite unchanged," Kick wrote, "food is very good—

blitzed areas are not obvious—Americans every place who pay through the eyes and get all the good things such as steak which I had my first night in London. Have seen Janie [Kenyon Slaney]—she looks marvelous and is quite determined to get out to India and to join her husband. . . . Lady Astor wrote me a note of welcome but she's at Plymouth at the moment. Everyone is surprised & I do mean surprised to see me." She herself was surprised by the strident amount of anti-Kennedy feeling she'd encountered. "I am determined to get my stories straight as I think I'll get it on all sides." She hoped for an assignment doing public relations out of the Red Cross's central office in London. "You know Jack how good I'd be there. Failing [that,] I'll be assigned to some Recreation Club somewhere in England . . . and one day off a week. This is war!" In the meantime, however, things were "terribly gay" with parties about once a week.

Kick did not get the PR job she wanted. She instead wound up, as she'd anticipated, at a Red Cross rest-and-recreation club. Situated on country estates and in city hotels from Glasgow to Dover, the clubs—forerunners to the USO—were meant to supply all manner of wholesome entertainment for GIs and sailors on leave. Most clubs were located in the hinterlands, far removed from the London society, nightlife, and friends Kick craved. Custom was to send new volunteers to the countryside before promoting them to London. Kick's father, however, pulled a few strings and Kick found herself immediately posted to the Hans Crescent Club, located in a posh Victorian hotel one block from Harrods and easily the most desirable assignment in the entire Red Cross club system.

Kick—who made her home in the hotel—was soon complaining to Frank Waldrop and other friends back in the States about having to spend so much of her time dancing, playing cards, and otherwise entertaining rough-around-the-edges country boys. She had just one day and a half off each week (never on the weekends) to socialize with *her* friends, and this, she told her old editor, was simply not enough. "The Director," she wrote her parents, "just had a little chat with me. . . . The first complaint was that I had too many phone calls. Second, I should cut down on my personal life. I don't see how I could possibly do it any more than I am already doing." It did not help Kick's popularity when Lady Astor rang up Harvey Dow Gibson, the American banker then serving as commissioner of the American Red Cross in Britain, to demand that Kick be released in the name of Anglo-American unity to attend a Saturday-night ball at Cliveden. (Nancy Astor subsequently dropped by the club a few times, where she proved a wearisome, meddlesome, and annoying volunteer. After sitting for five minutes with an American soldier from her home state of Virginia, Astor startled the beer-drinking man with the announcement: "You don't need to be entertained. I should give you a lecture on temperance.")

"Aren't you longing to hear about a day in the life of the Red Cross girl?" Kick wrote Billings. "Live here at the Club where I work. Am on the job at ten. There are always boys wanting information of various sorts— books out of the library, ping pong balls, etc. If there isn't too much doing I may sit down and have a chat with one of them or more. . . . You wouldn't recognize old Kick who used to walk around with her nose quite far in the air if she had to go in the subway to get to the Automat with you. I'd give my two tiny hands, covered as they are with warts, for a meal in the Automat and I wouldn't care if I had to sit with two dirty truck drivers. As a matter of fact they are probably the only people I know how to charm now."

In addition to not having enough time to spend with her friends, and being assigned so tawdry a task as mingling with the social equivalent of truck drivers, Kick was also out of sorts because her fellow volunteers—sensing Kick's special position and special treatment—resented her. A well-liked member of the staff had been summarily dispatched to distant Londonderry in order to make room for Kick. What was more, after just a few weeks on the job, Kick requested and received permission to take weekends off: a privilege afforded no other volunteer. According to some who served with her, Kick's lack of interest in her work (in fact, her outright dislike for it) was plainly evident and did not add to her popularity. Kick's fellow workers had come over to England to lend a hand. Kick, it was soon obvious, had come over to get closer to friends like Billy Hartington and Nancy Astor, to once again spend time at such fine estates as Chatsworth and Cliveden, and to immerse herself in the whirl and hubbub that surrounded London's social and financial elite. Kick had come to play. When play was denied, she pouted.

She did not pout, however, around Billy. They began seeing each other seriously in July. Together—joined by Tony Roslyn and other friends—they visited the 400 Club regularly and were also frequent guests at the home of Anthony Drexel Biddle, then posted to London as U.S. minister to the exiled governments of Poland, Belgium, Norway, Greece, the Netherlands,

Czechoslovakia, and Yugoslavia. "They have quite a small house," she wrote
her family after one visit to the Biddles, "and we had a buffet supper consisting of all the things I've been yearning for ever since I arrived: lobster,
ice cream, chocolate cake, chicken salad, etc. . . . Mr. and Mrs. Gibson [were
there] and told me about Lady Astor calling them and saying I must go to
the party Saturday night. Any minute I expect to be isolated to the Isle of
Man. . . . The hardest job Tony Biddle's Naval Attaché has here is pouring
out the cocktails every evening. We were also happy to find out that Ambassador Biddle was getting everything he needed in the food line because he's
got a tough war to fight."

· · ·

I T   D I D   N O T   H E L P Joe Jr. endure the boredom of his assignment with
VP-203 (first at San Juan and later, as of April, at Norfolk) to know that
even his little sister was closer to the war than he. Joe's seemingly endless
round of futile submarine hunts continued off the Virginia coast, just as they
had off Puerto Rico. He told friends glumly that he thought he was wasting
time while the war went on without him. What little action his unit saw
stemmed not from confrontations with German submarines, but rather
from mishaps, such as when a Mariner stalled on takeoff, killing three of
Joe's fellow aviators. Don Dirst, who served with Joe for a time, does not remember the names of the dead, only that "they were of three faiths: Protestant, Catholic, and Jewish." Dirst also recalls Joe, seemingly unfazed by the
accident, absentmindedly strolling in late for an ecumenical memorial service. When little brother Bobby—seventeen—showed up several weeks later
for a visit at Norfolk, Joe violated regulations and allowed the boy to come
along in his Mariner on a patrol. In fact, he even let Bobby pilot the aircraft
briefly, far out over the Atlantic, using the copilot's controls. Contemporaries who served with Joe at Norfolk remember him as frustrated but also
cocky after finally achieving the rank of lieutenant, junior grade. It was important to him, he admitted to at least one comrade, that his little brother
Jack no longer outranked him.

He seemed tense, unhappy, and—as usual—testy: his fuse as short and
the chip on his shoulder as big as ever. It appeared that if he could not be
combative against the real enemy, then he would be combative against his
cohorts: picking fights, making insulting comments, and pushing the emo-

tional envelope not only with enlisted personnel but also with officers. Many veterans of VP-203 remember him appearing especially frustrated, bitter, and unhappy in mid-June when one of his fellow Mariner pilots actually spotted a German sub—a first for their unit—and failed to sink it. Joe subsequently fumed at the loss, and loudly suggested that if the sighting had been his, so too would have been a kill. He spoke incessantly about his fellow pilot's incompetence, and suggested as well that the man and his crew might have been too scared to go in close and do the job that needed to be done. The insinuation eventually led to a fistfight from which Joe emerged the victor.

Commander Jim Reedy was not unaware of Joe's frustration, his anxiety to get into battle, his propensity for losing his cool, and his affinity for violence. Neither was he surprised, therefore, when he saw Joe standing at the back of Norfolk's Hangar Sp2, waving frantically with both hands, on the sweltering day in mid-July when Reedy called for volunteers to handle what he anticipated would be a very dangerous assignment. Reedy had lately been asked to establish a new patrol squadron—VP-110—for eventual duty hunting German submarines where they actually lived: near U-boat bases in the Bay of Biscay and along the French coast south of Brest. Manned by U.S. Navy Mariner pilots such as Joe, the squadron would not, however, fly Mariner aircraft. VP-110's pilots would instead fly an aircraft superior in all ways to the clunky Mariner: the Army's B-24 Liberator (reclassified for naval use as the PB4Y-1 Liberator). It was said that VP-110's missions would involve regular incursions of German-dominated airspace, and frequent altercations with the Luftwaffe. As Reedy described the program, Squadron VP-110 would train for several weeks and then depart for England in early autumn.

"The most excited man in the room was Joe Kennedy," recalled one of his cohorts. "He was bursting with enthusiasm." Another colleague remembers the same excitement in Kennedy. "I can recall quite well how enthused he was. . . . He was an eager beaver. He wanted to get with that war and get with it fast." Reedy accepted Joe immediately, along with many other pilots from VP-203. Before the war was over, VP-110 would lose two planes to enemy fighters and ten to weather and mechanical failure. Sixty-nine of the young men who so enthusiastically signed up with Reedy would die in action.

Joe had every reason to expect an excellent, exciting, and—above all—challenging ride. His biographer, Hank Searls, tells us: "The B-24 was an aircraft, in the eyes of a Mariner pilot, so hot, fast, and dangerous that it had always seemed beyond reach." It was also a very different aircraft from what Joe—who had never in his life flown anything bigger than a twin-engined seaplane—was used to. The Liberator presented one of the most complicated cockpits in aviation history: fifty dials, 150 switches. When not loaded with bombs, the overpowered aircraft felt like a fighter on takeoff. The plane featured a split tail, a wingspan of 110 feet, and the capacity to deliver no less than 8,000 pounds in explosives. Powered by four Pratt & Whitney Twin Wasp 14 engines, the Liberator had a cruising speed of 175 mph, a maximum speed of 300 mph, and a landing speed of 90 mph.

The Liberator boasted a cruising range of 3,000 miles when carrying a full bomb load (4,700 miles when empty) and had a service ceiling of 31,500 feet. Tricky for the most excellent of pilots, the plane must have been a special challenge for Joe, and there are reports that he always flew the Liberator with a dangerous sloppiness. Nevertheless he somehow managed to check out on the PB4Y-1 in just six days of intense work on Norfolk's East Field, after which Reedy put him to work flying a seemingly endless stream of the Liberators to Norfolk from the San Diego factory where they were engineered. Through August, Joe averaged five cross-country round trips every eight days and felt, he told a friend, much more like a Pan Am pilot than a warrior. He was glad he was finally scheduled to see some real combat, but at the same time he still felt outclassed by his younger brother out in the Solomons.

. . .

JOE SR., MEANWHILE, thought himself even more useless. A friend remembered him at about this time glumly surveying the ocean's destruction of a seawall near his home. "He wasn't going to fix it, he said. Let it go." He'd spent a fair amount of time and money in the previous months mounting criticisms of FDR that went widely unnoticed; he only stopped when he realized no one appeared to care about what he had to say. He was more marginalized now than ever before: still suspect as a fascist sympathizer, still criticized as a defeatist. If powerful men called at all, it was usually to provide disinformation. In June of 1943, when Kennedy's old protégé Beaverbrook—still influential in the Churchill government—came to the States for conferences with FDR, he made a visit to the highly complimented and almost pathetically grateful Kennedy, during which he whispered, confidentially, that there would never be a cross-Channel attack. Churchill, he said, opposed the entire concept.

23

Survival Time

L ATE THAT SPRING OF 1943, PT 109 and several other boats
from Squadrons 2 and 6 (all under Cluster's command) received orders to go into the Russell Islands—eighty miles west of Tulagi and
about one-third the distance to the Japanese stronghold of New Georgia,
which Bull Halsey called the next rung up the Solomons ladder. Here Jack
and his men bunked in an old farmhouse, played bridge and poker, and conducted relatively quiet patrols every other evening for a month and a half.
Jack's excellent relationship with Cluster paid dividends one night when,
playing chicken with another PT on his way back to base, Jack wound up
ramming the dock. Any other CO, including the one he was about to encounter, would have had Jack court-martialed, but Cluster let the incident
slide. The event earned Kennedy a new nickname. "Shafty" now disappeared in favor of "Crash."

Cluster was perhaps able to forgive Kennedy his attacking the pier because of the Keystone Cops antics of other PT squadrons in the region. Not
long before, near the start of the siege of New Georgia in May, six PTs from
Squadron 9 under Lieutenant Commander Robert Kelly attacked and sank
Admiral Turner's invasion-force flagship, the USS *McCawley*, in the Blanche

Channel on the east side of Rendova. (The unfortunate Kelly subsequently found himself demoted out of flotilla command.) Squadron 9 also had other mishaps, including having to abandon two grounded PT boats on two consecutive nights. (PT groundings were common. The antiquated maps used by their skippers—many of them World War I vintage—did not accurately reflect the changing, ever growing, and always dangerous coral reefs.)

More embarrassing (and more deadly) were the all too frequent altercations between PTs and the Allied B-25s charged with patrolling the waters of the Solomon and Russell Islands by day. Frequently stalling, the generally unreliable engines in the PTs often left the boats and their crews adrift in troubled waters well after sunrise, when they were not supposed to be there, and when it was easy for them to be mistaken for Japanese. On one particularly memorable morning, PT 166—on which Kennedy's friend Ensign George H. R. "Barney" Ross served as executive officer—wound up being attacked by B-25s as she stood by to help another PT stranded with engine trouble. PT 166 fired back in self-defense. One crew member died when the boat sank. At the same time, three of the B-25's crew drowned after the plane crashed. (Ross joked, darkly, that the B-25 was 166's first and only kill.) Shortly thereafter, three PTs commanded by a green lieutenant fired on a flotilla of U.S. destroyers off the west coast of Japanese-controlled Kolombangara, adjacent to New Georgia, forcing the Allied ships to briefly suspend their artillery support for infantry attacking Japanese positions at Munda Point on New Georgia.

Commenting wryly on these and other indiscretions, Jack wrote his parents in mid-July that he was moving to yet another base of operations up the line. Kennedy, his crew, and the 109 received orders on July 15 detaching them from Squadron 2 and reassigning them to Squadron 1 operating out of Lumbari, a small island next to newly liberated Rendova, off the south coast of hotly contested New Georgia. Here they would serve under a man Kennedy would quickly come to despise: Lieutenant Commander Thomas G. Warfield, a stiff, by-the-book career man who had put in many years as gunnery instructor at Annapolis. Much given to enforcing all the pretensions of military rank and formality, Warfield nevertheless seemed something of a coward. He refused to ride on PTs himself and instead commanded his squadron via high-frequency radio broadcasts made from the safety of a bunker on Lumbari. As Jack observed, Warfield's remote command method opened the door to miscommunication and potentially fatal mistakes. John Meade—one of Jack's fellow alums from Melville—told Nigel Hamilton in an interview many years later that Warfield was "the biggest shit in the Pacific."

All in all, by the time 109 arrived on the scene, the two-month-old New Georgia campaign had already proved far more costly in time and men than first anticipated. Throughout the early summer, the U.S. 43rd Infantry Division and 9th Marine Battalion failed repeatedly to capture Munda Point. Again and again bloody assaults were mounted with no result other than extensive Allied casualties from grueling combat—often hand-to-hand combat—with the Japanese. There was also one other result: a strange illness—a type of shell shock, perhaps—dubbed "war neurosis" by the doctors on the scene. The war neurosis came to infect no fewer than 2,500 New Georgia GIs. On one particularly bad evening, American soldiers of different divisions—exhausted, frustrated, and confused—savaged each other on the ground near Munda, knifing their comrades and tossing grenades at Allied units, all believing they were fighting the Japanese. On July 13, two days before Jack came to Lumbari, General Oscar W. Griswold publicly expressed his doubts as to whether the 43rd Division would ever succeed in taking Munda. And on the very day Jack and the PT 109 showed up, the key army and navy commanders previously in charge of the New Georgia effort received word they'd been relieved of command.

The Japanese held strong positions not just on New Georgia and Kolombangara, but also on Kolombangara's sister island Vella Lavella and many of the larger central Solomon islands to the east. PT commanders referred to the Ferguson Passage and Blackett Strait—which lay between the larger eastern islands and the string of New Georgia/Kolombangara/Vella Lavella—as "the Slot." Over recent weeks, the Slot had become the Japanese's preferred route for their nightly convoys (dubbed by Halsey "the Tokyo Express") charged with resupplying New Georgia. These parades of large ships traveled south each evening from their bases at Rabaul, Bourgainville, and the Shortland Islands loaded with troops and arms. Protected by float planes (the Japanese equivalents of the U.S. Navy's Mariners), the Japanese ships trudged through the Slot at about eighteen knots and then off-loaded on the shores of Kolombangara (from which men and materials could be moved easily across the narrow Kula Channel to New Georgia's

Munda Point) before returning north at twice the speed, their cargo holds empty. It was this supply channel through the Ferguson Passage and Blackett Strait that 109 and the other Lumbari PTs were meant to interdict.

"This work, once dull, has suddenly turned deadly," Jack wrote on July 28. The Japanese float planes watched for the PTs' V-shaped phosphorescent wakes (which Jack had once thought so beautiful) and dropped bombs at the junction of the Vs. Two of Kennedy's crew, Maurice Kowal and a new man, Leon Drawdy, received wounds from shrapnel during 109's first night out in the Vella Gulf (the evening of July 19). "We were well up in there— and lying to thinking this wasn't too tough," Jack wrote his parents, "when suddenly I heard a plane and looked up—and said it looks like one of our new ones to my exec. The next minute—was flat on my back across the deck. He had straddled us with a couple. The boat was full of holes . . . but we've had only minor hits on our boat since then. They usually drop a flare—of terrific brilliance—everything stands out for what seems miles around—you wait then as you can't see a thing up in the air—the next minute there's a heck of a craaack—they have dropped one or two. All in all, it makes for a certain loss of appetite." Japanese planes successfully bombed PT 105 a few nights later, on the 24th, killing that vessel's executive officer and just narrowly missing PT 109 and 106. Later that same evening, as 109, 106, and 161 escorted the broken 105 back to Lumbari, another Japanese plane attacked, dropping a 500-pound bomb that nearly blew 161 out of the water. As Jack well knew, each of these episodes was a close call. A direct hit to his or any other PT would mean immediate death for all hands.

One of Jack's men, Andrew Kirksey, took the attack of the 19th as an omen. "He never really got over it," Jack wrote, "he always seemed to have the feeling that something was going to happen to him. He never said anything about being put ashore—he didn't want to—but the next time we came down the line—I was going to let him work on the base force. When a fellow gets the feeling that he's in for it—the only thing to do is let him get off the boat—because strangely enough they always seem to be the ones that do get it. I don't know whether it's coincidence or what." Still, of all the crew, only Kirksey seemed depressed and pessimistic. All the others remained cheerful and confident despite the Spartan conditions under which they lived and labored.

Lumbari was nothing but a swamp surrounded by ocean. PT commanders and crews lived part of the time on their boats and part of the time in damp tents, the latter adjacent to a series of primitive slit trenches. The trenches—waterlogged, mosquito-infested—provided scant cover during air raids. "We mostly live on the boats," he wrote his parents, "eat canned army rations (beans, fried Spam!) and go out nearly every night—Try to grab a little sleep in the day. So far we have been lucky." He remained impressed with his men. Americans in general, he wrote, engaged in war the same way they engaged in football. "Those that don't like the game simply won't show up for practice—or if they are made to—are not worth a damn—Those that play—play like the devil—and do a great job . . ." All his men were players. "What is interesting though is that some of the mildest most unassuming fellows—stand up & do the best job—and another pleasant surprise—the tougher it gets—the less beefing you hear. . . . All in all its an education— and there is an undeniable interest and attraction to it."

· · ·

"WELL, TAKE CARE JOHNNY," Kick wrote Jack on July 29, adding, prophetically, "By the time you get this so much will have happened. . . . God bless you."

· · ·

JACK AND HIS MEN got a reprieve from patrol on the night of the 29th, when 109 had to undergo repairs for a defective rudder. While his boat was laid up, Jack took the initiative to try to fix at least one key deficiency in PT design: the vessel's limited deck-gun capability. On a quick trip to the nearby army base at Rendova he scrounged a surplus 37mm antitank gun, which he brought back with him to Lumbari. Securing it to the deck of the PT meant bolting the legs of the cannon to the deck and then tying the gun's wheels—on which it would recoil—to two large 2×8 coconut tree planks lashed down with rope. The crew removed 109's regulation life raft in order to make room for the new gun, and finished up work on the morning of August 1.

There were no stars and no moon as PT 109 slipped out to sea along with her sister craft at about six-thirty that night. In a breach of PT tradition, Kennedy's boat carried an unlucky thirteen souls—ten enlisted men plus Jack, executive officer Lennie Thom, and a guest: Barney Ross. His own boat, the 166, having been sunk by B-25s, Ross tagged along on PT 109 with instructions to man the deck cannon. Kennedy also asked Ross—who had evidently not mentioned his night blindness—to serve as forward lookout. The enlisted roster included the six remaining members of Jack's original crew, plus four only recently assigned to 109 from Warfield's personnel pool: Raymond Starkey (twenty-nine), Gerard E. Zinser (twenty-five), Harold Marney (nineteen), and Raymond Albert (twenty).

109 went out as part of a four-boat group under the command of Lieutenant Hank Brantingham, a venerated PT veteran who had served as executive officer to none other than Bulkeley himself and participated in MacArthur's rescue. Throughout the night, the PTs crept along slowly to keep the wake and noise to a minimum. Kennedy stood at the helm of 109. The Tokyo Express—consisting this evening of four destroyers transporting some nine hundred enemy troops—started to pass through the Blackett Strait around midnight. A skirmish—the PT boats firing on the destroyers and themselves being targeted by float planes—went on for about half an hour before the destroyers continued on their way. Two hours after midnight, PT 109 idled in the strait awaiting the return of the unloaded Japanese vessels. The details of what happened next remain vague. However, the bare incontestable fact is this: one of the homeward-bound Japanese ships—the destroyer *Amagiri* traveling at forty knots—emerged suddenly out of the dark night, rammed PT 109, and cut her in two. The impact tossed Kennedy into the cockpit, where he landed on his bad back.

Call it "Kennedy luck" that once the disaster of the 109 was over and Jack was called to account for his actions, his old friend Byron White (now assigned as a naval intelligence officer for MTB Flotilla One) wound up as one of the two investigators to whom he had to answer. In their formal report filed August 23, Lieutenant (j.g.) Byron White and Lieutenant (j.g.) James McClure soft-pedaled the question of how and why 109 got clipped by the *Amagiri*, instead choosing to emphasize Jack's brave behavior saving his crew once the 109 was lost. Toward this end, White and McClure described the actual accident succinctly and in a manner uncritical of 109's command:

> The time was about 0230. Ensign Ross was on the bow as lookout; Ensign Thom was standing beside the cockpit; Lt. Kennedy was at

the wheel, and with him in the cockpit was McGuire, his radioman; Marney was in the forward turret; Mauer, the quartermaster was standing beside Ensign Thom; Albert was in the after turret; and McMann was in the engine room. The location of other members of the crew upon the boat is unknown. Suddenly a dark shape loomed up on PT 109's starboard bow 200–300 yards distant. At first this shape was believed to be other PTs. However, it was soon seen to be a destroyer identified as of the Hibiki Group of the Fubuki Class bearing down on PT 109 at high speed. The 109 started to turn to starboard preparatory to firing torpedoes. However, when PT 109 had scarcely turned 30 degrees, the destroyer rammed the PT, striking it forward of the forward starboard tube and shearing off the starboard side of the boat aft, including the starboard engine. The destroyer traveling at an estimated speed of 40 knots neither slowed nor fired as she split the PT, leaving part of the PT on one side and the other on the other. Scarcely ten seconds elapsed between time of sighting and crash.

Evidence suggests a combination of conditions, inattentiveness, and lack of preparedness led to the disaster. Two of the crew of PT 109 were asleep when the *Amagiri* hit, and two more were lying down. By his own admission to White and McClure, Kennedy himself sighted the Japanese battleship only seconds before it hit. Zinser commented many years later: "It was so dark that night you couldn't hardly see a foot and a half in front of your nose. . . . this destroyer had the island of Kolombangara for a background and that's what made it that much more difficult for our lookout to spot." Barney Ross would recall that "we spotted [the *Amagiri*] at a distance of a quarter of a mile. First we thought it was a PT boat—that's what it seemed to be at first. Then we realized it was a destroyer, and then the skipper [Kennedy] started turning towards the destroyer. Had we had enough room, enough time, it's a good chance we would have been able to sink him instead of the destroyer getting us, because at this point—up until this point I don't believe the Japanese had seen us."

In violation of squadron policy, Jack had only one of three engines in gear at the time. Rapid movement on short notice was therefore impossible. After the sinking of PT 109, other PT men would not understand how

Kennedy could not have seen the *Amagiri* well before it closed on him. According to former PT skipper Leonard A. Nikoloric, "There was a lot of criticism in the Navy about the loss of 109. MacArthur is supposed to have said that Jack should have been court-martialed."

Ross believed that the destroyer crew spotted 109 about ten seconds before impact and that the *Amagiri* purposely turned into the smaller boat. He said it was a sight he would never forget: "the mast keeling over at about a 45 degree angle towards us—this destroyer mast—and at this distance it would probably be maybe 100 feet. If he [the commander of the *Amagiri*] hadn't turned he would just have missed us, but by turning he caught us on the starboard bow at about a 20 angle to the longitudinal center of the boat. So he split the boat sort of longways—not across the boat. He hit the bow up there about five feet from my right, and it continued on back, completely obliterating the starboard turret where I believe a young fellow named Kirksey was on watch, about two feet from the skipper's right. Just before the moment of impact I grabbed onto this 37mm army cannon and I was hanging on to that for dear life, and the boat of course lurched sharply to the right. It was like what I imagine it would be like to be hit by a train. . . . We were fortunate the destroyer was very narrow and sharp, because only two of us were killed, I guess, or disappeared anyway. And the next thing I know, the boat is at about a 45–50 degree angle and everything seems to be lit up. . . . The light I'd seen of course was the gasoline, which went up. This made a tremendous—not an explosion but a terrific roar that went up, I guess probably a hundred feet in the air." (Maguire later claimed that the Japanese on the *Amagiri* shelled the remains of the 109; other survivors disagreed.)

The next thing Ross remembered, he was afloat with Lenny Thom and Zinser. Thom "was talking like he was out of his mind. He didn't know where he was and he was trying to climb on top of me—thought I was a log or something—I remember Zinser and I were kind of slapping Lenny and trying to get him to realize where he was." Once Ross and Zinser got Thom to calm down, the three men began to swim toward the only part of the boat still afloat: the bow, from which other survivors flashed a blinker light. "I thought it was funny—the boat was drifting, and the wind was sort of blowing it away from us. So we were swimming toward the boat and it was floating away, that was just a little nerve-wracking." Zinser's arm and chest were badly burned; Maguire wound up swimming out to him from the wreck and helping him make it back to where he gratefully joined other survivors, Mauer and Albert among them. Meanwhile Thom, having gathered himself together, rescued Johnston, who had nearly been asphyxiated by gas fumes and, unconscious, had to be tied down to the wreck of 109 lest he fall off. "We lay on the front of the bow, right in front of the cockpit. As far as I know, the section with the engines sunk immediately," Zinser remembered. "The bow was sticking up at a very steep angle. It seemed to me the tide was taking us around in circles. Why the Japs over on Kolombangara didn't come out and get us I'll never know to this day. That was one of our biggest concerns." Kennedy rescued Pop McMahon, the most severely wounded of the crew, who had suffered major burns over 70 percent of his body, towing him back to the floating hulk; he then provided the same service for Starkey and Harris. Kirksey and Marney, meanwhile, were dead.

The men floated silently, glumly, for several hours, with no way of knowing a coast watcher for the New Zealand armed services—Lieutenant Arthur Reginald Evans, stationed behind enemy lines in the heights of Kolombangara—had already become aware of the accident and set the search for survivors in motion. "As dawn came up," Ross recalled, "we found ourselves on the boat with the boat under water all the way up to the bow. There was about 15 feet of the boat, which was 80 feet long, still sticking out of the water at a 45 degree angle, right side up. So we were hanging on to the boat, in the middle or toward the Gizo side of Blackett Strait. And we were quite exposed because over at Gizo there were, according to our intelligence, about 100 troops at the Gizo anchorage, which was the old British government house for that area of the Solomons." Worse, on the far side of the strait, Kolombangara served as home to more than ten thousand Japanese troops.

Ross remembered how Jack rather shrewdly and subtly asserted his authority over the group. He "discussed whether we should continue to operate as a unit, a military unit, or whether we should give every man for himself. I think Jack was just trying to sound us out because we all wanted to remain as a military unit and so he sort of, I think, established, reestablished his authority at this stage of the game. He was testing us out to see what shape our morale was in."

The PT took on additional water as the morning progressed, slowly starting to settle and turning her keel up so that it became hard for the crew to hold on. It seemed just a matter of time before she turned turtle for good; she also showed alarming signs of drifting toward Gizo, where they would be sure to be taken prisoner. Thus Kennedy made the decision they must strike out for an island barely visible, some four miles off in the opposite direction from Gizo. Jack ordered his poorest swimmers and more severely hurt crewmen lashed to a float rigged from one of the 2×8 planks that had previously anchored the 37mm gun. He then instructed the rest of the men to tow them. He himself towed the severely burned McMahon, holding the strap of the engineer's life jacket in his mouth and battling a strong easterly current all the way.

He and his crew had been in the water nearly fifteen hours—and swimming for a good five hours—before they finally made landfall at about 6 p.m. on August 2, collapsing on the beach of an island ("Plum Pudding Island"), the name of which they did not know. This was a tiny parcel about one hundred yards in diameter, surrounded by reefs. The small spit of sand boasted a grand total of six coconut trees—the bounty of which would last Kennedy and his men only about two days. Jack promptly took to calling the place "Bird Island" because of its many exotic seabirds, which, though plentiful, proved impossible to catch.

It was, Jack told his men, survival time. They had, between them, six loaded .45s, one loaded .38, one signal light, one large knife, one smaller knife, one pocketknife, and a lantern. The boat's first-aid kit had been lost in the collision. They had no water. And several of the men seemed in quite rough shape. Johnston could barely breathe. Ross recalled that Kennedy "had a situation where he didn't know how bad Johnston was. He sounded in terrible shape, he was coughing and retching." Also, Harris's leg had been severely banged up, and Zinser—though in much better shape than McMahon—nursed some burns. McMahon, they thought, would die soon. Robert Donovan, who interviewed McMahon, would write in the book *PT 109*: "Scabs forming over his burned eyelids made it difficult for him to see. The palms of his hands were swollen to a thickness of three inches. They were cracked like burned bacon, and he could look deeply into his own flesh. His misery was redoubled because his burns were giving off a terrible stench. . . ." Like the others, McMahon shivered in his damp clothes on the windy beach as the sun approached the horizon, the wind whipping up and chilling him to the bone. Sick and exhausted, they missed an opportunity that presented itself shortly after they made landfall: they failed to signal an Allied air patrol plane when it flew overhead.

Hyperactive, impatient, and psychologically indisposed to complacency, Kennedy was not on Bird Island more than half an hour before he decided to swim out to the Ferguson Passage in hopes of making contact with an American PT. "I think he felt that if he would just get out there," Ross remembered. "We were so near and yet so far. . . . Ferguson Passage was maybe a mile and a half away, and could be reached through shallow water and reefs with really not too much swimming. Of course . . . all of us tried to persuade him not to do it, but he was determined. If he could just get over there in about an hour's time . . . these boats would be going by. And here would be a chance to get us all out of the soup right away." Kennedy asked his crew to flash the signal light occasionally to give him a landmark in the darkness. He took off at just about 6:30 p.m., and by nine the next morning his comrades decided he must be dead.

They mourned silently, since their parched throats made speech nearly impossible. Later in the day, around noon, Lenny Thom thought for a moment he might be hallucinating, or perhaps seeing a ghost, when an exhausted (and yellow) Kennedy finally emerged from the water. He'd had no luck in the Ferguson Passage, but nevertheless ordered the unenthusiastic Ross to make a similar swim come sundown—a foray destined to prove just as futile as Jack's.

Back at Lumbari, the biggest shit in the Pacific refrained from putting out a search party, in large measure because of the story he'd been told by Lieutenant Phil Potter, commander of PT 169—a boat patrolling the same waters as 109 at the time of the crash. Potter claimed that he'd not turned tail and run at the first sight of the Japanese battleship, but in fact had remained on the scene and made a thorough though fruitless search for survivors. Of course, Potter lied: had he made a search, he would have found no fewer than eleven survivors plus more than half of 109. Based on Potter's testimony, things proceeded at Lumbari as though Kennedy and his men were dead; Warfield filled out the appropriate forms for MIAs and suggested that someone pack up the crew's things. At Tulagi, Johnny Iles arranged for Father McCarthy, the Catholic priest, to say a memorial mass. (One week later, when visiting the rescued Jack in the sick bay at Tulagi, Johnny would make the mistake of mentioning the mass, the very thought of which made

Jack furious. "He read the riot act to me. He said he wasn't ready to die just yet, and why the hell had I given up hope?")

Early on the 4th, with the coconuts on Bird Island dwindling, Jack decided his crew must make one more swim. Their destination this time was Olasana Island, considerably larger than Bird Island, lush with coconut trees, and only a half mile distant. The men used the same modus operandi now as they had two days before. Strong swimmers towed the weak on the plank, Kennedy hauled McMahon, and all of them fought the strong easterly current with everything they had. (Kennedy remembered years later that it seemed the current was actually stronger between the islands than it had been out in the middle of the strait. This may have been true, but more likely Jack and his men were simply more exhausted on the 4th than they had been on the 2nd.) The swim took two hours, with Kennedy and McMahon beating the others to the little beach on Olasana's southeastern end by about twenty minutes.

Here they at least had plenty of coconuts. Ross would remember how Harris, "the most nimble of our group, shinnied up the trees and got some green coconuts and threw them down." They also ate some of the ones on the ground "that weren't rotten, they were actually better than the ones up on the tree. . . . So, we kept going. In other words: Jack never allowed us to sit around and mope. . . . [Johnston] was in pretty good shape by now. So our main worry was McMahon. We all kept off the beach because we were afraid of being soloed—you could see for miles out there—silhouetted on the beach. So we all stayed in the bushes most of the time. Pappy [McMahon] lay in the water, and the salt water was apparently good for him. He kept moving his fingers so that he wouldn't lose the use of his hands. He instinctively did this. The doctor later told us that's what saved his hands."

Kennedy and Ross together took another swim on the afternoon of the 5th, going about a mile to Naru (sometimes called Cross) Island. They arrived on the island (where Japanese had at times been spotted) at about 3:30 p.m., and immediately ducked into the brush. White and McClure recounted in their report:

> Neither seeing nor hearing anything, the two officers sneaked through the brush to the east side of the island and peered from the brush onto the beach. A small rectangular box with Japanese writ-

ing on the side was seen which was quickly and furtively pulled into the bush. Its contents proved to be 30–40 small bags of crackers and candy. A little further up the beach, alongside a native lean-to, a one-man canoe and a barrel of water were found. About this time a canoe containing two persons was sighted. Light showing between their legs revealed that they did not wear trousers and, therefore, must be natives. Despite all efforts of Kennedy and Ross to attract their attention, they paddled swiftly off to the northwest. Nevertheless, Kennedy and Ross, having obtained a canoe, food and water, considered their visit a success.

What Jack had no way of knowing was that the natives he and Ross had tried to flag down were in fact scouts dispatched to Naru by coast watcher Evans for the purpose of surveying a Japanese wreck. Evans's Melanesians fled because they mistook Jack and Barney for Japanese soldiers.

That evening, leaving Ross concealed on Naru, Kennedy took the canoe—which turned out to be partially broken—and used it as a float for another expedition into the Ferguson Passage. He waited there until 10 p.m. in the futile hope of spotting some PTs. He then returned to Naru, where he found Ross asleep. ("He had a higher metabolism than I did," Ross would recall. "I slept right through until morning. He was up and at 'em, you know, back to the other guys. I remember he was kidding me about being lazy and I wouldn't wake up.") Leaving Ross behind to rise at his leisure and follow in the morning, Jack filled an old biscuit tin with fresh water, grabbed the box of food and candy, and returned to Olasana, once again using the broken canoe as a float.

Jack arrived on Olasana at about 11:30 p.m., where he found Lennie Thom chatting with the same two natives he and Ross had first spotted on Naru earlier in the day. Their names, Kennedy learned, were Biuku and Eroni, and they spoke just a little English. The two natives had been on Olasana for several hours already. One of them had even joined Thom in an aborted attempt to paddle to Lumbari, which lay some forty miles distant. Thom and his man Friday had turned back when the winds came up in the middle of the Ferguson Passage.

Kennedy, Biuku, and Eroni returned to Naru Island in the wee hours of the morning on August 6, intercepting Ross, whom they found swimming in the direction of Olasana. Once back on Naru, Biuku and Eroni revealed the hiding place of a large two-man canoe and then prepared to leave, promising to get word of the 109 survivors to American forces. At the suggestion of the islanders, Jack carved a brief and now famous message into a green coconut husk: NARU ISL NATIVE KNOWS POSIT HE CAN PILOT 11 ALIVE NEED SMALL BOAT KENNEDY.

After Biuku and Eroni left, Ross and Kennedy remained on Naru until evening. Then—perhaps suspecting the native men might not make it through or would not be listened to—Jack decided he and Barney should set out in the two-man canoe to once more try their luck intercepting PTs in the Ferguson Passage. Ross said as they left that he thought the water looked a little rough, but Jack insisted they'd be fine. With that, the two men paddled far out into the passage, saw nothing, and wound up being caught in a sudden rain squall, which eventually capsized the canoe, after which a wave dashed Ross against a coral reef, lacerating his right arm and shoulder. (His feet were already badly cut up, and infected, from walking on coral.) Swimming to land proved difficult and treacherous, but eventually both men managed to make it back onto Naru, where they remained the rest of the night. (As they labored back to the island, Kennedy turned to Ross and, grinning, said, "I guess this would be a fine time for you to say 'I told you so.' ")

Eight islanders appeared at Naru the next morning, the 7th, paddling a large war canoe. They carried food, medicine, and water. They also delivered a note on letterhead from Evans, who had now—after the fall of New Georgia to the Allies on the 5th—moved his base to a small offshore island near Wana Wana. Evans wrote that Biuku and Eroni had left in a canoe for Lumbari, carrying the coconut. He went on to suggest that Kennedy return with the natives to Evans's camp, from there to communicate by radio with Lumbari. Kennedy agreed to this but first insisted he and Ross be paddled to Olasana, where he dispensed the supplies to the men of the 109. Later, hidden under ferns in the war canoe so as not to be spotted by the Japanese, Kennedy allowed himself to be rowed to Evans's station. He arrived there at about 6:00 p.m., after which he communicated via coded radio transmissions with Lumbari. Forty miles away, the startled Warfield—who had by now spoken to Biuku and Eroni and seen the coconut—agreed to dispatch two PTs to rendezvous with Kennedy in the Ferguson Passage, near Patparan Island, at 10:30 p.m.

Some of Evans's islanders brought Kennedy to the place at the appointed time, where they waited a full hour for two PTs that, astonishingly, arrived late. One of the boats, Bill Liebenow's 157, carried not only the regular crew but also Biuku and Eroni, Jack's old friend Cluster, a pharmacist mate to give first aid, and two war correspondents (Lief Erikson of the AP and Frank Hewlett from UPI). Clambering aboard 157, Jack was at first less than cordial, demanding to know why Liebenow was running behind schedule. He turned down the offer of food, muttering: "Thanks, I've just had a coconut." Jack did, however, take a shot of whiskey, after which he embraced Biuku and Eroni. He subsequently made a gift to Eroni: a good-luck coin that Clare Boothe Luce had given him a year before and that he'd carried all through his ordeal. (He subsequently wrote Clare that the medallion "did service above and beyond its routine duties during a rather busy period.")

The men on Olasana Island were all asleep when 157—with Art Berndsten's 171 providing radar cover—showed up for the rescue. "As I remember it," Barney Ross told an interviewer many years later, "most of us were pretty exhausted by this time. Although we'd set a watch all night long, apparently we were all asleep at the critical moment when Jack and the PT boat arrived off of our little haven in the bushes. They weren't particularly anxious to make too much noise because they were in the restricted waters and we would have been sitting ducks for any Japanese that might have been coming by in patrol boats." Nevertheless, Jack was finally reduced to shouting in order to attract the attention of his sleeping crew. "They were hollering for us to wake. Finally we woke up in time to be rescued. I will never forget. I felt sort of foolish. We were all asleep!"

Rushing back to Lumbari on the 157, the men received first aid, food, and drinks served on the deck of the boat. In the midst of their celebration, they told their stories to Erikson and Hewlett. The crew all spoke highly of Lennie Thom, who had acted as surrogate leader during Kennedy's long absences in search of salvation. And they likewise heaped praise on their skipper, who did not bother to talk to the reporters, choosing instead to collapse into a bunk. One day later, at the little hospital back on Tulagi, navy physicians noted that Jack "at present time . . . shows symptoms of fatigue and many deep abrasions and lacerations of the entire body, especially the feet." They prescribed "hot soaks and alcohol and glycerin dressings and bed rest. Multiple vitamin tablets and high caloric diet." In other words, no coconuts.

Johnny Iles would recall how Jack, who'd always seemed skinny, appeared particularly emaciated following his rescue: emaciated and yellow.

His head, he told a friend, was in a bad place. He said he was annoyed that no other PTs had come to his aid immediately after the wreck: a fact about which he seemed genuinely bitter. Joe Kernell, a PT skipper from Squadron 5, remembered going to see Jack in his hospital bed at Tulagi. "He was in this hospital," Kernell recalled. "Not a real hospital, a tent affair, and wearing only skivvies. . . . I said, 'Jack, what went through your mind when you saw that destroyer coming and you thought you might be killed?' He looked real serious and asked, 'You really want to know? . . . I thought, my God, I owe Joe Kernell two hundred fifty dollars in bridge debts and I haven't paid him!' So, right there, he whipped out a check and paid me. Then, in that funny way of his, he made me feel terrible: that the only reason I'd come to the sick bay was to get my money!"

Cluster would remember Jack breaking down into tears and speculating that he might have been able to save the two men who died if only he'd received immediate aid from other PTs. Jack subsequently refused when Cluster offered him a ticket home. He wanted, he said, to get even with the Japanese. Cluster told Nigel Hamilton: "I think it was guilt of losing his two crewmen, the guilt of losing his boat, and of not being able to sink a Japanese destroyer. . . . I would say, if I tried to write a history of JFK's period in the Solomons, that Jack felt *very strongly* about losing those two men and his ship in the Solomons. He was *very, very bitter* that nobody had come to help him. And the second thing, *he wanted to pay the Japanese back*."

.   .   .

WORD OF 109's SINKING had not been publicized. Authorities had, however, notified the ambassador on the 6th that his son was missing: word the ambassador kept to himself, pending further news. "Several days later," Rose recalled, "when Joe had gone riding at 8 a.m., as was his custom, I turned on the radio and heard the announcement that Lieutenant j.g. John F. Kennedy, earlier reported missing, had been found. I waited for more news about him, but there was none. I called Joe, who was twenty minutes' distance away. He came home immediately and confirmed the details, and he told me what he had known, and that he had been trying to spare me until the facts were established."

Hewlett's and Erikson's accounts of the episode cleared Navy censors on August 18. The story made its way into national headlines. KENNEDY'S SON SAVES 10 IN PACIFIC, screamed the *Boston Globe*, with the subhead KENNEDY'S SON IS HERO IN PACIFIC. Writing shortly thereafter in the *New York Times*, Arthur Krock noted, "Former Ambassador and Mrs. Kennedy today shouted in joy when informed of the exploit of their son," but also "expressed deep sorrow for the two crewmen who lost their lives."

Jack promptly wrote his parents about the adventure. "On the bright side of an otherwise completely black time was the way that everyone stood up to it. Previous to that I had become somewhat cynical about the American as a fighting man. I had seen too much bellyaching and laying off. But with the chips down, that all faded away. I can now believe—which I never would have before—the stories of Bataan and Wake. For an American it's got to be awfully easy or awfully tough. When it's in the middle, then there's trouble. It was a terrible thing though, losing those two men. One had ridden with me for as long as I had been out here. . . . He had a wife and three kids. The other fellow had just come aboard. He was only a kid himself. It certainly brought home how real the war is—and when I read the papers from home, how superficial is most of the talking and thinking about it!"

· · ·

JOE JR. WROTE his parents on the 29th after receiving a letter in which his father scolded him, saying he was "considerably upset" not to have heard from Joe "during those days after news of Jack's rescue. . . . I thought that you would very likely call up to see whether we had any news as to how Jack was." Pleading his busy schedule ferrying Liberators from San Diego, Joe apologized and implied that he did not need to call home for word of Jack. All the information he needed—and more—seemed to be in the press. "With the great quantity of reading material coming in on the actions of the Kennedys in various parts of the world," he continued, "and the countless number of paper clippings about our young hero—the battler of the wars of Banana River, San Juan, Virginia Beach . . . will now step to the microphone and give out with a few words of his own activities."

Just a few weeks later, with a few days' leave on his hands before finally departing for Europe, Joe Jr. brought Commander Jim Reedy home for a visit to Hyannis during which a crowd of friends and family celebrated the ambassador's fifty-fifth birthday. Other guests included Boston police commissioner Joe Timilty and Judge John Burns, the old friend of the ambassador's who had helped tutor Joe Jr. during his time at Harvard Law. In the midst of dinner, Judge Burns raised his glass to toast "Ambassador Joe Kennedy, father of our hero, our own hero, Lieutenant John F. Kennedy of the United States Navy." Joe Jr. drank, but seemed unenthusiastic. Later that night, Timilty heard him sobbing in his room.

═ 24 ═

A Great Deal in
the Way of Death

JOE AND THE REST OF VP-110 arrived at the Dunkeswell airfield, Honiton—on the Devon coast—at the end of September, just in time for the rainiest autumn in Cornish history. The sixty-four officers and 106 men of VP-110 soon took to calling the place "Mudville Heights." Living two to a room in tiny Nissen huts made of corrugated iron, they found it impossible to stay warm because of the total dampness with which they were constantly surrounded. Also, the iron walls of their huts did not insulate against the cold, but rather conducted it. "A small stove which takes about an hour to get going serves as the only means for keeping us from catching pneumonia," Joe wrote his parents. "For a bath you have to go several miles and you must make it in the morning for all the hot water has been taken by evening. . . . So at long last, I'm really beginning to fight the war."

Joe's bomber wing worked as part of, and under the direction of, the Coastal Command of the British Royal Air Force. Nevertheless, all the planes, all the flying personnel, and most of the administrative and ground personnel were American. One visiting reporter observed of the Dunkeswell base: ". . . men and women of the Royal Air Force do all the 'housekeeping' at the station. RAF men and WAAF women keep the place clean, look after the heating stoves, tend to the water supply, cook, and dish out the food in the mess, which is run on the cafeterial system. In addition, WAAF women serve at telephone switchboards, work in signals, drive cars and trucks, do office work, and even help overhaul the motors of the big Liberator bombers." Many of Joe's cohorts were glad to have the women of the WAAF around. The nearest town, many miles away, couldn't produce half a dozen suitable dance partners on its own. "You get a good idea of how boring this life can be," wrote the reporter, "when you loaf around in the mess lounge waiting for your turn for what's technically termed an 'ops hop,' which means an operational flight. Sitting there before an open fire big enough to roast a side of beef, home feels very far away."

Joe's primary stock in trade consisted of twelve-hour search-and-destroy missions scouting the Bay of Biscay for U-boats on a schedule that most often ran from midnight to noon. Zipped into electrically heated leather flying suits and wearing Mae West life jackets for good measure, Joe and his crew went about a set routine with workmanlike precision. First, they tested their Liberator's machine guns shortly after takeoff, firing quick bursts from each. In the distance they could usually see other planes doing the same thing: red tracer bullets decorating the darkness in all directions. Then, for the balance of the night, Joe would illuminate the sea with a steady barrage of parachute flares—painstakingly identifying vessels as friendly or otherwise and then taking the appropriate action. (Joe had to be on guard after daybreak, as German Junkers 88s had a nasty habit of screaming down on Liberators from out of the sun.)

.   .   .

IN LONDON ON HIS days and nights off, Joe socialized with a host of old and new friends in a group anchored by his sister Kick. Other members of the gang included Billy Hartington, Bill Hearst, Jr. (now serving as a foreign correspondent for his father's newspapers), Hearst's wife, Lorrelle, Bebe and Chiquita Carcano, Nancy Astor's son Jakey (John Jacob Astor V, who would shortly wed the Catholic Chiquita over his mother's objections), and Joe's onetime girlfriend Virginia Gilliat, now Lady Sykes.

The group made the usual rounds, hitting the 400 and other clubs that had thus far survived German bombing. Joe was at the 400 with the Hearsts one night when Virginia Gilliat introduced him to a beautiful, brash, and witty Australian with whom he quickly became infatuated. The divorced and remarried mother of two children, Pat Wilson was also Protestant. She had been raised the daughter of a prosperous sheep rancher and had come to London more than ten years before, at the age of seventeen, to marry the twenty-one-year-old Earl of Jersey. Later, at age twenty-five, she married Robin Wilson, a banker in his late thirties. Joe observed in a letter to Jack that Pat's tile-roofed home in Woking (a town conveniently located one hour south of London on the same train line that serviced Dunkeswell) bore no trace of Major Wilson, currently stationed far away in Libya. Wilson's clothes did not fill the closet; his portrait did not adorn the wall. By late November, Joe was able to tell Jack—confidentially—that he felt quite the man of the Woking household, where Pat kept his pipe ready for him on the mantel.

Kick often wound up here as well, along with Billy Hartington, who—still with the Coldstream Guards—spent his weekdays at a base in Alton, Hampshire. Gathering for frequent weekends, each member of the foursome brought along whatever he or she had succeeded in hoarding in the way of foodstuffs the previous week: an egg here, a slab of bacon there, or perhaps even a can of cherished grapefruit juice. Billy—whose position as a future duke required that he avoid any hint of adverse publicity or scandal—usually showed up with the lightest load. Confident Joe and Kick, on the other hand, could be counted upon to appear with numerous goodies filched with impunity from the Dunkeswell canteen and the Hans Crescent Club. Enjoying these luxuries, the couples spent many hours listening and dancing to records, challenging each other in doubles tennis, and playing gin rummy out on the patio. At night, Joe retired with Pat while Kick took a guestroom. Billy, in turn, made himself comfortable on the living-room couch.

"There's heavy betting on when we're going to announce it," Kick quipped coyly to her mother. "Some people have gotten the idea I'm going to give in. Little do they know. Some of those old Devonshire ancestors would jump out of their graves if anything happened to some of their ancient traditions. It just amuses me to see how worried they all are." The dangling threat of marriage to Billy was, however, ever present. While the devout Rose languished in denial, the ambassador took a more indulgent view of things. "As far as I'm concerned," he wrote his daughter, "I'll gamble with your judgment. The best is none too good for you, but if you decide it's a Chinaman, it's okay with me. That's how much I think of you."

. . .

SEPTEMBER FOUND JACK out of the sick bay and stationed at Tulagi. The base had a new commandant, Mike Moran, former captain of the *Boise*, "and a big harp if there ever was one," Jack wrote his parents. "He's fresh out from six months in the States and full of smoke and vinegar and statements like—it's a privilege to be here and we should be ashamed to be back in the States—and we'll stay here ten years if necessary. That all went over like a lead balloon. However, the doc told us yesterday that Iron Mike was complaining of head-aches and diarrhea—so we look for a different tune to be thrummed on that harp of his before many months." Sardonic jokes aside, Jack at least respected Moran for one thing. The man appeared to understand a hard-won lesson that others in the PT fleets had yet to figure out: wooden ships armed with antiquated torpedoes simply did not have a place in modern warfare. Jack thought it an excellent idea when he learned that the Tulagi PT fleet would shortly be converted to heavily armed gunboats customized to fight small Japanese auxiliaries which, as Jack wrote his parents, "the Japs are using now instead of bigger stuff."

Navy mechanics spent several weeks stripping Jack's new boat, PT-59, of its torpedo tubes and depth charges. They then fitted the vessel with armor plating on both sides of the gas tanks and gunwale and installed fourteen .50-caliber armored guns along with two 40mm guns. Once the work was done, PT-59 would become Gunboat No. 1, and Jack the first gunboat commander in the Pacific. Five former crewmen from the 109—Mauer, Maguire, Drewitch, Kowal, and Drawdy—looked Kennedy up as he was getting his new boat ready at Guadalcanal. "Mauer and I went down to the dock," Maguire remembered. "Kennedy said, 'What are you doing here?' We said, 'What kind of a guy are you? You got a boat and didn't come get us?' Kennedy got choked up. The nearest I ever seen him come to crying." Lennie Thom would have come with Kennedy as well but for his promotion to command what would become Gunboat No. 2; Johnny Iles in turn became skipper of Gunboat No. 3.

Jack received promotion to full lieutenant on October 8. Perhaps more important so far as he was concerned, he received a letter from Inga the same day informing him that she'd dumped Nils Blok and would shortly move to Los Angeles, there to write the *Los Angeles Times* gossip column formerly authored by Sheilah Graham. He took the letter from Inga with him—and his crew noticed him reading it quite often—after No. 1 and the rest of the squadron moved up the line to remote Lumba Lumba, the new forward PT base at the island of Vella Lavella, on October 18. ". . . I am in a bad spot for getting out as I am now Captain of a gun-boat," he told his father. ". . . Have a picked crew—all volunteers—and all very experienced. Every man but one has been sunk at least once, and they have all been in the boats for a long time. It was sort of a dubious honor to be given the first [gunboat], so I will have to stick around and try to make a go of it. . . . Don't worry at all about me—I've learned to duck—and have learned the wisdom of the old naval doctrine of keeping your bowels—and your mouth—shut, and never volunteering."

Nevertheless, he still wanted to pay the Japanese back. He struck his crew as being all business on successive missions through the end of October and into early November: weeks that were, he wrote later, "packed with a great deal in the way of death." November 2 saw him rescuing marines trapped by Japanese ground forces on the island of Choiseul. After he'd gotten the men off the beach, Jack watched several severely wounded soldiers struggle and die in the main cabin of the gunboat, one of them in his very bunk. On the same night, after Jack had occasion to request air cover, he saw the Japanese systematically shoot down four Australian P-40s. Three nights later—with Byron White tagging along for the ride—No. 1 destroyed three Japanese barges that had become beached on Moli Island. It seemed to White that Jack clearly delighted in the sight of the barges going up in smoke.

Still, Jack remained ravenous for action. He was anxious to lash out at the Japanese with a furor that seemed almost religious in its intensity. His furor was tempered only by his poor health, which had grown steadily and decidedly worse since the sinking of the 109. The pains in both his back and stomach intensified. His fits of fever sprang up with increasing frequency, and "the yellow man"—as some of his cohorts took to calling him—dropped to 120 pounds. A navy doctor directed him to leave No. 1 on November 18, just a few days after another friend died in action. "Tough accident happened the other day," he wrote his family. "One of the boys who had ridden with me [on PT 109, but now serving on another boat] got killed. They picked up some Jap prisoners and he went forward . . . to give one of them a drink of water—as they had been floating around all night. He reached out his canteen—the Jap sprang forward—grabbed a tommy gun he held in the other hand, and in spite of the fact that he had four slugs poured into him, shot the boy. It is tough to go through what he went through and then get it that way—but you can't just fool around with these babies. They're murderous."

At Tulagi on November 23 a navy doctor x-rayed Jack and found, among other things, "a definite ulcer crater" which "would indicate an early duodenal ulcer." Prohibited from further duty, Jack wandered around Tulagi wearing a sacroiliac belt to help with his bad back, and even sometimes leaned on a cane. He wrote to his parents on the second anniversary of Pearl Harbor to say he'd received "fairly definite dope that I'm heading back in the very near future. . . . I should get back sometime in January according to the present arrangement. I am going to get sent to Melville as an instructor but there is a PT school at Miami that I'd like to get sent to—naturally." Torb Macdonald, serving with Harllee in MTB Squadron 12, wrote Jack the same day to say: "Life is just about the same here except that I've had a boat of my own since Dec. 1st or thereabouts. . . . Harllee thinks all I live for is to kill Japs & that I'm stupid enough to take the boat right on the beach. . . . However don't be alarmed & think I've gone Navy. I still am rather concerned with seeing to it that the art it has taken 10 years to develop gets a real chance to show its worth & full development, & any close runs I've made have been purely out of boredom & once because I wasn't any too sure where the hell I was. . . ."

While Jack waited for his orders home, he spent a great deal of time with Red Fay, whose PT 167 had come to Tulagi for repairs after receiving severe damage in battle. Both Jack and Fay seemed to have plenty of time on their hands. "He was trying to get his health back up," Fay recalled, "and that's when I spent a lot of time, every single day, practically, with him." Meanwhile, Jack's doctor ordered up still more x-rays, these revealing "chronic disc disease of the lower back."

After having spent nine months in the Solomons, Jack finally received his orders home on December 14, 1943. He was instructed to take thirty days' leave upon arrival in the United States and thereafter report to Melville

for unspecified duties. Jack departed Tulagi on the 21st and, arriving at Espíritu Santo, boarded the USS *Breton*—a fast escort carrier—for the journey
home. The *Breton* arrived in San Francisco on January 7. Jack saw Inga in
Los Angeles one day later for a visit that seems to have been purely platonic.
(In fact, Inga made a point of inviting her new boyfriend, a naval doctor, to
sit in on her conversation with Jack.) Afterward, she told friends that Jack
seemed both unhealthy and unhappy. She adopted a different tone, however,
in writing up her exclusive interview with him for the *Boston Globe*. TELLS
STORY OF PT EPIC read the page-one headline in the January 11 edition;
KENNEDY LAUDS MEN, DISDAINS HERO STUFF. "None of that hero stuff about
me," he told Inga. "The real heroes are not the men who return, but those
who stay out there, like plenty of them do, two of my men included." Inga
also interviewed the LA-based wife of Pop McMahon, who visited Jack
while he was stopping at her apartment. Mrs. McMahon told Inga: "When
my husband wrote home, he told me that Lt. Kennedy was wonderful, that
he saved the lives of all the men and everybody at the base admired him
greatly."

Jack went from LA to Rochester, Minnesota, for a quick consultation
with Mayo Clinic doctors, the Mayo experts warning him that it would take
a great deal of time and work before he'd be back in shape. Subsequently, he
headed to Palm Beach, where he made halfhearted attempts to nightclub
with Chuck Spalding and other old friends. The old ease, however, seemed
to have evaporated. Spalding said later he thought the quick transition from
the horrors of war to the pleasures of Palm Beach was too much for Jack to
negotiate.

Jack appeared out of place—dislocated—and he seemed to disdain many
of the simple joys of civilian life, all of them so trivial after the life-and-death
realities of battle. His mother noticed a change and commented on "his
bronze tired face which is thin & drawn." He did not seem able to eat much,
and would say apologetically to the old family cook: "Just can't take it yet,
Margaret." He also seemed nervous: hyper. The Kennedys' friend Barry
Shannon—publisher of a Palm Beach newspaper and owner of a stud farm—
said Jack in his present state reminded him of a highly geared racehorse. He
had to be unwound slowly, gradually, carefully. He was, in fact, in terrible
shape both emotionally and physically. During his stay in Palm Beach he was
twice rushed by ambulance to St. Mary's Hospital, his yellow body shivering with cold in the midst of eighty-five-degree heat.

Still, he was alive. Jack was with his father when the ambassador re-ceived word that the son of his old friend Harry Hogan had been killed in action. "Regardless of what some of us older fellows feel about the war," the ambassador wrote Hogan, "the reasons for it, and what it is to accomplish, we all know that our youngsters have had a firm determination to make the world a better place." There was, he said, satisfaction to be taken in that.

=== 25 ===

Just like Lazarus

BILLY HARTINGTON took a leave from the Coldstream Guards in January 1944 to stand for Parliament as a Conservative. The Derbyshire seat for which he ran was one that had been occupied by Cavendishes for 205 of the previous 210 years. Despite this history, Billy's election was by no means a sure thing. It was ebb tide for the Conservatives nationally. Even Churchill himself would be voted out of office the following year. Billy's rival, fifty-three-year-old alderman Charles White, whose father had beaten Billy's father many years before, ran on the Independent Socialist ticket. White prided himself on being a cobbler's son, and he sought to portray the election as a battle between the classes. Kick spent many a weekend campaigning. "Billy made about ten speeches a day and did very well with the odds against him," she reported to Lem Billings once the election was over and Billy had been trounced. Billy returned to his regiment in mid-February.

Taking as much time as possible off from the Hans Crescent Club, Kick continued to make her usual social rounds. The stark realities of the war, however, seemed hard to escape. In fact, they were beginning to invade even the most rarefied precincts, and finest homes, of England. Visiting Yorkshire that February, Kick spent some days with Lord Halifax's daughter, Anne Feversham, and Halifax's youngest son, Richard Wood, who had been badly wounded in the Middle East and was still getting used to his two new wooden legs. Wood met Kick at the train station and was "most efficient driving a car etc." Part of what Kick discussed with Anne and Richard that weekend was the dilemma of her love life with Billy, and the desperate turmoil in which they, and their families, found themselves.

Kick and Billy were by now quite candid—with themselves, their families, and their friends—about their desire to marry. This decision having been made, they began slowly and methodically to confront the religious and political quagmire that stood a good chance of keeping them apart. The Kennedys—although wary of the long-term Boston political implications of having a Protestant lord in the family—had no major objection to Billy so long as Kick's marriage to him was conducted by a priest of the Roman Catholic Church. Such a ceremony, however, would be possible under canon law only if Kick and Billy promised to raise all children of the union as Roman Catholics. The Cavendish family, in turn, did not have any problem with Billy's marrying Kick—nor even with Kick's remaining a practicing Catholic—so long as children of the union (particularly any heir to the Devonshire title) be brought up in the Church of England.

Had Billy been just any Anglican—or even a low-ranking noble like his cousin David Ormsby-Gore—the problem might have been more easily resolved. Kick wrote her family, "Poor Billy is very, very sad but he sees his duty must come first. He is a fanatic on the subject and I suppose just such spirit is what has made England great." All told, the Devonshires constituted the highest-profile Anglican family in England after the royals. The duchess was considered the first lady of the realm after royalty and, as Mistress of Robes to the Queen, served as chief lady-in-waiting. All of these positions held religious as well as social significance. What was more, Billy's ancestors had played pivotal roles in spreading Protestantism—and stifling Catholicism—throughout Britain and Ireland. A forebear on Billy's mother's side, Robert Cecil, chief minister to James I, had personally refused to allow the Prince of Wales to marry the Spanish infanta on grounds of her Catholicism. As well, many generations of Billy's paternal relatives had not only participated in but led the orchestrated domination of Irish Catholics. In 1870 the eighth duke, then serving as secretary of state for Ireland, defied his prime minister, broke with the Liberals, and formed his own party to oppose Irish home rule. In 1882 that same duke's younger brother (and successor as secretary of state for Ireland) died by assassination at the hands of nationalist militiamen in Dublin. Clearly, given the prominence of the Devonshires in the Anglican Communion, if there was to be compromise on the issue of marriage it would have to be the Catholic Church—and the Kennedys—that would do the compromising.

From his base of operations in the States, Joe Kennedy did his best to see what sort of dispensation, if any, could be got from the Vatican. What Joe sought was a Church-sanctioned marriage that would allow Kick and Billy's children to be raised as Anglicans while at the same time allowing Kick to remain a Catholic in good standing. This circle-squaring ambition was doomed from the start. The ambassador, so good at finding loopholes for himself and his children in every other area of life, had finally run across something he could not fix. Even high-powered friends like Francis Cardinal Spellman, archbishop of New York, appeared unable to arrange a solution.

In England, Kick visited David James Matthew, the Catholic auxiliary bishop of Westminister, to make her own personal, if futile, argument for a dispensation. When she failed in her task, she arranged an appointment for her brother Joe, who engaged in the same conversation with the same gentleman and came away with the same dismal result. Both Kick and Joe found it ironic that up until a relatively recent revision of Church law—a change made just fifteen years before, according to Matthew—Billy and Kick's marriage could have been solemnized by the Church with just one simple stipulation: that girl children be raised in their mother's Catholic faith. This compromise, no longer an option, was the type Kick believed might have actually succeeded in drawing Billy to a Catholic altar, as under the arrangement male heirs to the Devonshire title would still be safe from the wiles of Rome.

During mid-February—right about the time Kick sat chatting in Yorkshire with Anne and Robert—the ambassador looked back on a succession of failed attempts to gain a dispensation and, it seems, made a decision. Jotting a note to his daughter, he circled the question of marriage and quietly signaled that Kick might still, as usual, have whatever she wanted. He hinted she should proceed as she saw fit, saying he would bet on her judgment "anytime for any amounts." A similar signal went to Joe Jr. when the old man announced: "Kick can do no wrong." Rose, on the other hand, fully expected her daughter to abide by the ruling of the Church and, for the sake of religious principle, go for the first time in her life without a thing she desperately craved. How ironic it was, wrote Rose, for two people who had always been handed everything they ever wanted to now be denied the one thing they both wanted most.

.   .   .

JACK FLEW FROM Palm Beach to New York on February 5, where, despite his continuing ill health, he mustered the stamina for a fling with Flo Pritchett, the very beautiful fashion editor of the *New York Journal-American*, a former model, and the recently divorced wife of a conspicuously rich New York Catholic. One evening late that week, Flo and Jack emerged from his hotel room long enough to team up with Frances Ann Cannon and her husband, John Hersey, for drinks at the Stork Club, where Jack regaled the party with his own (by now much-rehearsed) version of the PT 109 story.

Hersey—who, as Kennedy well knew, had already written quite a bit about PT boats—was captivated by Jack's first hand account and asked if he might write it. If Jack cooperated, Hersey said, he believed he could probably place the piece with *Life* magazine. Intrigued with the idea of Hersey immortalizing his story in a high literary manner—and intrigued, too, with the notion of Hersey's account being distributed to millions of *Life* readers—Jack agreed. He insisted, however, that the writer speak not only with him but also with those other veterans of the affair who were now stateside, most of them based at Melville. He also asked that royalties from the piece go to the widow Kirksey.

The hero of the 109 was late to arrive at Boston's Parker House Hotel on the 11th, where Honey Fitz and some Democratic boosters—in fact, three hundred paying guests—had gathered to celebrate the old mayor's eighty-first birthday. Snow had delayed Jack's plane from New York. Midway into the proceedings, Clem Norton of the Boston Schools Committee—one of Honey Fitz's closest and oldest political cronies—interrupted the steady round of tributes to the mayor in order to reassure the increasingly restive crowd that young Kennedy (the real star of the show) would soon arrive. "He's the boy they thought was lost in the South Pacific," Honey Fitz shouted happily from the head table. "He came back, just like Lazarus from the dead. . . ." The old man broke down with happy tears when Jack—in dress uniform—turned up a few minutes later. First taking a moment to eye his grandson's emaciated frame and jaundiced complexion, he then hugged him hard and long. "I haven't seen this boy for more than a year, and he's been through hell since that time."

Proud Honey Fitz posed delightedly with his grandson. The photographs, which ran in all the Boston papers the next day, did much to boost attendance at yet another Kennedy appearance. Jack proved highly successful as the featured draw at the Lincoln's Birthday War Bond Rally (held in the Jordan Marsh department store downtown). Governor Saltonstall and Mayor Tobin also showed up, but played only supporting roles in the program that starred Jack. "Come and buy YOUR bonds," read newspaper ads and posters, "and hear Lieut. John Fitzgerald Kennedy—son of a former Ambassador to Great Britain, grandson of a former Mayor of Boston—of whom James Morgan of the *Boston Globe* said, 'his resourcefulness after his PT boat was rammed and sunk by a Japanese destroyer is one of the great stories of heroism in this war.' " An enormous crowd turned out, and Jack sold a half million dollars' worth of war bonds. Jack told a friend later he came away from the event feeling "like Sinatra."

Or at least like Sinatra with a badly beaten body. Given his frail condition, Jack requested and received a change in his orders, which had called for him to report to Melville on February 15. Instead he took leave and went to New England Baptist Hospital for two weeks, during which a team of Lahey Clinic doctors studied him carefully and agreed that major surgery on the spine—the same surgery that had been discussed and then put off in South Carolina the previous year—was now absolutely necessary. Without it, Jack could count on using crutches at best, or a wheelchair at worst, for the rest of his life. The doctors scheduled Jack's surgery for early June. Until then, Jack was to report to the Submarine Chaser Training Center (essentially a PT-boat shakedown base) at Miami, where he would be assigned "limited duties" and permitted to bunk at his father's Palm Beach mansion.

Before his release from the hospital, Jack gave Hersey an extensive interview during which he described—in far more detail than he had over drinks at the Stork Club—his version of the 109 affair: a version carefully calibrated to make both the crew and their commander look absolutely perfect in just about every way. Several weeks later, eyeing Hersey's first draft, Kennedy would request just three small changes, all of them designed to make various of his cohorts in the 109 affair show up better against Hersey's larger-than-life, heroic portrayal of JFK. Kennedy suggested, first of all, that Hersey expound more on the role played by Lennie Thom, who had been instrumental in saving Johnston and done so much to keep the eight surviving crew organized while Kennedy and Ross explored. Ross, too, needed more attention than Hersey had given him in the first draft. After all, it was Ross who had been personally responsible for towing the engineer Zinser. Most important, perhaps, Jack requested that Hersey delete a specific reference to one crew member, subsequently killed in other Solomons action, who had been conspicuous in losing his nerve at one key point during the long ordeal. The seaman went unnamed in Hersey's draft—as he will here— but Kennedy wanted the entire circumstance of the man's "lack of guts" stricken from the record. "I feel," wrote Kennedy, ". . . that our group was too small, that his fate is so well-known both to the men in the boats and to his family and friends that the finger would be put too definitely on his memory—and after all he *was* in my crew."

Of course, Hersey's account purposely obfuscated with regard to the role of coast watcher Evans, whose presence in the Solomons still remained secret. Perhaps somewhat less purposely—for Hersey could only know what Kennedy and company told him—the piece failed to explain just how 109 came to be rammed in the first place. Hersey's article came no closer than had Byron White's official report. "I read the piece . . ." Joe Jr. would write Jack after Hersey's piece appeared not in *Life* but *The New Yorker*, "and thought it was excellent. The whole squadron got to read it, and were much impressed by your intestinal fortitude. What I really want to know, is where the hell were you when the destroyer hove into sight, and exactly what were your moves, and where the hell was your radar?" (An older-model Elco boat, PT 109 had no radar.)

. . .

JACK REPORTED TO the Submarine Chaser Training Center, Miami, on March 14, 1944. Here he quickly fell into the habit of mocking the Florida locals, and he commented frequently on their witless lack of appreciation for the real war. "[They] all wait anxiously for D-day," he wrote a friend, "and you can find the beaches crowded every day with people—all looking seaward and towards the invasion coast."

In mid-April, when asked to conduct drills designed to simulate unlikely naval attacks on Miami by enemy forces, Kennedy perhaps took a secret pleasure when he and his fellow Miami PT commanders inadvertently threw a good scare into civilians at a dogtrack not far from Miami Beach. As part of their exercises for the day, several PT boats (Kennedy piloting one) approached the shore and began laying smoke. Meanwhile, unexpected breezes blew the smoke inland. When the smoke and fumes reached the dogtrack—where several thousand spectators sat watching dogs chase a mechanical rabbit—someone shouted "Poison gas!" and there was a panic. It was presumed the Germans were at that moment landing on the beach. A rush to the exits followed. Neither Jack nor any of his compatriots in the escapade ever received a reprimand.

In the midst of all this, Jack monitored the news from Europe closely, and noted with alarm the high number of casualties in Joe's squadron: not so much from enemy fire—although two planes had been lost to the Germans—as from accidents. "Heard from Joe a while back," he wrote Billings. "They have had heavy casualties in his squadron. I hope to hell he gets through OK. . . . I really think that Bobby [just graduated from Milton Academy and recently enrolled in the Naval Reserve] shouldn't go into aviation. I don't see where it is any more fun than P.T.s or D.D.'s or any other small ship—particularly as Bobby has spent so much of his life on small boats. I'm going to write him to that effect + I wish you would advise the same thing. It would be just his luck to get hit when old worn out bastards like you + me get through with nothing more than a completely shattered constitution."

26

Squaring the Circle

KICK VISITED HER FRIEND Jean Lloyd (the former Lady Victoria Jean Marjorie Mabell Ogilvy, eldest daughter of the ninth Earl of Airlie) in late April, and marveled at how Jean and her husband had downsized their lives to adjust to the rationed and tax-impoverished Great Britain of wartime. Their home was very small, with no phone, and was all in all very "domestic." Kick wrote her family it was "really fantastic" to "think how Jean lived before the war at Cortachy Castle [now requisitioned, like so many of Britain's great houses, for use by the army] and how easily she has taken on this role. Neither she or her husband think they will ever go back to the luxury of pre-war days. . . . Billy doesn't ever expect to live at Chatsworth I don't think really. . . ."

In the same letter, written April 24, Kick told her parents she would still very much like to marry Billy but that *when* depended on a lot of things—primarily finding a way to square the circle. Subsequently, Kick's friend Evelyn Waugh would say it was a case of "second front nerves" that caused the girl, just five days later, to recant and make up her mind to outrage her God. Indeed, all of Kick's surviving friends agree that the imminent invasion of Europe—with the Coldstream Guards likely to be in the first wave—figured largely in Kick's calculations when, exasperated by the long struggle to find a way to marry Billy and yet keep her soul, she at last decided that if forced to choose between the two she'd go with the man she loved.

This was not a decision that Kick—a devoutly believing and sincerely practicing Catholic—took lightly. It was, in fact, in many ways, the most radical departure from ancient beliefs that she or any of her clan had ever made; and she knew her decision would shock and cause pain to those she loved most. Cabling Hyannis on April 29, she named May 6 as the date when she would lapse into mortal sin: pledging herself under marriage vows administered by someone other than a Catholic priest and agreeing to allow her children to be raised as Anglicans. After that, Kick would not be able to make a true Act of Contrition or take Holy Communion.

As Father Martin D'Arcy—Kick's Jesuit parish priest at the Church of the Immaculate Conception, Mayfair, and a man famous for having converted both Edith Sitwell and Evelyn Waugh—reminded her, the catechism's uncompromising language on the subject of mixed marriages left very little to the imagination: "It is sacrilege to contract marriage in mortal sin, or in disobedience to the laws of the Church, and, instead of a blessing, the guilty parties draw down upon themselves the anger of God." Also, from the Catholic perspective, she would be damning her children when she allowed them to be raised Protestant.

As a practical matter, D'Arcy suggested that Kick insist on a civil ceremony over an Anglican service. The priest said both rituals were equally invalid in the eyes of the Church, but the civil ceremony would be preferable to Kick's complete conversion and marriage as an Anglican. (Archbishop William Godfrey—apostolic delegate and most senior Catholic curate in Great Britain—shortly declined when the archbishop of Canterbury suggested they both attend the civil wedding and say a shared blessing. Subsequent to this, during a prenuptial meeting with Joe Jr., the Duke of Devonshire proposed a "completely secret" blessing by the archbishop. "I said I didn't think it was a good idea," Joe wrote his parents, while the duke said "it would make the Duchess feel so much better. We left it at that, and Kick will have to decide.")

Ignorant of the time constraints under which the young couple labored, Rose could not understand their sudden rush in the face of religious issues that she believed might yet, with a little time, find a solution. "Heartbroken," she cabled Kick. "Feel you have been wrongly influenced—sending

Arch Spellman's friend [Archbishop Godfrey] to talk to you. Anything done for our Lord will be rewarded hundred fold." Another cable—evidently a condemnatory one—went to Rose's London friend Marie Bruce, whom Rose suspected of encouraging and facilitating Billy's match with Kick. "Marie Bruce is most upset about your cable," Kick wrote her mother on the 4th. "She has been more than kind. Please do not be angry with her."

On the same day, Billy sent Rose a letter in which he reminded her of his position in British society and explained he would be justified in allowing his children to be brought up as Roman Catholics only if he believed it desirable for England to become Roman Catholic, which he did not. "I do feel terribly keenly the sacrifices I'm asking Kick to make," he wrote, "but I can't see that she will be doing anything wrong in the eyes of God. . . . I shall never be able to get over my amazing good fortune in being allowed to have Kick as my wife, it still seems incredibly wonderful. Please try not to think too harshly of me." (When asked to do so, Kick refused to sign a formal document promising to raise her children in the Church of England. Nevertheless she did promise that she would not interfere with their religious instruction and would leave the manner of that instruction up to Billy. According to Hank Searls, the biographer of Joseph P. Kennedy, Jr., Billy likewise assured Kick that he would agree to the children's being raised Catholic if, after the war, the British aristocracy become so undermined by socialism that tradition no longer mattered.)

"Parnell's ghost must be smiling sardonically . . ." editorialized the London *Evening News* on the 5th. "It was Lord Hartington of the eighties who headed the Liberal-Unionist revolt that wrecked Gladstone's Home Rule Bill. Hartington it was who moved the second rejection of the Bill, and the hopes of Parnell and Irish-America vanished in the division lobbies. Now a Hartington is to marry a Catholic Irish-American who comes from one of the great Home Rule Families of Boston." Interviewed by reporters for the Astor-owned *Observer*, Lady Astor announced her delight with the prospective union, which she'd been assured would not result in the Romanizing of the House of Devonshire. Back in Massachusetts, Honey Fitz—caught by surprise when grinning reporters informed him of his granddaughter's impending marriage—chose to emphasize one key fact. No matter what happened, he said, Kathleen was "apart from her family training . . . by choice and conviction a Catholic."

. . .

JOE JR. EXPLAINED Kick's financial position as best he could—trying to remember the complex terms of the Kennedy family trust without having the relevant documents at hand—during a two-hour meeting with the Duke of Devonshire's attorney on May 5. "Customarily the wife places her money with the husband," Joe wrote his father after the wedding, "but in this case with the vagueness of my knowledge, [the lawyer] decided to leave her money alone" while at the same time adding quite a bit to it.

Through his attorney, the duke offered to make approximately the same settlement on Kick as had been made by his father on the present duchess. Billy was to receive £6,000 a year, which would actually amount to about £3,000 after income taxes. He would also have access to capital on demand through application to the corporation in charge of his father's estates, these amounts to be advanced against Billy's eventual inheritance. In the event Billy died, Kick would receive an income of £3,000 a year until such time as she remarried, at which point her income from the Devonshires would drop to just £1,000 annually. If Kick and Billy endured, and Kick wound up becoming the duchess, she would receive an increased income of £5,000 per year.

Children of the marriage were to receive a lump sum of £25,000 and income of £1,000 a year for education and maintenance. These sums, however, were contingent on the children's *not* becoming Catholics; should they be raised in or convert to the Church of Rome, they would be disqualified from receiving both the gift and the income.

. . .

SOME WOULD LOOK BACK and think it an ill omen. Certainly it did not foretell good luck: Kick's old black dress—the widow's dress, they called it later—that one of London's premier fitters used as a pattern for the girl's wedding outfit. The seamstress stayed up all night on the evening of the 5th—sequestered behind thick blackout curtains—laboring away on the dress so carefully contrived to match the pink camellias being brought from the gardens at Chatsworth: Kick's bouquet. Hard to come by, the pink fabric had been acquired just that afternoon with clothing coupons begged by Joe from his Dunkeswell comrades. (These were in turn supplemented—for the sake of having a hem—with still more coupons advanced by Marie Bruce's milkman.)

In the end, the outfit proved far nicer than required for the sparse ceremony transacted the next morning. The setting could not have been less
wonderful: a dingy office in the Registry of Births and Deaths for the Royal
Borough of Kensington and Chelsea. Billy wore his Coldstream Guards uniform, Kick the freshly minted dress together with a hat of pink and blue
plumes with a pink veil. The witnesses standing to one side included Billy's
grandmothers Devonshire and Salisbury; his best man, Charles Manners
(the Marquess of Granby); his parents; and his sisters, Anne and Elizabeth.
(Anne, horrified at having to show up in badly torn stockings, apologetically
explained she had no coupons with which to purchase new ones.) On Kick's
side stood only Lady Astor, Marie Bruce, and Joe Jr., who gave away the
bride. Double-decker buses rumbled by outside as a gray civil servant—a
duly appointed and apparently bored deputy of the registrar—administered
the stark, perfunctory, state-sanctioned vows by which Kick and Billy bound
themselves as man and wife. The whole procedure took less than ten minutes. Joe and the duke signed as witnesses.

Unlike the wedding ceremony itself, the party afterward bore traces of
elegance. With the Devonshires' London townhouse a casualty of German
bombing, Billy and Kick held their wedding reception at the home of a Devonshire relative near Eaton Square. The chef from Claridge's provided an
enormous chocolate wedding cake (albeit without icing) and the duke supplied copious amounts of champagne. Guests (of which there were two hundred) included Laura Mae McMartin Corrigan, founder of the Wings Club
(a London lodging place for on-leave Allied air officers). Mrs. Biddle attended as well, presenting Kick with a ruby sapphire clip from Cartier. (This
went nicely with the square-cut sapphire engagement ring, with diamonds on
each side, that Billy had given her several days earlier.) The "Dukie"—as Kick
took to calling her new father-in-law behind his back—gave his daughter-
in-law a beautiful diamond bracelet. Marie Bruce, meanwhile, made Kick a
gift of her own Porthault lingerie. Of course, not everyone came through
with elegant presents. Mr. and Mrs. Gibson showed up bearing nothing more
than thirty Red Cross girls and a gaggle of GIs—a few of that day's guests at
the club. The party ended with boozy soldiers from the Bronx and Peoria
carrying on long, rambling conversations with the likes of Lady Cunard.

Kick received no good wishes from the American Kennedys—at least
not at first. Joe Jr. quite uncharacteristically protested this with a terse cable
to his father, which he sent the day after the wedding: "The power of silence

is great." In response, the ambassador sent Kick a reassuring message: "With your faith in God, you can't make a mistake. Remember you are still and always will be tops with me." Despite his wife's rabid displeasure, at least a part of him had to be delighted at the idea that his Irish-American daughter had married into one of the most important families among the Protestant British nobility.

Rose, however, would never see things that way. The marriage truly shocked and outraged her. She had retreated to New England Baptist Hospital on the 3rd, there to stay for several days in order to get a checkup by Sara Jordan of the Lahey Clinic. When asked by reporters to comment on the impending nuptials, she sent word through the hospital staff that she was too sick to discuss the marriage. When she emerged on Kick's wedding day—escorted by Joe Timilty, who shooed away reporters and saw her onto a plane for New York—Rose wore black as though in mourning. "I'm sorry it has to be this way," she told the gentlemen from the press.

"As far as Kick's soul is concerned," Joe Jr. wrote the family, "I wish I had half her chance of seeing the pearly gates. As far as what people will say, the hell with them. I think we can all take it. It will be hardest on Mother, but I do think it will be all right." Marie Bruce in turn cabled Rose: "You would rejoice in their young happiness. Only grief your sorrow. Kathleen looked lovely."

Back in England, the Cavendish clan remained equally mute before the press. Only one had something to say. This was Adele Marie Astaire, who in 1932 had left her dancer partner and brother, Fred, to marry Lord Charles Cavendish, younger brother of Billy's father. Reporters cornered Adele at London's Rainbow Corner Red Cross Canteen, where she volunteered three days a week. Her comment was brief but enthusiastic. She said it was simply splendid to finally have another American in the family.

Time magazine commented the following week that the marriage had hit like an earthquake in many British quarters, and "One of England's oldest and loftiest families swayed perceptibly." So too, of course, did the Kennedys and Fitzgeralds. When Joe Jr. saw himself in wedding photos, happily smiling, he told Kick the pictures would finish him when published in Boston. As long as two years later, when Jack ran for Congress in Boston's eleventh district, the family would still be struggling to explain to outraged Catholics just why Kick had married a Protestant lord. At Compton Place,

Eastbourne, where the Marquess of Hartington and his bride spent six delicious honeymoon days, it was Billy and not Kick who dealt with the piles of letters from irate Catholics accusing Kick of selling her soul for a title.

To friends in Florida, Jack wryly commented on how absurd all the brouhaha was, at least as viewed from the distance of Palm Beach. He had little patience with pious hand-wringing, and he joked about his overly devout sister Eunice, who, "from the depths of her righteous Catholic wrath so truly said: 'It's a horrible thing—but it will be nice visiting her after the war, so we might as well face it.' "

·   ·   ·

THE SWAN HOTEL—a modest inn near Alton, not far from Billy Hartington's base—could not even attempt to compete with the luxuries of Compton Place, Chatsworth, or, for that matter, Palm Beach. Still, it was most suitable for the young couple who arrived there in mid-May. Their suite, the best the Swan had to offer, was smaller than the usual size for servants' apartments in any one of the many Devonshire homes. And the staff of the Swan—though accommodating—were often overwhelmingly so. Billy was their first marquess, after all, and they took great delight in calling him that at the top of their lungs. He confessed to Kick he enjoyed trading his title for his rank each morning when, in full uniform, he returned to base on his motorcycle. Kick, in turn, grew tired of being called "marchioness" almost as fast as she tired of being a celebrity. The marchioness took to using a bicycle to escape the Swan and explore the little hamlet whenever her husband was otherwise engaged.

She quickly found a sympathetic friend—a priest. As it happened, she'd encountered the man several times before. He'd previously been at the church in Maidenhead, close to Cliveden. "He confessed that he was unorthodox," she wrote her family, "but he said he admired my courage and he sympathized with my stand. He went on to say that I would be amazed at the number of people who also felt the same way. He told me not to worry and he was quite sure that prayer and trust in God's holy will would bring everything right." Kick and Billy entertained the priest for dinner, and Kick prayed hard that her mother might soon become as unorthodox as the monsignor.

She looked daily for a letter from her mother, but instead the packets of mail handed her at the front desk held only nonsense. *Life* magazine wanted to photograph her and the marquess and run the picture as a portrait of the "greatest gesture of Anglo-American unity since the Atlantic Charter." *Vogue* wanted her—and her alone—in its studios for an "artistic study" to be shot by Cecil Beaton. A letter from the Dukie flattered her, saying one of the streets in Eastbourne—a town he virtually owned—would be named in her honor. Kick planned to have flowering cherry trees planted up and down the thoroughfare, but then became dejected when Aunt Adele explained that the new Kennedy Street wound through the very same bad slum as the adjacent road: Astaire. It seemed the Cavendish ancestors had all the good streets, and newcomers to the family just had to make do with what was left.

27

Anvil

Joe Jr. had flown more than his quota of missions by early May 1944. Orders home were his for the asking, but he would have none of it. Fully briefed on the upcoming June 6 invasion of Normandy, he understood the importance of having aerial patrols scout for the U-boats that might otherwise disrupt the Allied armada. Thus Joe eagerly volunteered for "Operation Cork" and agreed to stay in England for another month. Throughout June, he spent an average of eleven and a half hours a day in the air flying monotonous loops between Dover and Cherbourg as wave after wave of Allied transports crossed the channel beneath him, one of them carrying his new brother-in-law, Billy. "I now have 39 missions and will probably have 50 by the time I leave," he wrote his mother and father in mid-June. "It is far more than anyone else on the base, but it doesn't prove a hell of a lot. . . ." As he was acutely aware, he had not yet earned any medals. Jack, meanwhile, had been awarded the Navy and Marine Corps Medal for heroism, and was in line for a Purple Heart.

He spent virtually all of his free time with Pat Wilson, but—now as before—wrote nothing of her to his parents. Both he and Kick continued to frequent Pat's little country cottage. In fact, they much preferred Pat's place to the city that summer, happy to avoid Hitler's latest experiment in murder: the V-1 flying bomb. Most Brits referred to the rockets as "doodlebugs" or "buzz-bombs" because of the peculiar buzzing noise to be heard right before one of them struck. The Germans launched the unmanned jets—gyro-controlled and loaded with dynamite—from massive and (so far) impregnable concrete bunkers positioned near the French coast. No amount of conventional bombing seemed capable of knocking out the highly fortified launching sites. Meanwhile, London's civilian casualties became immense: more than 2,500 killed and 7,000 wounded by the end of July.

· · ·

Jack returned to Chelsea Naval Hospital on June 11 for extensive x-rays and tests; he subsequently entered the Lahey Clinic at New England Baptist Hospital for back surgery that took place on the 24th. "The patient did well following the operation for a period of two weeks," Jack's surgeon, James L. Poppen, wrote in a report to Jack's navy doctors. "Upon having the patient get up and about, however, severe muscle spasms in the low back took place. These necessitated fairly large doses of narcotics to keep him comfortable." In fact, the surgery had made things worse. Torbert Macdonald—just returned from the Pacific—visited Jack during the second week of July. He found his old friend quite yellow (no surprise to Macdonald) and strapped into the bed as a form of traction. "His weight had dropped from 160 to about 125 pounds," Macdonald recalled. "When I came into his room, he raised a bony wrist and gave me a shaky wave. I asked him how he felt. He tried to lift his head. I had to lean over to hear him. 'I feel great,' he said. 'Great?' I echoed. 'Well,' he smiled, 'great considering the shape I'm in.'"

In addition to the back, Jack's other problems—primarily his ulcers and related ailments—still bothered him and complicated his recovery from the surgery. "As you know," the Lahey Clinic's Sara Jordan wrote to the navy physicians on July 14, "it is now his twentieth post-operative day, following operation for a ruptured intervertebral disc. Both before and since the operation, he has had exceedingly severe abdominal pain, intermittently at first but now almost constant, and at the present time relieved only by codeine. We carried out an X-ray study before the operation, which again showed extreme spasm and irritability of the duodenum, without a definite ulcer crater, but with a lipping of the base of the cap which was suggestive of a duodenal ulcer scar. There was also again rather marked spasm of the colon, and on Tuesday of this week we again X-rayed the colon with the same visualization of spastic colitis which had been constantly present, but which seemed accentuated at this observation."

He showed little improvement two weeks later. "Lt. Kennedy has continued to have low abdominal distress rather constantly," Jordan wrote the navy doctors on August 1. "The pain has been quite severe at times. We have used the antispasmodic medicines such as pavatrine, trasentin, as well as a mixture of belladonna, Phenobarbital and elixir of pepsin, and while I think there may be some improvement in his condition, I feel that he is still far from completely relieved of symptoms referable to the spastic colitis. He has had very few symptoms during his stay in the hospital which I think could be attributable to the duodenal ulcer or duodenitis."

Composing his own report the same day, Jack's surgeon, Dr. Poppen, took the unusual step of outright apologizing for what, in retrospect, seemed clearly to have been a failed surgery. He told the navy doctors he'd operated on more than five hundred ruptured intravertebral discs in his career and had only nine failures. Poppen said he was "indeed sorry that this had to happen with Lieutenant Kennedy. . . . At the present time the neurological examination still shows considerable tenderness. . . . The patient has definite pain in the standing position. . . . It is my impression that, in view of the postoperative course of Lieutenant Kennedy, it will be at least six months before he can return to active duty." In other words, Jack Kennedy's war was over.

One of the naval neurosurgeons, eyeing Jack's file, subsequently wondered if Poppen's surgical approach had been correct or warranted. The navy neurosurgeon noted that Jack was "obviously incapacitated by pain in low back & down L[eft] leg. *Impression*: This is a high strung individual (peptic ulcer) who has been through much combat strain. He may have recurrent disc [pain owing to] an incomplete removal, but better bet is that there is some other cause for his neuritis."

"In regard to the fascinating subject of my operation," Jack wrote a friend, "I should naturally like to go on for several pages . . . but will confine myself to saying that I think the Doc should have read just one more book before picking up the saw." His physicians moved him back to Chelsea

Naval Hospital during the last week of July. He was well enough a few days later—on August 7, a year to the day after the end of the 109 affair—to sneak out with a nurse to a room at the Ritz-Carlton Hotel. There, while Jack and his nurse made love, thieves stole the Buick he had bought with his *Why England Slept* royalties.

. . .

 EARLY IN THE SUMMER, with the D-Day invasion and Operation Cork done with, Joe still searched the horizon for action. He seemed wound-up, fixated on getting into dangerous situations no matter what. Colleagues commented later on his intense preoccupation with putting himself in harm's way, and thus on the path to publicly recognized heroism. "When I tried to make casual conversation," remembered a navigator, "I got the positive impression that I was talking about firecrackers to a man valiantly trying to perfect the atom bomb before an impossible deadline." Joe's fellow flier Louis Papas would recall: "There was never an occasion for a mission that meant extra hazard that Joe did not volunteer. He had everybody's unlimited admiration and respect for his courage, zeal and willingness to undertake the most dangerous missions."

He made full lieutenant, and celebrated his twenty-ninth birthday, at the end of July, just as Jack was being transferred back to Chelsea Naval Hospital from New England Baptist. Kick joined him at Pat Wilson's house for a small birthday bash. All those assembled—among them Esmon Harmsworth (Viscount Rothermere), the newspaper publisher and Conservative MP—lifted flutes of champagne to toast Joe's health and wish him a long, successful life. He spotted his first gray hairs that evening. "I'm getting on," he wrote his folks, "and I had better get a gal while there is some life in the old boy." The parents did not see much cause for alarm when, in the midst of the same breezy, lighthearted note, he casually mentioned his next enterprise. "I am going to do something different for the next three weeks. It is secret and I am not allowed to say what it is, but it isn't dangerous," he lied. "So don't worry."

. . .

JOE AND SEVERAL COHORTS flew a specially configured PB4Y-1 Liberator—a plane stripped down to the bare fuselage and, for the moment, very light and fast—from Dunkeswell to the army air base at Winfarthing-Fersfield (East Anglia) on July 30. He brought all his gear with him, including a recent and cherished acquisition: his new Raleigh English racing bike. "At two thousand feet," wrote Joe's biographer Hank Searls, "Joe frisked the unburdened plane two hundred miles north over the Salisbury Plain and across the Thames to the gentle East Anglican hills, buzzing Oxford and Cambridge en route. Below, the fields were green and blazed with harvest gold; when they spotted the giant Army air base at Fersfield it looked sterile and ominous in contrast to the soft English countryside."

His colleagues thought he seemed remarkably calm and happy considering the dangerous assignment for which he had volunteered both his plane and his person. Within a matter of days, Joe would see his Liberator packed from floor to ceiling with Torpex explosives—25,000 pounds of the stuff. Then he would pilot the heavy flying bomb down a runway and coax her slowly into the air. Once aloft, Joe and his copilot would throw switches surrendering control of their Liberator to remote control from a nearby "mother" aircraft and activate fuses associated with the detonator for the Torpex. Then, finally, if all went well, they would parachute out, leaving the Liberator—now a drone aircraft—to fly on under remote control to a worthy target, into which it would be crashed.

The army called this unlikely technology Aphrodite (after the butterfly, not the goddess). The navy—brought in recently by General Jimmy Doolittle, the new commander of the Eighth Air Force—referred to their version as Anvil. Doolittle, in turn, said he didn't give a damn which name won out so long as the concept, with its vast potential for taking out V-1 launch bunkers on the French coast, came to fruition soon. Doolittle believed it would be healthy to let the army fliers feel the navy boys breathing down their necks. The general said he did not care who won the race, so long as those V-1 bunkers wound up rubble in the near future. In fact, the only real difference between the army and navy approaches was the army's use of Liberator-class aircraft as mother ships and the navy's use of them as drones.

Arriving at Fersfield, Joe taxied past a large flock of the army's Aphrodite B-17s parked alongside their B-24 mother ships. It took a bit of exploring before he found the navy ghetto on the far side of the army's field, where he slowed his rolling Liberator to a stop beside two other naval aircraft: the Lockheed Venturas destined to serve as his own mother ships. He then moved into the simple Quonset hut he'd been assigned to share with a man he'd never met before: Ensign Jim Simpson, one of several navy radio-control experts in residence.

Joe's new roommate hailed from the Bible Belt, had been raised a hard-rock Baptist, and didn't have (or want) much experience with Roman Catholics. He looked on silently as Joe went to his knees to pray each evening before going to bed, and soon surprised himself by deciding he actually liked the papist, the son of the church his old minister back home was so fond of describing as "the whore of Rome." Joe had always gotten along better with roommates than he had with underlings. Though he lacked the ability to develop effective relationships with those who reported to him, he frequently won the hearts of those who did not. Now Joe and Simpson spent several long evenings talking religion and politics with the doors and windows of their hut thrown open to combat the oppressive heat, and the lights out so as not to signal the location of the base to enemy bombers. In the midst of their conversations, Simpson told Joe he liked him fine, but—nothing personal—he would never vote for him or any other Catholic for anything. Joe in turn observed that no one had seemed hesitant to vote for a Catholic to undertake Project Anvil, one of the most hazardous assignments of the war.

Joe took his first trial run on August 2, as soon as enlisted personnel finished loading his Liberator with sandbags to simulate the weight of the Torpex. Accompanied by Simpson and several other experts in aircraft radio control, Joe slowly moved the newly fat, lumbering drone plane off the ground. Once in the air, Wilford "Bud" Willy—a lanky Texan from Fort Worth who would serve as copilot during Joe's mission—showed Joe the complex procedure for activating the remote-control pilot system. After the system went live, it took the men a few minutes to get used to the uneven, unfluid motion of a large plane being flown by someone not actually aboard, someone not able to feel the flow of the aircraft. Simpson told Joe's biographer that the plane flew "like a spastic sea gull" until it reached cruising altitude at three hundred feet, where—amid little turbulence—things smoothed out. Joe and his colleagues repeated this exercise every day for a week, working diligently toward the time when they'd feel confident enough to try it for real, with genuine explosives and an actual target.

Joe made sure to be on hand the evening of August 4 when the army

sent out four Aphrodite B-17s (fully loaded with RDX, somewhat less powerful than the navy's preferred explosive, Torpex, the latter being 1.7 times
more powerful than TNT). He smoked a pipe and sat on the green grass
near a hangar as he watched the army pilots flog their heavy planes down the
runway and into the sky. The four B-17 Snowbirds—so nicknamed because
of the white-painted wings and fuselages designed to make them easily visible to controllers in the mother aircraft—had assignments to hit four separate V-1 launch sites near Calais, if they got that far. Joe shortly heard the
report when the first of the B-17s rolled and crashed—issuing a thunderous
explosion—not long after takeoff with its pilot still aboard. Later on, he
heard that all the other crews had come through their failed missions relatively unscathed, bailing out before misfortune struck. But not one plane
reached its target. One unmanned B-17 exploded for no apparent reason
near the coast of France; two others were shot down just short of their intended targets. As Joe observed to Simpson, getting out of the drone plane
sooner rather than later "would appear to be *key*."

. . .

Joe's training flights ended on the 9th, at which point technicians
sequestered his aircraft and began packing the Torpex. He called Lorelle
Hearst late on the 11th. "I'm about to go into my act," he told her. "If I don't
come back, tell my dad that I love him very much."

Joe's two Lockheed Ventura mother planes took off from Fersfield a little after 6 p.m. on the 12th. These circled the field at two thousand feet. A
navigation ship rushed down the runway next, followed by the drone Liberator piloted by Joe. The mother ships fell in behind the drone as it left the
field, these tailed by a small Mosquito aircraft carrying Colonel Elliott Roosevelt—son of the president—who had orders to document the mission on
film.

Elliott caught some footage of Joe in the cockpit and copilot Willy in
the bubble just before one of the mother planes took control of the robot.
The first turn at the first control point of the mission was made by remote
signal from the mother aircraft. Approximately two minutes after comple-
tion of this turn—at about six-twenty, with little more than ten minutes to
go before Joe and Willy were to jump—the drone exploded.

Elliott Roosevelt's Mosquito—approximately three hundred feet behind and slightly to the right of Joe's aircraft—received several hits from flying pieces of the robot plane, causing minor injuries to the crew. The badly damaged Mosquito was just barely able to limp home. "[It was] the biggest explosion I ever saw until the pictures of the atom bomb," said a pilot of one of the mother ships. In Newdelight Woods, the tiny British coastal town over which the blast occurred, fifty-nine buildings suffered damage.

First word of the tragedy came in a telegram from General Jimmy Doolittle to General Carl Spaatz. The telegram, marked "Top Secret," went out in cipher:

ATTEMPTED FIRST APHRODITE ATTACK TWELVE AUGUST WITH ROBOT TAKING OFF FROM FERSFIELD AT ONE EIGHT ZERO FIVE HOURS PD ROBOT EXPLODED IN THE AIR AT APPROXIMATELY TWO THOUSAND FEET EIGHT MILES SOUTHEAST OF HALESWORTH AT ONE EIGHT TWO ZERO HOURS PD WILFORD J. WILLY CMA SR GRADE LIEUTENANT AND JOSEPH P. KENNEDY SR GRADE LIEUTENANT CMA BOTH USNR CMA WERE KILLED PD COMMANDER SMITH CMA IN COMMAND OF THIS UNIT CMA IS MAKING FULL REPORT TO US NAVAL OPERATIONS PD A MORE DETAILED REPORT WILL BE FORWARDED TO YOU WHEN INTERROGATION IS COMPLETED

What caused the disaster? The navy impaneled an informal board of review two days after the explosion. Following a week of study, the board decided it was possible that, because of the design of the circuit and the particular type of fuse used, jamming or a stray signal could have armed the circuit and caused detonation of the charge. Joe had in fact been warned of this danger the day before his mission by an electronics officer who had cause to know about such things. The officer—Earl Olsen—had mentioned the problem to his superiors and been rebuffed. He then mentioned it to Joe in the hope Joe would scrub the flight, something the lieutenant refused to do. Then there was also the inherent instability of the explosive used for the mission: Torpex. Other possibilities included a short circuit, explosion of gas fumes, a fire in the aircraft, or flak or direct hit by small-caliber bullet. The board of review rejected the possibility of pilot error (the drone pilots prematurely arming the circuit and causing the detonation) "mainly because of the experience of the pilots and their familiarity with the equipment."

In the final analysis, the board listed jamming as the "primary probable cause" of the accident, and recommended measures to prevent this in future. As regards the explosive charge, Torpex would henceforth be abandoned in favor of the more stable TNT—this despite the fact that TNT was only 60 percent as powerful as Torpex and much harder to come by. The change would do nothing to enhance the effectiveness of the Aphrodite/Anvil programs, which would be shut down in the near future after a total of seventeen failed missions.

.   .   .

THE NEXT DAY, Sunday, came on quite hot and muggy at Hyannis. The family—including Jack, home on a day pass from Chelsea Naval Hospital—did not seem to mind. "I remember," wrote Rose, "that . . . we had all lunched outside, picnic style, on our big porch." Following lunch, the ambassador went upstairs for his customary nap. He had not been sleeping long, however, when Rose burst into his room, saying two priests were at the door with news of Joe.

After a private consultation with the fathers, the ambassador and Rose walked out onto the porch to speak to the family. "Your brother Joe has been lost," the ambassador announced, choking back tears. "He died flying a volunteer mission. I want you all to be particularly good to your mother." He then told them to go ahead and participate in sailboat races scheduled for that afternoon: *and to win*, in honor of their brother. As Rose recalled, most of the children obeyed their father's order, glumly trudging off to the yacht club, "but Jack could not. Instead, for a long time he walked on the beach in front of our house." The ambassador, meanwhile, retreated to his room and broke down.

In what would become a macabre tradition through the years, newspapers closely chronicled the family's grief. EX-ENVOY KENNEDY, CRUSHED BY SON'S DEATH, REMAINS IN SECLUSION, announced the *Boston Globe* on the 14th. " 'What can I say?' the father said tonight. 'We received word yesterday. All my younger children are here, and young John (Lt. John F. Kennedy, the PT boat hero) came down from Chelsea Naval Hospital, but had to go right back.' "

Reporters from the *Boston Herald* made sure to be on the scene two days later when Kick arrived from England after having been granted emergency priority air travel status. "It was quite a reunion, with the family bowed in grief," reported the *Herald*. ". . . The girl had seen her brother a short time before he left on his fatal flight. He was the only member of the family in England at the time of her marriage, and he witnessed the ceremony. Now the Lady Hartington, Miss Kennedy arrived at La Guardia Field, N.Y. in an Army transport plane early this afternoon and transferred immediately to a plane for Boston. Lt. John Kennedy, PT boat hero of the South Pacific, now recuperating from injuries at the Chelsea Naval Hospital, met his sister at Logan airport and accompanied her to Hyannis." The *Boston Globe* described Kick running up the ramp at Logan alone, "to be greeted by her brother, Lt. John F. Kennedy, holder of the Navy and Marine Corps Medal for heroism aboard a PT boat in the Southwest Pacific. 'Hello, Kat!' called John. In a robin's egg blue American Red Cross Summer uniform, the . . . prospective Duchess of Devonshire smiled wearily for an instant. Then she ran into John's arms and wept. After a moment, she squared her jaw, faced the crowd and walked resolutely up the ramp, arm in arm with her brother."

Beyond the gawking public, people who actually knew the family grieved not just for Joe, but for what they believed was to have been a grand life, now cut short. "I know that great things were awaiting Joe," wrote Dick Flood, one of the aviator's old law school roommates and a close friend from undergraduate days, "but God must have a still greater mission for him." Family friend Max Truitt wrote Jack from Washington: "I have talked with your father two times since hearing the tragic and profoundly sad news yesterday. There is really nothing one can say under such circumstances that adequately expresses feelings so keenly felt—so deeply embedded—but you must know that you, your wonderful father and your gracious and charming mother have my own deep and heartfelt sympathy. . . . And for you, Jack, may you soon be healed of your own afflictions so that you may be able to carry on—yes, carry on with some of those parental hopes and aspirations which had with great affection and care been planned for Joe."

Many struggled to doubt the tragic news. Various Catholic friends said prayers to the Lady of the Miraculous Medal, petitioning for word that Joe had bailed out to safety. "You, no doubt, know some of the details of the tragedy," Jack's friend Margaret Prior wrote him, "and I know I must be in the minority, but I can't seem to accept the fact there isn't a slight chance of Joe being alive. I wish God willed it so. I know Torbie will be deeply affected when he learns of it, and I hope when peace does come to us again, young men such as Torb and you will have a voice in formulating just punishment to the war lords and not allow the would-be pacifists to stir up sympathy for Germany. . . . Then other fine American boys, the cream of our country as Joe, will not have died in vain."

The Rev. Richard J. Cushing of Boston—auxiliary bishop and apostolic administrator of Boston who would one day, as cardinal, say the funeral mass for John Kennedy—sent the same printed card to the Kennedys that he routinely sent all families of fallen Catholic boys, a card which quoted Cardinal Mercier in addressing the question "Are Soldiers Martyrs?" ". . . if I am asked what I think concerning the eternal salvation of a brave man who voluntarily lays down his life in defense of his country's honor and in vindication of violated justice," said Mercier, "I do not hesitate to reply that one cannot doubt in the least that Christ will crown his military valor, . . . death, accepted in this Christian spirit, will assure the salvation of that man's soul."

Trying to make his own sense of what fate had wrought, Jack would write of his brother: "He had great physical courage and stamina, a complete confidence in himself which never faltered, and he did everything with a great verve and gusto, and though these very qualities were in the end his undoing, yet they made his life a wonderful one to live."

No traces of Joe or his copilot were ever found. Both men received the Navy Cross and the Air Medal posthumously. Back in England, Pat Wilson had barely started mourning for Joe Kennedy when she received word that her husband had been killed as well: ambushed by German soldiers while fighting in Italy.

28

Nothing Will Ever
Be the Same

ROSE HANDLED THE LOSS of her son in what was for her the most obvious and practical manner, retreating to her rosary and relying on her steadfast faith. The ambassador instead retreated into bitterness and anger—anger, by turns, at fate, at God, and at Roosevelt. The son's last letter arrived—posted only a few days before his deadly flight. "Don't get worried about it," he'd written of his mission, "as there is practically no danger." After reading Joe's missive from the grave, the ambassador collapsed in a chair, buried his head in his hands, and moaned that nothing would ever be the same again. The best part of his life was over. "When the young bury the old," he told a friend, "time heals the pain and sorrow; but when the process is reversed the sorrow remains forever."

On Labor Day, 1944—in the midst of a party on the porch at Hyannis where Jack and Kick entertained Jack's PT comrades Red Fay, Jim Reed, Lennie Thom, and Barney Ross—the ambassador interrupted the gay proceedings to shout down from an upstairs window: "Jack, don't you and your friends have any respect for your dead brother?" That Christmas, when Jack presented his parents with a privately printed memorial volume he'd edited entitled *As We Remember Joe*, his father thanked him but said he could not bear to read the many tributes. More than a decade later, when asked by his friend Bob Considine of the International News Service to comment on Joe Jr., Ambassador Kennedy—whom Considine described as "one of the top financiers of the age, a man known in many fields as cool beyond calculation under fire"—remained silent for a few moments and then suddenly "burst into tears at the luncheon-table, and for a full five minutes was wracked with grief that cannot be described. 'No,' he finally was able to say. 'No, Mrs. Kennedy can, but I'll never be able to.' "

Within days of learning about the loss of his eldest son, the ambassador began to sketch plans for a charitable foundation to honor the memory of his fallen boy. And he seemed gratified later, in July of 1945, when the navy named a new 2,200-ton destroyer after the fallen airman. Bobby Kennedy served on the vessel briefly in 1946, and the ship eventually played a key role in President John F. Kennedy's 1962 naval blockade of Cuba during the Missile Crisis.

. . .

KICK SAID A TRUE Act of Contrition and received the Host—her first since May—on September 16. Word of Kick's salvation—nothing less, so far as her mother was concerned—had arrived that morning in the form of a telegram announcing the death of Billy Hartington: shot through the heart by a German sniper near the town of Heppen, Belgium, on the 9th.

"If anything should happen to me," he'd written her two months before, "I shall be wanting you to try to isolate our life together, to face its finish, and to start a new one as soon as you feel you can. I hope that you will marry again, quite soon—someone good & nice." She did not, at first, think this would be possible. "If Eunice, Pat & Jean marry nice guys for fifty years they'll be lucky if they have five weeks like I did," she told her parents. She added that it seemed Billy had grown "much holier" after they were married. "Now he is the one to bring me closer to God—what a funny world." As for her apostasy, she said only: "God has taken care of that matter in his own way." She revealed her deepest sadness to her diary: "And so ends the story of Billy and Kick. I can't believe that the one thing I feared might happen should have happened. . . . Life is so cruel. I am on my way to England. Writing is impossible."

She joined the duke and duchess for a memorial service on the 30th, where they prayed in unison as Christians for the repose of Billy's soul. "I'm looking pleasant about life," she wrote Jack, "but it will be a long time before I get reconciled inside about this whole thing. Little things happen every day that make me think 'what would Billy have thought of that?' Mrs. Mead wrote that one must think of what one has had and has still got and not of what one hasn't got. I think she's got the idea but it will take time for it really to sink in. I know that there were a lot of difficulties in front of me if Billy had lived but somehow now none of those things seem to matter. It just seems that the pattern of life for me has been destroyed. At the moment I don't fit into any design. When I'm with people I like and know well it's alright for awhile and then I just start thinking and it's no good. I'm much better down here [at Chatsworth] just with the family and I can't face going out in London with a crowd which everyone thinks would cheer me up. . . . I just read in the paper this morning that Archie Spell brought back a tremendously high [Vatican] decoration to Daddy. What was that for? His children's war record?"

In the final analysis, the frequently superficial Kick had found an occasion for transforming bravery when she stared down her family and her church for the sake of her passion. She would, in future, continue to strain at the bit of the Catholic Church: never wholly rejecting it, but never again subjecting herself blindly and slavishly to the authority of Rome. She would also do most of her living in Britain. (A friend of Jack's who met Kick for the first time in 1945 described her as "very . . . English, or British, oriented. I felt that she had really melded herself into the city of London and England, as though it were her adopted home—that was my distinct impression.") Returning to the States only occasionally, she came to cherish the idea of the ocean that divided the land of her youth from the land of her maturity just as she plainly cherished the memory of those precious days with Billy: days that served as yet another border between her guileless, unquestioning girlhood and the woman she'd now become. She would always be a seeker after God; but she would also always be a seeker after love.

·   ·   ·

IN THE WAKE of his son's death, the ambassador became more vocally and violently anti-Roosevelt than ever before, telling reporters candidly that the president was the archvillain of America's recent history: the founder of all her troubles. When he bumped into Harry Truman—FDR's running mate in the 1944 election—he greeted him with the words "Harry, what the hell are you doing campaigning for that crippled son of a bitch who killed my son Joe?" (To which Truman, by his own account, replied: "If you say another word about Roosevelt, I'm going to throw you out a window.")

Subsequently, when FDR invited Kennedy to the White House to see if they could not yet again try to iron things out between them, Kennedy came away appalled by Roosevelt's poor physical condition. "If I hadn't been warned by the stories of his illness," Kennedy wrote after his visit, "I would have been shocked beyond words. He sat behind his desk and his face was as gray as his hair. . . . He is thin. He has an unhealthy color. His hands shake violently when he tries to take a drink of water." Neither did FDR enunciate well, and his memory—once his greatest strength—seemed at times to be strained, as when he expressed condolences on the death of Kick's husband, whom he called "Billy Harkshire." Kennedy seemed to take some satisfaction in FDR's pathetic state, although he admitted he was concerned that the "Rosenmans and Frankfurters" could now pretty much run the country without any objection from the invalid President.

"For a fellow who didn't want this war to touch your country or mine," Kennedy wrote Beaverbrook not long afterward, "I have had rather a bad dose—Joe dead, Billy Hartington dead, my son Jack in the Naval hospital. I have had brought home to me very personally what I saw for all the mothers and fathers of the world." He had not changed. He was still out for himself and his own. He was still disquieted about the war. He was still unable to understand the very real evils against which the war had been fought, and he was still more wary of the Rosenmans and Frankfurters—that is, the Jews—than he was of Hitler. It would be part of his tragedy that he would never be able to understand the worthiness of the fight in which his firstborn son had died.

· · ·

JACK EFFECTIVELY ENDED his military service on December 27, 1944, when he faced the Retirement Board of the Navy Department. At the end of a brief meeting at which the board quickly reviewed his dismal medical transcript, Jack received instructions to go home. The navy would send him his formal release from active duty—a medical discharge—on or about March 1. In the meantime, he should consider himself free to engage in any occupation he'd care to. Thus, early in 1945, Jack signed on as special columnist for the newspaper chain owned by his father's good friend William Randolph Hearst.

As one of his first outings, he drafted a short thesis in rebuttal to Harry Hopkins's plea—recently published in the *American Magazine*—for postwar rearmament. Kennedy titled his piece "Let's Try an Experiment in Peace." Jack argued against Hopkins's judgment that "we did everything possible to prevent war—except prepare for it." Concerned about Hopkins's notion that the United States should hereafter be the strongest nation in the world, Kennedy insisted that Hopkins's "plan for super-armament" in a postwar arms race would mean heavy taxes and thus the stifling of the economy. Instead, Kennedy proposed an agreement among the postwar Big Three (Britain, Russia, and the United States) for limiting postwar rearmament plans. "There will, of course, have to be a strong growth of mutual trust between these countries before any comprehensive plan can be worked out."

For all his talk about postwar unity, Jack soon got a firsthand feel for how elusive such unity was to be—at least with regard to the Soviets. That April the young Hearst correspondent attended the founding convention of the United Nations in San Francisco. Promoted by the Hearst syndicate as a "PT boat hero" out to express "the GI viewpoint" on political events, Jack chronicled Vyacheslav Molotov's "belligerent" performance with grim distaste. Soviet Russia, it seemed, was not prepared to entrust her safety to any other organization than the Red Army. "The Russians may have forgiven," wrote Jack, "but they haven't forgotten, and they remember very clearly those years before the war when Russia was only looking in the kitchen window. Hence, any organization drawn up here will be merely a skeleton. Its powers will be limited. It will reflect the fact that there are deep disagreements among its members." As the conference continued, Jack's pessimism increased. While stating plainly his view that humanity could not afford another war, he nevertheless reported "talk of fighting the Russians in the next ten or fifteen years." When the conference ended, Jack wrote approvingly of the UN as an institution, but insisted that in joining, the United States should do nothing to surrender her territorial interests or diminish the idea of the Monroe Doctrine.

A few weeks later, in June, Jack found himself in London covering the British elections. Intuitively sensing the direction things were headed, Jack surprised his editors by predicting the great war leader Churchill would be defeated, along with a host of other Conservatives. His editors printed his contrarian viewpoint, but few of Jack's colleagues believed him right. "This may come as a surprise to most Americans, who feel Churchill is as indomitable at the polls as he was in war," wrote Kennedy. "However, Churchill is fighting a tide that is surging through Europe, washing away monarchies and conservative governments everywhere, and that tide flows powerfully in England. England is moving towards some sort of social-ism. . . ." After the Labour upset the year before, Jack said, the Socialists "pulled out all the stops on the 'campaign oratory' and it was 'happy days are here again for everyone.' " But Churchill was only offering his old prescrip-tion of "toil and sweat," insisting the Tories would make no unkeepable promises. "Unfortunately for the Conservatives," observed Kennedy, "the people of this island have been on a diet of toil and sweat for the past five years."

And they were finished with it, just as Kennedy—after six months—was finished with his career in journalism. He told a friend later the job was sim-ply too passive for him. He was thinking, he said, about entering politics.

·   ·   ·

DURING LATE January of 1946—eight months after the close of hostil-ities in Europe—the ambassador came face to face with his past on a sunny afternoon in Palm Beach. "I remember," said Winston Churchill, but-tonholing the grim Kennedy at Hialeah Race Track, "that one of the last times we met we were having dinner during an air raid. It didn't bother us very much, though, did it?" Then, pausing for a moment to refresh himself with a mouthful of whiskey and soda, Churchill continued: "You had a ter-rible time during the war; your losses were very great. I felt so sad for you and hope you received my messages." Kennedy, who very well might not have been at Hialeah that day had he known it meant the risk of bumping into Winston, thanked the now out-of-power prime minister and said he'd received the messages but had been in no condition to respond at the time. "The world seems to be in a frightful condition," said Churchill. "Yes," Kennedy answered sharply, adding: "After all, what did we accomplish by this war?" Churchill shrugged. "Well, at least, we have our lives," he said, to which the ambassador responded: "Not all of us."

.   .   .

LEM BILLINGS OBSERVED that up until 1944, Jack's competition with Joe Jr. had, to a considerable extent, defined his personality. Indeed, the brothers' constant rivalry had always seemed their main point of contact: their primary bond. Now, with Joe gone, the bond nevertheless continued, with the rivalry taking on new and impossible dimensions from Jack's perspective. It is, after all, virtually impossible to win in any comparison with a martyr. Death is a tough act to follow. "I am now," Jack told Billings not long after Joe's death, "shadowboxing in a match the shadow is always going to win." As he contemplated a run for Congress in 1946, Jack said he felt "terribly exposed and vulnerable" without Joe there to serve as the focus of his father's ambitions, without Joe on-site to be pushed into the political arena while Jack bided his time and considered his options. In other moods, however, he clearly relished the idea of a campaign; he had, after all, spoken frequently in the past about the prospect of a political career. And the ambassador himself had told John Bulkeley as early as 1942 that he thought Jack had the stuff to be president. So we know the idea of Jack in politics was not a new one born of Joe's death, although it may well have been honed and sharpened by the fallout from that explosion over the British coast in 1944.

When Jack ran for Congress in Boston's 11th District during the fall of 1946, he did so—just as his father, his own good political instincts, and the truth of his personal experience would have him do—as a hero home from the wars. "Men who pushed back the Japs," read one press release, "island by island in the Pacific, men who stormed the blazing Normandy on D-Day and who hammered their way across France and Germany to blunt the Nazi military might are now fighting a different kind of campaign—a political battle on behalf of a young man who at one time during the war was reported missing in action. . . . One of the impressive features of his campaign has been the manner in which veterans of all branches have rallied behind his candidacy."

Jack often worked the story of PT 109 into his speeches, but did not do so cynically. When he spoke of 109, it was always with great and sincere emotion, as on the night he cited the bravery of Pappy McMahon, the eldest and most severely wounded of his men. "I felt," Kennedy said in an ex-temporaneous speech, "his courage was the result of his loyalty to the men around him. Most of the courage shown in the war came from men's under-standing of their interdependence on each other. Men were saving other men's lives at the risk of their own simply because they realized that perhaps the next day their lives would be saved in turn. And so there was built up dur-ing the war a great feeling of comradeship and fellowship and loyalty." He reflected that this comradeship was one of the few aspects of war that he and other returning soldiers and sailors missed: "that sense of working together for a common cause."

In the last days of the campaign, Jack's father arranged for John Hersey's account of PT 109—already reprinted once in *The Reader's Digest*—to be reprinted yet again in a pamphlet edition. One hundred thousand copies went out through the mails, along with a press release signed by Kennedy's old 109 crewmate William Johnston, the Dorchester truck driver. "I'm not a politician," Johnston wrote, "and I don't know much about politics. But, if the people of this district want a congressman with real abilities, with great qualities of leadership and with unusual courage, then John Fitzgerald Kennedy is their man. . . . Somebody [in fact, Kennedy's opponent] has talked about the need for a seasoned congressman. Kennedy was seasoned enough to command a PT boat in action. He was seasoned enough for the lives of his crew to be entrusted to him. . . . We may not know too much about politics, but we know a lot about John Fitzgerald Kennedy."

. . .

LIKE SO MANY of Britain's great country houses, Chatsworth today, as a matter of necessity, stands open to the public from late March through the end of October. Tourists from London and other towns roll up by the busload, walk through the mansion, and explore the eleven-hundred-acre park landscaped by Capability Brown so many centuries ago. (We don't know what Brown would think of the latest addition in the nearby woods: a "Farmyard and Adventure Playground" for children, who are also invited to explore a maze in the garden. The eleventh duke—Billy Hartington's brother Andrew—advertises a hut overlooking the playground as being available for birthday parties.) Additionally, the Chatsworth House Trust (a registered national charity) plays host to both a cooking school (conducted by the Chatsworth chef) and a sewing school (conducted by the Chatsworth seamstresses).

In return for a large tax discount, the duke invites the public to enjoy the large park for free. Nevertheless, the house, garden, and children's attractions come at a price: £7 and an additional £1 charged for parking. Special fees apply to the angling fair held annually on the banks of the River Dewent in May and the country fair hosted by the duke and duchess each September. Chatsworth also offers conference facilities, such as the Hartington Room, a fully equipped lecture and meeting room set in the old stable block designed by architect James Paine in 1758 at the behest of the fourth duke. Not far away, the eleventh duke's Carriage House Restaurant seats 250 and offers a full luncheon menu. The Carriage House Gift Shop, in turn, tempts visitors with everything from postcards to costume reproductions of the duchess's personal jewelry and copies of Chatsworth's art treasures. The shop also offers several cookbooks written by the current duchess—Kick's old friend, the former Deborah ("Debo") Mitford.

All of this activity—combined with the occasional sale of a masterpiece from the extensive family collection—enables the eleventh duke to hang on to Chatsworth, albeit by a thread. As no one knows better than the duke, the war against Hitler marked the final border between survival and surrender for many of Britain's noble families. Death duties in Britain increased to a whopping 65 percent on the largest estates during the early 1940s. Dispensations for deaths of heirs to titles on active service only kicked in for second and subsequent instances. Thus the House of Devonshire absorbed a brutal financial blow when its heir apparent—Billy Hartington—died in 1944. The Cavendishes then faced a death duty yet again with the demise of Billy's father in 1950.

To make matters worse, the years immediately following World War II saw the emergence of the least landed and most radical government in British history. "The end of the war," writes David Cannadine, "left most surviving landowners in circumstances more reduced and distressed than they had ever known; and in the austere and egalitarian world of Welfare State socialism that followed, there was a distinct feeling that their remaining economic privileges, political influence, and social status were no longer acceptable." The long process of dismantling and disenfranchising Britain's hereditary nobles continued with a vengeance after Hitler's defeat. Under

firm and committed legislative attack, aristocratic wealth and privilege with-
ered, and many landed families now joined the Mitfords as victims of the
Labourite urge against the old order. (One wonders if, looking back during
the years immediately following the war, Kick remembered Billy's promise
made before their wedding. Hadn't he said he would allow their children to
be raised Catholic if, eventually, the British aristocracy become so undermined by socialism that tradition no longer mattered?)

Today, very near Chatsworth, you may tour the graveyard of St. Peter's
Church, Edensor, without charge. Here you'll find many generations of
Cavendishes dating back to the fourteenth century. One of the newer stones
marks the resting place for Billy's and Andrew's father, the tenth duke. There
is no sign, however, of Billy, who lies far from here, in Belgium, with other
fallen British soldiers. The only hint of Billy at St. Peter's is the grave occupied by his widow, Kathleen Kennedy Hartington, the Marchioness of Hartington, who died with her new love—a divorced Protestant, Lord Peter
Fitzwilliam—in the crash of a plane carrying them from Britain to Cannes
during the spring of 1948.

The couple may have been eloping, or they may have simply been going
to Cannes for a romantic tryst. No one knows for sure. Kick's acquaintance
Evelyn Waugh believed the latter, which he considered preferable to marriage outside the church. "If you want to commit adultery," he told her not
long before she died, "or fornication & can't resist, do it, but realize what
you are doing, and don't give the final insult of apostasy." Not long after the
tragedy, Nancy Astor voiced the opinion that the crash had been engineered
by Vatican agents who were intent on stopping Kick before she embarked
upon yet another sacrilegious union. A mass card commissioned by Rose after Kick's death featured a portrait of the daughter Rose thought lost in
more ways than one. It also offered the text of a plenary indulgence—a
prayer designed to redeem damned souls from purgatory if said often
enough before a crucifix after Holy Communion.

· · ·

A SMALL STONE at the foot of Kick's grave commemorates the visit
made here in June of 1963 by President John Fitzgerald Kennedy, who
later paid a courtesy call to Chatsworth. He, of all the Kennedys, was the
one most changed by the war and the years that immediately preceded the

war. He had learned much in that time. He had learned that his father—whom he'd started out viewing as infallible—was more than capable of human error. He had learned that death is real: a genuine possibility just a breath away, not to be trifled with or taken for granted. He had also learned that God is not knowable through any process so numbingly simple as merely memorizing a catechism: a realization that seems to have made him reach for God even more devotedly, albeit in his own way and in his own time. "[The] faith you are born with is an empty one," Inga had written him. "The one you acquire later in life, when God has risen the curtain and showed you life, showed you all its beauties and many of its miseries—well, if you have faith then—that is worth something." He likewise learned—as was mentioned at the start of this narrative—that there was "nothing inevitable" about his prospects.

Inherently smarter and more congenial than his brother Joe (who seems to have been changed very little by his time in the service), and more generous and democratic (with a small *d*) than his sister Kick, Jack experienced the reinforcing of all his most interesting and compelling qualities during the war years. Indeed, the dedicated but perhaps inept youth who worked so sincerely to aid *Athenia* survivors in 1939 emerged from the war with greatly enhanced capabilities and compassion. He likewise emerged shorn of the mundane bigotries he'd been taught to accept since childhood, yet with both his fatalism and his pragmatism sharpened to a fine edge: both to serve him well in the coming years. (Interestingly, he soon adopted as his favorite poem the frighteningly prophetic World War I–era elegy entitled "I Have a Rendezvous with Death." This had been composed by another Harvard man, Alan Seeger, who died while fighting with the French in 1916.)

In the end, after surviving what he once called "the sea of death that swamped Mead, Bill H[artington], Joe, and so many others," Jack emerged a man in full: someone who looked at life and the world in a new and unique way, operating from a perspective he could not have previously imagined. The war changed him as it did his family, his generation, and his world. And nothing was ever the same again.

Acknowledgments

I wish to thank my agent, Chris Calhoun, and my editor, Bill Thomas, for their early and enthusiastic support. I would also like to thank my family—my wife, Christa, and our children, Bill and Katherine—for tolerating both me and the warring Kennedys for close to three years. The staff of the John F. Kennedy Library (in particular William Johnston, Megan Desnoyers, Allan Goodrich, and James Hill) proved unfailingly helpful, as did fellow sojourners on the Kennedy trail who aided me with enlightening correspondence, conversation, and inspiration, among them Arthur Schlesinger, Richard Reeves, Doris Kearns Goodwin, and Robert Dallek. I am also indebted to Jeffrey Flannery, Mary Wolfskill, and David Wigdor at the Library of Congress's Manuscript Division; F. Kennon Moody at the Franklin D. Roosevelt Library; Dave Maslyn at the University of Rhode Island Library; and Mike Bott, Keeper of Archives and Manuscripts at the Reading University Library, Sussex, United Kingdom. At the offices of Doubleday, Bill Thomas's assistant Kendra Harpster has proved an unfailingly efficient administrator, liaison, and ally. I would also like to thank Ted Johnson for an uncompromisingly thorough copy-edit.

Fellow writers and friends—among them Ben Cheever and Arthur Goldwag—helped me focus my thoughts, my prose, and my spirit. Tweed Roosevelt, as has become his generous habit, offered me sanctuary in his Boston guestroom during my frequent trips to consult archives in that city.

My Rhode Island neighbor Henry Morgenthau III chatted willingly and engagingly about the skirmishes between his father, Secretary of the Treasury Henry Morgenthau, Jr., and Ambassador Joseph P. Kennedy through 1938 and 1939. Henry's Princeton classmate Senator Claiborne Pell—another Rhode Island neighbor, who honors me with his friendship—spoke warmly about both Jack and Kick Kennedy, whom he knew well before, during, and after the war.

Ambassador Samuel Campiche generously shared his recollections of Jack, Kick, and their group in Washington during the days immediately preceding World War II. Samuel Hall Whitley II offered a splendid reminiscence of his passage to the South Pacific aboard the *Rochambeau* with his fellow Cape Codder Jack Kennedy in 1943. John Jerome Cabitor (Harvard '38), John Edward Regan, Jr. (Harvard '39), and William Pratt Tillinghast (Harvard '40) spoke at length about both Jack and Joe Jr. in their college days. Martha Good gave me details with which to put flesh on the young John Kennedy who greeted her and fellow American survivors after the sinking of the *Athenia* in 1939. Jakie Astor (Major Sir John Astor, a.k.a. John Jacob Astor VI) lent copies of correspondence between his mother, Nancy Astor, and Joseph P. Kennedy, Sr. And lastly, my friends Frank and Chris Roosevelt helped sort out the details of the interesting plane trip their father, Franklin D. Roosevelt, Jr., shared with Joseph P. Kennedy, Sr., from Palm Beach to New York in January of 1941.

EDWARD J. RENEHAN, JR.
Wickford, Rhode Island
August 2001

Source Notes

CHAPTER 1 (PAGES 1–14)

1. "It was easy . . .": Richard Reeves, *President Kennedy* (New York: Simon & Schuster, 1993), 27.
1. "more screwed-up . . .": Herbert Parmet, *Jack: The Struggles of John F. Kennedy* (New York: Dial Press, 1980), 111–12.
1. "Everything dates from that adventure": *Los Angeles Times*, 20 September 1962.
2. "I firmly believe . . .": John F. Kennedy to Lady Nancy Astor, 12 September 1954, copy lent by Major Sir John Astor.
2. "savaged . . .": John F. Kennedy to Claiborne Pell, 6 October 1947, Claiborne Pell Papers, Special Collections, University of Rhode Island Library.
2. "like a wrecking ball": Richard D. Mahoney, *Sons and Brothers* (New York: Arcade Publishing, 1999), 9.
3. "Finish First . . .": Ralph G. Martin, *A Hero for Our Time* (New York: Macmillan, 1983), 31.
3. "didn't like anyone . . .": Ronald Kessler, *The Sins of the Father* (New York: Warner Books, 1996), 43.
3. "could be pretty caustic . . .": Ralph G. Martin, *Seeds of Destruction: Joe Kennedy and His Sons* (New York: G. P. Putnam's Sons, 1995), 12.
3. "The aim . . ." Ronald Kessler, *The Sins of the Father*, 41.
3. the new main ran nine inches . . . : Richard J. Whalen, *The Founding Father* (New York: New American Library, 1964), 95.
4. "It's touch . . .": Gail Cameron, *Rose* (New York: G. P. Putnam's Sons, 1971), 105–6.
4. "I grew up . . .": Arthur Schlesinger, *Robert Kennedy and His Times* (Boston: Houghton Mifflin, 1978), 16.
4. "We all had the feeling . . .": Rose F. Kennedy, *Times to Remember* (Garden City, N.Y.: Doubleday, 1974), 155.
5. "On the way home . . .": John F. Kennedy, ed., *As We Remember Joe* (privately printed, 1944), 59.
5. breathed a sigh of relief . . . : Author interview with Julian Bach, Choate '32.
5. "permanent enemies . . .": Hank Searls, *The Lost Prince* (New York: New American Library, 1971), 69.
5. "He was with me . . .": John F. Kennedy, ed., *As We Remember Joe*, 44.
6. "I am just getting to the point . . .": Doris Kearns Goodwin, *The Fitzgeralds and the Kennedys* (New York: Simon & Schuster, 1987), 469.
6. "I had been to Laski's . . .": *Ibid.*, 471–72.
7. "Is that really the way it was?": John F. Kennedy to Harold Laski, 14 October 1944, Harold Laski Papers, University of Hull/Brynmoor-Jones Library Special Collections.
7. hated *Kikes*: Hank Searls, *The Lost Prince*, 97.
7. "older, bigger, stronger, . . .": Rose Kennedy Interview, Audiovisual Archives, JFK Library.

7. "and hear the sound of Joe banging . . .": Evan Thomas, *Robert Kennedy: His Life* (New York: Simon & Schuster, 2000), 39.
7. "He had a pugnacious personality. . . .": James M. Burns, *John Kennedy: A Political Profile* (New York: Harcourt, Brace, 1960), 28.
7. "At least one half of the days . . .": Rose F. Kennedy, *Times to Remember*, 85.
8. "elfin": *Ibid.*, 94.
8. "lying in bed . . .": Kay Halle Oral History, JFK Library.
9. "Jack made up for what he lacked . . .": Joan Meyers, ed., *John Fitzgerald Kennedy: As We Remember Him* (New York: Atheneum, 1965), 13.
9. "Guts is the word. . . .": Torbert Macdonald Interview, Audiovisual Archives, JFK Library.
9. lost his virginity to a white prostitute in a Harlem brothel: Thomas C. Reeves, *A Question of Character: A Life of John Kennedy* (New York: Free Press, 1991), 44.
9. brisk and businesslike sex: Author interview with John Edward Regan, Jr., Harvard '39.
9. "Went down to the Cape . . .": Nigel Hamilton, *JFK: Reckless Youth* (hereafter *Reckless Youth*) (New York: Random House, 1992), 165–66.
9. dated a succession of actresses, dancers, and older married women: Hank Searls, *The Lost Prince*, 74.
10. "had the best sense of humor . . .": Joan Blair and Clay Blair, Jr., *The Search for JFK* (New York: Berkley Books, 1976), 24.
11. "We just had awful experiences . . .": Nigel Hamilton, *Reckless Youth*, 193.
11. "very, very complex . . .": K. LeMoyne Billings Interview, Audiovisual Archives, JFK Library.
11. "My mother never hugged me, . . .": Ralph G. Martin, *Seeds of Destruction*, 7.
11. "I think half of this activity . . .": Ronald Kessler, *The Sins of the Father*, 111.
11. "She was either at Paris . . .": *Ibid.*, 11.
11. "Gee, you're a great mother . . .": Rose F. Kennedy, *Times to Remember*, 93.
12. "We always had a rosary . . .": Ralph G. Martin, *Seeds of Destruction*, 7.
12. Jack's sinner's faith seemed . . . : K. LeMoyne Billings Interview, Audiovisual Archives, JFK Library.
12. voiced open skepticism . . . : Joan Blair and Clay Blair, Jr., *The Search for JFK*, 27.
12. "I figured the boys could get . . .": Victor Lasky, *JFK: The Man and the Myth* (New York: Macmillan, 1963), 68.

CHAPTER 2 (PAGES 15–26)

16. "so hard he almost . . .": Ralph G. Martin, *Seeds of Destruction*, 65.
16. "a very dangerous man": Henry Morgenthau, Jr., Diary, 8 December 1937, FDR Library.
17. "The trouble with Kennedy . . .": *Ibid.*, 15 April 1935.
17. "Send a thief . . .": Michael R. Beschloss, *Kennedy and Roosevelt: The Uneasy Alliance* (hereafter *Kennedy and Roosevelt*) (New York: Norton, 1980), 88.
17. "I think it but fair . . .": John Flynn, "Other People's Money," *The New Republic*, 9 October 1935.
17. "I have no political ambitions . . .": Joseph P. Kennedy, Sr., *I'm for Roosevelt* (New York: Reynal & Hitchcock, 1936), 3.
18. "the dim and dull-eyed masses . . .": Richard J. Whalen, *The Founding Father*, 97.
18. "she bothered us more . . .": *Boston Globe*, 10 November 1940.
18. "I think . . .": Nigel Hamilton, *Reckless Youth*, 510.
19. "I wanted power. . . .": Arnold A. Hutschnecker, *The Drive for Power* (New York: M. Evans, 1974), 55.
19. "figured out not at all": Harold Ickes Diary, 13 March 1938, Harold Ickes Papers, Library of Congress.
20. had to settle for lowly Pi Eta: Several previous biographers have claimed that Joe made it into the Spee. The records of the Spee Club indicate otherwise.
20. "It was better than nothing . . .": Nigel Hamilton, *Reckless Youth*, 163.
21. "slender and handsome, . . .": John Kenneth Galbraith, *A Life in Our Times* (Boston: Houghton Mifflin, 1981), 53.
21. "a base and a social standing . . .": Nigel Hamilton, *Reckless Youth*, 208.
22. "With six minutes to go . . .": Hank Searls, *The Lost Prince*, 92.
22. "All those others . . .": Author interview with John Edward Regan, Jr., Harvard '39.
22. "England is a most important post . . .": Henry Morgenthau, Jr., Diary, 8 December 1937, Henry Morgenthau Papers, FDR Library.
23. "pouring his conservative ideas . . .": Harold Ickes Diary, 17 March 1938, Harold Ickes Papers, Library of Congress.

23. "he came back to me . . .": Arthur Krock, *Memoirs: Sixty Years on the Firing Line* (New York: Funk & Wagnalls, 1968), 333.

23. "needs skill brought by years . . .": Nigel Hamilton, *Reckless Youth*, 213.

24. "Just got news . . .": Joseph P. Kennedy, Sr., to Franklin D. Roosevelt, n.d. (1937), President's Personal Files, FDR Library.

24. "FDR did not hesitate . . .": Victor Lasky, *JFK: The Man and the Myth*, 51.

24. "he was going to send . . .": Henry Morgenthau, Jr., Diary, 8 December 1937, Henry Morgenthau Papers, FDR Library.

24. he did not think Kennedy would stay: Ronald Kessler, *The Sins of the Father*, 149.

24. "Don't go buying . . .": Peter Collier and David Horowitz, *The Kennedys: An American Drama* (New York: Summit Books, 1984), 82.

24. chiefly to please his wife: Harold Ickes Diary, 17 March 1938, Harold Ickes Papers, Library of Congress.

26. "must ultimately be faced down": Michael R. Beschloss, *Kennedy and Roosevelt*, 161.

Chapter 3 (pages 27–35)

27. "Well, I am here after a very nice . . .": Joseph P. Kennedy, Sr., to James Roosevelt, 3 March 1938, James Roosevelt Papers, FDR Library.

27. "You can't expect . . .": *Time*, 14 March 1938.

27. "I can tell you . . .": Joseph P. Kennedy, Sr., to James Roosevelt, 3 March 1938, James Roosevelt Papers, FDR Library.

28. "looks and acts like a Cardinal . . .": *Ibid.*

28. "Chamberlain believes . . .": Joseph P. Kennedy, Sr., to John Boettiger, 12 March 1938, Anna Roosevelt Halstead Papers, FDR Library.

28. "realistic, practical mind" . . . : Joseph P. Kennedy, Sr., to Cordell Hull, 4 March 1938, Cordell Hull Papers, Library of Congress.

29. "the only trousers . . .": London *Evening Standard*, 12 May 1938.

30. "It was an exciting and slightly hectic sailing . . .": Rose F. Kennedy, *Times to Remember*, 216–17.

30. "Now our family returned . . .": *Ibid.*

30. "It's so silly . . .": Lynne McTaggart, *Kathleen Kennedy: Her Life and Times* (New York: Dial Press, 1980), 24.

30. "Kathleen Kennedy, Aged 18 . . .": *Ibid.*

32. "I hate like hell . . .": Joseph P. Kennedy, Sr., to Joseph Breen, 31 December 1937, Archives of the Motion Picture Producers and Distribution Association of America.

32. "There is little doubt . . .": Washington Chancery to British Foreign Office, American Department, February 1938, Cable F0371/21530/A1564/60/45, Public Records Office, London.

32. "I have a beautiful blue silk room . . .": Joseph P. Kennedy, Sr., to James Roosevelt, 3 March 1938, James Roosevelt Papers, FDR Library.

33. "watched me daily . . .": Joseph P. Kennedy, Sr., "Diplomatic Memoirs" (unpublished manuscript), Chapter 2, p. 2, James Landis Papers, Library of Congress.

33. "the fundamental basis of British foreign policy . . .": William Manchester, *The Last Lion: Alone 1932–1940* (Boston: Little, Brown, 1988), 243.

33. "masterpiece . . . there will be no war . . .": Joseph P. Kennedy, Sr., to Arthur Krock, 28 March 1938, Arthur Krock Papers, Princeton University Library.

33. "the U.S. would be very foolish . . .": Joseph P. Kennedy, Sr., to Franklin D. Roosevelt, cable, 11 March 1938, President's Personal Files, FDR Library.

34. "the great majority of Americans . . .": Joseph P. Kennedy, Sr., "Diplomatic Memoirs," Chapter 3, p. 9.

34. "no plan to seek or offer . . .": *Ibid.*

34. "as much as I dislike . . .": Joseph P. Kennedy, Sr., to Bernard Baruch, 21 March 1938, Baruch Papers, Princeton University Library.

35. "on this score in vigorous language . . .": Joseph P. Kennedy, Sr., "Diplomatic Memoirs," Chapter 2, p. 8.

Chapter 4 (pages 36–45)

36. "[Kennedy's] bouncing offspring make . . .": "The Nine Kennedy Kids Delight Great Britain," *Life*, 11 April 1938.

37. "Even though his own . . .": New York *Daily News*, 10 May 1938.

37. "America's most important debutante": "Miss Kathleen Kennedy," *Queen*, 12 May 1938, 12.

38. "a fine ride": Joseph P. Kennedy, Sr., "Diplomatic Memoirs," Chapter 2, p. 5.
38. "It was a wonderful time . . .": Rose F. Kennedy, *Times to Remember*, 221.
39. "Churchill was scornful . . .": Joseph P. Kennedy, Sr., "Diplomatic Memoirs," Chapter 2, p. 8.
39. "the high point in Mr. Chamberlain's foreign policy . . .": Joseph P. Kennedy, Sr., to Arthur Krock, 14 April 1938, Arthur Krock Papers, Princeton University Library.
40. "There is no question of the power . . .": Anne Morrow Lindbergh, *The Flower and the Nettle: Diaries and Letters of Anne Morrow Lindbergh 1936–1939* (New York: Harcourt Brace Jovanovich, 1976), 100.
40. "German air strength is greater . . .": Charles A. Lindbergh, *The Wartime Journals of Charles A. Lindbergh* (New York: Harcourt Brace Jovanovich, 1970), 73.
40. "England seems hopelessly behind . . .": *Ibid.*, 22.
40. "treated as omniscient . . .": William Manchester, *The Last Lion: Alone, 1932–1940*, 317.
41. "I'm glad you are smart enough . . .": Lady Nancy Astor to Joseph P. Kennedy, Sr., n.d., copy lent by Major Sir John Astor.
42. "I like her very much. . . .": Amanda Smith, ed., *Hostage to Fortune* (New York: Viking, 2000), 250.
42. "If I were your wife . . .": William Manchester, *The Last Lion: Alone, 1932–1940*, 85.
42. "After two years . . .": John Halperin, *Eminent Georgians* (New York: St. Martin's Griffin, 1988), 185.
42. "very like a pacifist": Nancy Astor, *My Two Countries* (Garden City, N.Y.: Doubleday, 1923), 23.
42. "That this House will in no circumstances . . .": William Manchester, *The Last Lion: Alone, 1932–1940*, 48.
43. "Day after day . . .": William L. Shiner, *The Rise and Fall of the Third Reich* (New York: Simon & Schuster, 1960), 327.
43. "give a rough time" . . . : Nancy Astor to Joseph P. Kennedy, Sr., 13 April 1938, copy lent by Major Sir John Astor.
43. "Jewish pundits . . .": Joseph P. Kennedy, Sr., to Nancy Astor, 5 May 1938, copy lent by Major Sir John Astor.
43. "Spent Easter weekend . . .": Kathleen Kennedy to K. LeMoyne Billings, 29 April 1938, John F. Kennedy Personal Papers, Box 4A, folder of K. LeMoyne Billings correspondence, JFK Library.
44. "Rose, this is a helluva . . .": Rose F. Kennedy, *Times to Remember*, 221.
44. "Palm Sunday. . . .": Amanda Smith, ed., *Hostage to Fortune*, 252–53.
44. "like a watchman": *Ibid.*
45. "If he means economic penetration . . .": Joseph P. Kennedy, Sr., "Diplomatic Memoirs," Chapter 3, p. 4.
45. "Although Kennedy promised . . .": Michael R. Beschloss, *Kennedy and Roosevelt*, 165.
45. "Germany's best friend": Nigel Hamilton, *Reckless Youth*, 236.

CHAPTER 5 (PAGES 46–58)

47. "I felt like Cinderella": Rose F. Kennedy, *Times to Remember*, 228.
47. "Will Kennedy Run . . .": "Will Kennedy Run for President?" *Liberty*, 21 May 1938.
48. "Did Joe Kennedy Sr. want to be President . . .": Arthur Krock interview with Joan and Clay Blair, Joan and Clay Blair Papers, University of Wyoming Archives.
48. "Mr. Roosevelt had made no announcement . . .": Joseph P. Kennedy, Sr., "Diplomatic Memoirs," Chapter 9, p. 3.
49. "Crown Prince . . .": New York *Daily News*, 20 May 1940.
49. "I enlisted under President Roosevelt . . .": Joseph P. Kennedy, Sr., "Diplomatic Memoirs," Chapter 9, p. 3.
49. "moral authority": *Ibid.*, Chapter 10, p. 4.
49. "Joe Kennedy, if he were in power . . .": Harold Ickes Diary, 3 July 1938, Harold Ickes Papers, Library of Congress.
50. "I am once again confounding . . .": John F. Kennedy to Claiborne Pell, 17 June 1938, Claiborne Pell Papers, Special Collections, University of Rhode Island Library.
51. "positive evidence that Kennedy . . .": *Chicago Tribune*, 23 June 1938.
51. "true Irish anger" . . . : Joseph P. Kennedy, Sr., "Diplomatic Memoirs," Chapter 9, p. 7.
52. "Jimmy has helped Kennedy . . .": "Jimmy's Got It," *The Saturday Evening Post*, 28 June 1938.
52. "I'll admit I am the American Ambassador . . .": *Baltimore Sun*, 29 June 1938.
52. "and that annoyed his father . . .": Arthur Krock Oral History, JFK Library.
53. "sexual aggressiveness . . .": Lynne McTaggart, *Kathleen Kennedy: Her Life and Times*, 43.

53. "Joe looked much more mature . . .": Hugh Fraser Oral History, JFK Library.
54. "a nice boy . . .": Hank Searls, *The Lost Prince*, 103.
54. "The whole family is taking to London . . .": London *Times*, 24 May 1938.
56. "a lanky, coltish charm": Lynne McTaggart, *Kathleen Kennedy: Her Life and Times*, 45.
57. "She is very sharp . . .": The Duke of Devonshire to Lady Astor, 12 September 1938, copy lent by Major Sir John Astor.

CHAPTER 6 (PAGES 59–71)

59. "the conventional prejudices of his rank and station": David Cecil, *The Young Melbourne* (London: Constable, 1939), 62.
60. "I went over with very little money . . .": Rose F. Kennedy, *Times to Remember*, 215.
60. "Joe was an awful good-looking young fellow . . .": Hank Searls, *The Lost Prince*, 107.
60. "quite necessary to keep around . . .": Hugh Fraser Oral History, JFK Library.
61. Jack, in turn, bragged about Dietrich: Author interview with Claiborne Pell.
61. learning to water-ski: *Ibid.*
62. "I should like to ask . . .": Joseph P. Kennedy, Sr., to Cordell Hull, Diplomatic Dispatch, 18 August 1938, Cordell Hull Papers, Library of Congress.
63. "I can't for the life of me . . .": John Morton Blum, ed., *From the Morgenthau Diaries*, vol. 1 (Boston: Houghton Mifflin, 1959), 518.
64. "quite unwell . . .": Joseph P. Kennedy, Sr., to Cordell Hull, Diplomatic Dispatch, 30 August 1938, Cordell Hull Papers, Library of Congress.
64. "The Foreign Secretary says that the French . . .": Joseph P. Kennedy, Sr., to Cordell Hull, Diplomatic Dispatch, 31 August 1938, Cordell Hull Papers, Library of Congress.
65. "would not be practicable . . .": Cordell Hull to Joseph P. Kennedy, Sr., Diplomatic Dispatch, 1 September 1938, Cordell Hull Papers, Library of Congress.
65. "keep cool . . .": *Boston Herald*, 31 August 1938.
65. "Frankly, I think Joe Kennedy's attention . . .": Franklin D. Roosevelt to Cordell Hull, 1 September 1938, Cordell Hull Papers, Library of Congress.
65. "[Kennedy] believes it his business . . .": *Washington Star*, 15 September 1938.
65. "a miserable pygmy race . . .": William L. Shirer, *The Rise and Fall of the Third Reich* (New York: Simon & Schuster, 1959), 383.
66. "if these tortured creatures . . .": *New York Times*, 13 September 1938.
67. "on the highest authority": *Washington Evening Star*, 29 September 1938.
67. "He felt it absolutely imperative . . .": Joseph P. Kennedy, Sr., to Cordell Hull, Diplomatic Dispatch, 14 September 1938, Cordell Hull Papers, Library of Congress.
67. "The whole plan . . .": Joseph P. Kennedy, Sr., to Cordell Hull, Diplomatic Dispatch, 19 September 1938, Cordell Hull Papers, Library of Congress.
68. "there was little doubt . . .": Joseph P. Kennedy, Sr., "Diplomatic Memoirs," Chapter 14, p. 23.
69. "All over London . . .": *Ibid.*, Chapter 15, p. 11.
69. "very blue . . .": Joseph P. Kennedy, Sr., to Arthur Krock, 26 September 1938, Arthur Krock Papers, Princeton University Library.
69. "horrible, fantastic, [and] incredible . . .": London *Times*, 27 September 1938.
70. "I have now been informed . . .": London *Daily Mail*, 29 September 1938.
70. "I hope this doesn't mean . . .": Joseph P. Kennedy, Sr., to Cordell Hull, Diplomatic Dispatch, 28 September 1938, Cordell Hull Papers, Library of Congress.
71. "Well boys, the war is off": Joseph P. Kennedy, Sr., "Diplomatic Memoirs," Chapter 16, p. 16.
71. "sustained a total and unmitigated defeat": William Manchester, *The Last Lion: Alone, 1932–1940*, 361.

CHAPTER 7 (PAGES 72–82)

72. "in disregard of treaty obligations . . .": *Parliamentary Debates, 1937–1938*, Vol. 339, p. 36.
73. "Isn't it wonderful": James Laver, *Between the Wars* (Boston: Houghton Mifflin, 1961), 221.
73. "Kennedy sent in a speech . . .": Jay Pierrepont Moffat Diary, 17 October 1938, Jay Pierrepont Moffat Papers, Library of Congress.
73. "For Mr. Kennedy to propose . . .": *New York Post*, 20 October 1938.
73. "amateur and temporary diplomats . . .": *New York Herald Tribune*, 22 October 1938.
74. "I wonder if Joe Kennedy understands . . .": Max Freedman, ed., *Roosevelt and Frankfurter: Their Correspondence, 1928–45* (Boston: Little, Brown, 1967), 463–64.
74. "Mr. Lippman article shows . . .": Amanda Smith, ed., *Hostage to Fortune*, 301.

74. "taking orders and working for hours . . .": *Ibid.*, 305.
74. "a number of Jewish publishers and writers . . .": Joseph P. Kennedy, Sr., "Diplomatic Memoirs," Chapter 18, p. 4.
74. "Jewish columnists . . .": Amanda Smith, ed., *Hostage to Fortune*, 305.
75. "Foolishly, he had no prepared speech . . .": Philip Kaiser, *Journeying Far and Wide: A Political and Diplomatic Memoir* (New York: Scribner's, 1992), 127.
75. "I was embarrassed . . .": Dennis J. Hutchinson, *The Man Who Once Was Whizzer White* (New York: Free Press, 1998), 135.
75. "I am somewhat embarrassed . . .": Joseph P. Kennedy, Sr., to Cordell Hull, Diplomatic Dispatch, 28 October 1938, Cordell Hull Papers, Library of Congress.
75. "I don't know who spread poison . . .": Amanda Smith, ed., *Hostage to Fortune*, 298–99.
76. "Isn't there some way . . .": Joseph P. Kennedy, Sr., "Diplomatic Memoirs," Chapter 20, p. 11.
76. "add new luster to a reputation . . .": *Life*, 16 January 1939.
77. "get rid of theirs as well": Joseph P. Kennedy, Sr., to Cordell Hull, Cable, 31 August 1938, Cordell Hull Papers, Library of Congress.
77. "While [the speech] seemed unpopular with the Jews . . .": James M. Burns, *John Kennedy: A Political Profile*, 37.
77. "I don't think . . .": Torbert Macdonald Interview, Audiovisual Archives, JFK Library.
78. "It's pretty funny . . .": John F. Kennedy to parents, n.d. (1938), Box 1, John F. Kennedy Personal Papers, JFK Library.
78. "The White House has on its hands a fighting Irishman . . .": *New York Daily Mirror*, 12 November 1938.
78. "I am going home to face the President . . .": *New York Times*, 16 December 1938, p. 13.
79. "terribly peeved with Joe. . . .": Henry Morgenthau, Jr., Diary, 5 December 1938, Henry Morgenthau Papers, FDR Library.
79. "Father knew that Kennedy had to go . . .": Michael R. Beschloss, *Kennedy and Roosevelt*, 184.
79. "a virtual publicity bureau": *Boston Herald*, 26 March 1939.
80. "inevitably mean the destruction of the American form of government . . .": Joseph P. Kennedy, Sr., to Franklin D. Roosevelt, 3 March 1939, President's Personal Files, FDR Library.
81. "bucked the State Department and Mr. Roosevelt . . .": *Boston Globe*, 20 April 1939.
81. "wants to get out . . .": Michael R. Beschloss, *Kennedy and Roosevelt*, 184.
82. "rocked him . . .": Torbert Macdonald Interview, Audiovisual Archives, JFK Library.
82. "to begin his education": Hank Searls, *The Lost Prince*, 127.

CHAPTER 8 (PAGES 83–96)

83. "today, here in this shattered city . . .": Hank Searls, *The Lost Prince*, 117.
84. "Sorry I missed you. . . .": *Ibid.*, 116.
85. "Louella . . .": *Ibid.*, 111–12.
85. "Every house . . .": Amanda Smith, ed., *Hostage to Fortune*, 311–12.
85. "A skinny Spanish chap . . .": *Ibid.*, 312–14.
86. "We awoke to find soldiers . . .": *Ibid.*, 315–16.
88. "A more pompous ass . . .": Joseph P. Kennedy, Sr., to Cordell Hull, Diplomatic Dispatch, 17 March 1939, Cordell Hull Papers, Library of Congress.
88. "the family came in and all knelt . . .": Amanda Smith, ed., *Hostage to Fortune*, 316–20.
88. "I hope you will always . . .": *Ibid.*
89. "I have the evening papers in front of me . . .": Joseph P. Kennedy, Sr., "Diplomatic Memoirs," Chapter 24, p. 1.
89. "You caused it yourself!": John Halperin, *Eminent Georgians*, 219.
89. "The abdication of German political Catholicism . . .": John Cornwell, *Hitler's Pope* (New York: Penguin, 1999), 6–7.
90. "she could not see any reason . . .": Joseph P. Kennedy, Sr., to Cordell Hull, Diplomatic Dispatch, 17 March 1939, Cordell Hull Papers, Library of Congress.
90. "felt not only a sense . . .": Joseph P. Kennedy, Sr., "Diplomatic Memoirs," Chapter 27, p. 4.
91. "As I left . . .": *Ibid.*, Chapter 26, p. 6.
91. "His Majesty's government would feel themselves . . .": Michael R. Beschloss, *Kennedy and Roosevelt*, 186.
91. "The city came to life . . .": Amanda Smith, ed., *Hostage to Fortune*, 323–24.
92. "throughout the world hundreds of millions . . .": Michael R. Beschloss, *Kennedy and Roosevelt*, 189.

92. "Well, that was a real great job . . .": Joseph P. Kennedy, Sr., "Diplomatic Memoirs," Chapter 26, p. 14.
93. "It came down on a gold spoon . . .": *Ibid.*
93. "She is still pretty young . . .": John F. Kennedy to Claiborne Pell, n.d. (March 1939), Claiborne Pell Papers, Special Collections, University of Rhode Island Library.
93. "listening to telegrams being read . . .": Orville Bullitt, ed., *For the President, Personal and Secret: Correspondence Between Franklin Delano Roosevelt and William C. Bullitt* (Boston: Houghton Mifflin, 1972), 273.
94. "had not gone to an Eastern College": Lawrence Leamer, *The Kennedy Women* (New York: Villard Books, 1994), 261.
95. "the sun setting on a golden age . . .": Leo Damore, *The Cape Cod Years of John Fitzgerald Kennedy* (Englewood Cliffs, N.J.: Prentice Hall, 1967), 50.
95. "you had a feeling . . .": *Ibid.*
95. "just won't work": John F. Kennedy to Joseph P. Kennedy, Sr., n.d. (1939), JFK Presidential Office Files, JFK Library.
96. "Criticism of me had begun . . .": Joseph P. Kennedy, Sr., "Diplomatic Memoirs," Chapter 26, p. 11.
96. When FDR heard of Kennedy's unauthorized encounter: Charles Higham, *Trading with the Enemy* (New York: Delacorte, 1983), 168–70.
96. "perfectly certain he will be the compromise candidate . . .": Harold Ickes Diary, 29 April 1939, Harold Ickes Papers, FDR Library.
96. "the Democratic [party] policy in the United States . . .": Harold Ickes Diary, 2 July 1939, Harold Ickes Papers, FDR Library.

CHAPTER 9 (PAGES 97–106)

97. "See that? . . .": Peter Collier and David Horowitz, *The Kennedys*, 101.
98. "I went down to dinner . . .": Amanda Smith, ed., *Hostage to Fortune*, 333.
99. "I recall very well . . .": Torbert Macdonald Interview, Audiovisual Archives, JFK Library.
99. "There were a couple of German fellows . . .": Dennis J. Hutchinson, *The Man Who Once Was Whizzer White*, 137–38.
99. "We got along very well . . .": Torbert Macdonald Interview, Audiovisual Archives, JFK Library.
101. "No trains were running . . .": George F. Kennan, *Memoirs, 1925–50* (Boston: Atlantic Monthly Press/Little, Brown, 1967), 91.
101. "It's been damn interesting . . .": John F. Kennedy to K. LeMoyne Billings, n.d. (May 1939), John F. Kennedy Personal Papers, Box 4A, folder of K. LeMoyne Billings correspondence, JFK Library.
103. "Before Mr. Hull and Mr. Roosevelt . . .": Amanda Smith, ed., *Hostage to Fortune*, 338.
104. "Alderly, where they lived . . .": Nancy Mitford, ed., *The Stanleys of Alderley: Their Letters Between the Years 1851–1865* (London: Chapman & Hall, 1939), p. xvi.
104. "Head of bone and heart of stone": David Pryce Jones, *Unity Mitford: A Quest* (London: Weidenfeld & Nicolson, 1976), 262.
104. "[She] seems to be in a state . . .": Amanda Smith, ed., *Hostage to Fortune*, 355–56.
105. "I have done everything I can think of . . .": Joseph P. Kennedy, Sr., "Diplomatic Memoirs," Chapter 33, p. 2.
105. "Accommodations are now available . . .": London *Times*, 25 August 1939.
105. "to cut it up . . .": Joseph P. Kennedy, Sr., "Diplomatic Memoirs," Chapter 33, p. 2.
106. "You have to make your solution . . .": *Ibid.*
106. "The unfortunate thing . . .": *Ibid.*

CHAPTER 10 (PAGES 107–116)

108. "These boys and all the rest of the country . . .": Amanda Smith, ed., *Hostage to Fortune*, 365.
108. "The Prime Minister has just broadcast . . .": Joseph P. Kennedy, Sr., to Cordell Hull, Diplomatic Dispatch, 3 September 1939, 11:20 a.m., Cordell Hull Papers, Library of Congress.
109. "We all went down . . .": Amanda Smith, ed., *Hostage to Fortune*, 366–67.
110. "It's the end of the world . . .": Joseph Alsop and Robert Kintner, *American White Paper: The Story of American Diplomacy and the Second World War* (New York: Literary Guild, 1940), 68.
110. "reminded him of a dream . . .": Joseph P. Kennedy, Sr., to Cordell Hull, Diplomatic Dispatch, 4 September 1939, Cordell Hull Papers, Library of Congress.

111. "Remember . . . the Poles are not Czechs": John F. Kennedy to K. LeMoyne Billings, n.d. (May 1939), John F. Kennedy Personal Papers, Box 4A, folder of K. LeMoyne Billings correspondence, JFK Library.

111. "We spent a rainy, cold night . . .": Author interview with *Athenia* survivor Martha Good of Chariton, Iowa.

112. "the 18-year-old son . . .": London *Daily Telegraph & Morning Post*, 8 September 1939.

112. "a storm of protest . . .": *Buffalo Evening News*, 8 September 1939.

112. "Ambassador of mercy . . .": London *Evening News*, 7 September 1939.

113. "impossible and unnecessary": Joseph P. Kennedy, Sr., "Diplomatic Memoirs," Chapter 34, p. 5.

113. "Yesterday my son Jack went up . . .": Joseph P. Kennedy, Sr., to Cordell Hull, Diplomatic Dispatch, 8 September 1939, Cordell Hull Papers, Library of Congress.

113. "grudging, mindless, mechanized approach": John F. Kennedy to Claiborne Pell, 12 September 1939, Claiborne Pell Papers, Special Collections, University of Rhode Island Library.

114. "a new London . . .": Amanda Smith, ed., *Hostage to Fortune*, 371–72.

114. "offering my soul . . .": *Ibid.*

114. "The big men of Berlin and London . . .": John F. Kennedy to Claiborne Pell, 16 September 1939, Claiborne Pell Papers, Special Collections, University of Rhode Island Library.

114. "that America has talked a lot about . . .": Joseph P. Kennedy, Sr., to Franklin D. Roosevelt, 10 September 1939, President's Personal File, FDR Library.

115. "within a relatively brief period . . .": Joseph P. Kennedy, Sr., to Cordell Hull, 11 September 1939, Cordell Hull Papers, Library of Congress.

115. "silliest message": James Farley, *Jim Farley's Story: The Roosevelt Years* (New York: Whittlesey, 1948), 198–99.

115. "Joe has been an appeaser . . .": John M. Blum, ed., *From the Morgenthau Diaries*, Vol. 2, *Years of Urgency, 1938–1941* (Boston: Houghton Mifflin, 1964), 102.

115. "As I see it . . .": John Wheeler-Bennett, *King George VI: His Life and Reign* (New York: St. Martin's Press, 1958), 419.

116. "This Government, so long as the present . . .": Cordell Hull to Joseph P. Kennedy, Sr., 11 September 1939, Cordell Hull Papers, Library of Congress.

116. "to help England and France economically . . .": Amanda Smith, ed., *Hostage to Fortune*, 377.

CHAPTER 11 (PAGES 117–129)

117. "People are sleeping . . .": Rose F. Kennedy, *Times to Remember*, 256.

118. "She is much happier . . .": Lynne McTaggart, *Kathleen Kennedy: Her Life and Times*, 220.

118. "That son of a bitch . . .": Amanda Smith, ed., *Hostage to Fortune*, 378.

119. "I talk to Bullitt occasionally . . .": Arthur Schlesinger, Jr., *Robert Kennedy and His Times*, 29.

119. "England and France can't quit . . .": Joseph P. Kennedy, Sr., to Franklin D. Roosevelt, 30 September 1939, President's Personal Files, FDR Library.

120. "energy and brains . . .": Rose F. Kennedy, *Times to Remember*, 261.

120. "conniving mind . . .": Amanda Smith, ed., *Hostage to Fortune*, 392–93.

120. "The Naval person . . .": *Ibid.*

120. "I can't help feeling . . .": *Ibid.*

120. "Incidentally, Beaverbrook told me . . .": Joseph P. Kennedy, Sr., to Franklin D. Roosevelt, 3 November 1939, President's Personal Files, FDR Library.

120. "a professing Catholic . . .": Whitehall Minute Books, Charles Peake entry, 12 October 1939, Foreign Office Archives, Public Records Office, Kew Gardens, Surrey.

121. "I wish that I could resist . . .": Whitehall Minute Books, John Balfour entry, 20 September 1939, Foreign Office Archives, Public Records Office, Kew Gardens, Surrey.

122. "A complaint might make him shut up . . .": Whitehall Minute Books, Sir Berkeley Gage entry, 26 September 1939, Foreign Office Archives, Public Records Office, Kew Gardens, Surrey.

122. "Kennedy has been adopting . . .": Whitehall Minute Books, 3 October 1939, Foreign Office Archives, Public Records Office, Kew Gardens, Surrey.

122. "Goodlooking, articulate . . .": Hank Searls, *The Lost Prince*, 133.

123. "for he is afraid . . .": *Ibid.*

123. "condemned the empirical . . .": Amanda Smith, ed., *Hostage to Fortune*, 381–82.

123. "There is every possibility . . .": *Harvard Crimson*, 9 October 1939. Blair Clark, then editor of the *Crimson*, has repeatedly confirmed Jack's authorship of the editorial in interviews with Nigel Hamilton, Doris Goodwin, and other researchers.

124. "Everyone here is still ready . . .": John F. Kennedy to Joseph P. Kennedy, Sr., n.d., John F.

Kennedy Personal Papers, Box 4B, Correspondence 1933–50, folder of items relating to Gene Schoor's *Young John Kennedy*, JFK Library.

125. "failure to utter one word . . .": John F. Kennedy, "League of Nations," John F. Kennedy Personal Papers, Box 4, JFK Library.

126. "Get something that likes lovin' . . .": Nigel Hamilton, *Reckless Youth*, 295.

126. "He's just the same": Rose F. Kennedy, *Times to Remember*, 256.

127. "This party is probably going to stop . . .": John F. Kennedy to Claiborne Pell, 14 October 1939, Claiborne Pell Papers, Special Collections, University of Rhode Island Library.

127. "He thinks [Churchill] is better in the Cabinet than out . . .": Amanda Smith, ed., *Hostage to Fortune*, 399.

127. "didn't look well": *Ibid.*, 402.

128. "[He] asked me to have . . .": *Ibid.*

128. "Eunice would like to go . . .": *Ibid.*

129. "plates to keep spinning on sticks": Henry Morgenthau, Jr., Diary, 11 November 1939, Henry Morgenthau Papers, FDR Library.

129. "Supposing, as I do not for one moment . . .": Walter Lippman Oral History, Oral History Project, Columbia University.

129. "The London Embassy announced . . .": *New York Times*, 7 December 1939.

129. "There was only one thing I really wanted to do . . .": Joseph P. Kennedy, Sr., "Diplomatic Memoirs," Chapter 37, p. 28.

129. "I'm all through . . .": *New York Times*, 7 December 1939.

CHAPTER 12 (PAGES 130–140)

130. Kennedy surprised reporters: *New York Times*, 9 December 1939.

130. "He didn't flash . . .": Joseph P. Kennedy, Sr., "Diplomatic Memoirs," Chapter 38, pp. 1–9.

132. "Farley's efforts to force . . .": *Ibid.*, Chapter 38, p. 15.

132. "The talk that I gave . . .": *New York Times*, 11 December 1939.

132. "I should not have been surprised by worse": Whitehall Minute Books, Sir Alexander Cadogan entry, 14 December 1939, Foreign Office Archives, Public Records Office, Kew Gardens, Surrey.

132. "Mr. Kennedy is a very foul specimen . . .": David E. Koskoff, *Joseph P. Kennedy* (Englewood Cliffs, N.J.: Prentice Hall, 1974), 329.

132. "Although I had made it clear . . .": Joseph P. Kennedy, Sr., "Diplomatic Memoirs," Chapter 38, p. 12.

133. "I could see . . .": *Ibid.*, Chapter 38, p. 17.

134. "that Germany would win . . .": Harold Ickes Diary, 10 March 1940, Harold Ickes Papers, Library of Congress.

135. "knowing myself as I do . . .": Rose F. Kennedy, *Times to Remember*, 262.

135. "If you mean by isolation[ist feeling] . . .": London *Times*, 8 March 1940.

135. "which I believe correctly summarized . . .": Joseph P. Kennedy, Sr., "Diplomatic Memoirs," Chapter 37, p. 12.

136. "to tell the people of the USA . . .": *Sunday Graphic*, 10 March 1940.

136. "I don't think any of the children should come . . .": Lynne McTaggart, *Kathleen Kennedy: Her Life and Times*, 77.

136. "not because he wants to . . .": Michael R. Beschloss, *Kennedy and Roosevelt*, 204.

137. "I had a talk with Mother Isabel . . .": Amanda Smith, ed., *Hostage to Fortune*, 470.

137. "work like a slave": Hank Searls, *The Lost Prince*, 136.

137. "increasingly overwhelmed . . .": Thomas J. Bilodeau Oral History, JFK Library.

138. "Jack rushed madly around . . .": Hank Searls, *The Lost Prince*, 156.

139. "too long, wordy . . .": Report card for "Appeasement at Munich," John F. Kennedy Personal Papers, Box 2, JFK Library.

139. "I suppose the best plan . . .": John F. Kennedy to Joseph P. Kennedy, Sr., n.d. (Spring 1940), John F. Kennedy Personal Papers, Box 4B, Correspondence 1933–50, folder of items relating to Gene Schoor's *Young John Kennedy*.

CHAPTER 13 (PAGES 141–151)

141. "I thought this would give me . . .": Joseph P. Kennedy, Sr., "Diplomatic Memoirs," Chapter 40, p. 10.

142. "The Norwegian invasion by Hitler . . .": Amanda Smith, ed., *Hostage to Fortune*, 418.

143. "I got a letter from Kick . . .": Lynne McTaggart, *Kathleen Kennedy: Her Life and Times*, 77.
143. "I gathered from your last letter . . .": John F. Kennedy to Joseph P. Kennedy, Sr., n.d. (Spring 1940), John F. Kennedy Personal Papers, Box 4B, Correspondence 1933–50, folder of items relating to Gene Schoor's *Young John Kennedy*, JFK Library.
143. "the honourable member from Berlin": John Halperin, *Eminent Georgians*, 219.
144. "Tomorrow morning . . .": Joseph P. Kennedy, Sr., to FDR and Cordell Hull, Diplomatic Dispatch, 15 May 1940, Cordell Hull Papers, Library of Congress.
145. "the situation is deadly acute. . . .": Joseph P. Kennedy, Sr., to FDR and Cordell Hull, Diplomatic Dispatch, 16 May 1940, Cordell Hull Papers, Library of Congress.
145. "Rarely, if ever before . . .": *New York Times*, 17 May 1940.
145. "Everyone is unanimous . . .": Hank Searls, *The Lost Prince*, 135.
146. "The situation is terrible . . .": Amanda Smith, ed., *Hostage to Fortune*, 432–33.
147. "And if they do come . . .": William Manchester, *The Last Lion: Alone, 1932–40*, 320.
147. "Grandpa thought I did . . .": Doris Kearns Goodwin, *The Fitzgeralds and the Kennedys*, 601.
147. "I had been hoping . . .": *Ibid.*, 602.
148. "[I made an appointment] . . .": Joseph P. Kennedy, Sr., "Diplomatic Memoirs," Chapter 38, p. 14.
148. "jackal and betrayer . . .": *Ibid.*
148. "worried about Ireland. . . .": Winston Churchill to Franklin D. Roosevelt, 12 June 1940, President's Personal Files, FDR Library.
149. "Your message . . .": Franklin D. Roosevelt to Paul Reynaud, 11 June 1940, President's Personal Files, FDR Library.
150. "I realize the tragedy . . .": Joseph P. Kennedy, Sr., to Franklin D. Roosevelt and Cordell Hull, Diplomatic Dispatch, 13 June 1940, Cordell Hull Papers, Library of Congress.
150. "As I asked . . .": Franklin D. Roosevelt to Winston Churchill, Diplomatic Dispatch, 14 June 1940, Cordell Hull Papers, Library of Congress.
151. "seemed very optimistic . . .": Joseph P. Kennedy, Sr., to Cordell Hull, 24 June 1940, Cordell Hull Papers, Library of Congress.
151. "We have to get those . . .": Joseph P. Kennedy, Sr., "Diplomatic Memoirs," Chapter 38, p. 17.

Chapter 14 (pages 152–164)

152. "The desperate need of . . .": *Boston Herald*, 20 May 1940.
152. "In an editorial on . . .": *Harvard Crimson*, 9 June 1940.
153. "I have come down to New York . . .": John F. Kennedy to Joseph P. Kennedy, Sr., n.d., John F. Kennedy Personal Papers, Box 4B, Correspondence 1933–50, folder of items relating to Gene Schoor's *Young John Kennedy*.
154. "I can't say that I did more than polish . . .": Arthur Krock Oral History, JFK Library.
154. "the disastrous turn of events . . .": Bertram Aswell to Gertrude Algase, 18 June 1940, HarperCollins Archives.
154. "Any system of government will work . . .": John F. Kennedy, *Why England Slept* (New York: Wilfred Funk, 1940), 17.
155. "England . . . stood alone . . .": Henry Luce Oral History, JFK Library.
155. "America will never be ready for any war . . .": John F. Kennedy, *Why England Slept*, xiv.
156. "busily comes and goes . . .": John F. Kennedy to Claiborne Pell, 7 July 1940, Claiborne Pell Papers, Special Collections, University of Rhode Island Library.
156. "Jack was autographing . . .": Charles Spalding Oral History, JFK Library.
156. "Thanks a lot Daddy . . .": Doris Kearns Goodwin, *The Fitzgeralds and the Kennedys*, 606.
157. "At the moment . . .": Lynne McTaggart, *Kathleen Kennedy: Her Life and Times*, 78–79.
157. "the height of nonsense . . .": Joseph P. Kennedy, Sr., to Cordell Hull, 12 July 1940, Cordell Hull Papers, Library of Congress.
157. "I hope that at Washington . . .": Whitehall Minute Books, Sir John Balfour entry, 22 August 1940, Foreign Office Archives, Public Records Office, Kew Gardens, Surrey.
158. Jack told friends: K. LeMoyne Billings Oral History, JFK Library.
159. "a great argument for . . .": Franklin D. Roosevelt to John F. Kennedy, 27 August 1940, copy in Pre-Presidential Papers, JFK Library.
159. "the son of the Ambassador . . .": *New York Sun*, 2 August 1940.
159. "very immature . . .": Max Freedman, ed., *Roosevelt and Frankfurter: Their Correspondence, 1928–45*, 590.
160. "a self-centered, frightened rich man . . .": Kingsley Martin, ed., *New Statesman Years, 1931–45*, 313.

160. "The English people . . .": Amanda Smith, ed., *Hostage to Fortune*, 451.
160. "Saw Joe Kennedy . . .": Ian MacLeod, *Neville Chamberlain* (New York: Atheneum, 1962), 279.
161. "He just loved to go to church . . .": Hank Searls, *The Lost Prince*, 148.
161. "Young Kennedy pleads for immediate conscription . . .": *Boston Herald*, 5 August 1940.
162. Jack shortly complained to his brother: Nigel Hamilton, *Reckless Youth*, 341–42.
162. "John F. Kennedy, 23 . . .": *Boston Herald*, 10 September 1940.
163. "under the threat of bombing": Joseph P. Kennedy, Sr., "Diplomatic Memoirs," Chapter 48, p. 12.
163. "Regarding our last telephonic conversation . . .": Joseph P. Kennedy, Sr., to Franklin D. Roosevelt, 27 August 1940, File 123, State Department Archives.

CHAPTER 15 (PAGES 165–178)

165. "I have become one of Roosevelt's . . .": Joseph P. Kennedy, Jr., to Nancy Astor, 7 October 1940, copy lent by Major Sir John Astor.
165. "I don't like the idea of being summoned . . .": John F. Kennedy to Claiborne Pell, 6 October 1940, Claiborne Pell Papers, Special Collections, University of Rhode Island Library.
166. sunbathed constantly: Nigel Hamilton, *Reckless Youth*, 349.
166. "like a Jap": John F. Kennedy to Claiborne Pell, 6 October 1940, Claiborne Pell Papers, Special Collections, University of Rhode Island Library.
167. intended to hold on to his Catholic affiliation: Nigel Hamilton, *Reckless Youth*, 357.
167. "The holder of 2748 . . .": *Stanford Daily*, 30 October 1940.
167. "This draft has caused me a bit of concern . . .": John F. Kennedy to K. LeMoyne Billings, 14 November 1940, John F. Kennedy Personal Papers, Box 4A, folder of K. LeMoyne Billings correspondence, JFK Library.
167. "the unhappy political future . . .": John F. Kennedy to Claiborne Pell, 12 November 1940, Claiborne Pell Papers, Special Collections, University of Rhode Island Library.
168. "There has been plenty of bombing . . .": Rose F. Kennedy, *Times to Remember*, 272–74.
168. "The house . . . that I live in . . .": *Ibid.*
169. "wasn't very cordial . . .": Joseph P. Kennedy, Sr., "Diplomatic Memoirs," Chapter 48, p. 6.
169. "The people here keep saying . . .": Joseph P. Kennedy, Sr., to John F. Kennedy, 10 September 1940, John F. Kennedy Personal Papers, Box 4A, Correspondence 1933–50, folder of letters from Joseph P. Kennedy, Sr., to John F. Kennedy, 1940–45.
169. "To enter this war . . .": Joseph P. Kennedy, Sr., "Diplomatic Memoirs," Chapter 49, p. 10.
169. "if the English people thought . . .": *Ibid.*, Chapter 46, p. 29.
170. "the President regards Kennedy . . .": *Boston Globe*, 7 October 1940.
170. "put twenty-five million votes . . .": Michael R. Beschloss, *Kennedy and Roosevelt*, 16.
170. "When I asked him what would be . . .": Lord Halifax to Lord Lothian, 10 October 1940, FO 371/24251, Public Records Office, Kew Gardens, Sussex, England.
170. "The article which Mr. Kennedy has written . . .": Foreign Office Memorandum marked "Secret" and dated 18 October 1940, FO 371/24251, Public Records Office, Kew Gardens, Sussex, England.
171. "indignant": Joseph P. Kennedy, Sr., "Diplomatic Memoirs," Chapter 51, p. 1.
171. "Ah, Joe. It is good to hear . . .": Arthur Krock, *Memoirs: Sixty Years on the Firing Line*, 399.
172. as an ingrate . . .": *Ibid.*, 405.
172. At the White House . . . : James F. Byrnes, *All in One Lifetime* (New York: Harper & Brothers, 1958), 125.
173. "if I did that, my attitude . . .": Joseph P. Kennedy, Sr., "Diplomatic Memoirs," Chapter 51, p. 6.
173. "On Sunday, I returned from war-torn Europe . . .": *New York Times*, 29 October 1940.
173. "Kennedy has no depth . . .": James Leutze, ed., *The London Journals of General Raymond E. Lee*, 1940–1941 (Boston: Little, Brown, 1971), 115.
174. "welcome back to the shores of America . . .": *New York Times*, 1 November 1940.
174. "or the greatest horse's ass": Joseph P. Kennedy, Sr., "Diplomatic Memoirs," Chapter 51, p. 17.
175. "Democracy is all finished . . .": *Boston Globe*, 10 November 1940.
175. "unguarded talk": *New York Times*, 11 November 1940.
175. told FDR he must publicly condemn Kennedy: William H. Tuttle, Jr., "A Reappraisal of William Allen White's Leadership," *Journal of American History*, March 1970, 856.
175. "democracy is finished because it is making . . .": *New York Herald Tribune*, 5 December 1940.
175. "We can forgive wrongheadedness . . .": George Murray, "The Strange Case of Mr. Kennedy," London *Daily Mail*, 12 November 1940.

175. "the Lindbergh appeasement groups . . .": Douglas Fairbanks, Jr., to Franklin D. Roosevelt, 5 December 1940, President's Personal File, FDR Library.
176. "scare the Jews out of the film business . . .": Darryl Zanuck to Joseph Alsop, 16 December 1940, Joseph and Stewart Alsop Papers, Library of Congress.
176. "many people are beginning to feel . . .": Douglas Fairbanks, Jr., to Franklin D. Roosevelt, 5 December 1940, President's Personal File, FDR Library.
176. "After our talk with Joe in California . . .": John Boettiger to Franklin D. Roosevelt, 19 February 1941, Anna Roosevelt Halsted Papers, FDR Library.
176. Boettiger and Kennedy had nearly come to blows: Marion Davies, *The Times We Had* (New York: Bobbs-Merrill, 1976), 222–24.
177. "I never want to see that son of a bitch . . .": Joseph P. Lash, *Eleanor: The Years Alone* (New York: W.W. Norton, 1972), 287.
177. "an outstanding example . . .": Harold Ickes Diary, 13 December 1940, Harold Ickes Papers, Library of Congress.
178. "While our own defenses are weak . . .": *Washington Times Herald*, 20 December 1940.
178. "unwitting . . .": *New York Times*, 30 December 1940.

CHAPTER 16 (PAGES 179–186)

179. "international generosity . . .": Samuel I. Rosenman, ed., *The Public Papers and Addresses of Franklin D. Roosevelt, 1940* (New York: Random House, 1941), 663–72.
180. "I hate all those God-damned Englishmen . . .": J. J. Astor to Brendan Bracken, 19 February 1941, File 371, British Foreign Office Archives.
181. "He told me he would like to have a long talk . . .": Nigel Hamilton, *Reckless Youth*, 397.
181. "to be *and* not to be": *New York Herald Tribune*, 22 January 1941, 17.
181. "Many Americans . . .": *Washington Post*, 19 January 1941, 5.
182. "I would not want to answer . . .": *Hearings Before the Committee on Foreign Affairs, House of Representatives, 77th Congress, 1st Session, on H.R. 1776*, 221–315.
182. "almost as good a witness . . .": Michael R. Beschloss, *Kennedy and Roosevelt*, 240.
183. "prove wrong all those . . .": Hank Searls, *The Lost Prince*, 156.
183. "There is a real feeling here . . .": John F. Kennedy to Claiborne Pell, 11 December 1940, Claiborne Pell Papers, Special Collections, University of Rhode Island Library.
184. "the same sleep that brought England . . .": John F. Kennedy, "Should Ireland Give Naval and Air Bases to England?" *New York Journal-American*, 2 February 1941.
184. "would be strongly influenced by . . .": Rose F. Kennedy, *Times to Remember*, 279.
184. "unlimited national emergency": *New York Times*, 27 May 1941.
185. "the first and fundamental fact . . .": *New York Times*, 28 May 1941.
185. "a most historic and most solemn . . .": *New York Times*, 2 June 1941.
185. "Everyone feels that we are in the war . . .": Lynne McTaggart, *Kathleen Kennedy: Her Life and Times*, 90.
186. At some point during his stay: Nigel Hamilton, *Reckless Youth*, 404.

CHAPTER 17 (PAGES 187–200)

187. "Wouldn't you know it? . . .": Hank Searls, *The Lost Prince*, 162.
187. he was enthusiastic about joining a fighting force: Author interview with John Jerome Cabitor, Harvard '38.
188. A friend remembered him . . . : John F. Kennedy, ed., *As We Remember Joe*, 19.
190. "Don't they have souls? . . .": Hank Searls, *The Lost Prince*, 164.
191. "I am rapidly reaching a point where . . .": John F. Kennedy to Claiborne Pell, 27 July 1941, Claiborne Pell Papers, Special Collections, University of Rhode Island Library.
192. "a very unusual youngster. . . .": Office of Naval Intelligence, Investigative Report on John F. Kennedy, 10 September 1941, John F. Kennedy Personal Papers, JFK Library.
192. "Macdonald came down to crew . . .": Nigel Hamilton, *Reckless Youth*, 409.
193. "too much smarts . . .": Author interview with Senator Claiborne Pell.
193. "We let our hair down. . . .": Author interview with Ambassador Samuel Campiche.
193. "I have just had lunch with Dinah Brand . . .": Amanda Smith, ed., *Hostage to Fortune*, 532.
194. "Received letter from Billy last night. . . .": *Ibid.*, 533.
194. "There were six of us in the room . . .": Joan Blair and Clay Blair, Jr., *The Search for JFK* (New York: G. P. Putnam's Sons, 1976), 120.

195. "there was not a real emergency . . .": John F. Kennedy, Memorandum: "Dinner at Mrs. Patterson's," Speech and Book Materials, 11 November 1941–23 January 1942, Pre-Presidential Papers, Box 11, JFK Library.
195. "An old Scandinavian proverb . . .": *Washington Times Herald*, 27 November 1941.
197. share not only his cynicism, but his bed: Lynne McTaggart, *Kathleen Kennedy: Her Life and Times*, 102.
197. "Oh, Daddy considers . . .": Doris Kearns Goodwin, *The Fitzgeralds and the Kennedys*, 631.
197. sullen and hypercritical: Author interview with Senator Claiborne Pell.
198. "These unfortunates . . .": Marguerite Clark, "Surgery in Mental Cases," *American Mercury*, March 1941.
198. "The operation eliminated . . .": Rose F. Kennedy, *Times to Remember*, 287.
199. "Joe and I brought the most eminent . . .": *Ibid.*, 286.
199. "has returned to the surface of my character . . .": John F. Kennedy to Claiborne Pell, 5 December 1941, Claiborne Pell Papers, Special Collections, University of Rhode Island Library.
200. "I particularly disliked . . .": K. LeMoyne Billings Oral History, JFK Library.

CHAPTER 18 (PAGES 201–215)

201. "On the afternoon of December 12 . . .": Memorandum for the Director, 12 December 1941, Hoover Confidential Files, JFK Library.
203. "very pro-Nazi . . .": Ronald Kessler, *The Sins of the Father*, 259.
203. "One of ex-Ambassador Kennedy's eligible sons . . .": New York *Daily News*, 12 January 1942.
203. "came boiling down . . .": Nigel Hamilton, *Reckless Youth*, 440.
204. "Inga returned with an infected throat. . . .": Kathleen Kennedy to John F. Kennedy, 28 January 1942, John F. Kennedy Personal Papers, Box 4A, Correspondence 1933–50, folder of Kathleen Kennedy correspondence, 1942–47, JFK Library.
204. "He wants fame, the money . . .": Inga Arvad to John F. Kennedy, 26 January 1942, John F. Kennedy Personal Papers, Box 4A, Correspondence 1933–50, folder of letters from Inga Arvad, JFK Library.
205. "Distrust is a very funny thing . . .": *Ibid.*, 27 January 1942, JFK Library.
205. "[I] saw Inga [and] had a long chat with her . . .": Torbert MacDonald to John F. Kennedy, n.d., John F. Kennedy Personal Papers, Box 4B, Correspondence 1933–50, folder of Torbert MacDonald correspondence, JFK Library.
205. "You always say you have faith . . .": Inga Arvad to John F. Kennedy, 14 February 1942, John F. Kennedy Personal Papers, Box 4A, Correspondence 1933–50, folder of letters from Inga Arvad, JFK Library.
205. "Kennedy and Mrs. Fejos engaged in . . .": D. M. Ladd, "Memorandum for the Director," 6 February 1942, Hoover Confidential Files, JFK Library.
206. "more truth than poetry": Nigel Hamilton, *Reckless Youth*, 456.
206. "My plans are as usual varied . . .": John F. Kennedy to K. LeMoyne Billings, 14 February 1941, John F. Kennedy Personal Papers, Box 4A, folder of K. LeMoyne Billings correspondence, JFK Library.
207. "wasn't happy at all . . .": K. LeMoyne Billings Oral History, JFK Library.
207. "Have I discussed Southerners with you? . . .": John F. Kennedy to K. LeMoyne Billings, 14 February 1941, John F. Kennedy Personal Papers, Box 4A, folder of K. LeMoyne Billings correspondence, JFK Library.
207. "Kathleen [is] sweet . . .": Inga Arvad to John F. Kennedy, dated "Monday, 1942," John F. Kennedy Personal Papers, Box 4A, JFK Library.
208. "I may as well admit . . .": Inga Arvad to John F. Kennedy, 11 March 1942, John F. Kennedy Personal Papers, Box 4A, Correspondence 1933–50, folder of letters from Inga Arvad, JFK Library.
208. "The newspapers still go on printing . . .": John F. Kennedy to Ralph Horton, n.d., written from Charleston, John F. Kennedy Personal Papers, Box 4B, Correspondence 1933–50, folder of Ralph Horton correspondence, JFK Library.
209. "Have been offered commission . . .": Torbert Macdonald to John F. Kennedy, n.d., John F. Kennedy Personal Papers, Box 4B, Correspondence 1933–50, folder of Torbert Macdonald correspondence, JFK Library.
209. "Macdonald is up in Boston. . . .": John F. Kennedy to Claiborne Pell, 3 January 1942, Claiborne Pell Papers, Special Collections, University of Rhode Island Library.
210. "I swear to God Kennedy . . .": Torbert Macdonald to John F. Kennedy, 9 March 1942, John F.

Kennedy Personal Papers, Box 4B, Correspondence 1933–50, folder of Torbert Macdonald correspondence, JFK Library.

211. "Mr. Kaltenborn, do you think . . .": Lynne McTaggart, *Kathleen Kennedy: Her Life and Times*, 113–14.

211. "Name the battle post . . .": Joseph P. Kennedy to Franklin D. Roosevelt, 4 March 1942, President's Personal File, FDR Library.

211. "A funny thing happened . . .": Kathleen Kennedy to her parents, 20 March 1942, John F. Kennedy Personal Papers, Box 4A, Correspondence 1933–50, folder of Kathleen Kennedy correspondence, 1942–47, JFK Library.

212. "pessimistic on all fronts . . .": John F. Kennedy to Claiborne Pell, 12 March 1942, Claiborne Pell Papers, Special Collections, University of Rhode Island Library.

212. "has been greatly handicapped . . .": Nigel Hamilton, *Reckless Youth*, 490.

213. "This student does not . . .": Hank Searls, *The Lost Prince*, 168–69.

214. "I saw young Joe in Jacksonville . . .": Doris Kearns Goodwin, *The Fitzgeralds and the Kennedys*, 623.

214. "temporarily incapacitated": Hank Searls, *The Lost Prince*, 170–71.

214. "Student is tense in cockpit. . . .": *Ibid.*

214. "The sight of those boys . . .": Joseph P. Kennedy, Sr., to G. R. Fairlamb, 12 May 1942, G. R. Fairlamb Papers, Naval War College, Newport.

215. "I got an excited note . . .": Kathleen Kennedy to John F. Kennedy, 20 May 1942, John F. Kennedy Personal Papers, Box 4A, Correspondence 1933–50, folder of Kathleen Kennedy correspondence, 1942–47, JFK Library.

CHAPTER 19 (PAGES 216–226)

217. "At present I am teaching . . .": Hank Searls, *The Lost Prince*, 173.

217. "You wouldn't think this very important . . .": Doris Kearns Goodwin, *The Fitzgeralds and the Kennedys*, 625.

218. "I am awfully sorry to hear . . .": Joseph P. Kennedy, Jr., to Joseph P. Kennedy, Sr., October 1942, Joseph P. Kennedy Papers, JFK Library.

219. "I think it would be a mistake . . .": K. LeMoyne Billings to John F. Kennedy, n.d., 1942, "Friday," John F. Kennedy Personal Papers, Box 4A, folder of K. LeMoyne Billings correspondence, JFK Library.

219. nothing short of anxious: John W. Horner to John F. Kennedy, n.d., John F. Kennedy Personal Papers, Box 4A, Correspondence 1933–50, Joseph P. Kennedy, Jr., Condolence Mail, Folder 1, JFK Library.

219. "I understand you and Bunny Waters . . .": Joseph P. Kennedy, Jr., to John F. Kennedy, n.d., "Tuesday," John F. Kennedy Personal Papers, Box 4A, Correspondence 1933–50, folder of letters and telegrams from Joseph P. Kennedy, Jr., JFK Library.

219. "He has become disgusted with the desk jobs . . .": Doris Kearns Goodwin, *The Fitzgeralds and the Kennedys*, 634.

220. "[Jack] went through town . . .": Nigel Hamilton, *Reckless Youth*, 494.

220. "I think the break-up with Inga . . .": Torbert Macdonald Oral History, JFK Library.

220. to break faith with the father: Charles Spalding Oral History, JFK Library.

220. "Jack always had something to prove . . .": K. LeMoyne Billings Interview, Audiovisual Archives, JFK Library.

221. "a cross-section of American manhood . . .": *Chicago Herald-American*, 25 September 1942.

221. "a good bunch . . .": John F. Kennedy to K. LeMoyne Billings, n.d. (July 1942), John F. Kennedy Personal Papers, Box 4A, folder of K. LeMoyne Billings correspondence, JFK Library.

221. "They want me to conduct . . .": Doris Kearns Goodwin, *The Fitzgeralds and the Kennedys*, 635.

223. "may have gotten his big 'S' . . .": John F. Kennedy to K. LeMoyne Billings, n.d., John F. Kennedy Personal Papers, Box 4A, folder of K. LeMoyne Billings correspondence, JFK Library.

223. "magnetic and charismatic . . .": John F. Kennedy to Claiborne Pell, 5 September 1942, Claiborne Pell Papers, Special Collections, University of Rhode Island Library.

223. "surpassing courage . . .": "Bulkeley Asks 50—1,024 Volunteer!" *New York Herald-American*, 5 September 1942.

224. "quite ready to die for the USA . . .": Rose F. Kennedy to Family, 9 October 1942, John F. Kennedy Personal Papers, Box 4A, JFK Library.

224. "[The Ambassador] had a lot of bitter things to say . . .": William B. Breuer, *Sea Wolf: A Biography of John D. Bulkeley, USN* (Novato, Calif.: Presidio Press, 1989), 108.
225. "I've known Georgie almost longer . . .": Kathleen Kennedy to Nancy Astor, 24 September 1942, copy lent by Major Sir John Astor.

CHAPTER 20 (PAGES 227–237)

228. "But these things can't be faked. . . .": Author interview with Karen O. Jones.
228. "Jack came home . . .": Amanda Smith, ed., *Hostage to Fortune*, 548.
228. Rosen persuaded Kennedy . . . : Nigel Hamilton, *Reckless Youth*, 512.
229. "The first time I ever fired a torpedo . . .": Nigel Hamilton, *Reckless Youth*, 514.
230. "The Training Center . . . tried desperately . . .": Anonymous, "Administrative History of PTs," unpublished manuscript on deposit in the Naval Historical Collection, Naval War College Archives, Newport, Rhode Island.
230. "not to believe everything one is told . . .": John F. Kennedy to Claiborne Pell, 30 October 1942, Claiborne Pell Papers, Special Collections, University of Rhode Island Library.
230. "Add into that equation . . .": John F. Kennedy to Claiborne Pell, 27 October 1942, Claiborne Pell Papers, Special Collections, University of Rhode Island Library.
231. "a sincere and hardworking student . . .": John Harllee Oral History, JFK Library.
231. "receptive to everybody . . .": Nigel Hamilton, *Reckless Youth*, 512–13.
231. "[Jack] was such an outstanding student . . .": John Harllee Oral History, JFK Library.
232. "I got Torb in here yesterday . . .": John F. Kennedy to K. LeMoyne Billings, 19 November 1942, John F. Kennedy Personal Papers, Box 4A, folder of K. LeMoyne Billings correspondence, JFK Library.
232. "practical steps . . .": John F. Kennedy to Claiborne Pell, 12 November 1942, Claiborne Pell Papers, Special Collections, University of Rhode Island Library.
232. "ripping an operations manual . . .": Torbert Macdonald Oral History, JFK Library.
233. "outclassed the heavier one . . .": Paul B. Fay, *The Pleasure of His Company* (New York: Harper & Row, 1966), 135–37.
234. "gastro-enteritis, acute": Navy Medical Record, Lt. John F. Kennedy, John F. Kennedy Personal Papers, Box 11a, JFK Library.
234. "I'm now on my way to war . . .": John F. Kennedy to K. LeMoyne Billings, 30 January 1943, John F. Kennedy Personal Papers, Box 4A, folder of K. LeMoyne Billings correspondence, JFK Library.
235. "Having reached my limit on bullshit . . .": John F. Kennedy to Claiborne Pell, 23 February 1943, Claiborne Pell Papers, Special Collections, University of Rhode Island Library.
235. "proceed via government or commercial air . . .": Chief of Naval Personnel to Lt. (j.g.) John F. Kennedy, 19 February 1943, John F. Kennedy Personal Papers, Box 11, JFK Library.
236. "journeyed to the PBM Squadron . . .": E. G. Johnstone to JFK, n.d., John F. Kennedy Personal Papers, Box 9, Correspondence 1943–52, folder of items relating to Joseph P. Kennedy, Jr.'s, naval career, JFK Library.
236. "He [Joe] stood for perfection in himself . . .": Hank Searls, *The Lost Prince*, 175.
236. "I thought he was a typical . . .": *Ibid.*
237. "lived a good bit of his life . . .": John F. Kennedy to Parents, 10 May 1943, John F. Kennedy Personal Papers, Box 5, JFK Library.
237. "He had a certain aura of shyness . . .": Nigel Hamilton, *Reckless Youth*, 527.
237. "was very basic . . .": "Edgar Stephens Remembers JFK He Knew in Navy," *Albany Gazette* (New Albany, Missouri), 23 November and 25 November 1988.
237. "long and valuable chats with Jack . . .": Author interview with Samuel Hall Whitley II.

CHAPTER 21 (PAGES 238–245)

240. "As we were carrying . . .": John Kennedy to K. LeMoyne Billings, 6 May 1943, John F. Kennedy Personal Papers, Box 4A, folder of K. LeMoyne Billings correspondence, JFK Library.
241. "Have my own boat now . . .": John F. Kennedy to Rose and Joseph Kennedy, n.d., John F. Kennedy Personal Papers, Box 5, Family Correspondence Folder, JFK Library.
242. "good stuff": John F. Kennedy to K. LeMoyne Billings, n.d., John F. Kennedy Personal Papers, Box 4A, folder of K. LeMoyne Billings correspondence, JFK Library.

242. "greatly illusioned . . .": Nigel Hamilton, *Reckless Youth*, 533.
242. "gut and back . . .": John F. Kennedy to K. LeMoyne Billings, n.d., John F. Kennedy Personal Papers, Box 4A, folder of K. LeMoyne Billings correspondence, JFK Library.
243. "We had one in today . . .": John F. Kennedy to his parents, 15 May 1943, typescript copy, John F. Kennedy Personal Papers, Box 5, Family Correspondence Folder, JFK Library.
243. "We go out on patrol . . .": Doris Kearns Goodwin, *The Fitzgeralds and the Kennedys*, 648.
243. "On good nights it's beautiful . . .": John F. Kennedy to his parents, 15 May 1943, typescript copy, John F. Kennedy Personal Papers, Box 5, Family Correspondence Folder, JFK Library.
244. "Here he has none . . .": *Ibid.*
245. "they have been pretty good about relieving us . . .": John F. Kennedy to K. LeMoyne Billings, n.d., John F. Kennedy Personal Papers, Box 4A, folder of K. LeMoyne Billings correspondence, JFK Library.

Chapter 22 (pages 246–255)

246. "You will be pleased to know . . .": John F. Kennedy to Family, 24 June 1943, John F. Kennedy Personal Papers, Box 5, Family Correspondence Folder, JFK Library.
247. "buried near the beach where he fell . . .": John F. Kennedy to Rose and Joseph P. Kennedy, n.d., John F. Kennedy Personal Papers, Box 5, Family Correspondence Folder, JFK Library.
247. "the mingled bondage . . .": John Buchan, *Pilgrim's Way* (Boston: Houghton Mifflin, 1940), 50.
247. "bulge . . .": John F. Kennedy to his parents, n.d., April 1943, John F. Kennedy Personal Papers, Box 5, Family Correspondence Folder, JFK Library.
247. "and he polished off five scotches . . .": John F. Kennedy to Kathleen Kennedy, 3 June 1943, typescript copy, John F. Kennedy Personal Papers, Box 5, JFK Library. The Hersey article Jack references is "PT Squadron in the South Pacific," which appeared in the 10 May 1943 issue of *Life*.
248. "lying on a cool . . .": *Ibid.*
248. "figured an angle": Kathleen Kennedy to Nancy Astor, n.d., copy lent by Major Sir John Astor.
249. "It really is the most pathetic . . .": Kathleen Kennedy to family, 27 June 1943, John F. Kennedy Personal Papers, Box 5, Family Correspondence Folder, JFK Library.
249. "At the moment I am sunning myself . . .": Kathleen Kennedy to John F. Kennedy, 3 July 1943, John F. Kennedy Personal Papers, Box 5, JFK Library.
250. "The Director just had a little chat . . .": Doris Kearns Goodwin, *The Fitzgeralds and the Kennedys*, 666.
251. "You don't need to be entertained . . .": Lynne McTaggart, *Kathleen Kennedy: Her Life and Times*, 137.
251. "Aren't you longing to hear . . .": Kathleen Kennedy to K. LeMoyne Billings, 25 March 1943, John F. Kennedy Personal Papers, Box 4A, JFK Library.
252. "They have quite a small house . . .": Kathleen Kennedy to family, 14 July 1943, John F. Kennedy Personal Papers, Box 5, JFK Library.
252. "they were of three faiths . . .": Author interview with Don Dirst.
253. "The most excited man in the room . . .": Hank Searls, *The Lost Prince*, 180.
254. "The B-24 was an aircraft . . .": *Ibid.*
254. "He wasn't going to fix it . . .": Evan Thomas, *Robert Kennedy: His Life*, 33.

Chapter 23 (pages 256–273)

258. "the biggest shit . . .": Nigel Hamilton, *Reckless Youth*, 552.
259. "This work, once dull . . .": John F. Kennedy to Claiborne Pell, 29 July 1943, Claiborne Pell Papers, Special Collections, University of Rhode Island Library.
259. "He never really got over it . . .": Doris Kearns Goodwin, *The Fitzgeralds and the Kennedys*, 652.
260. "We mostly live on the boats . . .": John F. Kennedy to Family, n.d., received 10 August 1943, John F. Kennedy Personal Papers, Box 5, Family Correspondence Folder, JFK Library.
260. "Well, take care . . .": Kathleen Kennedy to John F. Kennedy, 29 July 1943, John F. Kennedy Personal Papers, Box 5, JFK Library.
261. "The time was about 0230. . . .": Lt. (jg) Byron R. White and Lt. (jg) J. G. McClure, six-page report entitled "Sinking of PT-109 and subsequent rescue of survivors," 24 August 1943, declassified April 1964, John F. Kennedy Personal Papers, Box 6, JFK Library.
262. "It was so dark . . .": Nigel Hamilton, *Reckless Youth*, 580.
262. "we spotted [the *Amagiri*] . . .": Barney Ross Interview, Audiovisual Archives, JFK Library.

263. "There was a lot of criticism . . .": Joan Blair and Clay Blair, Jr., *The Search for JFK*, 342.
263. "the mast keeling over . . .": Barney Ross Interview, Audiovisual Archives, JFK Library.
264. "We lay on the front of the bow . . .": Nigel Hamilton, *Reckless Youth*, 580.
264. "As dawn came up . . .": Barney Ross Interview, Audiovisual Archives, JFK Library.
265. "Scabs forming over his burned eyelids . . .": Robert J. Donovan, *PT 109* (New York: McGraw-Hill, 1961), 169.
266. "I think he felt that if . . .": Barney Ross Interview, Audiovisual Archives, JFK Library.
267. "He read the riot act . . .": Joan Blair and Clay Blair, Jr., *The Search for JFK*, 272.
267. "the most nimble of our group . . .": Barney Ross Interview, Audiovisual Archives, JFK Library.
267. "Neither seeing nor hearing anything . . .": Lt. (jg) Byron R. White and Lt. (jg) J. G. McClure, six-page report entitled "Sinking of PT-109 and subsequent rescue of survivors," 24 August 1943, declassified April 1964, John F. Kennedy Personal Papers, Box 6, JFK Library.
268. "He had a higher metabolism . . .": Barney Ross Interview, Audiovisual Archives, JFK Library.
269. "NARU ISL . . .": The original coconut is on display at the JFK Library, Boston.
269. "I guess this would be a fine time . . .": Barney Ross Interview, Audiovisual Archives, JFK Library.
270. "did service above and beyond . . .": John F. Kennedy to Clare Boothe Luce, n.d., Clare Boothe Luce Papers, Library of Congress.
270. "As I remember it . . .": Barney Ross Interview, Audiovisual Archives, JFK Library.
270. "at present time . . . shows . . .": Medical Report, Lieutenant John F. Kennedy, John F. Kennedy Personal Papers, Box 11a, JFK Library.
271. "He was in this hospital . . .": Joan Blair and Clay Blair, Jr., *The Search for JFK*, 272.
271. "I think it was guilt . . .": Nigel Hamilton, *Reckless Youth*, 608.
271. "Several days later . . .": Rose F. Kennedy, *Times to Remember*, 293.
272. "KENNEDY'S SON SAVES 10 . . .": *Boston Globe*, 19 August 1943.
272. "Former Ambassador and Mrs. Kennedy . . .": *New York Times*, 20 August 1943.
272. "On the bright side of an otherwise . . .": John F. Kennedy to Rose and Joseph P. Kennedy, n.d., letter received 12 September 1945, typescript copy, John F. Kennedy Personal Papers, Box 5, JFK Library.
272. "considerably upset . . .": Doris Kearns Goodwin, *The Fitzgeralds and the Kennedys*, 662.
273. "Ambassador Joe Kennedy, father of our hero . . .": Hank Searls, *The Lost Prince*, 183.

CHAPTER 24 (PAGES 274–281)

274. "A small stove which takes . . .": Doris Kearns Goodwin, *The Fitzgeralds and the Kennedys*, 671.
274. "men and women of the Royal Air Force . . .": John F. Kennedy, ed., *As We Remember Joe*, 7–8.
276. "There's heavy betting . . .": Doris Kearns Goodwin, *The Fitzgeralds and the Kennedys*, 669.
276. "As far as I'm concerned . . .": Lynne McTaggart, *Kathleen Kennedy: Her Life and Times*, 155.
277. "and a big harp if there ever was one. . . .": John F. Kennedy to his parents, n.d., received 12 September 1945, typescript copy, John F. Kennedy Personal Papers, Box 5, Family Correspondence Folder, JFK Library.
277. "the Japs are using now . . .": *Ibid.*
277. "Mauer and I went down to the dock . . .": *Boston Globe*, 21 June 1989.
278. "I am in a bad spot . . .": John F. Kennedy to Joseph P. Kennedy, Sr., letter mailed 30 October 1943, typescript copy, John F. Kennedy Personal Papers, Box 5, Family Correspondence Folder, JFK Library.
278. "packed with a great deal in the way of death": John F. Kennedy to Claiborne Pell, 10 November 1943, Claiborne Pell Papers, Special Collections, University of Rhode Island Library.
278. "Tough accident happened the other day. . . .": John F. Kennedy to his family, letter received 1 November 1943, typescript copy, John F. Kennedy Personal Papers, Box 5, Family Correspondence Folder, JFK Library.
279. "a definite ulcer crater": Report of Medical Survey for Retirement Board, 16 October 1944, John F. Kennedy Personal Papers, Box 11a, JFK Library.
279. "fairly definite dope . . .": John F. Kennedy to his family, 7 December 1943, John F. Kennedy Personal Papers, Box 5, Family Correspondence Folder, JFK Library.
279. "Life is just about the same here . . .": Torbert Macdonald to John F. Kennedy, 7 December 1943, John F. Kennedy Personal Papers, Box 4B, Correspondence 1933–50, folder of Torbert Macdonald correspondence, JFK Library.
279. "He was trying to get his health back up . . .": Nigel Hamilton, *Reckless Youth*, 629.

279. "chronic disc disease . . .": Report of Medical Survey for Retirement Board, 16 October 1944, John F. Kennedy Personal Papers, Box 11a, JFK Library.
280. "TELLS STORY OF PT EPIC . . .": *Boston Globe*, 11 January 1943.
280. "his bronze tired face . . .": Amanda Smith, ed., *Hostage to Fortune*, 573.
281. "Regardless of what some of us . . .": *Ibid.*, 574.

CHAPTER 25 (PAGES 282–288)

282. "Billy made about ten speeches . . .": Kathleen Kennedy to K. LeMoyne Billings, 23 February 1944, K. LeMoyne Billings Papers, JFK Library.
283. "most efficient driving a car etc.": Amanda Smith, ed., *Hostage to Fortune*, 574. Note: Kick and Wood briefly considered marriage after the war.
283. "Poor Billy is very, very sad . . .": Doris Kearns Goodwin, *The Fitzgeralds and the Kennedys*, 674.
284. "anytime for any amounts": Lynne McTaggart, *Kathleen Kennedy: Her Life and Times*, 155.
285. "Kick can do no wrong.": Ronald Kessler, *The Sins of the Father*, 321.
286. "He's the boy they thought was lost . . .": *Boston Globe*, 12 February 1944.
286. "Come and buy . . .": *Ibid.*
286. "like Sinatra": Author interview with Claiborne Pell.
287. "I feel . . . that our group . . .": Nigel Hamilton, *Reckless Youth*, 645.
287. "I read the piece . . .": Joseph P. Kennedy, Jr., to John F. Kennedy, 10 August 1944, John F. Kennedy Personal Papers, Box 4A, Correspondence 1933–50, folder of letters and telegrams from Joseph P. Kennedy, Jr.
288. "[They] all wait anxiously . . .": Nigel Hamilton, *Reckless Youth*, 645.
288. "Heard from Joe a while back . . .": John F. Kennedy to K. LeMoyne Billings, 3 May 1944, John F. Kennedy Personal Papers, Box 4A, folder of K. LeMoyne Billings correspondence, JFK Library.

CHAPTER 26 (PAGES 289–296)

289. "really fantastic . . .": Amanda Smith, ed., *Hostage to Fortune*, 583.
289. "second front nerves": Lynne McTaggart, *Kathleen Kennedy: Her Life and Times*, 167.
290. "It is sacrilege . . .": *Ibid.*, 155.
290. "I said I didn't think . . .": Amanda Smith, ed., *Hostage to Fortune*, 587.
290. "Heartbroken . . .": *Ibid.*, 586.
291. "Marie Bruce is most upset . . .": *Ibid.*, 589.
291. "I do feel terribly keenly . . .": *Ibid.*, 584–86.
291. According to Hank Searls . . . : Hank Searls, *The Lost Prince*, 207.
291. "Parnell's ghost . . .": London *Evening News*, editorial, 5 May 1944.
291. "apart from her family training . . .": *Boston Globe*, 4 May 1944.
292. "Customarily the wife . . .": Hank Searls, *The Lost Prince*, 208.
293. "The power of silence . . .": Lynne McTaggart, *Kathleen Kennedy: Her Life and Times*, 160.
294. "With your faith in God . . .": *Ibid.*
294. "I'm sorry it has to be this way.": *Boston Globe*, 6 May 1944.
294. "As far as Kick's soul is concerned . . .": Doris Kearns Goodwin, *The Fitzgeralds and the Kennedys*, 678–80.
294. "You would rejoice . . .": Lynne McTaggart, *Kathleen Kennedy: Her Life and Times*, 161.
295. "from the depths of her righteous Catholic wrath . . .": Nigel Hamilton, *Reckless Youth*, 652.
295. "He confessed that he was unorthodox . . .": Amanda Smith, ed., *Hostage to Fortune*, 594.

CHAPTER 27 (PAGES 297–307)

297. "I now have 39 missions . . .": Hank Searls, *The Lost Prince*, 232.
298. "The patient did well . . .": Dr. James Poppen to Captain Conklin, 1 August 1944, John F. Kennedy Personal Papers, Box 11a, JFK Library.
298. "His weight had dropped . . .": Gerald Walker and Donald A. Allan, "Jack Kennedy at Harvard," *Coronet*, May 1961.
298. "As you know . . .": Dr. Sara Jordan to Captain Conklin, 14 July 1944, John F. Kennedy Personal Papers, Box 11a, JFK Library.
299. "Lt. Kennedy has continued . . .": Dr. Sara Jordan to Captain Conklin, 1 August 1944, John F. Kennedy Personal Papers, Box 11a, JFK Library.

299. "indeed sorry that this had to happen . . .": Dr. James Poppen to Captain Conklin, 1 August 1944, John F. Kennedy Personal Papers, Box 11a, JFK Library.

299. "obviously incapacitated . . .": Clinical Notes, 4 August 1944, John F. Kennedy Personal Papers, Box 11a, JFK Library.

299. "In regard to the fascinating subject . . .": Herbert Parmet, *Jack: The Struggles of John F. Kennedy* (New York: Dial Press, 1980), 321.

300. "When I tried to make casual conversation . . .": Thomas C. Reeves, *A Question of Character* (New York: Free Press, 1991), 71.

300. "There was never an occasion . . .": Hank Searls, *The Lost Prince*, 245.

300. "I'm getting on . . .": Amanda Smith, ed., *Hostage to Fortune*, 598.

301. "At two thousand feet . . .": Hank Searls, *The Lost Prince*, 227.

302. "like a spastic sea gull": *Ibid.*, 230.

303. "would appear to be *key*": *Ibid.*, 233.

303. "I'm about to go into my act. . . .": *Ibid.*, 242.

304. "[It was] the biggest explosion . . .": After Action Report of Mission of 12 August 1944 authored by Air Corps Captain John M. Sande, John F. Kennedy Personal Papers, Box 9, JFK Library.

304. "the biggest explosion I ever saw . . .": Hank Searls, *The Lost Prince*, 250.

304. "ATTEMPTED FIRST APHRODITE . . .": Top Secret telegram from General Doolittle to General Spaatz concerning failure of the initial Aphrodite mission, John F. Kennedy Personal Papers, Box 9, JFK Library.

304. mentioned the problem: Jack Olsen, *Aphrodite: Desperate Mission* (New York: G. P. Putnam's Sons, 1970), 224.

304. "mainly because of the experience of the pilots . . .": Report on Accidental Loss of Robot Aircraft, 27 August 1944, John F. Kennedy Personal Papers, Box 9, JFK Library.

305. "I remember that . . .": Rose Fitzgerald Kennedy, *Times to Remember*, 301.

305. "EX-ENVOY KENNEDY, CRUSHED . . .": *Boston Globe*, 14 August 1944.

306. "It was quite a reunion . . .": *Boston Herald*, 17 August 1944.

306. "to be greeted by her brother . . .": *Boston Globe*, 17 August 1944.

306. "I know that great things were awaiting . . .": Richard Flood to John F. Kennedy, 15 August 1944, John F. Kennedy Personal Papers, Box 4A, Correspondence 1933–50, Joseph P. Kennedy, Jr., Condolence Mail, Folder 1, JFK Library.

306. "I have talked with your father two times . . .": Max Truitt to John F. Kennedy, n.d., John F. Kennedy Personal Papers, Box 4A, Correspondence 1933–50, Joseph P. Kennedy, Jr., Condolence Mail, Folder 1, JFK Library.

306. said prayers to the Lady of the Miraculous Medal: Gertrude Bateman to John F. Kennedy, n.d., John F. Kennedy Personal Papers, Box 4A, Correspondence 1933–50, Joseph P. Kennedy, Jr., Condolence Mail, Folder 1, JFK Library.

306. "You, no doubt, know some of the details . . .": Margaret Prior to John F. Kennedy, n.d., John F. Kennedy Personal Papers, Box 4A, Correspondence 1933–50, Joseph P. Kennedy, Jr., Condolence Mail, Folder 1, JFK Library.

307. ". . . if I am asked what I think concerning . . .": Card from the Rev. Richard J. Cushing, John F. Kennedy Personal Papers, Box 4A, Correspondence 1933–50, Joseph P. Kennedy, Jr., Condolence Mail, Folder 3, JFK Library.

307. "He had great physical courage . . .": John F. Kennedy, ed., *As We Remember Joe*, 5.

CHAPTER 28 (PAGES 308–318)

308. "Don't get worried about it . . .": Amanda Smith, ed., *Hostage to Fortune*, 598.

308. "When the young bury the old . . .": Doris Kearns Goodwin, *The Fitzgeralds and the Kennedys*, 693.

308. "Jack, don't you and your friends . . .": Lynne McTaggart, *Kathleen Kennedy: Her Life and Times*, 179.

309. "one of the top financiers . . .": Joan Blair and Clay Blair, Jr., *The Search for JFK*, 343.

309. "If anything should happen to me . . .": Amanda Smith, ed., *Hostage to Fortune*, 601.

309. "If Eunice, Pat & Jean . . .": *Ibid.*

309. "God has taken care of that matter . . .": Richard J. Whalen, *The Founding Father*, 375.

309. "And so ends the story . . .": Doris Kearns Goodwin, *The Fitzgeralds and the Kennedys*, 696.

310. "I'm looking pleasant about life . . .": Kathleen Kennedy to John F. Kennedy, 31 October 1944, John F. Kennedy Personal Papers, Box 4A, Correspondence 1933–50, folder of Kathleen Kennedy correspondence, 1942–47, JFK Library.

310. "very . . . English, or British, oriented . . .": Nigel Hamilton, *Reckless Youth*, 706.

311. "Harry, what the hell . . .": Ronald Kessler, *The Sins of the Father*, 287.

311. "If I hadn't been warned . . .": Doris Kearns Goodwin, *The Fitzgeralds and the Kennedys*, 701–2.

311. "For a fellow who didn't want this war . . .": *Ibid.*, 697.

312. "plan for super-armament . . .": John F. Kennedy, "Let's Try an Experiment in Peace," unpublished manuscript, John F. Kennedy Personal Papers, JFK Library.

312. "The Russians may have forgiven . . .": Nigel Hamilton, *Reckless Youth*, 696.

313. "This may come as a surprise . . .": *Ibid.*, 707.

313. "I remember that one of the last times we met . . .": Amanda Smith, ed., *Hostage to Fortune*, 622–23.

314. "I am now shadowboxing . . .": Doris Kearns Goodwin, *The Fitzgeralds and the Kennedys*, 698.

314. "Men who pushed back the Japs . . .": Kennedy for Congress Press Release, Pre-Presidential Papers, Box 11, JFK Library.

315. "I felt his courage . . .": Kenneth O'Donnell and David F. Powers, *Johnny, We Hardly Knew Ye* (Boston: Little, Brown, 1970), 66–67.

315. "I'm not a politician . . .": Press release dated 17 June 1946, Pre-Presidential Papers, Box 98, JFK Library.

316. "The end of the war . . .": David Cannadine, *The Decline and Fall of the British Aristocracy* (New Haven: Yale University Press, 1989), 637–38.

317. "if you want to commit adultery . . .": Martin Stannard, *Evelyn Waugh: The Later Years 1939–1966* (New York: Norton, 1992), 310.

318. "[The] faith you are born with . . .": Inga Arvad to John F. Kennedy, 14 February 1942, John F. Kennedy Personal Papers, Box 4A, Correspondence 1933–50, folder of letters from Inga Arvad, JFK Library.

318. "the sea of death that swamped . . .": John F. Kennedy to Claiborne Pell, 6 October 1947, Claiborne Pell Papers, Special Collections, University of Rhode Island Library.

Index